Logic, Argumentation & Reasoning

Interdisciplinary Perspectives from the Humanities
and Social Sciences

Volume 1

Series Editor

Shahid Rahman

For further volumes:
http://www.springer.com/series/11547

Logic, Argumentation & Reasoning

The Series is developed in partnership with the Maison Européenne des Sciences de l'Homme et de la Société (MESHS) at Nord - Pas de Calais and the UMR-STL: 8163 (CNRS). Aims & Scope: The scientific objectives of the series, where humanities and social sciences are conceived as building interdisciplinary interfaces, are:

This series publishes volumes that link practices in the Humanities and Social Sciences, with theories in Logic, Argumentation and Reasoning, such as: Decision theory and action theory, Argumentation Theories in: cognitive sciences, economy, sociology, law, logic, philosophy of sciences. The series is open towards research from the Analytic and the Continental traditions, and has four main focus areas: Pragmatic models and studies that develop a dynamic approach to reasoning in which argumentation is structured as an interaction or as a game, in which two or more participants play moves defined by the type of argumentation in question, communication, language and techniques of argumentation: studies between the practical and theoretical dimensions of argumentation, as well as the relationships between argumentation and other modes of communication, reception, persuasion and power: studies in which reasoning practice is considered from the point of view of its capacity to produce conviction of persuasion, and focusing on understanding what makes an argument performative, Diachronic transformations of reasoning practices studies that emphasize the invention and renewal of reasoning forms, with respect to its performance and its effectiveness.

General Editor
Shahid Rahman (Lille, UMR 8163)

Managing Editor
Laurent Keiff (Lille, UMR 8163)

Area Editors

Argumentation and Pragmatics
Marcelo Dascal (Tel Aviv)
Erik Krabbe (Groningen)
Frans H. van Eemeren (Amsterdam)
John Woods (British Columbia/King's College)

Argumentation and Rhetoric
Fabienne Blaise (Lille, MESHS-Nord Pas de Calais)
Gabriel Galvez-Behar (Lille, MESHS-Nord Pas de Calais)
André Laks (Sorbonne, Paris IV)
Ruth Webb (Lille, UMR 8163)

Decision Theory, Mathematics, Economy
Jacques Dubucs (IHPST-Paris 1)
Frederic Jouneau (Lille)
Richard Sobel (Lille)

Cognitives Sciences. Computer Sciences
Yann Coello (Lille)
Eric Gregoire (CRIL-Lens)
Henry Prakken (Utrecht)
François Recanati (ENS, Paris)

Epistemology and Philosophy of Science
André Fuhrmann (Frankfurt)
Gerhard Heinzmann (Nancy)
Göran Sundholm (Leyden)

Logic
Michel Crubellier (Lille, UMR 8163)
Dov Gabbay (King's College)
Sven Ove Hansson (Stockholm)
Tero Tulenheimo (Lille, UMR 8163)

Political Science and Sociology
Jean-Gabriel Contamin (Lille)
Franck Fischer (Rutgers)
Josh Ober (Stanford)
Marc Pichard (Lille, MESHS-Nord Pas de Calais)

Carlo Cellucci

Rethinking Logic: Logic in Relation to Mathematics, Evolution, and Method

Carlo Cellucci
Sapienza University of Rome
Rome
Italy

ISBN 978-94-024-0102-8   ISBN 978-94-007-6091-2 (eBook)
DOI 10.1007/978-94-007-6091-2
Springer Dordrecht Heidelberg New York London

© Springer Science+Business Media Dordrecht 2013
Softcover reprint of the hardcover 1st edition 2013
This work is subject to copyright. All rights are reserved by the Publisher, whether the whole or part of the material is concerned, specifically the rights of translation, reprinting, reuse of illustrations, recitation, broadcasting, reproduction on microfilms or in any other physical way, and transmission or information storage and retrieval, electronic adaptation, computer software, or by similar or dissimilar methodology now known or hereafter developed. Exempted from this legal reservation are brief excerpts in connection with reviews or scholarly analysis or material supplied specifically for the purpose of being entered and executed on a computer system, for exclusive use by the purchaser of the work. Duplication of this publication or parts thereof is permitted only under the provisions of the Copyright Law of the Publisher's location, in its current version, and permission for use must always be obtained from Springer. Permissions for use may be obtained through RightsLink at the Copyright Clearance Center. Violations are liable to prosecution under the respective Copyright Law.
The use of general descriptive names, registered names, trademarks, service marks, etc. in this publication does not imply, even in the absence of a specific statement, that such names are exempt from the relevant protective laws and regulations and therefore free for general use.
While the advice and information in this book are believed to be true and accurate at the date of publication, neither the authors nor the editors nor the publisher can accept any legal responsibility for any errors or omissions that may be made. The publisher makes no warranty, express or implied, with respect to the material contained herein.

Springer is part of Springer Science+Business Media (www.springer.com)

Preface

Despite strenuous efforts by its proponents, the contemporary form of logic, mathematical logic, has generally failed to convince mathematicians, natural scientists and human scientists of its relevance to their work, increasingly so in the last few decades. This contrasts with the reputation logic enjoyed in antiquity, not only as one of the main parts of philosophy, but also as a supplier of instruments for the sciences.

The purpose of this book is to explain how the present condition of logic came about and to propose an alternative to it. To this end, the book first gives an overview of how logic and its relation to the scientific method have been conceived in antiquity and in the modern age, because this provides indications for a new approach to the subject. Then the book proposes a new view of logic and its relation to evolution, language, reason, method and knowledge, particularly mathematical knowledge. It also proposes a new view of philosophy and its relation to knowledge, because seeing logic in a wider context helps to place it on a more satisfactory basis. In terms of the proposed new view, logic is primarily a logic of discovery. Accordingly, the book deals with the rules of discovery.

I am grateful to several people for the help they gave me in many ways. Some read a chapter and made remarks. Some raised questions in correspondence. Some made comments on views expressed in this book, presented at seminars or conferences. For their help in whatever form, I am especially indebted to Arthur Bierman, Mirella Capozzi, Riccardo Chiaradonna, Cesare Cozzo, Philip J. Davis, Michèle Friend, Donald Gillies, Norma Goethe, Emily Grosholz, Reuben Hersh, Jeff Kochan, Colin McGinn, Danielle Macbeth, Julien Murzi, Dan Nesher, Marwan Rashed, Stephen Read, Andrea Reichenberger, Stephen P. Schwartz, Giovanna Sillitti, Hourya Benis Sinaceur, Fabio Sterpetti, Philip Sullivan, Robert Thomas, Mario Vassalle, Johan van Benthem, Jan von Plato. This does not mean that they share the views expressed in this book or are in any way responsible for any remaining inaccuracies.

I am also grateful to two anonymous referees for their comments, and to Arlette Dupuis for reading the manuscript and suggesting several linguistic improvements. Moreover, I want to thank the Series Editor, Shahid Rahman, for supporting the book idea, for helping out in many ways, and for selecting the book to inaugurate the series Logic, Argumentation & Reasoning, and Christi Lue at Springer for her assistance in the publication process.

The views expressed in the book are a development of those presented in Cellucci 1998, 2003, 2008a, 2008b, 2012. Chapter 18 is a revised version of Cellucci 2011. I thank Cambridge Scholars Publishing for their kind permission to use this material.

A word about pronouns and gender. Constant use of 'he or she' may be clumsy, while constant use of 'she' may give rise to misunderstandings. Therefore, I have preferred to use the generic 'he' while stipulating here that I mean it to refer to persons of both genders.

Contents

1 Introduction 1
    1.1   The Intended Purpose of Mathematical Logic 1
    1.2   The Basic Assumptions of Mathematical Logic 1
    1.3   Inadequacy of the Basic Assumptions of Mathematical Logic ... 3
    1.4   The Reception of the Limitative Results 5
    1.5   Mathematics and Axiomatic Formal Theories 6
    1.6   Mathematics and the Loss of Certainty 7
    1.7   The Top-Down and Bottom-Up Approaches to Mathematics 10
    1.8   The Top-Down and Bottom-Up Approaches to Science 11
    1.9   Limitations of the Top-Down Approach 12
    1.10   Seeking a New Role for Mathematical Logic 13
    1.11   The Criticism of Scholastic Logic 14
    1.12   Scholastic Logic and Mathematical Logic 15
    1.13   Mathematical Logic and Discovery 16
    1.14   The Need for an Alternative Logic Paradigm 17
    1.15   Towards an Alternative Logic Paradigm 18
    1.16   Characters of the Alternative Logic Paradigm 18
    1.17   The Alternative Logic Paradigm and Philosophy 19
    1.18   The Reconstruction of Logic 19
    1.19   Organization of the Book 21
    1.20   Notations, Quotations, Transliterations 22

Part I   Ancient Perspectives

2 The Origin of Logic 25
    2.1   Six Claims by Greek Philosophers 25
    2.2   Universe, Mind and Divinity 26
    2.3   Human Mind and Divine Mind 26
    2.4   Method and Universe 27
    2.5   Method and Logic 27
    2.6   Logic and Discovery 28

2.7	Logic, Intuitive Thinking and Discursive Thinking	29
2.8	An Articulated View of the Origin of Logic	29
2.9	Origin of the Connection Between Universe, God and Mind	30
2.10	From Chaos to Order	31
2.11	Universe and *Eunomia*	31
2.12	Intuitive Thinking, Discursive Thinking and Greek Mythology	33
2.13	Origin of the Name 'Logic'	33
2.14	Aristotle's Names for Logic	34
2.15	Origin of the Name 'Method'	35

3 Ancient Logic and Science ... 37
- 3.1 Conceptions of Science ... 37
- 3.2 Parmenides' Conception of Science ... 37
- 3.3 Parmenides on the Role of Logic and Intuition in Science ... 38
- 3.4 Plato's Conception of Science ... 39
- 3.5 Plato and Knowledge as Justified True Belief ... 41
- 3.6 Plato on the Role of Logic and Intuition in Science ... 42
- 3.7 Plato on the Impediments of the Body ... 42
- 3.8 Plato's Criticism of the Axiomatic Method ... 43
- 3.9 Hippocrates of Cos' Criticism of the Axiomatic Method ... 44
- 3.10 Aristotle's Conception of Science ... 45
- 3.11 Aristotle's Conception of Demonstration ... 46
- 3.12 Aristotle on Role of Logic and Intuition in Science ... 47
- 3.13 Aristotle on Proper and Common Principles ... 49
- 3.14 Aristotle's Conception of Definition ... 49
- 3.15 Aristotle's Separation of Kinds and Principles ... 50
- 3.16 Aristotle on Truth as Correspondence ... 51
- 3.17 Aristotle on Truth as Intuition of the Essence ... 52
- 3.18 Aristotle on *Nous* and Intuition ... 52

4 The Analytic Method ... 55
- 4.1 Statement of the Analytic Method ... 55
- 4.2 Inference and Containment ... 55
- 4.3 The Plausibility Test Procedure ... 56
- 4.4 Plausibility and Probability ... 56
- 4.5 Non-deductive Rules, Plausibility and Experience ... 57
- 4.6 Deductive Rules, Plausibility and Experience ... 57
- 4.7 The Double Movement of the Analytic Method ... 58
- 4.8 The Analytic Notion of Demonstration ... 58
- 4.9 Origin of the Analytic Method ... 59
- 4.10 Basic Features of the Analytic Method ... 62
- 4.11 Analytic Method and Infinite Regress ... 63
- 4.12 Non-finality of Solutions to Problems ... 64
- 4.13 Original Formulation of the Analytic Method ... 65
- 4.14 Original Formulation of the Analytic Method and Intuition ... 67

	4.15	The Axiomatic Method	68
	4.16	The Axiomatic Notion of Demonstration	68
	4.17	Analytic Method vs. Axiomatic Method	69
	4.18	The Method of Ancient Medicine	70
	4.19	Limitations of the Original Formulation of the Analytic Method	71
	4.20	Fortune of the Analytic Method	72
5	**The Analytic-Synthetic Method**		**75**
	5.1	Aristotle's Changes to the Analytic Method	75
	5.2	Aristotle's Analytic-Synthetic Method	76
	5.3	Original Formulation of Aristotle's Analytic-Synthetic Method	76
	5.4	An Example of Aristotle's Analytic-Synthetic Method	78
	5.5	The Direction of Analysis in Aristotle's Analytic-Synthetic Method	80
	5.6	Aristotle's Analytic-Synthetic Method and Intuition	81
	5.7	Plausible Premises and *Endoxa*	81
	5.8	The Controversy Between Plato and Aristotle Concerning Method	82
	5.9	Pappus' Analytic-Synthetic Method	83
	5.10	Original Formulation of Pappus' Analytic-Synthetic Method	84
	5.11	An Example of Pappus' Analytic-Synthetic Method	85
	5.12	The Direction of Analysis in Pappus' Analytic-Synthetic Method	87
	5.13	Fortune of the Analytic-Synthetic Method	88
	5.14	Analytic-Synthetic Method and Axiomatic Method	89
	5.15	Relations with Reduction to the Impossible	90
	5.16	The Reason for Use of Reduction to the Impossible	91
	5.17	Analytic Method vs. Analytic-Synthetic Method	93
6	**Aristotle's Logic: The Deductivist View**		**95**
	6.1	The Deductivist View of Aristotle's Logic	95
	6.2	Assertions	97
	6.3	Logical Relations Between Assertions	99
	6.4	Syllogisms	100
	6.5	Concerning the Name 'Syllogism'	101
	6.6	Figures and Moods	102
	6.7	Singular and Indeterminate Assertions in Syllogisms	104
	6.8	Complete and Incomplete Syllogisms	104
	6.9	Conversion Rules and Strong Reduction to the Impossible	105
	6.10	The Completion of Syllogisms	107
	6.11	The Reduction of Syllogisms	108
	6.12	Syllogistic	110
	6.13	Limitations of the Deductivist View	112

7 Aristotle's Logic: The Heuristic View ... 115
- 7.1 The Ultimate Sources of Aristotle's Logic ... 115
- 7.2 The Proximate Source of Aristotle's Logic ... 117
- 7.3 The Heuristic View of Aristotle's Logic ... 119
- 7.4 Aristotle's Procedure for Finding Premises by Syllogism ... 120
- 7.5 Problem Dependence of Aristotle's Procedure ... 123
- 7.6 Finding Premises by Induction ... 123
- 7.7 Finding Premises in the Analytic-Synthetic Method ... 126
- 7.8 The Role of Plausibility in the Analytic-Synthetic Method ... 126
- 7.9 Plausibility and Essence ... 128
- 7.10 Finished Science and Science in the Making ... 128
- 7.11 Aristotle's Logic as a Logic of Discovery ... 129
- 7.12 Limitations of Aristotle's Logic ... 129
- 7.13 The Stoics' Deductivist Turn ... 132

Part II Modern Perspectives

8 The Method of Modern Science ... 137
- 8.1 Galileo's Method ... 137
- 8.2 Galileo and Pappus' Method ... 138
- 8.3 An Example of Galileo's Method ... 139
- 8.4 Newton's Method ... 142
- 8.5 Newton and Pappus' Method ... 144
- 8.6 Galileo vs. Idealization ... 144
- 8.7 Galileo's Philosophical Revolution ... 146
- 8.8 Galileo's Philosophical Revolution and Mathematics ... 146
- 8.9 Galileo's Great Book of the World vs. Aristotle's Books ... 147
- 8.10 Galileo's Distinction Between Primary and Secondary Qualities ... 148
- 8.11 Limitations of Galileo's Distinction ... 149
- 8.12 The Need for a New Kind of Mathematics ... 149
- 8.13 The Effectiveness of Mathematics in the Natural Sciences ... 150
- 8.14 Modern Science and Truth ... 151
- 8.15 Concept of Truth and Criterion of Truth ... 152
- 8.16 Mathematics and Truth ... 153
- 8.17 Plausibility in Place of Truth ... 154

9 The Quest for a Logic of Discovery ... 157
- 9.1 Logic and the Scientific Revolution ... 157
- 9.2 Bacon's Quest for a Logic of Discovery ... 157
- 9.3 Bacon's Induction ... 158
- 9.4 Limitations of Bacon's Attempt ... 160
- 9.5 Descartes' Quest for a Logic of Discovery ... 161
- 9.6 Descartes' Opposition of Analysis to Synthesis ... 163
- 9.7 Descartes' Appeal to Intuition ... 164

Contents xi

	9.8	Limitations of Descartes' Attempt	166
	9.9	Leibniz's Attempt to Keep a Foot in Two Shoes	168
	9.10	Leibniz's Universal Language and Calculus of Reasoning	169
	9.11	Limitation of Leibniz's Attempt	171
	9.12	Kant's View of Logic as a Canon	172
	9.13	Kant's Opposition of Artificial Logic to Natural Logic	174
	9.14	Kant's Divisions of Logic	175
	9.15	Kant on the Nature of the Scientific Method	176
	9.16	Kant's Closed World View of Science	177
	9.17	Kant on the Solvability of All Mathematical Problems	178
	9.18	Kant on Induction and Analogy	179
	9.19	The Twilight of the Quest for a Logic of Discovery	181
10	**Frege's Approach to Logic**		**183**
	10.1	Frege's Restriction of Logic to the Study of Deduction	183
	10.2	Frege's Assumptions Concerning the Nature of Logic	184
	10.3	Frege's Ideal of Atomizing Deduction	185
	10.4	Frege's View of Mathematical Practice and Mathematics	186
	10.5	Frege's Closed World View of Mathematics	187
	10.6	Frege's Analysis of Assertions	188
	10.7	Shortcomings of Frege's Concept of Function	189
	10.8	Frege's Analysis of Deduction	190
	10.9	Limitations of Frege's Analysis of Assertions and Deduction	190
	10.10	Frege's Logicist Programme	191
	10.11	Frege's Foundation of Logic	193
	10.12	Frege's Logicist Programme and Leibniz's Logicist View	194
	10.13	Frege's Primitive Laws of Logic	195
	10.14	Failure of Frege's Foundation of Mathematics	195
	10.15	Failure of Frege's Foundation of Logic	196
11	**Gentzen's Approach to Logic**		**199**
	11.1	Formal Languages	199
	11.2	Gentzen's Analysis of Deduction	200
	11.3	The Significance of Gentzen's Analysis	201
	11.4	Inferentialism	202
	11.5	Detour Contractions	203
	11.6	Permutation Contractions	204
	11.7	Simplification Contractions	206
	11.8	Normal Deductions	207
	11.9	The Case of Negation	207
	11.10	Limitations of Gentzen's Analysis of Deduction	208
	11.11	Failure of the Ideal of Atomizing Deduction	213
12	**The Limitations of Mathematical Logic**		**215**
	12.1	The Claims Concerning Mathematical Logic	215
	12.2	The Abandonment of Aristotle's Broad Conception of Logic	215

	12.3	The Abandonment of the Analytic-Synthetic Method	216
	12.4	Failure of the Ideal of a Universal Language	217
	12.5	Failure of the Ideal of a Calculus of Reasoning	217
	12.6	Inadequacy of the Closed World View	218
	12.7	Inadequacy of the Analytic-Synthetic Method	218
	12.8	The Unknowability of the Truth of Principles	219
	12.9	Failure of the Logicist Programme	219
	12.10	Failure of Hilbert's Conservation Programme	220
	12.11	Failure of Hilbert's Consistency Programme	221
	12.12	Inadequacy of Consistency as a Criterion of Truth	221
	12.13	Failure of Hilbert's Programme of Mechanizing Discovery	222
	12.14	Inadequacy of Logic as the Study of Deduction	223
	12.15	Failure of Inferentialism	224
	12.16	High Expectations, Modest Returns	224

13 Logic, Method and Psychology of Discovery ... 227
- 13.1 The Divorce of Logic from Method ... 227
- 13.2 The Collapse of the Discussion on Method ... 228
- 13.3 The Psychology of Discovery ... 229
- 13.4 Psychology of Discovery, Logic and Intuition ... 231
- 13.5 Limitations of Psychology of Discovery ... 231
- 13.6 Limitations of Self-Reports ... 233
- 13.7 The Romantic Myth of Genius ... 234
- 13.8 Analytic Method vs. Intuition ... 235

Part III An Alternative Perspective

14 Reason and Knowledge ... 239
- 14.1 The Need to Reconsider the Nature of Logic ... 239
- 14.2 The Origin of Logic and Reason ... 239
- 14.3 The Concept of Reason ... 240
- 14.4 The Metaphor of Choosing ... 241
- 14.5 Human Nature ... 242
- 14.6 Cultural and Biological Evolution ... 243
- 14.7 Essential Relativity of the Concept of Reason ... 244
- 14.8 Natural and Artificial Reason ... 245
- 14.9 Reason and Mind ... 245
- 14.10 The Sapient Paradox ... 246
- 14.11 The Extended Mind ... 246
- 14.12 Extended Mind and World ... 247
- 14.13 Extended Mind and Brain Plasticity ... 248
- 14.14 Biological Role of Knowledge ... 249
- 14.15 The Consciousness Argument ... 250
- 14.16 Unconscious Processes ... 251
- 14.17 Knowledge and the Unknowability of Things in Themselves ... 251

14.18	The Purpose of Knowledge	253
14.19	Cultural Role of Knowledge	254
14.20	Scientific Knowledge	255
14.21	Mathematical Knowledge	255

15 Reason, Knowledge and Emotion ... 257
15.1	Reason and Emotion	257
15.2	Emotion as a Compensation for the Limitations of Reason	258
15.3	Knowledge and Emotion	258
15.4	Solving Problems and Emotion	259
15.5	Choice of Problems or Hypotheses and Emotion	260
15.6	Scientific Knowledge and Emotion	261
15.7	Mathematical Knowledge and Emotion	262
15.8	Error and Emotion	262
15.9	Doubt and Emotion	264

16 Logic, Evolution, Language and Reason ... 265
16.1	Natural and Artificial Logic	265
16.2	Remarks on the Distinction Between Natural and Artificial Logic	266
16.3	Origin of the Distinction Between Natural and Artificial Logic	266
16.4	Anti-evolutionism in Logic	267
16.5	The Reducibility Thesis	268
16.6	The Need for Artificial Logic	269
16.7	Logic and Language	269
16.8	Perception as Inference	270
16.9	Non-propositional Inferences	271
16.10	The Origin of Perception as Inference	272
16.11	The Irresistibility of Inferences Involved in Perception	272
16.12	Objections to Perception as Inference	273
16.13	Discursive and Visual Logic	275
16.14	The Role of Visual Logic in Knowledge	276
16.15	Limitations of Visual Logic	276
16.16	Complementarity of Discursive and Visual Logic	277
16.17	Logic and Reason	278

17 Logic, Method and Knowledge ... 279
17.1	Logic and Method	279
17.2	Against Logic as a Normative Science	279
17.3	Spinoza's Hammer-and-Iron Argument	280
17.4	Solving Problems and Knowledge	281
17.5	*Meno*'s Paradox	281
17.6	Analytic Method and Knowledge	283
17.7	Logic and Knowledge	283
17.8	Non-ampliativity of Deductive Rules	284
17.9	The Paradox of Inference	285

	17.10	Rules for Finding Hypotheses	286
	17.11	Knowledge and Certainty	286
	17.12	Solving Problems and Intuition	287
	17.13	Objections Against the Possibility of a Logic of Discovery	288
	17.14	Hypotheses and the *A Priori*	291
	17.15	The Evolution of the *A Priori*	291
	17.16	The Open World View of Science	294
18	**Classifying and Justifying Inference Rules**		**295**
	18.1	The Standard Classification of Inference Rules	295
	18.2	Abduction	296
	18.3	Peirce on the Status of Abduction	296
	18.4	Peirce on Abduction and Intuition	297
	18.5	Peirce's Classification of Inference Rules	298
	18.6	Objections to the Non-ampliativity of Abduction	299
	18.7	Inference to the Best Explanation	300
	18.8	An Alternative Classification of Inference Rules	301
	18.9	Failures in Justifying Deductive Rules	302
	18.10	Validation and Vindication	305
	18.11	Vindication and Truth Preservation	305
	18.12	The Vindication of Deductive Rules	306
	18.13	Vindication of Deductive Rules and Usefulness	306
	18.14	Failures in Justifying Non-deductive Rules	307
	18.15	The Vindication of Non-deductive Rules	308
	18.16	Vindication of Non-deductive Rules and Usefulness	308
	18.17	The Vindication of Abduction	309
	18.18	The Asymmetry View	309
	18.19	Sextus Empiricus' Argument Concerning the Criterion of Truth	310
	18.20	Hume's Argument Concerning Induction	310
	18.21	Two Questions Concerning Hume	311
19	**Philosophy and Knowledge**		**313**
	19.1	Philosophy in the Face of Modern Science	313
	19.2	Analytic Philosophy and Knowledge	314
	19.3	The Armchair View of Philosophy	316
	19.4	Implications of the Armchair View	316
	19.5	The Demise of Philosophy	319
	19.6	An Alternative Philosophy Paradigm	320
	19.7	Distinguishing Features of Philosophy	321
	19.8	An Alternative View of Epistemology	322
	19.9	Comparison with Other Views of Philosophy	324
	19.10	Good and Bad Philosophy?	325
	19.11	The Way of Naturalism	325
	19.12	The Ultimate Reason of Supernaturalism	328

Part IV Rules of Discovery

20 Induction and Analogy 331
    20.1   The Rules of Discovery 331
    20.2   Induction from a Single Case 332
    20.3   Induction from Multiple Cases 333
    20.4   Some Misconceptions Concerning Induction 334
    20.5   Analogy 336
    20.6   Analogy by Quasi-Equality 337
    20.7   Analogy by Separate Indistinguishability 338
    20.8   Inductive Analogy 339
    20.9   Proportional Analogy 340
    20.10 Analogy by Agreement 342
    20.11 Analogy by Agreement and Disagreement 343
    20.12 A Refinement of Analogy by Agreement 344
    20.13 Some Misconceptions Concerning Analogy 344

21 Other Rules of Discovery 347
    21.1   Expanding the Rules of Discovery 347
    21.2   Generalization 347
    21.3   Specialization 348
    21.4   Metaphor 349
    21.5   Some Misconceptions Concerning Metaphor 351
    21.6   Metonymy 352
    21.7   Definition 353
    21.8   Definition as Abbreviation 353
    21.9   Definition as Analysis 355
    21.10 Diagrams 357
    21.11 Some Misconceptions Concerning Diagrams 359

22 Conclusion 365

References 367

Name Index 379

Subject Index 385

Chapter 1
Introduction

1.1 The Intended Purpose of Mathematical Logic

Although, throughout its history, logic has taken several forms, in 1931 the question 'What is logic?' would have received a straightforward answer: Logic is mathematical logic. For by that time mathematical logic, the new form of logic created by Frege, had completely superseded all other forms of logic.

In a book published in that year, Scholz expressed his enthusiasm for the new form of logic, claiming that it "gives us the complete inferential rules which the development of the tremendously exacting modern mathematics requires."[1] Scholz's claim is so much more significant as it was made the very same year that Gödel published his incompleteness theorems, which were ruinous for the intended purpose of mathematical logic: to give a secure foundation for mathematics.

1.2 The Basic Assumptions of Mathematical Logic

That this was the intended purpose of mathematical logic is apparent from Frege, who bases the subject on the following assumptions.

1) *The purpose of mathematical logic is to give a secure foundation for mathematics*. This is essential "to place the truth of a proposition beyond all doubt."[2]

2) *Mathematical logic pursues this purpose through the study of the method of mathematics*. This will show "the ultimate ground upon which rests the justification for holding" a proposition "to be true."[3]

---

[1] Scholz (1961, 67).
[2] Frege (1959, 2).
[3] *Ibid.*, 3.

3) *The method of mathematics is the axiomatic method.* We start from axioms "expressly declared as such, so that we can see distinctly what the whole structure rests upon," and proceed from them by rules of deduction "specified in advance."[4]

4) *Mathematical logic need only express what is necessary for the axiomatic method.* It may "forgo expressing anything that is without significance for the inferential sequence."[5] That is, "anything that it is not necessary for setting up the laws of deduction."[6] Everything "necessary for a correct inference is expressed in full, but what is not necessary is generally not indicated."[7] Thus mathematical logic will fail to express all aspects of mathematics. But mathematical logic "is a device invented for certain scientific purposes," that is, to give a secure foundation for mathematics, "and one must not condemn it because it is not suited to others."[8]

5) *Mathematical logic can actually give a secure foundation for mathematics.* Indeed, by means of it, "every gap in the chain of deductions is eliminated with the greatest care," so we can "say with certainty upon what primitive truths the proof depends."[9] Admittedly, to "the question why and with what right we acknowledge" that the primitive truths are actually truths, mathematical logic "can give no answer."[10] Trying to give an answer by means of it "would be as much as to judge without judging, or to wash the fur without wetting it."[11] But an answer to the question is given by intuition.[12]

Assumptions 1)–5) are the basic assumptions of mathematical logic, by which Frege shaped the discipline. Clearly the subject, as presented in current textbooks, is not a direct descendant of Frege, but rather of Hilbert and his school.[13] Nevertheless, it still rests on Frege's basic assumptions, as it is apparent from its leading representatives, such as Gödel and Tarski, who state:

1) The purpose of mathematical logic is to give a secure "foundation for mathematics."[14]

2) Mathematical logic pursues this purpose through the study of the method of mathematics, which alone can assure for mathematics the "highest possible degree of clarity and certainty."[15]

---

[4]Frege (1964, 2).
[5]Frege (1967, 6).
[6]Frege (1979, 5).
[7]Frege (1967, 12).
[8]*Ibid.*, 6.
[9]Frege (1959, 4).
[10]Frege (1964, 15).
[11]Frege (1959, 36).
[12]On intuition in Frege, see Chapter 10. Unless otherwise stated, here and in what follows 'intuition' means 'intellectual intuition', that is, an unmediated apprehension of intellectual objects, not to be confused with Kant's pure sensible intuition.
[13]Especially Hilbert and Ackermann (1950) and Hilbert and Bernays (1968–1970).
[14]Gödel (1986–2002, III, 45).
[15]Tarski (1994, 109).

3) The method of mathematics is the axiomatic method, because every mathematical "discipline begins with a list of a small number of sentences, called axioms" which "are recognized as true without any further justification."[16] Then "no other sentence is accepted in the discipline as true unless we are able to prove it with the exclusive help of axioms and those sentences that were previously proved."[17] Thus "every mathematical discipline" is "a deductive theory."[18]

4) Mathematical logic need only express what is necessary for the axiomatic method, because it serves "exclusively for the purpose of studying deductive sciences."[19] Thus mathematical logic will fail to express all aspects of mathematics. In particular, the idea "to replace mathematical intuition by rules for the use of symbols fails."[20] But mathematical logic is only intended to be a tool to give a secure foundation for mathematics.

5) Mathematical logic can actually give a secure foundation for mathematics, because "the problem of giving" a secure "foundation for mathematics" falls "into two different parts."[21] First, the methods of demonstration "have to be reduced to a minimum number of axioms" and deductive "rules of inference."[22] This is obtained through "the so-called 'formalization' of mathematics."[23] Secondly, "a justification in some sense or other has to be sought for these axioms."[24] Admittedly, such a justification cannot be given by mathematical logic. But it is given by intuition, because axioms "can directly be perceived to be true (owing to the meaning of the terms or by an intuition of the objects falling under them)."[25]

1.3 Inadequacy of the Basic Assumptions of Mathematical Logic

However reasonable the basic assumptions 1)–5) may seem, by Gödel's incompleteness theorems they are untenable.[26]

---

[16]Tarski (1969, 70).
[17]*Ibid.*
[18]Tarski (1994, 112).
[19]Tarski (1983, 166).
[20]Gödel (1986–2002, III, 346).
[21]*Ibid.*, III, 45.
[22]*Ibid.*
[23]*Ibid.*
[24]*Ibid.*
[25]*Ibid.*, III, 347.
[26]For a precise statement of Gödel's incompleteness theorems see, for example, Cellucci (2007, 175–178, 184–185) (Gödel's first incompleteness theorem); *Ibid.*, 180–184 (Gödel's second incompleteness theorem); *Ibid.*, 185–187 (Gödel's third incompleteness theorem).

The assumption 3), that the method of mathematics is the axiomatic method, conflicts with Gödel's first incompleteness theorem, by which, for any consistent, sufficiently strong, deductive theory T, there is a sentence G of T which is true, specifically true in the natural numbers, but undemonstrable in T.[27] Therefore, mathematical reasoning cannot be reduced to deductive reasoning, and the method of mathematics cannot be identified with the axiomatic method. It is no way out to identify mathematics with an infinite sequence of axiomatic systems, rather than a single one, on the basis that, by Gödel's first incompleteness theorem, the concept of demonstration "cannot be exhausted by any single formalization."[28] For then mathematical demonstration would be "that sort of growing thing which the intuitionists have postulated for certain infinite sets."[29] But this is incompatible with the axiomatic method, it is only compatible with the analytic method; see Chapter 4.

The assumption 2), that mathematical logic pursues the purpose to give a secure foundation for mathematics through the study of the method of mathematics, conflicts with the fact that, by Gödel's first incompleteness theorem, the method of mathematics cannot be identified with the axiomatic method, therefore the study of the method of mathematics is not the same as the study of the axiomatic method.

The assumption 4), that mathematical logic need only express what is necessary for the axiomatic method, conflicts with the fact that, by expressing only what is necessary for the axiomatic method, mathematical logic will fail to express what is necessary for the method of mathematics, since the latter cannot be identified with the axiomatic method.

The assumptions 1) and 5), that the purpose of mathematical logic is to give a secure foundation for mathematics and mathematical logic can actually give such a foundation, conflict with Gödel's second incompleteness theorem, by which, for any consistent, sufficiently strong, deductive theory T, the sentence canonically expressing the consistency of T, Con(T), is undemonstrable in T.[30] Then *a fortiori* Con(T) is undemonstrable by absolutely reliable means. Therefore, the purpose of mathematical logic to give a secure foundation for mathematics cannot be achieved. In particular intuition, being subjective and unreliable, cannot assure us that the axioms are true.

Actually, the view that there could be a secure foundation for mathematics was no more reasonable than the Hindu's view, mentioned by Russell, "that the world

---

[27]Throughout this book, 'deductive theory' means 'axiomatic formal theory', and 'sufficiently strong deductive theory' means 'deductive theory containing first-order Peano arithmetic'. 'Demonstration' is used as a general name for both axiomatic and non-axiomatic arguments. Similarly for 'demonstrable' and 'undemonstrable'.

[28]Curry (1977, 15).

[29]*Ibid.*

[30]A sentence canonically expressing the consistency of a deductive theory is one satisfying the conditions of Löb (1955). A simpler condition, however, is sufficient; see Cellucci (2007, 180–181).

rested upon an elephant and the elephant rested upon a tortoise; and when they said, 'How about the tortoise?' the Indian said, 'Suppose we change the subject'."[31]

1.4 The Reception of the Limitative Results

It has been stated above that, however reasonable the basic assumptions 1)–5) may seem, by Gödel's incompleteness theorems they are untenable. This, however, is something several mathematical logicians and mathematicians are unwilling to accept.

For example, Murawski states that, although Gödel's incompleteness theorems indicate "certain weaknesses of the axiomatic-deductive method," the latter "makes it possible to specify" the notion of a demonstration and of "the correctness of methods admissible in mathematics."[32] If "we resigned from it," then the notion of a demonstration and "consequently that of a theorem would become entirely subjective."[33]

This is unwarranted. It is unjustified to say that the axiomatic-deductive method makes it possible to specify the notion of a demonstration. By Gödel's first incompleteness theorem, the axiomatic notion of demonstration is inadequate for mathematics. It is unjustified to say that the axiomatic-deductive method makes it possible to specify the correctness of methods admissible in mathematics. By Gödel's second incompleteness theorem, there is no absolutely reliable way of establishing the correctness of such methods. It is unjustified to say that, if we resigned from the axiomatic-deductive method, then the notion of a demonstration and consequently that of a theorem would become entirely subjective. From antiquity there has been an alternative to the axiomatic notion of demonstration, the analytic notion of demonstration, which is by no means subjective, and moreover is not affected by Gödel's incompleteness results; see Chapter 17.

As another example, Gowers states that every mathematical argument can be expressed as a deduction which "starts with axioms that are universally accepted and proceeds to the desired conclusion by means of only the most elementary logical rules."[34] This "means that any dispute about the validity" of a mathematical demonstration "can always be resolved."[35] Of course, there remains the question "why should one accept the axioms proposed by mathematicians," but what a mathematical demonstration "actually does is show that certain conclusions" follow

---

[31] Russell (1996, 4).
[32] Murawski (1999, 338).
[33] *Ibid.*
[34] Gowers (2002, 39).
[35] *Ibid.*, 40.

"from certain premises."[36] The "validity of these premises is an entirely independent matter which can safely be left to philosophers."[37]

This is unwarranted. It is unjustified to say that every mathematical argument can be expressed as a deduction which starts with axioms that are universally accepted and proceeds to the desired conclusion by means of only the most elementary logical rules. By Gödel's first incompleteness theorem, this is untenable. It is unjustified to say that any dispute about the validity of a mathematical demonstration can always be resolved. By Gödel's second incompleteness theorem, there is no absolutely reliable way of establishing its validity. It is unjustified to say that what a mathematical demonstration actually does is show that certain conclusions follow from certain premises. By Gödel's first incompleteness theorem, mathematical demonstration cannot be reduced to deduction. It is unjustified to say that the validity of the premises is an entirely independent matter which can safely be left to philosophers – meaning that it is irrelevant to mathematics. If the premises were inconsistent, any conclusion would follow. Therefore, if mathematics is not to be a vacuous exercise, the validity of the premises is essential.[38]

A notable exception to this dismissive attitude towards Gödel's incompleteness theorems is Post. Already in 1941 he expressed his "continuing amazement that, ten years after Gödel's remarkable achievement," the "current views on the nature of mathematics are thereby affected only to the point of seeing the need of many formal systems, instead of a universal one."[39] On the contrary, "has it seemed to us to be inevitable" that Gödel's achievement "will result in a reversal of the entire axiomatic trend of the late nineteenth and early twentieth centuries."[40] Axiomatic "thinking will then remain as but one phase of mathematical thinking."[41]

1.5 Mathematics and Axiomatic Formal Theories

It has been claimed above that the assumption that the method of mathematics is the axiomatic method conflicts with Gödel's first incompleteness theorem. Against this claim, it might be objected that it is based on a statement of Gödel's first incompleteness theorem which is metaphysical: For any consistent, sufficiently strong, deductive theory T, there is a sentence G of T which is true, specifically, true in the natural numbers, but undemonstrable in T. This statement is metaphysical because it refers to the notion of truth in the natural numbers. Thus Floyd and Putnam state: "That the Gödel theorem shows that (1) there is a well-defined

---

[36] Ibid., 41.
[37] Ibid.
[38] See the answer to objection 3) in the next section.
[39] Post (1965, 345).
[40] Ibid.
[41] Ibid.

notion of 'mathematical truth' applicable to every formula of PM" – the system of *Principia Mathematica* – "and (2) that, if PM is consistent, then some 'mathematical truths'" G "are undecidable in PM, is not a mathematical result but a metaphysical claim."[42] What Gödel actually showed, as subsequently improved by Rosser, is the following 'syntactic' result: if PM is consistent, there is a sentence G of PM, specifically, an arithmetical sentence, such that, both G and $\neg G$ are undemonstrable in PM.

This objection, however, is unjustified. For any consistent, sufficiently strong, deductive theory T, the sentence G and the sentence canonically expressing the consistency of T, $\mathrm{Con}(T)$, are equivalent, and their equivalence can be established in T. Then we have as much, or as little, reason to believe that G is true as we have reason to believe that T is consistent. Therefore, if we know that the deductive theory T is consistent, we also know that the sentence G is true. Thus the truth of G is already implicit in the assumption that T is consistent.

Moreover, a syntactic deductive theory T capable of talking about demonstrations in T, as required by the construction of the sentence G, will need to talk about expressions. Now, the syntax of expressions and arithmetic are interpretable into each other.[43] Therefore, anyone who had reservations about the notion of truth in the natural numbers ought to have reservations about syntax.

The objection rests on the assumption that, if natural numbers are accessible to knowledge, all their properties will be so accessible. This assumption is as unwarranted as the assumption that, when a painter paints a picture, he will know all properties of his painting. If so, there would be no need for art critics.

1.6 Mathematics and the Loss of Certainty

Since, as it has been argued above, by Gödel's second incompleteness theorem, the purpose of mathematical logic to give a secure foundation for mathematics cannot be achieved, mathematics cannot be said to be absolutely certain. Nevertheless, against this claim, the following objections could be raised.

1) If mathematics cannot be said to be absolutely certain, then Gödel's second incompleteness theorem, being a mathematical result, cannot be said to be absolutely certain. But the claim that mathematics cannot be said to be absolutely certain is based on Gödel's result. Then this claim too cannot be said to be absolutely certain. Therefore, the claim that, by Gödel's second incompleteness theorem, mathematics cannot be said to be absolutely certain, is self-defeating.[44]

---

[42]Floyd and Putnam (2000, 632).

[43]See, for example, Quine (1946).

[44]This objection was raised in correspondence by Reuben Hersh, acting as *advocatus diaboli*, not because he shared it.

But this objection is unjustified, because the argument that, by Gödel's second incompleteness theorem, mathematics cannot be said to be absolutely certain, does not depend on the assumption that Gödel's second incompleteness theorem can be said to be absolutely certain. It is a reduction to the impossible, because it is of the following kind. Let us suppose, for argument's sake, that mathematics can be said to be absolutely certain. Then Gödel's second incompleteness theorem, being a mathematical result, can be said to be absolutely certain. But, by Gödel's second incompleteness theorem, mathematics cannot be said to be absolutely certain. Thus mathematics cannot be said to be absolutely certain. Contradiction. Therefore mathematics cannot be said to be absolutely certain.

2) Gödel's second incompleteness theorem is irrelevant to the question of the absolute certainty of mathematics. For, either (A) "we have no doubts about the consistency of" Zermelo-Fraenkel set theory with the axiom of choice ZFC, in which case "there is nothing in the second incompleteness theorem to give rise to any such doubts."[45] Or (B) "we do have doubts about the consistency of ZFC," but then "we have no reason to believe that" a demonstration of the consistency of ZFC "formalizable in ZFC would do anything to remove those doubts."[46] For "the consistency of ZFC is precisely what is in question."[47]

But this objection is unjustified, because case (A), that we have no doubts about the consistency of ZFC, might occur only if we could give a demonstration of the consistency of ZFC by absolutely reliable means. Now, by Gödel's second incompleteness theorem, this is impossible. On the other hand, case (B) is misstated. For if we do have doubts about the consistency of ZFC, then the question is not whether a demonstration of the consistency of ZFC formalizable in ZFC would do anything to remove those doubts. It is, rather, whether a demonstration of the consistency of ZFC given by absolutely reliable means would do anything to remove them, and the answer is yes, definitely.

That, by Gödel's second incompleteness theorem, a demonstration of the consistency of ZFC given by absolutely reliable means is impossible, means that the doubts about the consistency of ZFC cannot be removed. Then it is unjustified to say that "nothing in Gödel's theorem is in any way incompatible with the claim that we have absolutely certain knowledge of the truth of the axioms" of "any of the formal systems that we use in mathematics," and "therewith of their consistency."[48] By Gödel's second incompleteness theorem, we are not entitled to make this claim.

3) Gödel's second incompleteness theorem is irrelevant to the question of the absolute certainty of mathematics, because we can adopt Wittgenstein's rule: "Don't draw any conclusions from a contradiction: make that a rule."[49] Then, if we get to

---

[45]Franzén (2005, 105).
[46]*Ibid.*, 105–106.
[47]*Ibid.*, 105.
[48]*Ibid.*
[49]Wittgenstein (1976, 209).

1.6 Mathematics and the Loss of Certainty

a contradiction, we will "simply say, 'This is no use – and we won't draw any conclusion from it'."[50] Thus the contradiction is sealed off, and a "contradiction is harmless if it can be sealed off."[51]

But this objection is unjustified. Contradictions usually arise from use of poorly formulated concepts, and their discovery is a powerful incentive to reformulate them. Thus the paradoxes of the calculus of infinitesimals led to reformulate the concept of infinitesimal, and Russell's paradox led to reformulate the concept of set. On the contrary, Wittgenstein's rule leaves everything as it is. It simply prevents the contradiction from being "applied to produce arbitrary results," which would make "the application of mathematics into a farce."[52] But it does not explain the cause of the contradiction, nor does anything to remove it, thus it does not contribute to reformulate poorly formulated concepts. Had it been for Wittgenstein, the axioms of ZFC would never have been formulated.[53] Then appealing to Wittgenstein's rule is not a philosophically significant objection.[54]

Since the above objections are unjustified, there seems to be no valid argument against the claim that mathematics cannot be said to be absolutely certain. Thus there seems to be no valid argument against the claim that mathematical knowledge is not infallible, in the sense that it cannot be ruled out that it might lead to error. In order to rule out such possibility, we should at least be able to give a demonstration of the consistency of ZFC by absolutely reliable means. But, by Gödel's second incompleteness theorem, this is impossible.

Simpson claims that today "the validity of mathematics is under siege."[55] In particular, "Gödel supplied heavy artillery for all would-be-assailants of mathematics."[56] Therefore, "mathematicians and philosophers of mathematics ought to get on with the task of defending their discipline."[57] The "attack on mathematics is part of a general assault against reason."[58] Actually, almost the opposite is the case. What is against reason is, rather, to place mathematics in an unlikely paradise of eternal, unrevisable truths, instead of taking it for what it really is, fallible, revisable, and evolving, like natural science.

---

[50] *Ibid.*

[51] Wittgenstein (1978, III.80).

[52] *Ibid.*, VII.15.

[53] A brilliant parody of Wittgenstein's rule is implicit in Calvino's fictional dialogue between Marco Polo and Kublai Kahn; see Calvino (1974, 69).

[54] This does not mean that inconsistency handling is not a technologically relevant question. As Wagner states, while in mathematics "the contradictions in a theory must not be tolerated and have to be removed, otherwise the theory as a whole should be rejected as meaningless," in artificial intelligence "inconsistency handling plays a crucial role" (Wagner 1991, 538). But one thing is a technologically relevant question, and another thing is a philosophically relevant question.

[55] Simpson (1988, 357).

[56] *Ibid.*, 362.

[57] *Ibid.*, 358.

[58] *Ibid.*

After decades of fruitless attempts to establish the absolute certainty of mathematics, Russell admitted: "I wanted certainty in the kind of way in which people want religious faith. I thought that certainty is more likely to be found in mathematics than elsewhere."[59] But, "having constructed an elephant upon which the mathematical world could rest, I found the elephant tottering" and, "after some twenty years of very arduous toil, I came to the conclusion that there was nothing more that I could do in the way of making mathematical knowledge indubitable."[60] The "splendid certainty which I had always hoped to find in mathematics was lost in a bewildering maze."[61] Recognizing that one cannot find splendid certainty in mathematics is the starting point for any realistic philosophy of mathematics.[62]

1.7 The Top-Down and Bottom-Up Approaches to Mathematics

An argument which is often used against the significance of Gödel's incompleteness theorems is that they are irrelevant to mathematical practice. For example, Davies states: "I got the dread seeing yet another discussion of Gödel's theorems and their importance, when I knew that they had almost no relevance to the work of most mathematicians."[63] As a matter of fact, after the discovery of Gödel's incompleteness theorems, several mathematicians have continued to do mathematics as if Gödel's results did not exist. Even their view of the nature of mathematics has been unaffected by Gödel's results, because they have continued to believe that "the axiomatic method is 'the' method of mathematics, in fact, it is mathematics."[64]

This is due to the fact that most mathematicians follow the top-down approach to mathematics, which has been the mathematics paradigm for the past one and a half century. According to the top-down approach:

1) A mathematics field is developed from above, that is, from general principles concerning that field.

2) It is developed by the axiomatic method, which is a downward path from principles to conclusions derived deductively from them.

An example of the top-down approach is Leibniz's approach to the calculus of infinitesimals, as presented by de l'Hospital's in the first textbook on the subject.[65] Another example is Church's approach to computability in terms of

---

[59]Russell (1971, III, 220).
[60]*Ibid.*
[61]Russell (1995b, 157).
[62]See Cellucci (2013a).
[63]Davies (2008, 88).
[64]Naylor and Sell (2000, 6).
[65]See de l'Hospital (1696, 1–2).

the lambda calculus.[66] That the top-down approach has been the mathematics paradigm for the past one and a half century is due to the influence of the Göttingen school and Bourbaki. But, identifying the method of mathematics and science with the axiomatic method, the top-down approach is incompatible with Gödel's incompleteness theorems. And, identifying mathematical reasoning with deductive reasoning, it conflicts with the fact that "deduction plays only a small role in human reasoning."[67]

The alternative to the top-down approach is the bottom-up approach, according to which:

1) A mathematics field is developed from below, that is, from problems of that field or from problems of other mathematics, natural science or social science fields.

2) It is developed by the analytic method, which is an upward path from problems to hypotheses derived non-deductively from them.[68]

An example of the bottom-up approach is Newton's approach to the calculus of infinitesimals; see Chapter 21. Another example is Turing's approach to computability, which is based on an analysis of the actions of a human being who is making a calculation.[69]

While Gödel's incompleteness theorems affect the axiomatic method, they do not affect the analytic method. On the contrary, they provide evidence for it; see Chapter 17.

1.8 The Top-Down and Bottom-Up Approaches to Science

The top-down and bottom-up approaches extend from mathematics to natural and social science fields.

According to the top-down approach, a natural or social science field is developed from above, that is, from general principles concerning that field, and is developed by the axiomatic method. For example, Dirac states that one has a "physical theory when all the axioms and rules of manipulation governing the mathematical quantities are specified and when in addition certain laws are laid down connecting physical facts with the mathematical formalism."[70] In an application of a physical theory "one would be given certain physical information, which one would proceed to express by equations between the mathematical quantities. One would then deduce new equations with the help of the axioms and rules of manipulation."[71]

---

[66] See Church (1936, 346–349).
[67] Oaksford and Chater (2007, 56).
[68] On the distinction between top-down and bottom-up approaches to mathematics, see Cellucci (2013b).
[69] See Turing (1936–1937, 249–252).
[70] Dirac (1958, 16).
[71] *Ibid.*

Conversely, according to the bottom-up approach, a natural or social science field is developed from below, that is, from problems of that field or of other natural or social science fields, and is developed by the analytic method. For example, Grosholz states that "certain important areas of scientific activity have not been, and may never be, reformulated in terms of axiomatic theories."[72] And yet "they come to stand in deep and interesting relations to other areas of science in complex ways that contribute to scientific explanation," and "the derivation may fail to be deductive."[73] These areas of science are investigated by analysis, which is "the search for the conditions of solvability of a problem."[74] Such conditions are found by means of "non-deductive derivations," which "may themselves be powerful vehicles of scientific explanation."[75]

The top-down and bottom-up approaches correspond to two different views of the world. The top-down approach corresponds to the view that all facts are to be explained in terms of some higher principle. In the theological version of this view, the higher principle is God or something like God. The bottom-up approach corresponds to the view that the world is to be explained in terms of physical processes, moving from the less complex to the more complex.

1.9 Limitations of the Top-Down Approach

In addition to being incompatible with Gödel's incompleteness theorems, the top-down approach has other limitations. Here are some of them as regards mathematics.

1) *It does not permit to distinguish between mathematical theories in terms of their significance.* As Bourbaki acknowledges, being based on arbitrary axioms, subject only to the requirement of consistency, the top-down approach leads to "a whole crop of monster-structures, entirely without applications."[76]

2) *It leads to a fragmentation of the research.* As Bourbaki acknowledges, because of such an approach, "many mathematicians take up quarters in a corner of the domain of mathematics," and "are unable to understand the language and the terminology used by colleagues who are working in a corner remote from their own."[77]

3) *It is not very successful in the application of mathematics to several non-mathematics fields.* Dieudonné even claims that, "of all the striking progress" in recent mathematics, almost "not a single one" had "anything to do with physical

---

[72] Grosholz (2000, 81).
[73] *Ibid.*
[74] Grosholz (2007, 34).
[75] Grosholz (2000, 82).
[76] Bourbaki (1996, 1275, footnote 9).
[77] *Ibid.*, 1266.

applications."⁷⁸ This is due to the fact that several mathematics fields are developed from within, that is, from principles concerning their own basic concepts, rather than from without, that is, from the peculiarities of the non-mathematics fields.

4) *It cannot explain the success of the application of mathematics to physics.* As Bourbaki acknowledges, such an approach makes us "completely ignorant as to the underlying reasons" for the "intimate connection between experimental phenomena and mathematical structures."⁷⁹ It "so happens – without our knowing why – that certain aspects of empirical reality fit themselves into" mathematical structures "as if through a kind of preadaptation."⁸⁰ One may ask "why do such applications ever succeed," but, "fortunately for us, the mathematician does not feel called upon to answer such questions."⁸¹

1.10 Seeking a New Role for Mathematical Logic

As a response to the failure of mathematical logic to give a secure foundation for mathematics, mathematical logicians have developed logic into a more and more mathematical discipline, giving up the ambition to contribute to the philosophical understanding of the foundations of mathematics. This attempt, however, has not been very successful. As Wang points out, mathematical "logicians find themselves attracted into the whirl of mathematical activity. At the same time," their contribution "to the philosophical understanding of the foundations of human knowledge (and mathematics in particular) appears to decrease rather than increase."⁸² A reason why they have developed logic into a more and more mathematical discipline "may be the sociopsychological pull toward more definite results. This has produced the effect that the philosophically more relevant aspects of logic are left underdeveloped and consequently driven underground by the less relevant but more impressive mathematical advances."⁸³ Moreover, although today, "as practiced, mathematical logic is but a special branch of mathematics," in fact "it is not often regarded as a very central branch."⁸⁴

As another response to the failure of mathematical logic to give a secure foundation for mathematics, other people have sought a new role for the subject, particularly in mathematics or in computer science. McCarthy even claimed that "it is reasonable to hope that the relationship between computation and mathematical logic will be as fruitful in the" twenty first "century as that between analysis and

---

[78] Dieudonné (1964, 248).
[79] Bourbaki (1996, 1275).
[80] *Ibid.*, 1276.
[81] Bourbaki (1949, 2).
[82] Wang (1974, 28).
[83] *Ibid.*
[84] *Ibid.*, 21.

physics in the last."[85] This is unconvincing. On the one hand, few mathematicians would acknowledge the relevance of mathematical logic to their own discipline. Thus Dieudonné states that the trouble with the formal systems of mathematical logic is that "no mathematician as far as I know has ever found any use for these systems at all."[86] Indeed, "even if mathematical logic had completely ceased to exist in 1925, no mathematician would ever have missed it."[87] On the other hand, mathematical logic has played no major part in the most significant technological developments of real computing in the last decades. For example, large investments by Japan's Ministry of International Trade and Industry in a Fifth Generation Computer Systems project, heavily dependent on mathematical logic, ended in failure and the project was eventually terminated.

This is no surprise because the intended purpose of mathematical logic, the one for which it was created, was to give a secure foundation for mathematics. This shaped the subject and deeply affected its further development. It would have been extraordinary if mathematical logic had turned out to be fit to a completely different purpose. As we have seen, Frege himself stated that mathematical logic is a device invented for certain scientific purposes, and one must not condemn it because it is not suited to others.

1.11 The Criticism of Scholastic Logic

The failure of the attempts to seek another role for mathematical logic reproposes the question: What is logic? Is it merely the study of deductive reasoning, or has it a wider scope? In the seventeenth century the then current logic paradigm, Scholastic logic, fell under the blows of Bacon, Galileo, Descartes, and Locke.

Thus Bacon stated that Scholastic logic "is useless for the discovery of sciences."[88] It "is good rather for establishing and fixing errors (which are themselves based on vulgar notions) than for inquiring into truth; hence it is more harmful than useful."[89]

Galileo stated that Scholastic "logic teaches how to know whether or not reasonings and demonstrations already made and discovered are conclusive," but not "to find conclusive reasonings and demonstrations."[90]

Descartes stated that Scholastic logic "contributes nothing whatsoever to the knowledge of truth."[91] It "does not teach the method by which something has been

---

[85] McCarthy (1963, 69).
[86] Dieudonné (1979, 32).
[87] Ibid., 33.
[88] Bacon (1961–1986, I, 158).
[89] Ibid.
[90] Galilei (1968, VIII, 175).
[91] Descartes (1996, X, 406).

discovered."[92] Therefore, it "is entirely useless for those who wish to investigate the truth of things."[93]

Locke stated that Scholastic logic "discovers no new proofs," it is merely "the art of marshalling, and ranging the old ones we have already."[94] Therefore, it "has been thought more proper for the attaining victory in dispute, than for the discovery or confirmation of truth, in fair enquiries."[95]

Bacon, Galileo, Descartes, and Locke highlighted a serious weakness of Scholastic logic: its inadequacy to the needs of modern science, being useless to discover anything new. At least in this respect, the present logic paradigm, mathematical logic, does not fare much better.

1.12 Scholastic Logic and Mathematical Logic

In fact, the condition of mathematical logic appears dangerously similar to that of Scholastic logic. Admittedly, mathematical logic can account for inferences that Scholastic logic could not account for, such as: All horses are animals, therefore all heads of horses are heads of animals. But the uselessness Bacon, Galileo, Descartes, and Locke ascribed to Scholastic logic did not stem from a deficiency later removed by technical refinements. It was due to the fact that Scholastic logic was not an instrument of discovery, and this charge affects mathematical logic as well. It is untouched by the latter being a technical refinement over Scholastic logic.

To address the incapacity of Scholastic logic to be an instrument of discovery, Bacon and Descartes tried to develop a logic of discovery. Since the effort was focused on that direction, in the seventeenth and eighteenth centuries there was a marked decline of interest in Scholastic logic.

In this connection, it is significant that historians of logic inspired by mathematical logic blame the Scientific Revolution for the decline of interest in logic during the seventeenth and eighteenth centuries, and consider logically irrelevant Bacon's and Descartes' attempts to develop a logic of discovery. In their view, the copious and passionate discussions on the scientific method during the Scientific Revolution were extrinsic to logic and even opposed to it.

Thus the Kneales state that "the rise of modern physics" and "the recognition that logic was not an instrument of discovery" led to "the marked decline of interest in formal logic which occurred during the seventeenth and eighteenth centuries."[96] In particular, "logic was divorced at this time from mathematics."[97] Mathematicians

---

[92]*Ibid.*, VII, 156.
[93]*Ibid.*, X, 406.
[94]Locke (1975, 679).
[95]*Ibid.*, 677–678.
[96]Kneale and Kneale (1962, 307).
[97]*Ibid.*, 308.

focused their attention on "algebra and analysis" which "were not elaborated in axiomatic fashion."[98] They "came to think of their new methods as independent of traditional logic," since "the new branches of mathematics were supposed to contain a technique of discovery."[99] Blanché states that, "as a result of the scientific revolution carried out, most of all, by Galileo," a "radical transformation takes place: the sharp rejection of logic" and its replacement with "the making theoretically explicit of the method practiced by science."[100] The "best representative of this new attitude is Descartes," a philosopher who, like Bacon, "has given no real contribution to logic."[101] In fact, in Bacon's and Descartes' work "there is strictly nothing to keep for the history of logic."[102]

1.13 Mathematical Logic and Discovery

That, like Scholastic logic, mathematical logic is useless to discover anything new, is not an accident, but rather a consequence of Frege's assumption that the question of discovery is merely subjective.

According to Frege, "we can inquire, on the one hand, how we have gradually arrived at a given proposition and, on the other, how we can finally provide it with the most secure foundation."[103] The first question, discovery, is merely subjective, because it "may have to be answered differently for different persons," only the second question, justification, "is more definite."[104] Therefore, logic must concern itself "not with the way in which" mathematical propositions "are discovered but with the kind of ground on which their" justification "rests."[105] The "task of logic is to set up laws according to which a judgment is justified by others."[106] These are the laws of deduction, therefore, according to Frege, logic must concern itself only with deduction.

Frege's view is shared by most mathematical logicians. According to them, while deducing conclusions from given principles is a logical task, there is no logical way to scientific hypotheses, the latter can be reached only by intuition. Therefore, logic must concern itself only with deduction. In the last century, this has been the prevailing view, which does not mean that it is a sound one. Indeed, one of the aims of this book is to show that it is not.

---

[98] *Ibid.*, 309.
[99] *Ibid.*
[100] Blanché (1970, 175).
[101] *Ibid.*
[102] *Ibid.*, 174.
[103] Frege (1967, 5).
[104] *Ibid.*
[105] Frege (1959, 23).
[106] Frege (1979, 175).

1.14 The Need for an Alternative Logic Paradigm

Consistently with Frege's assumption that no logic of discovery is possible, mathematical logic has been useless to discover anything new. Frege himself states: "There are no new truths in my work."[107] This exposes mathematical logic to the very same charge of uselessness that Bacon, Galileo, Descartes, Locke brought against Scholastic logic.

Not only mathematical logic has been useless to discover anything new, but it has not been significantly helpful even as a means of justification. A proposition cannot be more justified than the axioms from which it is deduced, and, by Gödel's second incompleteness theorem, no absolutely reliable justification for the axioms is generally possible.

As a result, mathematical logic has had little impact on scientific research. A discipline earns its keep if it proves capable of solving problems, first of all, those arising from the world around us and our participation in it. If it fails to do so, there is a sense of unreality about the whole discipline. Davis even states that, although "it would be invidious to mention a specific example of exhaustion of a field when there are people working very happily in it," the "following example and opinion is in the open literature. Classical mathematical logic" has "lost its connection to reality and has produced mathematical monsters."[108]

An alternative logic paradigm is necessary if logic is to play any significant role in scientific research. Thus Rota states that "that magnificent clockwork mechanism that is mathematical logic is slowly grinding out the internal weaknesses of the system."[109] Its concepts "were invented one day for the purpose of dealing with a certain model of the world" which is "inadequate to the needs of the new sciences."[110] Today, "in all circumstances imaginable, including mathematical reflection (the true one, not the one of *a posteriori* reconstructions), logic shines for its absence."[111] If "we are to set the new sciences on firm, autonomous, formal foundations, then a drastic overhaul" of "logic is in order."[112]

An alternative logic paradigm is also necessary if logic is to play any significant role in philosophy. Thus Wang states that, "as we understand the nature of mathematical logic better, we find that the early belief in its philosophical relevance was largely an illusion."[113] Mathematical logic "is rather detached from actual knowledge" because, instead of being concerned with the process of knowledge

---

[107] Frege (1967, 6).
[108] Davis (2006, 176).
[109] Kac et al. (1992, 180).
[110] *Ibid.*
[111] Rota (1999, 94).
[112] Kac et al. (1992, 180).
[113] Wang (1974, 28).

acquisition, it "seems to be concerned only with end results."[114] Insofar as "it has been influential in philosophy, I am not sure the influences have been good ones."[115]

1.15 Towards an Alternative Logic Paradigm

Towards an alternative logic paradigm, this book examines the limitations of mathematical logic and outlines a new approach to logic.

In this respect, it is illuminating to compare mathematical logic with earlier views about logic and its relation to the scientific method. To this end, this book gives an overview of how logic and its relation to the scientific method have been conceived in antiquity and in the modern age. This does not mean that this book is a history of logic. It only focuses on certain crucial steps in the development of logic and its relation to the scientific method that may provide useful indications for a new approach to the subject. From the overview it appears that, contrary to a widespread opinion, mathematical logic represents a substantial restriction on the scope of logic with respect to Plato, Aristotle, Descartes and Kant.

Since one of the most serious limitations of mathematical logic is that it is useless to discover anything new, in the alternative logic paradigm logic is intended, first of all, to provide rules of discovery, that is, non-deductive rules for finding hypotheses to solve problems. While mathematical logic, being a logic of justification, is only aimed at systematizing and justifying what is already known – and, by Gödel's incompleteness theorems, fails even to do that – in the alternative logic paradigm logic aims at providing means to discover something new. This is essential if logic is to play any relevant role in mathematics, science and even philosophy.

1.16 Characters of the Alternative Logic Paradigm

The alternative logic paradigm outlined in this book is not merely an expansion of mathematical logic. It has different presuppositions, it uses different rules and develops aspects that previously received little notice. In particular, it involves a new view of the relation of logic to evolution, language, reason, method and knowledge.

1) *Evolution*. According to mathematical logic, logic is totally independent of biological evolution. According to the alternative logic paradigm, logic is a continuation of the problem solving processes with which biological evolution has endowed all organisms.

2) *Language*. According to mathematical logic, logic is essentially dependent on language, since it is only concerned with propositional inferences, that is, inferences

---

[114] *Ibid.*
[115] *Ibid.*, 51.

from propositions to propositions. According to the alternative logic paradigm, logic is also concerned with non-propositional inferences.

3) *Reason.* According to mathematical logic, logic is the whole of reason. According to the alternative logic paradigm, logic is only a part of reason.

4) *Method.* According to mathematical logic, logic does not originate from method. According to the alternative logic paradigm, method is the source of logic.

5) *Knowledge.* According to mathematical logic, logic does not provide means to acquire knowledge. According to the alternative logic paradigm, logic provides such means.

These differences between the alternative logic paradigm and mathematical logic will be discussed in Chapters 16 and 17.

1.17 The Alternative Logic Paradigm and Philosophy

The alternative logic paradigm outlined in this book also involves a new view of the relation of philosophy to knowledge.

According to mathematical logic, and analytic philosophy which is strictly related to it, philosophy does not provide means to acquire knowledge, it only clarifies what we already know.[116] According to the alternative logic paradigm, philosophy may provide such means. This extends the relation of logic to knowledge to the whole of philosophy.

This difference between the alternative logic paradigm and analytic philosophy will be discussed in Chapter 19.

1.18 The Reconstruction of Logic

About a century ago Dewey published a book entitled *Reconstruction in philosophy*. Some twenty-five years later, in a new Introduction to the book, he stated: "Today Reconstruction *of* philosophy is a more suitable title than Reconstruction *in* philosophy."[117] In particular, the reconstruction of philosophy involved a reconstruction

---

[116]Here and in what follows, 'analytic philosophy' means 'classical analytic philosophy', a philosophical movement including Cambridge philosophers, such as Russell, Moore, and Wittgenstein; Vienna Circle philosophers, such as Schlick, Carnap, and Neurath; Berlin philosophers, such as Reichenbach and Hempel; Oxford philosophers, such as Ryle, Austin, Strawson, and Dummett; American philosophers, such as Quine and Sellars. It does not mean neo-analytic philosophy, the eclectic, heterogeneous and often conflicting variety of doctrines that today go by the name of 'analytic philosophy'. For an overview of the historical development of analytic philosophy see, for example, Schwartz (2012).

[117]Dewey (2004, iii).

of logic, because "contemporary logical theory is the ground upon which all philosophical differences and disputes are gathered together and focussed."[118]

Dewey's problem is still with us. A reconstruction of logic is necessary if logic is not to become an anachronism. The alternative logic paradigm outlined in this book is intended to suggest a way towards this goal.

In view of its substantial differences from mathematical logic, the alternative logic paradigm is likely to meet opposition from mathematical logicians. But they should listen to van Benthem, who states that "we cannot keep singing hymns to Gödel and Tarski forever – unless we are already in Heaven."[119] I "have never been able to understand this defense of the status quo," by which "innovative 'agents provocateurs' like Lakatos in his mind-opener *Proofs and refutations* were subjected to torrents of abuse, rather than the lively interest in new ideas one would expect from a vigorous community."[120] In fact, "I have always found many outspoken critics" of mathematical "logic (Blanshard, Perelman, Toulmin, Lakatos) extremely interesting and well-worth reading, and a useful reminder of the many doors our Founding Fathers have closed historically – doors that could be opened again now."[121]

Such doors should be opened again today, if logic is to recover the role it had in antiquity. As Barnes states, in antiquity no one who considered logic "a legitimate object of study in its own right, disputed the idea that logic also supplied the sciences with its instruments."[122] On the other hand, "logic was not an esoteric discipline, reserved – like medicine or the higher mathematics – for a few specialists. Rather, it was a standard part of the school curriculum."[123] Thus "every educated man was soaked in logic," and, on the other hand, "logic was an uncontested basis for the study of science and philosophy."[124]

To recover the role logic had in antiquity, an alternative logic paradigm is necessary. This is by no means intended to diminish the importance of mathematical logic. Frege's creation stands up as a monument to which we must always return in thought. But, as it happens with even the most splendid intellectual creations, it has shown its limitations.

Having been a mathematical logician myself, I can only repeat what Descartes said: "It is some years now since I realized how numerous were the false opinions that I had admitted as true in my youth, and how dubious was whatever I had since built on them," and "hence that it was necessary, at least once in my life, to demolish everything from the ground and begin again from the first foundations."[125]

---

[118] *Ibid.*, 77.
[119] van Benthem (2008, 40).
[120] *Ibid.*
[121] *Ibid.*
[122] Barnes (2003, 22).
[123] *Ibid.*
[124] *Ibid.*, 23.
[125] Descartes (1996, VII, 17).

1.19 Organization of the Book

The book is divided into four parts, after the present Chapter 1: Ancient Perspectives, Modern Perspectives, An Alternative Perspective, Rules of Discovery.

Part I, 'Ancient Perspectives', considers some basic perspectives on logic in antiquity, especially in Plato and Aristotle.

Chapter 2 deals with the origin of logic and its relation to method, as well as with the origin of the names 'logic' and 'method'. Chapter 3 deals with Plato's and Aristotle's conceptions of science, which involve two different methods, the analytic method and Aristotle's analytic-synthetic method, respectively. Chapter 4 deals with the analytic method. Chapter 5 deals with Aristotle's analytic-synthetic method and Pappus' variant of it. Chapter 6 deals with the deductivist view of Aristotle's logic, which interprets it as the study of deduction. Chapter 7 deals with the heuristic view of Aristotle's logic, which interprets it as primarily a logic of discovery. It is argued that only this view is adequate.

Part II, 'Modern Perspectives', considers some basic perspectives on logic in the modern age, from the originators of modern science to mathematical logic.

Chapter 8 deals with the method of modern science, as stated by Galileo and Newton, showing that it is essentially the same as Aristotle's analytic-synthetic method. Chapter 9 deals with Bacon's, Descartes', Leibniz's and Kant's conceptions of logic, in particular, with their views on the logic of discovery. Chapter 10 deals with Frege's conception of logic, in particular with Frege's ideal of splitting up deduction into a few logically simple modes of inference, and his failure in achieving this ideal. Chapter 11 deals with Gentzen's analysis of deduction and his failure in achieving that very same ideal. Chapter 12 deals with the impact of Gödel's incompleteness theorems, and other limitative results, on the tenets of mathematical logic. Chapter 13 deals with the divorce of logic from method operated by Frege, and with the limitations of the psychology of discovery which originated from that divorce.

Part III, 'An Alternative Perspective,' outlines a perspective on logic hopefully not subject to the limitations of mathematical logic.

Chapter 14 deals with the nature of reason and knowledge. Chapter 15 deals with the relation of reason and knowledge to emotion. Chapter 16 deals with the relation of logic to evolution, language and reason. Chapter 17 deals with the relation of logic to method and knowledge. Chapter 18 deals with the question of the classification and justification of inference rules, both deductive and non-deductive. Chapter 19 deals with the relation of philosophy to knowledge.

Part IV, 'Rules of Discovery', considers rules of discovery, namely, non-deductive rules for finding hypotheses to solve problems.

Chapter 20 deals with induction and analogy, indeed, various kinds of them. Chapter 21 deals with generalization, specialization, metaphor, metonymy, definition, and diagrams.

The book is the result of a constant struggle between scope and depth. There is scarcely a chapter that would not be worthy of further expansion, but this would make the book too bulky and unwieldy. Moreover, as Sterne says, "no author, who understands the just boundaries of decorum and good-breeding, would presume to think all: The truest respect which you can pay to the reader's understanding, is to halve this matter amicably, and leave him something to imagine, in his turn, as well as yourself."[126]

1.20 Notations, Quotations, Transliterations

The following notations are used for logical constants: $\neg$ (not), $\wedge$ (and), $\vee$ (or), $\rightarrow$ (if... then), $\leftrightarrow$ (if and only if), $\forall$ (for all), $\exists$ (for some, there exists).

When quoting from ancient Greek philosophers, and even from some modern ones, translations are original unless otherwise stated. This is motivated by the fact that, first, every translation is an interpretation, and the interpretations proposed in this book are often different from those on which current translations are based; secondly, current translations of different works by different translators may be inconsistent with each other, so quoting from them would lead to misunderstandings.

When quoting Greek expressions, the so-called scientific transliteration from the Greek to the Latin alphabet is used.

---

[126] Sterne (1997, 88).

Part I
Ancient Perspectives

Chapter 2
The Origin of Logic

2.1 Six Claims by Greek Philosophers

When dealing with logic, the following three questions naturally arise:

What is the origin of logic and its relation to method?
What is the origin of the name 'logic'?
What is the origin of the name 'method'?

Let us first consider the question: What is the origin of logic and its relation to method? In order to answer this question, it is useful to focus on the following six claims by Greek philosophers.

(1) The universe is a *kosmos*, namely an order, because it is governed by a divine mind.

(2) The human mind mirrors the divine mind, which makes it potentially capable of acquiring knowledge of the universe.

(3) In order to acquire knowledge of the universe, the human mind needs a method.

(4) The method is implemented by developing logical means, so logic arises from method.

(5) Logic is a logic of discovery, because it provides means to acquire knowledge of the universe.

(6) Logic is discursive thinking but, in order to acquire knowledge of the universe, the human mind also needs intuitive thinking, which is the highest faculty.

Parmenides, Plato and Aristotle were the first to make all of the claims (1)–(6). The next few sections will present their formulations.

2.2 Universe, Mind and Divinity

(1) The universe is a *kosmos*, namely an order, because it is governed by a divine mind.

a) Parmenides states that the universe is an "order [*diacosmos*]."[1] For it is ruled by the mind of "the Goddess who governs all things."[2]

b) Plato states that the universe is not "left to the guidance of the irrational, the chance and the fortuitous" but "is governed by a mind [*nous*] and a marvellous ordering wisdom."[3] This is "the reason why this universe is called an order [*kosmos*]."[4] The mind in question is the mind of the God who is the "maker and father of this universe."[5] He modelled it "after that which is apprehended by reason and mind."[6]

c) Aristotle states that there is a first mover on which "depend the heavens and the world of nature."[7] The first mover is a mind, because he "thinks."[8] By thinking, he moves the heavens, being their "moving or efficient principle" without which "there would be no movement."[9] Then the first mover is God, since "it is God that moves everything in the whole universe."[10]

2.3 Human Mind and Divine Mind

(2) The human mind mirrors the divine mind, which makes it potentially capable of acquiring knowledge of the universe.

a) Parmenides presents the Goddess who governs all things as saying: "I will tell you" the order of the universe, "and you listen and receive my word."[11] Human beings will be able to receive the Goddess' word because the human mind mirrors the Goddess' mind. This makes the human mind potentially capable of acquiring knowledge of the universe because, the Goddess says, "I describe this order of the universe, completely truthlike, to you."[12]

---

[1] Diels and Kranz (1964, 28 B 8.60).
[2] *Ibid.*, 28 B 12.3.
[3] Plato, *Philebus*, 28 d 6–9.
[4] Plato, *Gorgias*, 508 a 3.
[5] Plato, *Timaeus*, 28 c 3–4.
[6] *Ibid.*, 29 a 6–7.
[7] Aristotle, *Metaphysica*, Λ 7, 1072 b 14.
[8] *Ibid.*, Λ 7, 1072 b 19–20.
[9] *Ibid.*, Λ 7, 1071 b 12–13.
[10] Aristotle, *Ethica Eudemea*, Θ 2, 1248 a 26–27.
[11] Diels and Kranz (1964, 28 B 2.1).
[12] *Ibid.*, 28 B 8.60.

b) Plato states that the human mind is "the divine part in us," and the revolutions of the human mind have affinity with "the revolutions of the universe."[13] The latter are the "revolutions of the God."[14] This makes the human mind potentially capable of acquiring knowledge of the universe.

c) Aristotle states that the human mind "rules and guides us and has insight into matters noble and divine, either because it is divine or just the most divine element within us."[15] This makes the human mind potentially capable of acquiring knowledge of the universe, although we only "sometimes are" in "that good state in which" God "always is."[16]

2.4 Method and Universe

(3) In order to acquire knowledge of the universe, the human mind needs a method.

a) Parmenides states that, in order to acquire knowledge of the universe, the human mind needs to follow "the much-informing way [*hodos*] of the Goddess, that leads the wise man through all."[17] This "is the way of conviction, since it attends upon true reality."[18]

b) Plato states that, in order to acquire knowledge of the universe, the human mind needs a method, because "this is how one must reason about the nature of anything."[19] Proceeding without method "would be like walking with the blind. But someone who goes about his subject skilfully must not be like the blind."[20]

c) Aristotle states that, in order to acquire knowledge of the universe, the human mind needs a method because, to that purpose, "one must have been educated in the method by which each thing should be demonstrated."[21]

2.5 Method and Logic

(4) The method is implemented by developing logical means, so logic arises from method.

---

[13] Plato, *Timaeus*, 90 c 7–d 1.

[14] *Ibid.*, 47 c 3.

[15] Aristotle, *Ethica Nicomachea*, K 7, 1177 a 13–16.

[16] Aristotle, *Metaphysica*, Λ 7, 1072 b 24–25.

[17] Diels and Kranz (1964, 28 B 1.2–3).

[18] *Ibid.*, 28 B 2.4.

[19] Plato, *Phaedrus*, 270 c 10–d 1.

[20] *Ibid.*, 270 d 9–e 2.

[21] Aristotle, *Metaphysica*, α 3, 995 a 12–13.

a) Parmenides states that the method is implemented by developing logical means such as the principle of non-contradiction, $\neg(A \wedge \neg A)$, which states that "this shall never prevail, that what is not is."[22] Or the principle of the excluded middle, $A \vee \neg A$, which states that what is "must either be altogether or be not at all."[23] Or the rule of reduction to the impossible, by which, if an assumption A yields a contradiction, B and $\neg B$, then one can infer $\neg A$. An example of Parmenides' use of this rule will be considered in Chapter 3.

b) Plato states that the method is implemented by developing logical means, because knowledge cannot be acquired "without a logical art."[24] Therefore, the method must be a "method of logic."[25]

c) Aristotle states that the method is implemented by developing logical means, because they give the "ability to syllogize about any problem proposed, on the basis of the things which are given as the most accepted opinions."[26]

2.6 Logic and Discovery

(5) Logic is a logic of discovery, because it provides means to acquire knowledge of the universe.

a) Parmenides states that logic is a way through which we come to "learn everything" and reach "the unshaken heart of the well-rounded truth."[27]

b) Plato states that, if a man "does not give up until" he "reaches the end of the intelligible," logic will enable him "to arrive at what each thing itself is."[28]

c) Aristotle states that we not only can know "how syllogisms come about" but also "have the ability to discover [*euriskein*] them."[29] This enables us to acquire scientific knowledge, because it is by means of a certain kind of syllogism that "we have scientific knowledge."[30]

---

[22] Diels and Kranz (1964, 28 B 7.1).
[23] *Ibid.*, 22 B 8.11.
[24] Plato, *Phaedo*, 90 b 7.
[25] Plato, *Sophista*, 227 a 8.
[26] Aristotle, *Sophistici Elenchi*, 34, 183 a 37–38.
[27] Diels and Kranz (1964, 28 B 1.28–29).
[28] Plato, *Respublica*, VII 532 a 7–b 2.
[29] Aristotle, *Analytica Priora*, A 32, 47 a 2–4.
[30] Aristotle, *Analytica Posteriora*, A 2, 71 a 19.

2.7 Logic, Intuitive Thinking and Discursive Thinking

(6) Logic is discursive thinking but, in order to acquire knowledge of the universe, the human mind also needs intuitive thinking, which is the highest faculty.

a) Parmenides states that logic is discursive thinking, because it makes the human mind "judge by reasoning [*logos*]."[31] But, in order to acquire knowledge of the universe, the human mind also needs intuitive thinking, which is the highest faculty because "intuiting [*noein*]" what is and "what is [*einai*] are the same thing."[32] This does not mean that what is exists only insofar as it is intuited. For "without the being to which it refers, you will not find intuiting."[33] Rather, it means that intuiting is an act of mind by which the content of that act and what is are the same thing. Therefore, if you want to know what is, "look [*leusse*] with intuition [*nooi*]."[34]

b) Plato states that logic is discursive thinking, because it "concerns those things which are especially apprehended by argument."[35] But, in order to acquire knowledge of the universe, the human mind also needs "intuitive thinking [*noesis*]," which is "the highest faculty."[36]

c) Aristotle states that logic is discursive thinking, because it is based on syllogism, and "syllogism is discourse [*logos*]."[37] But, in order to acquire knowledge of the universe, the human mind also needs intuitive thinking, which is the highest faculty, because "intuition" is "always true."[38]

2.8 An Articulated View of the Origin of Logic

On the basis of claims (1)–(6), it is possible to give an answer to the question: What is the origin of logic and its relation to method? Or rather, it is possible to give three different, though complementary, answers.

The first answer is that logic is:

(A) That rational faculty which all human beings have.

---

[31] Diels and Kranz (1964, 28 B 7.5).

[32] *Ibid.*, 28 B 3.1.

[33] *Ibid.*, 28 B 8.35–36.

[34] *Ibid.*, 28 B 4.1. Clement of Alexandria, through whom we know this passage, comments on it by saying that intuition is necessary because there are things which are never seen "with our eyes, but only with our intuition [*nooi*]" (*Ibid.*, 28 B 4). Empedocles echoes the passage in question: "Gaze [*derkeu*] with intuition [*nooi*]" (*Ibid.*, 31 B 17.21).

[35] Plato, *Parmenides*, 135 e 2–3.

[36] Plato, *Respublica*, VI 511 d 8.

[37] Aristotle, *Topica*, A 1, 100 a 25.

[38] Aristotle, *Analytica Posteriora*, B 19, 100 b 7–8.

For if the human mind mirrors the divine mind which governs the universe, then all human beings have a rational faculty, and logic is that faculty. Parmenides, Plato and Aristotle were the originators of logic in sense (A), because they were the first to suggest that logic is that rational faculty which all human beings have.

The second answer is that logic is:

(B) The development of procedures for acquiring knowledge.

For if, in order to acquire knowledge, the human mind needs a method, thus procedures adequate to that purpose, then the development of such procedures is essential, and logic is such a development. Hippocrates of Chios and Hippocrates of Cos were the originators of logic in sense (B), because they were the first to develop procedures for acquiring knowledge, in mathematics and medicine, respectively. This will be discussed in Chapter 4.

The third answer is that logic is:

(C) The systematic study of procedures for acquiring knowledge.

For, once again, if, in order to acquire knowledge, the human mind needs a method, thus procedures adequate to that purpose, then it may be useful to undertake a systematic study of such procedures, and logic is such a study. Aristotle was the originator of logic in sense (C), because he was the first to make a systematic study of procedures for acquiring knowledge. This will be discussed in Chapters 5, 6, and 7. Being a systematic study, logic in sense (C) is logic as a subject.

2.9 Origin of the Connection Between Universe, God and Mind

While Parmenides, Plato and Aristotle were the first to make all of the claims (1)–(6), some of those claims are anterior to them.

For example, claims (1) and (2) already occur in Heraclitus, who "connects human reason with the divine reason which governs and controls everything in the universe."[39] According to Heraclitus, "all things happen according to" the divine "reason."[40] And "we do and think everything by partaking in the divine reason."[41] Because human reason partakes in the divine reason, "reason is common to all."[42]

Claims (1) and (2) are even anterior to Greek philosophy. They occur in an inscription made by order of the pharaoh Shabaka around 710 BC, which was a copy of a much older text, at least 1292–1075 BC. The inscription states that the Memphis God "Ptah is the very great, who has given life" to every thing "through

---

[39]Diels and Kranz (1964, 22 A 20).
[40]*Ibid.*, 22 B 1.
[41]*Ibid.*, 22 A 16.
[42]*Ibid.*, 22 B 2.

this heart."[43] Thus every thing was born, "all the faculties were made and all qualities determined."[44] Thus the heart is in all bodies, "thinking whatever the heart wishes."[45]

For ancient Egyptians, the heart was the seat of the mind, so 'heart' also meant 'mind'. Therefore, what the inscription actually states is that a God has given life to every thing through his mind. Thus every thing was born, all the faculties were made and all qualities determined. Thus the mind is in all bodies, thinking whatever the mind wishes.

2.10 From Chaos to Order

Claim (1) often goes together with the claim that, before the divine intervention, everything was in a state of chaos.

For example, Plato states that, "before the universe was generated, there were three distinct things, that is, being, space, and generation."[46] The nurse of generation, "being filled with dissimilar and imbalanced powers, was thoroughly imbalanced" and, "swaying irregularly in every direction, was shaken by them, and its motion in its turn shook them."[47] Then the God, "finding everything visible not in a state of rest, but of inharmonious and disorderly motion, brought it from chaos to order."[48]

Plato also states that, after bringing everything visible from chaos to order, the God gave the universe a mind in order to maintain that order. But since "mind can never come to anything except in the company of soul," he "constructed the universe by putting mind into soul and soul into body."[49] Then "this universe is a living thing, endowed with soul and mind thanks to the providence of the God."[50]

2.11 Universe and *Eunomia*

Claim (1) implies that the universe is an *eunomia*, that is, a good order. There is an *eunomia* in stars, seasons and nature generally.

---

[43] *The Shabaka Stone*, col. 53.
[44] *Ibid.*, col. 57.
[45] *Ibid.*, col. 54.
[46] Plato, *Timaeus*, 52 d 3–4.
[47] *Ibid.*, 52 e 1–5.
[48] *Ibid.*, 30 a 3–5.
[49] *Ibid.*, 30 b 3–5.
[50] *Ibid.*, 30 b 7–c 1.

The claim that the universe is an *eunomia* has great political significance. The birth of Greek science and philosophy was by and large coeval with an important change in Greek society: the transition from the arbitrary powers of the aristocratic magistrates to a written or customary law which limited their powers and regulated social conflict. This transition was a step towards a lawful order, or *eunomia*. It was to be modelled upon the *eunomia* of the universe because, as Solon stated, only "*eunomia* brings order and makes everything proper."[51] Thus the *eunomia* of the universe was an ideal to strive towards for the Greek society as a whole.

The *eunomia* of the universe was an ideal to strive towards also for the individual, who had to conform to it in order to be in harmony with nature. Comprehending the order of the universe was essential to harmonize the individual's life with the conditions of nature, which was necessary to attain wisdom rather than merely knowledge. Thus Euripides stated: "Blessed is he who has gained knowledge in nature," who "contemplates the ageless order of immortal nature, how it has been formed, in what way and manner."[52] He "seeks neither to harm his fellow-citizens nor rushes into unjust actions."[53]

This statement is significant, not only because it implies that the contemplation of the order of nature is essential to harmonize the individual's life with the conditions of nature, but also in another respect. The transition of the Greek society, from the arbitrary powers of the aristocratic magistrates to a lawful order mirroring the *eunomia* of the universe, was not without opposition. An example of this is Anaxagoras' trial and sentencing to death.

Anaxagoras held that "the mind is infinite and self-ruled, and is mixed with no thing, but is alone, itself by itself."[54] It is "the thinnest of all things and the purest, and has perfect knowledge of everything and the greatest strength."[55] It "set in order all things that were to be, and all things that were and are not now, and all things that are now or will be."[56] Therefore, "the orderly disposition of all things was designed and realized by the rational power of an infinite mind."[57]

Thus Anaxagoras implicitly denied the divinity of all Gods except an infinite mind. For such reason he was accused of impiety, cast into prison, sentenced to death, and only thanks to Pericles' intervention the death sentence was commuted to exile. Since Euripides is said to have been, like Pericles, a pupil of Anaxagoras, Euripides' statement that he who has gained knowledge in nature seeks neither to harm his fellow-citizens nor rushes into unjust actions, appears to be a vindication of Anaxagoras.

---

[51] Solon 4.32 (West).

[52] Euripides, *Tragicorum Graecorum Fragmenta* (Nauck), fr. 910.

[53] *Ibid.*

[54] Diels and Kranz (1964, 59 B 12).

[55] *Ibid.*

[56] *Ibid.*

[57] *Ibid.*, 59 A 48.

2.12 Intuitive Thinking, Discursive Thinking and Greek Mythology

Claim (6) can be put into relation to two aspects of Greek mythology.

1) *Zeus and Apollo*. In Greek mythology, Zeus is the intuiting mind [*nous*], bringing forth all things. Apollo is the universal word [*logos*], expressing the thoughts of Zeus through the oracle in the inner sanctum of Apollo's temple at Delphi. Since Apollo is the son of Zeus, there is a hierarchy between them, with Zeus at the top. Similarly, according to (6), there is a hierarchy between intuitive thinking and discursive thinking, with intuitive thinking at the top.

2) *Seers*. In Greek mythology seers, such as Cassandra, in addition to eyesight, have a second sight, which allows them to see truths that elude the eyesight. Similarly, according to (6), human beings, in addition to discursive thinking, have a second kind of thinking, intuitive thinking, which allows them to see truths that elude discursive thinking.

2.13 Origin of the Name 'Logic'

After considering the question of the origin of logic and its relation to method, let us consider the question: What is the origin of the name 'logic'?

'Logic' translates *logike*, an adjective which derives from *logos* and is often attached to *techne* [art] or *episteme* [science]. Now *logos* means discourse, argument, reasoning, faculty of reasoning, reason. Therefore *logike techne* means the art of reasoning, or reason, and *logike episteme* the science of reasoning, or reason.

Use of the term *logike* goes back at least to Democritus, author of a work entitled *On Logic or Canons* [*Peri logikon e kanons*]. This work is lost, but at least we know that Democritus "spoke strongly against" demonstration "in his *Canons*."[58] This suggests that Democritus' work was not concerned with demonstration, except perhaps for criticizing it.

Aristotle uses the term *dialektike* [dialectic], rather than *logike*, to mean logic as a subject, that is, logic in the sense (C) above. For example, he states that, "of this subject," namely *dialektike*, "it is not the case that part had been worked out before and part had not, instead, nothing existed at all."[59] In particular, "on syllogizing we had absolutely nothing of an earlier date to speak of at all, before we strove for a long time, trying with an expenditure of energy."[60] Thus Aristotle claims to be the originator of logic as a subject.

---

[58] Sextus Empiricus, *Adversus Dogmaticos*, II.328.
[59] Aristotle, *Sophistici Elenchi*, 34, 183 b 34–36.
[60] *Ibid.*, 34, 184 b 1–3.

The Stoics use the term *logike* to mean any inquiry concerning *logos*. They divide *logike* into "two sciences, rhetoric and dialectic," where the former is "the science of speaking well in continuous discourse", the latter "the science of correct discussion conducted by question and answer."[61] Thus the Stoics use *logike* as a general name for both dialectic and rhetoric.

The term *logike* becomes synonymous with *dialektike* only at the time of Cicero. Cicero himself speaks of that "part of philosophy that deals with inquiry and argument, which is called *logike*."[62]

The Greek commentators on Aristotle use *logike* to mean logic as a subject. For example, Alexander of Aphrodisias says that "logic [*logike*] or syllogistic is the study now before us. Under it fall demonstrative, and dialectical, and examinatory, and also sophistical procedures."[63]

2.14 Aristotle's Names for Logic

Although Aristotle does not generally use *logike* to mean logic as a subject, he states that "there are three classes of questions and problems. Some questions are ethical, some are scientific, and some are logical [*logikai*]."[64] This raises the issue in what relation does *logikos* [logical] stand to *dialektikos* [dialectical].

Now, by *logikos* Aristotle means 'general', in the sense of not employing principles proper to any given science. For example, he states: "I call it 'logical' [*logikos*] because, the more general it is, the further is it removed from the proper principles."[65] On the other hand, Aristotle states that "dialectic [*dialektike*] is not concerned with any determinate set of things, nor with any one kind."[66] From this Barnes concludes that, for Aristotle, *logikos* "is more or less synonymous with *dialektikos*."[67] For *dialektike*, not being concerned with any determinate set of things nor with any one kind, is general in the sense of not employing principles proper to any given science.

This, however, seems to be unjustified. By saying that *dialektike* is not concerned with any determinate set of things nor with any one kind, Aristotle does not mean to say that *dialektike* is general in that sense. Rather, he means to say that *dialektike* is not limited to problems of any particular science but can be used to solve problems

---

[61] Diogenes Laertius, *Vitae Philosophorum*, VII.41.
[62] Cicero, *De Finibus Bonorum et Malorum*, I.22.
[63] Alexander of Aphrodisias, *In Aristotelis Analyticorum Priorum Librum Primum Commentarium* (Wallies), 1.3–5.
[64] Aristotle, *Topica*, A 14, 105 b 19–21.
[65] Aristotle, *De Generatione Animalium*, B 8, 747 b 28–30.
[66] Aristotle, *Analytica Posteriora*, A 11, 77 a 31–32.
[67] Barnes (1993, 173).

2.15 Origin of the Name 'Method'

in any area, since "this is the task of dialectic in itself."[68] But solving problems is not problem-independent. As it will be argued in Chapter 7, Aristotle's problem solving procedure requires experience specific to the problem, so it is problem-dependent. Thus the use of *dialektike* depends on the subject, and hence is not general in the sense of not employing principles proper to any given science. Therefore, *logikos* and *dialektikos* are not synonymous.

To designate logic as a subject, in addition to 'dialectic', Aristotle also uses 'analytics'. Indeed, he refers to his work about problem solving – what today we know as *Prior Analytics* and *Posterior Analytics* – as *ta analutika*.[69] For example, he says: "How the questioner asks for the initial thing and for contraries has been described in accordance with truth in the *Analytics* [*ta analutika*]."[70]

The term *analutikos* comes from *analusis*, a compound of *ana* and *lusis*. One of the meanings of *ana* is 'upward', and one of the meanings of *lusis* is 'solution', so one of the meanings of *analusis* is 'upward solution'. Indeed, the title *ta analutika* is reminiscent of the analytic method used by Hippocrates of Chios and Hippocrates of Cos for solving problems in mathematics and medicine, respectively, where analysis is an upward solution. The analytic method will be discussed in Chapter 4. Aristotle's choice of the title *ta analutika* was intended to suggest a connection with the analytic method of Hippocrates of Chios and Hippocrates of Cos. In fact, in the *Analytics*, Aristotle develops a variant of the analytic method which is aimed at solving problems in any science; see Chapter 7.

Aristotle's use of the term 'analytics' is not an alternative to 'dialectic' but rather refers to a part of it. Solving problems, which is the task of dialectic, requires a procedure, and in the *Analytics* Aristotle describes such a procedure. Analytics is the part of dialectic which is concerned with the development of a problem solving procedure.

2.15 Origin of the Name 'Method'

Let us now consider the question: What is the origin of the name 'method'?

'Method' translates *methodos*, a compound of *meta* and *hodos* whose literal meaning is 'way with'. As a technical term, *methodos* does not appear before Plato. Nevertheless, as we have seen, Parmenides uses *hodos* [way], and this term is used, with the same meaning, by others as well, including Aristotle.[71]

In Plato, the term *methodos* occurs in the context of a comparison between medicine and rhetoric. Indeed, Plato states that "the manner of the medical art is

---

[68] Aristotle, *Sophistici Elenchi*, 34, 183 a 39.

[69] Aristotle never uses the titles *Prior Analytics* and *Posterior Analytics*. They were probably added by later editors to designate two parts of a single work. Aristotle only uses *ta analutika*.

[70] Aristotle, *Topica*, Θ 13, 162 b 31–32.

[71] For example, Aristotle uses *hodos* in *Analytica Priora*, A 30, 46 a 3.

somehow the same as that of rhetoric."[72] In both cases "you have to analyse the nature of something, the body in medicine, the soul in rhetoric."[73] Just as the doctor must analyse the nature of the body, so the rhetorician must analyse the nature of the soul. And just as, according to Hippocrates of Cos, one cannot analyse the nature of the body without a method, so one cannot analyse the nature of the soul "without this method [*methodos*]."[74]

This passage reveals the idea of method at its very formation, because it suggests that there exists a procedure common to two distinct fields, medicine and rhetoric. Undoubtedly, Plato's views about method were stimulated by the procedures of Hippocrates of Chios and Hippocrates of Cos for solving problems in mathematics and medicine, respectively, as well as by the philosophical practice of Socrates and of Plato's school; see Chapter 7. From these particular procedures, however, Plato extracted the general idea of method, and established the use of *methodos* as a technical term.

Plato's reference to medicine and rhetoric was not without following. For example, Aristotle states that "we shall possess the method completely when we shall be in the same condition as in the case of rhetoric, medicine, and other such abilities."[75]

---

[72] Plato, *Phaedrus*, 270 b 1–2.
[73] *Ibid.*, 270 b 4–5.
[74] *Ibid.*, 270 c 4–5.
[75] Aristotle, *Topica*, A 3, 101 b 5–6.

Chapter 3
Ancient Logic and Science

3.1 Conceptions of Science

In Chapter 2 we have seen that, for Parmenides, Plato and Aristotle, logic is discursive thinking but, in order to acquire knowledge of the universe, the human mind also needs intuitive thinking, which is the highest faculty.

This is the foundation of their conceptions of science and the role of logic and intuition in science. The present chapter outlines such conceptions, because they will be needed for reference in the following chapters.

3.2 Parmenides' Conception of Science

According to Parmenides, scientific knowledge is about what is [*to eon*], namely, the universe. The latter is "ungenerated and imperishable, whole, unique, motionless and completed."[1] It is "one, continuous."[2] And it is "like the mass of a well-rounded sphere, pushing out equally in every direction from the centre."[3] Thus, in trying to get scientific knowledge, "it matters not at all from which point I begin, for to that same place I shall come back again."[4]

With respect to what is, Parmenides distinguishes between what appears to the senses and what lies behind appearances. Scientific knowledge is only about the latter, because the senses may lead you to believe that "things which are not are."[5] Relying on the senses is the way of "the opinions of mortals, in which there is no

---

[1] Diels and Krantz (1964, 28 B 8.3–4).
[2] *Ibid.*, 28 B 8.6.
[3] *Ibid.*, 28 B 8.43–45.
[4] *Ibid.*, 28 B 5.1–2.
[5] *Ibid.*, 28 B 7.1.

truthful certainty."[6] Therefore, if you want to obtain scientific knowledge, "restrain your thinking from this way of inquiry."[7]

Rather than relying on the senses, you must judge by reasoning, because only in this way you may avoid being deceived. For example, the senses may lead you to believe that the moon increases and wanes during the course of time. Judging by reasoning, you will realize that this is an illusion, that the moon is a globe which is always the same size and shape. Its apparent bodily changes are only a play of shadows, which arises from the fact that the moon is "shining at night with a light not of its own, wandering around the earth."[8] It is shining at night with a light not of its own, because it is "always gazing towards the rays of the sun."[9]

As another example, the senses incline you to believe that what is is generated. Judging by reasoning, and specifically by reduction to the impossible, you will realize that this is not the case; see Chapter 5.

3.3 Parmenides on the Role of Logic and Intuition in Science

By stating that you must judge by reasoning since only in this way you may avoid being deceived, Parmenides brings a new element into reason: discursive thinking. In the previous tradition starting with Homer, this element is not recognized, and reason is supposed to consist only in intuitive thinking.

Homer himself uses *noein* only to refer to a sudden recognition of something behind the appearances. For example, he says that Helen realized the true identity of Aphrodite, appearing to her disguised as an old woman, "when she recognized [*enoese*] the round sweet throat of the Goddess and her desirable breasts and her eyes that were full of shining."[10] Likewise he says that the old dog Argos realized the true identity of Odysseus, appearing to him disguised as a beggar, when "he recognized [*enoesen*] Odysseus who was standing near" and, as a sign of recognition, "wagged his tail and dropped his ears."[11]

Starting with Parmenides, reason is no longer supposed to consist only in intuitive thinking, but also in discursive thinking. The latter is a precondition for arriving at knowledge of what is, because only with discursive thinking you can avoid being deceived. Thus discursive thinking and intuitive thinking are both part of reason. On the other hand, as we have seen in Chapter 2, according to Parmenides, discursive thinking is not sufficient to arrive at knowledge of what is. In order to arrive at that knowledge you also need intuitive thinking, which is the highest faculty.

---

[6] *Ibid.*, 28 B 1.30.
[7] *Ibid.*, 28 B 7.2.
[8] *Ibid.*, 28 B 14.
[9] *Ibid.*, 28 B 15.
[10] Homer, *Ilias*, III.396–397.
[11] Homer, *Odyssea*, XVII.301–302.

3.4 Plato's Conception of Science

Since knowledge of what is essentially requires intuitive thinking, for Parmenides the role of logic in science cannot be to obtain knowledge of what is. It is rather to remove obstacles from getting such knowledge, by refuting wrong opinions derived from the senses.

3.4 Plato's Conception of Science

According to Plato, "scientific knowledge refers to what is [*to on*], in order to know, about what is, how it is."[12] Now, what is consists of "two kinds of reality," or worlds, "one visible, the other invisible."[13] The visible world is what surrounds us, what we see, what we hear, what we experience. It "is perceived by sense, generated, always in motion, coming to be in a certain place and again vanishing out of it, and is apprehended by belief, which goes together with sense perception."[14] Being always in motion, the visible world is "never the same."[15] On the other hand, the invisible world consists of "the ideas in themselves of things."[16] It "is always the same, ungenerated and imperishable."[17] It "is not visible nor perceptible by any sense, and only intuition has been granted to contemplate it."[18] Thus Plato transforms Parmenides' distinction between what appears to the senses and what lies behind appearances into a distinction between two worlds, the visible and the invisible one.

The visible world is a copy of the invisible world, having "been fashioned on the model of that which is apprehended by reason and is unchanging, and, if this is admitted, it must therefore of necessity be a copy of something."[19] But, while "doing their best to be like" what belongs to the invisible world, the things of the visible world "fall short of it."[20] So the visible world is only an imperfect copy of the invisible one.

The visible and the invisible world can be represented as arranged on "a line divided into two unequal sections."[21] The visible world is the lower section, the invisible world the upper section. Each of these sections is divided in its turn into two subsections, "in the same ratio."[22]

---

[12] Plato, *Respublica*, VI 477 b 11–12.
[13] Plato, *Phaedo*, 79 a 6–7.
[14] Plato, *Timaeus*, 52 a 5–7.
[15] Plato, *Phaedo*, 79 a 10.
[16] Plato, *Parmenides*, 135 a 2.
[17] Plato, *Timaeus*, 52 a 1–2.
[18] *Ibid.*, 52 a 3–4.
[19] *Ibid.*, 29 a 6–b 2.
[20] Plato, *Phaedo*, 75 b 7–8.
[21] Plato, *Respublica*, VI 509 d 6–7.
[22] *Ibid.*, VI 509 d 7–8.

The lower subsection of the visible world "consists of images," first "shadows, then reflections on the surface of water or on the surface of compact, smooth and shiny things, and everything of that sort."[23] The upper subsection of the visible world consists of "that of which" the lower subsection "is the image, that is, the animals around us, all the plants, and the whole kind of artefacts."[24]

The lower subsection of the invisible world consists of ideas in themselves. But, in this subsection, reason "is forced to investigate" them "from hypotheses" for which no justification is given, proceeding from hypotheses "to a conclusion."[25] That is, it is forced to investigate them by the axiomatic method. The upper subsection of the invisible world consists again of ideas in themselves, and also in this subsection reason investigates them from hypotheses. But it "does not consider these hypotheses as principles" for which no justification is given; rather, it considers them "truly as hypotheses" for which a justification must be given, that is, "as stepping stones from which to take off and proceed" to the summit of the invisible world, "the unhypothetical principle [*arche anupothetos*] of everything."[26] The latter is the idea of the Good, which is higher than all the other ideas in themselves, since "not only do the objects of knowledge owe their being known to the Good, but their being and essence are also due to it."[27]

With the four subsections of the line Plato associates four distinct affections of the soul. With the lower subsection of the visible world, he associates "perception of images [*eikasia*]," with the upper subsection, "belief [*pistis*]."[28] On the other hand, with the lower subsection of the invisible world, he associates "discursive thinking [*dianoia*]," with the upper subsection "intuitive thinking [*noesis*]."[29]

Of these four affections of the soul, only intuitive thinking yields knowledge. Indeed, perception of images and belief do not yield knowledge because the visible world, which is their object, "comes to be and passes away but never really is."[30] Thus it can only be "an object of belief through unreasoning sense perception."[31] Those who observe things of the visible world "have beliefs about these things but have no knowledge of that about which they have beliefs."[32] At best, they have "justified [*meta logou*] true belief."[33] But justified true belief is still belief, and "belief is different from knowledge."[34] Indeed, "belief opines," and does not

---

[23] *Ibid.*, VI 509 d 10–510 a 3.
[24] *Ibid.*, VI 510 a 5–6.
[25] *Ibid.*, VI 510 b 5–6.
[26] *Ibid.*, VI 511 b 4–6.
[27] *Ibid.*, VI 509 b 5–7.
[28] *Ibid.*, VI 511 e 1–2.
[29] *Ibid.*, VI 511 d 8.
[30] Plato, *Timaeus*, 28 a 3–4.
[31] *Ibid.*, 28 a 2–3.
[32] Plato, *Respublica*, V 479 e 3–4.
[33] Plato, *Theaetetus*, 202 c 7–8.
[34] Plato, *Respublica*, V 478 a 1–2.

opine "about the same things as knowledge knows."[35] It opines about things of the visible world. On the other hand, discursive thinking does not yield knowledge, being "something intermediate between" mere "belief and intuition."[36] Starting from hypotheses for which no justification is given, those who investigate ideas in themselves by discursive thinking "do not grasp these things."[37]

Only "about those who can see each of these things in itself" by intuitive thinking, "will we say that they have knowledge, and are not merely entertaining beliefs."[38] Thus knowledge is obtained only by intuitive thinking. Intuitive thinking grasps "the nature itself of each thing which is, with the part of the soul which is fit to grasp a thing of that sort; and is fit to grasp it because it is akin to it."[39] Therefore, intuitive thinking is infallible.

3.5 Plato and Knowledge as Justified True Belief

Although Plato makes it quite clear that knowledge is different from justified true belief, several people interpret him as identifying them. For example, Chisholm states that the definition of knowledge "proposed in Plato's dialogue, the *Theaetetus*, is that knowledge is justified true belief."[40] This is unwarranted. Admittedly, in the *Theaetetus* Plato considers the view that "true belief accompanied by an account [*logos*] is knowledge."[41] But he considers this view only to reject it. He rejects it on two grounds.

First, Plato points out that the account, or justification, would have to be knowledge itself. Then, saying that knowledge is true belief accompanied by an account would amount to saying that knowledge is true belief accompanied by knowledge. But "nothing could be sillier than to say that" knowledge is true "belief accompanied by knowledge."[42] The circle would be too blatant.

Secondly, Plato holds that knowledge must be most certain and infallible. But justified true belief, being belief, is about things that we perceive through the body, and "plainly, whenever the soul sets about examining anything with the participation of the body, it is deceived by it."[43] Therefore, justified true belief cannot be most certain and infallible. It follows that knowledge cannot be identified with justified

---

[35]*Ibid.*, V 478 a 9–11.
[36]*Ibid.*, VI 511 d 4.
[37]*Ibid.*, VI 511 d 1–2.
[38]*Ibid.*, V 479 e 6–7.
[39]*Ibid.*, VI 490 b 3–4.
[40]Chisholm (1989, 90).
[41]Plato, *Theaetetus*, 202 c 7–8.
[42]*Ibid.*, 210 a 7–8.
[43]Plato, *Phaedo*, 65 b 9–11.

true belief. And indeed, "how could any reasonable being ever identify that which is infallible with that which is not infallible?"[44] Identifying them is impossible. Knowledge is obtained only by intuitive thinking.

3.6 Plato on the Role of Logic and Intuition in Science

Since, according to Plato, knowledge is obtained only by intuitive thinking, and intuitive thinking is about ideas in themselves and the unhypothetical principle of everything, knowledge requires an ascent from the visible world to the summit of the invisible world. Such an ascent can be performed only "by the power of" the dialectical method, or "dialectic."[45] The "dialectical method alone, doing away with the hypothetical character of the premises, proceeds this way up" to the ideas in themselves and the unhypothetical principle of everything, "and is thereby consolidated."[46] This is the "turning of the soul, from a day that is a kind of night, to the true day, the ascent to what is."[47] Now, the dialectical method is the analytic method, which will be discussed in Chapter 4. Thus Plato's conception of science is based on the view that the analytic method is the scientific method.

Nevertheless, while capable of raising the soul up to the ideas in themselves and the unhypothetical principle of everything, the dialectical method cannot give knowledge of them. Such knowledge is given "only by intuition."[48] The ideas in themselves and the unhypothetical principle of everything are "visible only by the pilot of the soul, intuition."[49]

Since knowledge of the ideas in themselves and the unhypothetical principle of everything is obtained only by intuition, for Plato the role of logic in science cannot be to obtain knowledge of the ideas in themselves and the unhypothetical principle. It is rather to ascend to them, and then to descend from them to conclusions.

3.7 Plato on the Impediments of the Body

According to Plato, however, the soul can obtain knowledge of the ideas in themselves, and the unhypothetical principle of everything, by intuition only after death, when the soul is separated from the body. Indeed, in *Phaedo* he states that, "as

---

[44] Plato, *Respublica*, V 477 e 7–8.
[45] *Ibid.*, VI 511 b 3.
[46] *Ibid.*, VII 533 c 8–d 1.
[47] *Ibid.*, VII 521 c 6–7.
[48] Plato, *Timaeus*, 51 d 5.
[49] Plato, *Phaedrus*, 247 c 7–8.

long as we have the body and our soul is contaminated by such an evil, we will never adequately gain the possession of what we desire, and that, we say, is truth."[50] Thus, "if we want to know anything clearly, we must leave our body and contemplate the things themselves with the soul by itself."[51] For "only then, namely when we have died, in other words when we are outside life, we will get what we desire."[52] That is, truth.

Chen claims that, while in *Phaedo* "a pessimistic conclusion is drawn: Men cannot attain to this knowledge in the present life," in the *Republic* "an optimistic answer to the same question is given."[53] Plato goes "into detail about how the prospective rulers of the ideal state are led to apprehend the idea of the Good."[54] Chen, however, overlooks that in the *Republic* Plato describes an ideal state, which could be realized only in a City not of this world. He makes it quite clear that "the City whose foundation we have been discussing" is one "which cannot be accommodated anywhere in this world," it is put "in Heaven as a model [*paradeigma*] for those who desire to see it and, having it as their end, want to base themselves on it."[55]

In fact, after the *Republic*, in *Phaedrus*, Plato reasserts that only after death we can behold "the happy vision and contemplation" of the ideas in themselves and the unhypothetical principle of everything, and can have "calm and happy visions, in pure light."[56] For only then we are not enshrined in "this tomb which we now carry about and we call body, imprisoned in it like an oyster in its shell."[57] Thus Plato reaffirms his pessimistic view about the capacity of men to attain knowledge during life.

3.8 Plato's Criticism of the Axiomatic Method

That, according to Plato, in the lower subsection of the invisible world, reason investigates ideas in themselves by the axiomatic method, on the basis of hypotheses for which no justification is given, is at the origin of his criticism of the axiomatic method in the *Republic*.

Mathematicians who use the axiomatic method take their hypotheses for granted, and "don't feel any further need to give a justification [*didonai logon*] for them, either to themselves or to anyone else, as if they were axiomatic principles; then, starting from these, they draw their consequences, and agree on the conclusions about

---

[50] Plato, *Phaedo*, 66 b 5–7.
[51] *Ibid.*, 66 d 8–e 2.
[52] *Ibid.*, 66 e 2–4.
[53] Chen (1992, 2).
[54] *Ibid.*
[55] Plato, *Respublica*, IX 592 a 9–b 2.
[56] Plato, *Phaedrus*, 250 b 8–c 4.
[57] *Ibid.*, 250 c 4–6.

the matter of their inquiry."[58] Moreover, they "use visible forms and make their arguments about them, though not thinking about them but about those others of which they are images."[59] These "figures that they make and draw, they now use as images, seeking to see those things in themselves that one can see only by thought."[60]

Such mathematicians "only dream about what is, and are unable to have a waking view of it as long as they make use of hypotheses that they do not bring into question, since they are unable to give any justification for them."[61] But "will those who are unable to give or follow a justification, ever have knowledge of what we say should be known?"[62] They do not "carry out the investigation going up to a principle," but only on the basis of unjustified hypotheses, so they do "not get an intuition of those objects, even though they are intuitive objects when related to a principle."[63] Therefore, they do not really know the principle. But "when a man does not know the principle, and when the conclusion and intermediate steps are also constructed out of what he does not know, how can he imagine that such a fabric of convention can ever become science?"[64]

Yielding a fabric of convention, the axiomatic method is unable to give knowledge of what is. This, however, does not mean, as Bailey states, that "in the *Republic* Plato contrasts dialectic with mathematics on the grounds that the former but not the latter gives justifications of some kind for its hypotheses, pursuing this process until it reaches 'an unhypothetical principle'."[65] Plato contrasts dialectic not with mathematics, but only with mathematics developed by the axiomatic method. He cannot contrast dialectic with mathematics developed by the analytic method because, as it has been stated above, dialectic is the analytic method. Mathematics developed by the analytic method gives justifications for its hypotheses pursuing this process until it reaches the unhypothetical principle of everything. What Plato criticizes is not mathematics, as such, but only the practice of certain mathematicians.

3.9 Hippocrates of Cos' Criticism of the Axiomatic Method

Plato's criticism of the use of the axiomatic method in mathematics in the *Republic*, is akin to Hippocrates of Cos' criticism of the use of the axiomatic method in medicine in *De Vetere Medicina*.

---

[58] Plato, *Respublica*, VI 510 c 6–d 3.
[59] *Ibid.*, VI 510 d 5–7.
[60] *Ibid.*, VI 510 e 3–511 a 2.
[61] *Ibid.*, VII 533 c 1–3.
[62] *Ibid.*, VII 531 e 3–4.
[63] *Ibid.*, VI 511 c 8–d 2.
[64] *Ibid.*, VII 533 c 3–6.
[65] Bailey (2006, 101).

Hippocrates of Cos states that, "all those who have undertaken to speak or write about medicine, having laid down as a hypothesis for their account hot or cold or wet or dry or anything else they want, narrowing down the primary cause of diseases and death" and "laying down the same one or two things as the cause in all cases, clearly go wrong in much that they say."[66] Medicine has no need of an unjustified hypothesis, and anyone who tries to investigate on the basis of it "and says that he has discovered something, has been deceived and continues to deceive himself."[67]

Thus Hippocrates of Cos criticizes those who carry out an inquiry in medicine by the axiomatic method, for the very same reason for which Plato criticizes those who carry out an inquiry in mathematics by that method. They take their hypotheses for granted and do not give any justification of them.

3.10 Aristotle's Conception of Science

According to Aristotle, "scientific knowledge is directed at what is [*to on*]."[68] Now, what is consists of individuals. Therefore, scientific knowledge is about individuals. Each individual belongs to some kind. There exist several kinds, because "the kinds of the things that there are, are different."[69] Moreover, the different kinds are separated, so each individual belongs to one and only one kind.

Each science is concerned with one and only one kind, because a "science is one if it is concerned with one kind."[70] The latter is said to be the kind of that science. Since each science is concerned with one and only one kind, kinds serve as principles of individuation for sciences. Being concerned with one and only one kind, each science is about individuals of one and only one kind.

However, a science is not about individuals of one and only one kind *qua* individuals. For individuals have accidental properties – properties they happen to have but they could lack – and "there is no scientific knowledge of the accidental."[71] But, in addition to accidental properties, individuals have essential properties, that is, properties without which they could not exist. For example, being pedestrian is an essential property of man because, "if 'pedestrian' does not exist, 'man' will not exist."[72] Now, essential properties are universals, and "scientific knowledge is always knowledge of universals."[73] Therefore, while there is no scientific knowledge of the accidental, there can be scientific knowledge of

---

[66] Hippocrates (2005, 75).

[67] *Ibid.*, 75, 77.

[68] Aristotle, *Analytica Posteriora*, B 19, 100 a 9.

[69] *Ibid.*, A 32, 88 b 1–2.

[70] *Ibid.*, A 28, 87 a 38.

[71] Aristotle, *Metaphysica*, E 2, 1027 a 20.

[72] Aristotle, *Topica*, Z 6, 145 a 8.

[73] Aristotle, *Metaphysica*, M 10, 1086 b 33.

essential properties of individuals, because they are universals. Then, that each science is about individuals of one and only one kind means that it is about their essential properties.

The essential properties of an individual form its essence, where the "essence [*to ti en einai*] of a thing is what the thing is said to be in itself."[74] Then, "to have knowledge of a thing is to have knowledge" of "the essence of the thing."[75] On the other hand, "for all things, essence is the cause [*aitia*] of what they are."[76] So, to know the essence of a thing is to know the cause of it. Then to have scientific knowledge of a thing is to know the cause of it. Indeed "we think we have scientific knowledge of a thing" when "we think we know the cause why that thing is, that it is the cause of that thing, and that it cannot be otherwise."[77] But, to know the cause of a thing is to have a demonstration of it, since a "demonstration is a deduction that shows the cause and the 'why'."[78] Therefore, "to have scientific knowledge" of a thing is "to have a demonstration [*apodeixis*] of it."[79]

3.11 Aristotle's Conception of Demonstration

What is a demonstration? According to Aristotle, it is a deduction which proceeds "from premises which are true, and prime, and immediate, and better known than, and prior to, and the causes of the conclusion."[80]

1) *The premises must be true*. If they were false, there would be a demonstration, and hence scientific knowledge, of what is not. But "it is not possible to have scientific knowledge of what is not, for example, that the diagonal" and side of a square are "commensurate."[81] Therefore, the premises must be true. Then the conclusions too will be true, because "a conclusion from truths is always true."[82]

2) *The premises must be prime*. That is, they must be principles, because "I call the same thing prime and principle."[83] Being principles, they must be "indemonstrable, otherwise one would not have scientific knowledge without having

---

[74] *Ibid.*, Z 4, 1029 b 13–14.

[75] *Ibid.*, Z 6, 1031 b 20–21.

[76] Aristotle, *De Anima*, B 4, 415 b 12–13. Although perhaps 'reason' would be a better translation for *aitia*, this would be awkward in some contexts, so the traditional translation 'cause' seems to be preferable.

[77] Aristotle, *Analytica Posteriora*, A 2, 71 b 9–13.

[78] *Ibid.*, A 24, 85 b 23–24.

[79] *Ibid.*, B 3, 90 b 9–10.

[80] *Ibid.*, A 2, 71 b 20–22.

[81] *Ibid.*, A 2, 71 b 25–26.

[82] *Ibid.*, A 6, 75 a 5–6.

[83] *Ibid.*, A 2, 72 a 6–7.

a demonstration of them."[84] But, if one had a demonstration of principles, the premises of such demonstration would have to be demonstrable, otherwise one could simply say that the original conclusion depended on these indemonstrable premises. Now, if the premises were demonstrable, the premises of their demonstration would have to be demonstrable, and so on, *ad infinitum*. Then there would be an infinite regress. The regress can be stopped only by recognizing that the premises must be prime.

3) *The premises must be immediate.* That is, there must be no other proposition prior to them, since a premise is "immediate if there is no other proposition prior to it."[85] If the premises were not immediate, there would be some propositions prior to them, the premises would be demonstrable from such proposition, and hence would not be prime.

4) *The premises must be better known than the conclusion.* We "must not only already know the prime premises," but "must actually know them better."[86] Indeed, "if we know and are convinced of something because of the prime premises, then we know and are convinced of the latter better, since it is because of them that we know and are convinced of what is posterior."[87]

5) *The premises must be prior to the conclusion.* We must "already know them, not only in the sense of understanding them, but also in sense of knowing that they are the case."[88]

6) *The premises must be the causes of the conclusion.* The cause of a thing is "that from which a thing comes to be."[89] Now, the premises are that from which the conclusion comes to be. Therefore, "the premises are the causes of the conclusion, in the sense of 'that from which'."[90]

3.12 Aristotle on Role of Logic and Intuition in Science

According to Aristotle, however, a further condition must be added to conditions 1)–6) considered in the previous section.

7) *The premises must not only be true but also known to be true.* For if they were true but not known to be true, we could not "have scientific knowledge of what follows from them, absolutely and properly."[91] This raises the question of how the premises "become known" to be true, and "what is the state which gets to know

---

[84] *Ibid.*, A 2, 71 b 27–28.
[85] *Ibid.*, A 2, 72 a 8.
[86] *Ibid.*, A 2, 72 a 27–29.
[87] *Ibid.*, A 2, 72 a 30–32.
[88] *Ibid.*, A 2, 71 b 31–33.
[89] Aristotle, *Physica*, B 2, 194 b 24.
[90] *Ibid.*, B 3, 195 a 18–19.
[91] Aristotle, *Analytica Posteriora*, A 3, 72 b 14.

them."[92] Now, the premises cannot become known to be true by demonstration, nor can the state which gets to know them be discursive thinking, because then the premises would be an object of scientific knowledge. But the premises are principles, and the principles "of what is an object of scientific knowledge cannot be an object of scientific knowledge itself," because "what is an object of scientific knowledge is demonstrable."[93] On the contrary the premises, being principles, "are indemonstrable, so it will not be scientific knowledge but intuition [*nous*] that is concerned with the principles."[94] Thus "it is intuition, and not discursive thinking, that apprehends the prime things," it "is intuition that apprehends the unchanging and first terms in the order of demonstrations."[95] That is, it is "intuition [*nous*] that apprehends the principles."[96] Then, the premises become known to be true by intuition, and the state which gets to know them is intuitive thinking.

Thus, like Plato, Aristotle holds that knowledge that the premises are true is obtained only by intuition. Unlike Plato, however, he believes that we can obtain such knowledge while we are still living. For we have a capacity of intuition which "enters from outside and is divine."[97]

Also like Plato, Aristotle holds that the knowledge that the premises are true, which is obtained by intuition, is infallible. For the premises are concerned with the essence of things, and "with respect to essence it is impossible to be in error, except accidentally."[98] One may "either intuit it or not."[99] But not to intuit it is to have no knowledge of it, and hence to be in error, because "everyone is in error on matters about which he has no knowledge."[100] Then, with respect to the premises, "falsity does not exist, nor error, but only ignorance; and ignorance that is not like blindness, for blindness would be like the case in which someone does not possess the ability to think at all."[101] Rather, it is like possessing sight but being momentarily unable to see, because a bandage covers one's eyes.

Since knowledge that the premises are true is obtained only by intuition, for Aristotle the role of logic in science cannot be to know that the premises are true. It is rather to ascend to them, and then to descend from them to conclusions.

---

[92] *Ibid.*, B 19, 99 b 17–18.
[93] Aristotle, *Ethica Nicomachea*, Z 6, 1140 b 34–35.
[94] Aristotle, *Magna Moralia*, A 34, 1197 a 22–23.
[95] Aristotle, *Ethica Nicomachea*, Z 11, 1143 a 36–1143 b 3.
[96] Aristotle, *Analytica Posteriora*, B 19, 100 b 12.
[97] Aristotle, *De Generatione Animalium*, B 3, 736 b 27–28.
[98] Aristotle, *Metaphysica*, Θ 10, 1051 b 25–26.
[99] *Ibid.*, Θ 10, 1051 b 31–32.
[100] *Ibid.*, Γ 3, 1005 b 13–14.
[101] *Ibid.*, Θ 10, 1052 a 1–4.

3.13 Aristotle on Proper and Common Principles

According to Aristotle, among the premises or principles, "some are proper [*idia*] to each science and others are common [*koina*]."[102]

The proper principles are about "those things which are assumed to be, and concerning which the science investigates what holds of them in themselves, for example, units in arithmetic, or points and lines in geometry."[103] The proper principles are either hypotheses or definitions. A "hypothesis [*hupothesis*]" states "that something is, or that something is not."[104] A "definition [*horismos*]" states "what something is," thus "its essence."[105] For example, it is a definition to state that "a unit is what is quantitatively indivisible."[106] It is a hypothesis to state that a unit is. Thus, stating "what a unit is" and stating "that a unit is are not the same thing."[107] Therefore, definitions and hypotheses are different.

On the other hand, the common principles are principles which are common to all the sciences, for "all the sciences share with one another in the use of the common principles."[108] Common principles are logical principles, that is, principles which "hold good for every thing that is," thus for every kind, "and not for some special kind apart from others."[109] They are "necessary for anyone to have, if he is going to learn anything at all."[110] Such is the principle of non-contradiction, which states that "it is impossible to affirm and deny at the same time."[111] Or the principle of excluded middle, which states that "it is necessary to affirm or deny one thing of any one thing."[112]

3.14 Aristotle's Conception of Definition

Actually, Aristotle considers two concepts of definition. According to one of them, a definition states the essence of something, so it is "a discourse about what something is."[113] Therefore, it is a 'definition of thing'. According to the other one, a definition

---

[102] Aristotle, *Analytica Posteriora*, A 10, 76 a 38.
[103] *Ibid.*, A 10, 76 b 4–5.
[104] *Ibid.*, A 2, 72 a 20.
[105] *Ibid.*, B 3, 90 b 30.
[106] *Ibid.*, A 2, 72 a 22–23.
[107] *Ibid.*, A 2, 72 a 23–24.
[108] *Ibid.*, A 11, 77 a 26–27.
[109] Aristotle, *Metaphysica*, Γ 3, 1005 a 21–22.
[110] Aristotle, *Analytica Posteriora*, A 2, 72 a 16–17.
[111] *Ibid.*, A 11, 77 a 10.
[112] Aristotle, *Metaphysica*, Γ 7, 1011 b 24.
[113] Aristotle, *Analytica Posteriora*, B 10, 93 b 29.

states "what a name, or some other name-like expression, means."[114] Therefore, it is a 'definition of name'.

But, although Aristotle considers two concepts of definition, for him the definition of thing is the only genuine kind of definition. Indeed he argues that, if the definition of name were a genuine kind of definition, it would be "a discourse that signifies the same as a name. But this is absurd. For" then, "first, there would be definitions of non-substances and of things which do not exist, since one can signify even things which do not exist."[115] This is impossible because, "of that which does not exist, no one knows what it is."[116] For example, "when I say 'goat-stag', I might know what the expression or name signifies" – a fabulous creature, half-goat, half-stag – "but it is impossible to know what a goat-stag is."[117] Secondly, "all discourses would be definitions. For one can associate a name to any expression whatsoever, so that we would all talk expressing definitions."[118]

3.15 Aristotle's Separation of Kinds and Principles

Aristotle's view that kinds are separated has the following implications as regards principles.

1) *A thing of a given kind must be demonstrated from principles of that kind.* It "is not possible to demonstrate anything by crossing from another kind [*ex allou genous metabainein*], for example, something geometrical by arithmetic."[119] For in a demonstration "the extremes and the middle terms must be from the same kind," otherwise the demonstration would contain "accidental things."[120] Then it would not be a demonstration. Therefore, "the indemonstrables," that is, the principles, "must be in the same kind [*en to auto genei*] as the things demonstrated."[121]

2) *There cannot be principles capable of demonstrating things of every kind.* Such principles "would be principles of every thing."[122] Demonstrations based on them would then be applicable to every kind, whereas every demonstration concerns a given kind and "is not applicable to another kind."[123]

---

[114] *Ibid.*, B 10, 93 b 30–31.
[115] *Ibid.*, B 7, 92 b 27–29.
[116] *Ibid.*, B 7, 92 b 5–6.
[117] *Ibid.*, B 7, 92 b 6–8.
[118] *Ibid.*, B 7, 92 b 30–32.
[119] *Ibid.*, A 7, 75 a 38–39.
[120] *Ibid.*, A 7, 75 b 10–12.
[121] *Ibid.*, A 28, 87 b 2–3.
[122] *Ibid.*, A 9, 76 a 17–18.
[123] *Ibid.*, A 9, 76 a 22–23.

3) *Even common principles belong to a given science only insofar as they are restricted to the kind of that science.* For common principles are only "common by analogy, since they are only useful insofar as they bear on the kind underlying the science."[124]

3.16 Aristotle on Truth as Correspondence

There is a strict connection between Aristotle's view that knowledge that the premises are true is obtained only by intuition and his concept of truth. Aristotle considers two concepts of truth, truth as correspondence and truth as intuition of the essence.

According to the concept of truth as correspondence, "truth is to say of what is that it is, and of what is not that it is not," while "falsity is to say of what is that it is not, and of what is not that it is."[125] This concept of truth, however, does not provide a criterion of truth, namely, a means to decide whether a specific statement is true. For, without a faculty capable of apprehending the essence of things, we cannot ascertain whether a statement corresponds to "any nature existing objectively outside thinking."[126] We can only compare the statement with a representation of some thing existing outside thinking. But a representation is only "an affection of thinking."[127] It is something which does not exist "in things" but only "in thinking."[128] For such reason, the concept of truth as correspondence does not provide a criterion of truth. From this Aristotle concludes that this concept of truth cannot be used in practice, and hence "must be set aside."[129]

Despite this, Aristotle is often credited as being a supporter of the concept of truth as correspondence, even its originator. For example, Tarski states that "the earliest explanation" of the concept of truth as correspondence "can be found in Aristotle's *Metaphysics*."[130] Such concept of truth was "put forward by Aristotle."[131] This is unjustified. First, the concept of truth as correspondence already occurs in Plato, who states that "the discourse that says of the things that are that they are, is true, the one that says of the things that are that they are not, is false."[132] Secondly, as we have seen above, for Aristotle, the concept of truth as correspondence cannot be used in practice because it does not provide a criterion of truth, and hence must be set aside.

---

[124] *Ibid.*, A 10, 76 a 38–40.
[125] Aristotle, *Metaphysica*, Γ 7, 1011 b 26–27.
[126] *Ibid.*, E 4, 1028 a 2.
[127] *Ibid.*, E 4, 1027 b 34–1028 a 1.
[128] *Ibid.*, E 4, 1027 b 26–27.
[129] *Ibid.*, E 4, 1027 b 34.
[130] Tarski (1969, 63).
[131] *Ibid.*
[132] Plato, *Cratylus*, 385 b 7–8.

It might be objected that since, according to Aristotle, we do have a faculty – intuition – capable of apprehending the essence of things, for him truth as correspondence must be a genuine concept of truth. This objection, however, is unjustified because, if we have a faculty capable of apprehending the essence of things, then truth does not consist in the correspondence of a statement with something existing outside thinking, but rather in the direct apprehension of the essence of the thing. By such apprehension, intuition and the essence of the thing are the same. For then intuition "becomes the object of thought by the act of apprehension and thinking, so that intuition and the object of thought are the same."[133] If intuition and the essence of the thing are the same, speaking of correspondence is misleading. While truth as correspondence merely involves a parallelism between thinking and something existing outside thinking, truth involves an identity between intuition and its object.

3.17 Aristotle on Truth as Intuition of the Essence

Because of the inadequacy of the concept of truth as correspondence, for Aristotle the concept of truth as intuition of the essence is the only genuine one. According to the concept of truth as intuition of the essence, truth is to intuit the essence of a thing. Or rather, "truth is to intuit and to state" the essence of a thing, while "not to intuit is not to know."[134] For in order to have truth, one must not only intuit the essence of a thing but also state it. Now, to state the essence of a thing is to give a definition of it – in the sense of a definition of thing – because, for Aristotle, a definition of thing states its essence, what the thing is. Therefore, truth is to intuit the essence of a thing and to give a definition of it.

Since, as we have seen, for Aristotle the premises are the causes of the conclusion and hence express the essence of a thing, from the fact that truth is to intuit and to state the essence of a thing it follows that knowledge that the premises are true can be obtained only by intuition. This explains why, as it has been stated in the previous section, there is a strict connection between Aristotle's view that knowledge that the premises are true is obtained only by intuition and his concept of truth.

3.18 Aristotle on *Nous* and Intuition

In Chapter 2 and in the present one, 'intuition' has been used as a translation for *nous*. Barnes objects that "'intuition' will not do as a translation for *nous*."[135] For intuition "implies a sort of mental 'vision': intuition is mental sight; intuited truths

---

[133] Aristotle, *Metaphysica*, Λ 7, 1072 b 20–21.
[134] *Ibid.*, Θ 10, 1051 b 24–25.
[135] Barnes (1993, 268).

3.18 Aristotle on *Nous* and Intuition

are just 'seen' to be true."[136] But Aristotle implicitly denies "the identification of *nous* of the principles with quasi-perceptual *nous*."[137] For him, *nous* "is not intended to pick out some faculty or method of acquiring knowledge."[138]

This objection, however, is unjustified. Of course, Aristotle uses *nous* in different senses. Sometimes he uses it in a broader sense, to indicate the mind, meant as the seat of the various mental faculties. Sometimes he uses it in a more restricted sense, to indicate one of these mental faculties. With respect to scientific knowledge, however, Aristotle uses *nous* in the more restricted sense, to indicate a faculty capable of directly apprehending the essence of things and the truth of principles. Thus *nous* is really mental sight and a quasi-perception. In fact Aristotle explicitly associates intuition with sight, because he says that "as sight is in the body, so *nous* in the soul."[139] Indeed, "the activities of *nous* are *noeseis*, which are the seeing of intelligible things, just as the activity of the faculty of sight is the seeing of sensible things."[140]

Of course, that Aristotle associates intuition with sight does not mean that he considers *nous* to be identical to sight, or generally to perception. For "perception is of particulars."[141] Conversely *nous*, apprehending essences, is of universals. Moreover, "the faculty of perception is not capable of perceiving after a too intense sensible; for example, it cannot perceive sound after too loud sounds, nor see or smell after too strong colours or odours."[142] Conversely "*nous*, when it has intuited something highly intelligible, is not less, but rather more capable of intuiting things that are less intelligible."[143] Therefore, *nous* is not identical to sight. Nevertheless, *nous* and sight are similar insofar as they are both kinds of seeing, sight being the seeing of sensible things, *nous* the seeing of intelligible things.

---

[136] *Ibid.*, 267.

[137] *Ibid.*, 269.

[138] *Ibid.*, 268.

[139] Aristotle, *Ethica Nicomachea*, A 6, 1096 b 28–29.

[140] Aristotle, *Protrepticus* (Düring), 24.

[141] Aristotle, *De Anima*, B 5, 417 b 22.

[142] *Ibid.*, Γ 4, 429 a 31–429 b 3.

[143] *Ibid.*, Γ 4, 429 b 3–4.

Chapter 4
The Analytic Method

4.1 Statement of the Analytic Method

As it has been said in Chapter 3, Plato's conception of science is based on the view that the analytic method is the scientific method.

The analytic method is the method according to which, to solve a problem, one looks for some hypothesis that is a sufficient condition for solving it. The hypothesis is obtained from the problem, and possibly other data already available, by some non-deductive rule, and must be plausible, in a sense to be explained below. But the hypothesis is in its turn a problem that must be solved, and is solved in the same way. That is, one looks for another hypothesis that is a sufficient condition for solving the problem posed by the previous hypothesis, it is obtained from the latter, and possibly other data already available, by some non-deductive rule, and must be plausible. And so on, *ad infinitum*. Thus solving a problem is a potentially infinite process.

Therefore, in the analytic method, there are no principles, everything is a hypothesis. The problem and the other data already available are the only starting points for solving the problem.

4.2 Inference and Containment

That, in the analytic method, a hypothesis is obtained from the problem, and possibly other data already available, by some non-deductive rule, rather than by some deductive rule, is because deductive rules are non-ampliative, that is, the conclusion is contained in the premises. This means that the conclusion either is literally a part of the premises, or implies nothing that is not already implied by the premises. Therefore, deductive rules have no heuristic power.

Conversely, non-deductive rules are ampliative, that is, the conclusion is not contained in the premises, in the above sense. Therefore, non-deductive rules have heuristic power.

The ampliativity of non-deductive rules and the non-ampliativity of deductive rules will be further discussed in Chapters 17 and 18.

4.3 The Plausibility Test Procedure

That, in the analytic method, a hypothesis must be plausible, means that the arguments for the hypothesis must be stronger than those against it on the basis of experience, so, for the moment, the hypothesis can be approved. Indeed, 'plausible' comes from the Latin *plausibilis*, which derives from *plaudere* that means 'to applaud', 'to approve'.

In order to show that a hypothesis is plausible it may be useful to use the following plausibility test procedure:

(1) Deduce conclusions from the hypothesis.

(2) Compare the conclusions with each other, in order to see that the hypothesis does not lead to contradictions.

(3) Compare the conclusions with other hypotheses already known to be plausible, and with results of observations or experiments, in order to see that the arguments for the hypothesis are stronger than those against it on the basis of experience.

If the hypothesis passes the plausibility test procedure, then for the moment it is approved. Only for the moment, because new data may always emerge with which the hypothesis may turn out to be incompatible. If the hypothesis does not pass the plausibility test procedure, then, while not being rejected outright, it is put on a waiting list, subject to further investigation.

4.4 Plausibility and Probability

According to a widespread opinion, plausibility is strictly connected with probability. For example, Pólya states that one can "use the calculus of probability to render more precise our views on plausible reasoning."[1] Indeed, "the calculus of plausibilities obeys the same rules as the calculus of probabilities."[2]

This is unjustified. As Kant points out, "plausibility is concerned with whether, in the cognition, there are more grounds for the thing than against it."[3] Conversely,

---

[1] Pólya (1954, II, 116).
[2] Pólya (1941, 457).
[3] Kant (1992, 331).

"probability is a fraction, whose denominator is the number of all the possible cases, and whose numerator contains the number of winning cases."[4] Plausibility and probability are distinct, because plausibility "rests merely on the subject," while "probability rests on the object."[5] While plausibility is not a mathematical concept, "there is a mathematics of probability."[6]

Kant's distinction between plausibility and probability is justified because, as it will be argued in Chapter 20, there are hypotheses which are plausible but, in terms of the classical concept of probability to which Kant refers, have zero probability. On the other hand, there are hypotheses which are not plausible but, again in terms of the classical concept of probability, have a non-zero probability. The same holds on other concepts of probability.

4.5 Non-deductive Rules, Plausibility and Experience

The plausibility of a hypothesis obtained by some non-deductive rule is not guaranteed by that rule but only by experience.

According to a widespread opinion, non-deductive rules are plausibility preserving, that is if the premises are plausible, so is the conclusion. For example, Pólya states that the following pattern of plausible inference holds: From 'A analogous to B' and 'B more credible' we may infer 'A somewhat more credible', that is, "a conjecture becomes somewhat more credible when an analogous conjecture becomes more credible."[7]

This is unjustified. Non-deductive rules are not plausibility preserving, because the arguments for the conclusion go beyond those for the premises.

That non-deductive rules are not plausibility preserving implies that, as it has been stated above, the plausibility of a hypothesis obtained by some non-deductive rule is not guaranteed by that rule but only by experience.

4.6 Deductive Rules, Plausibility and Experience

The same holds of deductive rules. The plausibility of a hypothesis obtained by some deductive rule is not guaranteed by that rule but only by experience.

Once again, according to a widespread opinion, deductive rules are plausibility preserving. For example, Pólya states that the following pattern of plausible

---

[4]*Ibid.*, 328.

[5]*Ibid.*, 153.

[6]*Ibid.*, 331. On Kant's distinction between plausibility and probability, see Capozzi (2002), Chapter 7, Section 5, and Chapter 15.

[7]Pólya (1954, II, 12).

inference holds: From "A implied by H" and "H more credible" we may infer "A more credible."[8]

This is unjustified. For example, let A and B be two rival scientific hypotheses. In order to be accepted, A and B must both be plausible. This is possible because the arguments for and against A need not coincide with the arguments for and against B. On the other hand, being rival, A and B must be mutually incompatible. This means that certain arguments for A must be arguments against B, and vice versa. Then, although A and B are both plausible, their conjunction, $A \wedge B$, will not be plausible. Thus the conjunction introduction rule, 'From A and B infer $A \wedge B$', is not plausibility preserving.

That deductive rules are not plausibility preserving implies that, as it has been stated above, the plausibility of a hypothesis obtained by some deductive rule is not guaranteed by that rule but only by experience.

4.7 The Double Movement of the Analytic Method

The analytic method involves not only an upward movement, from problems to hypotheses, but also a downward movement, from hypotheses to problems, because the plausibility test procedure described above involves considering conclusions deduced from the hypothesis. In fact, each upward movement will be followed by a downward movement. Therefore, the analytic method can be schematically represented as follows.

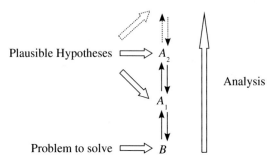

4.8 The Analytic Notion of Demonstration

The analytic method leads to the analytic notion of demonstration, according to which a demonstration consists, first, in a non-deductive derivation of a hypothesis from a problem, and possibly other data already available, where the hypothesis is a sufficient condition for solving the problem and is plausible; then, in a

---

[8] *Ibid.*, II, 27.

non-deductive derivation of another hypothesis from this hypothesis, and possibly other data already available, where this other hypothesis is a sufficient condition for solving the problem posed by the former hypothesis and is plausible; and so on, *ad infinitum*. The goal of a demonstration is to discover hypotheses that are sufficient conditions for solving a problem and are plausible. Thus demonstration has a heuristic role.

A demonstration should serve two functions: 1) it should generate new knowledge from old knowledge; 2) it should give an explanation and provide an understanding of the problem. The analytic notion of demonstration serves both these functions. Indeed, by supplying plausible hypotheses which are sufficient conditions for solving the problem, it generates new knowledge from the problem, and possibly other data already available, thus from old knowledge. On the other hand, by supplying plausible hypotheses which are obtained from the problem and hence are strictly related to it, it gives an explanation and provides an understanding of the problem.[9]

4.9 Origin of the Analytic Method

The analytic method was originally used by Hippocrates of Chios to solve several geometric problems, such as the duplication of the cube and the quadrature of certain lunules.

1) *The duplication of the cube*: Find the side of the cube double of a given cube. To solve this problem, Hippocrates of Chios states the following hypothesis:

(A) Given any two straight lines, a and b, we can always find two other straight lines, x and y, which are the mean proportionals in continued proportion between a and b, that is $a{:}x = x{:}y = y{:}b$.

$$\begin{array}{l}\rule{4cm}{0.4pt}\ a \\ \rule{3cm}{0.4pt}\ x \\ \rule{2.5cm}{0.4pt}\ y \\ \rule{2cm}{0.4pt}\ b\end{array}$$

Hypothesis (A) is a sufficient condition for solving the problem. For, by (A), for any given straight lines a and b, we can find two other straight lines, x and y, such that $a{:}x = x{:}y = y{:}b$. Then $(a{:}x)^3 = (a{:}x)(x{:}y)(y{:}b) = (a{:}b)$. For $b = 2a$ this yields $(a{:}x)^3 = 1{:}2$, hence $x^3 = 2a^3$, that is, a cube double of the given cube of side a. Thus "the cube will be doubled."[10] This solves the problem.

But hypothesis (A) is in its turn a problem that must be solved. It is solved by Menaechmus stating the following hypothesis:

---

[9] On the relation of the analytic notion of demonstration to explanation and understanding, see Cellucci (forthcoming).

[10] Eutocius (1881, 104.15).

(A′) The mean proportionals, x and y, in continuous proportion between two straight lines, a and b, are the coordinates of the meeting point of the parabola satisfying the condition $x^2 = ay$ and the hyperbola satisfying the condition $xy = ab$.

Hypothesis (A′) is a sufficient condition for solving the problem. For let a, b be the two given straight lines. Draw a parabola with vertex O and axis Ox, such that its parameter is equal to a. Then draw a hyperbola with Ox, Oy as asymptotes, such that the rectangle under the distance of any point of the hyperbola from Ox, Oy respectively is equal to the rectangle ab. The hyperbola will meet the parabola. Let P be their meeting point. Let PQ, PR be drawn parallel to Ox, Oy respectively. So PQ, PR are the coordinates of the point P.

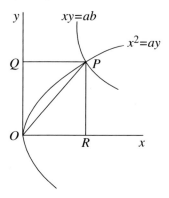

Take PQ as x and PR as y. By the hypothesis $x^2 = ay$ we have $PQ^2 = a \cdot PR$, hence $a:PQ = PQ:PR$. On the other hand, by the hypothesis $xy = ab$ we have $PQ \cdot PR = ab$, hence $a:PQ = PR:b$. Then $a:PQ = PQ:PR = PR:b$, that is, $a:x = x:y = y:b$, which is "what was to be found."[11] That is, (A). This solves the problem.

But hypothesis (A′) is in its turn a problem that must be solved. And so on, *ad infinitum*.

The process by which the problem of the duplication of the cube has been solved can be schematically represented as follows.

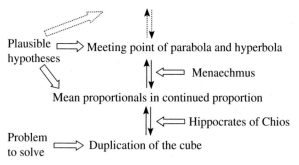

---

[11] *Ibid.*, 96.4.

7) *The process of justification of hypotheses essentially depends on experience.* This follows from the fact that, as it has been stated above, the plausibility of a hypothesis obtained by some non-deductive rule is not guaranteed by that rule but only by experience.

8) *Solving a problem is a dynamic process.* First a problem is formulated. Then a hypothesis is found by some non-deductive rule, and is shown to solve the problem and to be plausible. Successively a new hypothesis is found to solve the problem posed by the former hypothesis. And so on.

9) *Solving a problem yields something new.* Being obtained from the problem, and possibly other data already available, by some non-deductive rule, a solution is not contained in the problem or the other data already available, but possesses novelty with respect to them since non-deductive rules are ampliative. This explains why solving a problem can yield something new.

10) *Intuition has no role in solving a problem.* It has no role in the discovery of hypotheses, because hypotheses are obtained from the problem, and possibly other data already available, by some non-deductive rule, so not by intuition but by argument. It has no role in the justification of hypotheses, because their plausibility is established by means of the plausibility test procedure, so not by intuition but by argument.

11) *Solving a problem is a potentially infinite process, so no solution is final.* At any stage, the inquiry may bring up new data incompatible with the hypothesis on which the solution is based. Then the hypothesis, while not being rejected outright, is put on a waiting list, subject to further inquiry. Even when the inquiry does not bring up incompatible data, the hypothesis remains a problem to be solved, and is solved by looking for another hypothesis, and so on. Thus every solution is provisional.

12) *Hypotheses are neither true nor certain, but this does not diminish the value of the analytic method.* Hypotheses can only be plausible, and plausibility does not guarantee truth or certainty. But plausibility is the best we can achieve, because there is no special source of knowledge capable of guaranteeing absolute truth or certainty. As Plato says, human beings can only "adopt the best and least refutable of human hypotheses, and embarking on it as on a raft, risk the dangers of crossing the sea of life."[14]

4.11 Analytic Method and Infinite Regress

Since, in the analytic method, solving a problem is a potentially infinite process, it may be objected that the analytic method leads to an infinite regress, hence it cannot yield knowledge. For example, Tarski states that, in the analytic method, "in order to

---

[14]Plato, *Phaedo*, 85 c 8–d 2.

establish the validity of a statement, it is necessary to refer back to other statements," and this leads "to an infinite regress."[15]

This objection, however, is unwarranted because, that in the analytic method no hypothesis is absolutely justified, does not mean that such method cannot yield knowledge. It can yield knowledge, albeit fallible knowledge. The analytic method would not yield knowledge only if hypotheses were arbitrary. But they are not arbitrary, because they must be plausible. Therefore, the analytic method can yield knowledge. On the other hand, the knowledge it yields is fallible, in the sense that it cannot be ruled out that it may lead to error. New data may always emerge with which the hypotheses on which knowledge is based may turn out to be incompatible.

Lewis claims that "to speak of fallible knowledge, of knowledge despite uneliminated possibility of error, just sounds contradictory."[16] But, as it has been argued in the Introduction, even mathematical knowledge is not infallible, in the sense that it cannot be ruled out that it might lead to error. A fortiori, so is non-mathematical knowledge. Thus, if Lewis were right, knowledge would be impossible.

4.12 Non-finality of Solutions to Problems

Since, in the analytic method, no solution to a problem is final, it may be objected that this does not account for the fact that mathematical results are final and forever. For example, Jaffe states that, while "scientific hypotheses come and go," mathematics "is different from science because it lasts an eternity."[17]

This objection, however, is unjustified. As Davis says, "problems, questions, and solutions are not static entities" but "change throughout history, throughout our own lifetimes," thus "there is no finality in the creation, formulation and solutions of problems."[18] For this reason "we frequently settle for provisional, 'good enough' solutions."[19] This applies also to mathematical problems. Even in mathematics "a solved problem is still not completely solved but leads to new and profound challenges."[20] In fact, "discovering a sense in which" this is the case "is one important direction that mathematical research takes."[21]

The analytic method suggests such a sense. A solved problem is still not completely solved since no hypothesis is absolutely justified. Any hypothesis which provides a solution to the problem is liable to be replaced with another hypothesis when new data emerge, so every solution is always provisional.

---

[15]Tarski (1994, 110).
[16]Lewis (1996, 549).
[17]Jaffe (1997, 139).
[18]Davis (2006, 164).
[19]*Ibid.*
[20]*Ibid.*, 177.
[21]*Ibid.*

4.13 Original Formulation of the Analytic Method

Although Hippocrates of Chios used the analytic method to solve several geometric problems, it was Plato who gave its first explicit formulation. This does not mean, as Cornford states, that "Plato 'discovered' the method of Analysis, in the same sense as Aristotle discovered the syllogism."[22] Already Hippocrates of Chios used that method.

Plato states that, to solve a problem, you "should take refuge in certain hypotheses, and consider the truth of matters in them."[23] Then, "if anyone attacked the hypothesis, you would not dismiss him and would not avoid answering to him until you had examined its consequences, to see whether they are in accord, or are not in accord, with each other."[24] Even if the consequences were in accord with each other, this would not mean that the hypothesis is conclusively founded, but only that it does not lead to contradiction. Therefore, you would "give an account [*didonai logon*] of the hypothesis itself," and "you would give such an account in the same way, positing another hypothesis, whichever should seem best of the higher ones, and so on until you came to something adequate."[25] But the hypothesis thus reached will always be a problem that eventually will have to be solved by positing a new hypothesis. And so on, *ad infinitum*. For, as we have seen in Chapter 3, according to Plato, as long as we have a body, we will never adequately gain possession of truth. Thus solving a problem is "an endless task."[26] Husserl claims that the ancients did not "grasp the possibility of an infinite task."[27] Plato's formulation of the analytic method shows how unjustified is this claim. For Plato, solving a problem is an infinite task.

Plato uses the analytic method to solve several philosophical problems. Let us consider two of them, the teachability of virtue and the immortality of the soul.

1) *The teachability of virtue*: Show that virtue is teachable.

To solve this problem, Plato states the following hypothesis:

(C) "Virtue is science."[28]

Hypothesis (C) is a sufficient condition for solving the problem. For every science is teachable, so "if virtue is science, clearly it is teachable."[29] From this, by (C), it follows that virtue is teachable. This solves the problem.

---

[22] Cornford (1932, 47).
[23] Plato, *Phaedo*, 99 e 5–6.
[24] *Ibid.*, 101 d 3–5.
[25] *Ibid.*, 101 d 5–e 1.
[26] Plato, *Parmenides*, 136 c 7.
[27] Husserl (1970, 21).
[28] Plato, *Meno*, 87 c 12.
[29] *Ibid.*, 87 c 5–6.

But hypothesis (C) is in its turn a problem that must be solved, and is solved by Plato in the same way, stating the following hypothesis:

(C′) "Virtue is something good."[30]

Hypothesis (C′) is a sufficient condition for solving the problem. For "science embraces everything that is good."[31] From this, by (C′), it follows that virtue is science, that is, (C). This solves the problem. Then, "stating the hypothesis that virtue is science, we hypothesize correctly."[32]

But hypothesis (C′) is in its turn a problem that must be solved. And so on, *ad infinitum*.

2) *The immortality of the soul*: Show that the soul is immortal.
To solve this problem, Plato states the following hypothesis:

(D) "Each of the ideas exists."[33] That is, "there exists a beautiful in itself, a good in itself, a large in itself, and so on."[34]

Hypothesis (D) is a sufficient condition for solving the problem. For, by (D), "the reason why a given thing is," say, "beautiful" is not "its having a lovely colour, or its shape or anything else of the sort," but rather "the presence or communion of that beautiful in itself."[35] The thing in question "is beautiful for no other reason than because it participates in the beautiful in itself; and the same goes for all other things."[36] Thus all "things participate in ideas."[37] But all things "do not admit whatever idea may be opposite to the one that is in them."[38] Therefore, nothing can participate in an idea and in its opposite. Now, the soul participates in the idea of life because "the soul, whatever it occupies, always comes to that bringing life."[39] On the other hand, the "opposite of life" is "death."[40] Then, since nothing can participate in an idea and in its opposite, the soul cannot participate in the idea of death. Therefore "the soul is immortal."[41] This solves the problem.

But hypothesis (D) is in its turn a problem that must be solved, and is solved by Plato in the same way, stating the following hypothesis:

---

[30] *Ibid.*, 87 d 2–3.
[31] *Ibid.*, 87 d 6 7.
[32] *Ibid.*, 87 d 7–8.
[33] Plato, *Phaedo*, 102 b 1.
[34] *Ibid.*, 100 b 6–7.
[35] *Ibid.*, 100 d 1–2, 5–6.
[36] *Ibid.*, 100 c 5–6.
[37] *Ibid.*, 102 b 2.
[38] *Ibid.*, 104 b 9–10.
[39] *Ibid.*, 105 d 3–4.
[40] *Ibid.*, 105 d 6, 9.
[41] *Ibid.*, 105 e 6.

(D′) Justified "true belief" and "intuition [*nous*]" are "two different kinds."[42] Each of them "by nature is associated with different things."[43]

Hypothesis (D′) is a sufficient condition for solving the problem. For, by (D′), justified true belief and intuition are two different kinds, and each of them by nature is associated with different things. Now, as we have seen in Chapter 3, justified true belief is associated with the things of the visible world. Then, from (D′), it follows that, as there really exist the things of the visible world, so there really exist the things of the invisible world. Thus "there really exist these ideas in themselves, forms that cannot be perceived by senses but only by intuition."[44] That is, (D). This solves the problem.

But hypothesis (D′) is in its turn a problem that must be solved. And so on, *ad infinitum*.

4.14 Original Formulation of the Analytic Method and Intuition

While intuition plays no role in the analytic method as stated at the beginning of this chapter, it plays an essential role in Plato's original formulation of the analytic method. Indeed, as we have seen in Chapter 3, according to Plato, while the analytic method is capable of raising the soul up to the ideas in themselves and the unhypothetical principle of everything, it cannot give knowledge of them. Only intuition can give such knowledge. Therefore, according to Plato, the analytic method needs intuition.

Popper claims that Plato advocates "two opposed views on science."[45] According to one view, science is based on the analytic method, which is described "in some detail in Plato's *Republic*," in "the *Meno*," and "in the *Phaedo*."[46] According to the other view, science is based on "the intuitive grasp of the essence," namely, on intuition, as stated, for example, in "Plato's *Phaedo*."[47] But this claim is unjustified. According to Plato, on the one hand, as it has been stated above, the analytic method needs intuition. On the other hand, intuition needs the analytic method, because only the analytic method is capable of raising the soul up to the ideas in themselves and the unhypothetical principle of everything. Therefore, contrary to Popper's claim, for Plato, the analytic method and intuition do not lead to two opposed views of science, but are part of one and the same view of science.

---

[42] Plato, *Timaeus*, 51 d 3–4.
[43] Plato, *Respublica*, V 478 4–5.
[44] Plato, *Timaeus*, 51 d 4–5.
[45] Popper (1998, 243).
[46] *Ibid.*, 244.
[47] *Ibid.*

4.15 The Axiomatic Method

That, in the analytic method, solving a problem is a potentially infinite process, distinguishes the analytic method from the axiomatic method. The latter is the method according to which, to demonstrate a statement, one starts from some given primitive premises, which are supposed to be true, in some sense of 'true', and deduces the statement from them.

Mathematicians of Plato's school used the axiomatic method, which, being an effective means of organizing a body of mathematical knowledge, ended up prevailing among them. This explains Plato's harsh criticism of the axiomatic method, which we have seen in Chapter 3. Nevertheless, it was Aristotle who gave its first explicit formulation. This does not mean that "Aristotle introduced the 'synthetic way' of introducing new structures: the axiomatic method."[48] Already mathematicians of Plato's school used it.

The axiomatic method became popular through Euclid's *Elements*. Then, in the modern and contemporary age, especially Pascal, Hilbert and Padoa modified Aristotle's original formulation, bringing the axiomatic method to its present form. In particular, they dropped Aristotle's condition that the primitive premises must be true in the sense that they must state the essence of the mathematical entities involved.[49]

The axiomatic method is what results from the analytic method when the hypotheses, stated at a certain stage, are assumed as principles for which no justification is given. Indeed, this is the substance of Plato's criticism of the axiomatic method.

4.16 The Axiomatic Notion of Demonstration

The axiomatic method leads to the axiomatic notion of demonstration, according to which a demonstration consists in a deduction of a statement from given prime premises which are supposed to be true, in some sense of 'true'. The goal of a demonstration is to give a justification for a statement. Thus demonstration has a validation role.

There is a basic difference between the analytic and the axiomatic notion of demonstration. According to the analytic notion, a demonstration is the basic tool for acquiring knowledge. According to the axiomatic notion, a demonstration is merely a sort of super spell checker that validates a statement relative to given prime premises.

---

[48]Barendregt (2009, 2287).

[49]For more on these changes, see, for example, Cellucci (1998), Chapters 4 and 5.

The point of the analytic notion of demonstration, with respect to the axiomatic one, is vividly expressed by Hamming as follows: "If the Pythagorean theorem were found to not follow from postulates, we would again search for a way to alter the postulates until it was true. Euclid's postulates came from the Pythagorean theorem, not the other way."[50] In mathematics "you start with some of the things you want and you try to find postulates to support them."[51] The idea that you simply lay down some arbitrary postulates and then make deductions from them "does not correspond to simple observation."[52]

4.17 Analytic Method vs. Axiomatic Method

The use of the axiomatic method in mathematics gave rise to animated debates within Plato's school. Some of its members, "such as the mathematicians of the school of Menaechmus, thought it correct to call" all propositions "problems."[53] Other members, "such as the followers of Speusippus and Amphinomous, thought it correct to call all propositions 'theorems', holding such designation more appropriate than the designation 'problems' for the theoretical sciences."[54]

The question whether mathematical propositions were to be called problems or theorems was not a merely terminological one. It was the expression of a conflict between two different views of the method of mathematics. For those, like the mathematicians of the school Menaechmus, who thought it correct to call all propositions problems, mathematics was problem solving, and the method of mathematics was the analytic method. Conversely, for those, like the followers of Speusippus and Amphinomous, who thought it correct to call all propositions theorems, mathematics was theorem proving, and the method of mathematics was the axiomatic method.

In view of this, it is then significant that, in the *Republic*, Plato takes a stand in favour of the view that mathematics is problem solving, by stating: "We will therefore do astronomy as in geometry, through problems."[55] This is a declaration in favour of the analytic method, as opposed to the axiomatic method.

---

[50]Hamming (1980, 87).
[51]Hamming (1998, 645).
[52]Hamming (1980, 87).
[53]Proclus, *In Primum Euclidis Elementorum Librum Commentarii* (Friedlein), 78.8–9.
[54]*Ibid.*, 77.15–19.
[55]Plato, *Respublica*, VII 530 b 6–7.

4.18 The Method of Ancient Medicine

As it has been mentioned above, the axiomatic method ended up prevailing among mathematicians of Plato's school, which explains Plato's harsh criticism of the method in the *Republic*. It also explains why, after the *Republic*, in *Phaedrus*, Plato considers Hippocrates of Cos' method of medicine as paradigmatic for philosophy, advising philosophers to "look and see what Hippocrates" of Cos "and true argument say about nature."[56]

It seems likely that Hippocrates of Cos' work to which Plato refers is *De Vetere Medicina*, because "no other Hippocratic work explicitly sets out a method of discovery that is so similar to the method described at *Phaedrus* 270c."[57] Then the reason why, in *Phaedrus*, Plato considers Hippocrates of Cos' method of medicine, rather than the method of mathematics, as paradigmatic for philosophy, is that Hippocrates of Cos' method of medicine, as stated in *De Vetere Medicina*, is the analytic method, whereas the method of mathematics had become the axiomatic method.

That Hippocrates of Cos' method of medicine is the analytic method can be seen, for instance, by considering his solution to the problem: Explain why "the human being is affected and altered" by different foods "in one way or another."[58]

To solve this problem, Hippocrates of Cos introduces the following hypothesis:

(E) The substances which are in the food "are also in the human being."[59]

Hypothesis (E) is a sufficient condition for solving the problem. For, when the substances which are in the human being are well "mixed and blended with one another," they do not "cause the human being pain," while, when one of the substances which are in the human being "separates off and comes to be on its own," it "causes the human being pain."[60] So the human being is affected and altered by the substances which are in him. Then, by (E), the human being is affected and altered by the substances which are in the food. Since different foods contain different substances, it follows that the human being is affected and altered by different foods in one way or another. This solves the problem.

But hypothesis (E) is in its turn a problem that must be solved. It is solved by Empedocles stating the following hypothesis:

(E′) "Living beings feed on that which is homogeneous to them."[61]

---

[56] Plato, *Phaedrus*, 270 c 9–10.
[57] Schiefsky (2005, 71).
[58] Hippocrates (2005, 91).
[59] *Ibid.*, 93.
[60] *Ibid.*
[61] Diels and Kranz (1964, 31 A 77).

4.19 Limitations of the Original Formulation of the Analytic Method

Hypothesis (E′) is a sufficient condition for solving the problem. For, by (E′), nutrition takes place by the assimilation of like to like, so the substances which are in the food are also in the human being, that is, (E). This solves the problem.

But hypothesis (E′) is in its turn a problem that must be solved. And so on, *ad infinitum*.

4.19 Limitations of the Original Formulation of the Analytic Method

Plato's original formulation of the analytic method has some basic limitations.

1) Plato gives no indication as to how to find hypotheses to solve problems.

2) He only asks that the consequences of hypotheses agree with each other, which does not guarantee that they agree with experience.

3) He assumes that knowledge must be most certain and infallible. Since, about the things of the visible world, there can only be belief, which is fallible, this leads him to identify knowledge with the intuition of ideas in themselves. Then he is confronted with the problem of establishing that such ideas exist. Moreover, the intuition of ideas in themselves can be reached only after death. So Plato's assumption that knowledge must be most certain and infallible implies that we cannot reach knowledge during life.

The analytic method, as stated in the first section of this chapter, is not subject to these limitations.

It is not subject to limitation 1), because it specifies that hypotheses are found by non-deductive rules. Several non-deductive rules for finding hypotheses are given in the last part of this book.

It is not subject to limitation 2), because it asks that hypotheses are plausible, which guarantees that they agree with experience.

It is not subject to limitation 3), because it does not assume that knowledge must be most certain and infallible. Then one no longer needs to establish that ideas in themselves exist, one may allow that the upward process from the problem to hypotheses can be potentially infinite. The price to be paid for this is that knowledge is not infallible. On the positive side, as it has been just mentioned, one no longer needs to establish that ideas in themselves exist. Rather than by ideas in themselves, hypotheses are guaranteed by their plausibility, hence by experience.

That one no longer needs to establish that ideas in themselves exist is no small advantage, for at least two reasons.

First, as we have seen earlier in this chapter, in order to establish hypothesis (D), that ideas in themselves exist, Plato needs hypothesis (D′), that justified true belief and intuition are two different kinds and each of them is associated with different things. Then, in order to establish hypothesis (D′), he needs the hypothesis that intuition exists. But he provides no justification for this hypothesis, so his whole argument is based on an unwarranted hypothesis.

Secondly, ideas in themselves are an idealization, or divinization, of the objects of experience, obtained by assuming that all their limitations be removed. In this respect, they parallel Greek Gods, who are an idealization, or divinization, of human beings, obtained by assuming that all their limitations be removed. As the Greeks projected all the perfections they would have liked human beings to have upon their Gods, Plato projects all the perfections he would have liked objects of experience to have upon ideas in themselves. But such projections were made only to meet the demand of desire where actual experience was disappointing, and the fact that they subjectively satisfied that desire does not bestow reality upon them.

4.20 Fortune of the Analytic Method

As it has been mentioned above, being an effective means of organizing a body of mathematical knowledge, the axiomatic method ended up prevailing among the mathematicians of Plato's school, and Aristotle gave its first explicit formulation in the *Posterior Analytics*.

Aristotle does not completely dismiss the analytic method, but replaces it with the analytic-synthetic method, which differs from it in some essential respects. The axiomatic method is the synthetic part of Aristotle's analytic-synthetic method. When, in the modern age, interest in method revived, attention focused on Aristotle's analytic-synthetic method and on a variant of it, Pappus' analytic-synthetic, which also differs from the analytic method in some essential respects. Thus the analytic method was replaced with Aristotle's or Pappus' analytic-synthetic method. Both these forms of the analytic-synthetic method will be dealt with in Chapter 5.

As a result of the replacement of the analytic method with Aristotle's or Pappus' analytic-synthetic method, the influence of the analytic method faded. And yet it continued to have an underground life, remaining alive until this day. An example is Fermat's problem, also known as Fermat's Last Theorem: Show that there are no positive integers x, y, z such that $x^n + y^n = z^n$ for $n > 2$. It is usually said that Fermat's problem was solved by Wiles. This is not literally correct, because the problem was solved by Ribet, using the following hypothesis of Taniyama and Shimura:

(F) Every elliptic curve over the rational numbers is modular.

In fact, Ribet showed: "Conjecture of Taniyama-Shimura $\Rightarrow$ Fermat's Last Theorem."[62] Namely, he showed that (F) is a sufficient condition for solving Fermat's problem. But hypothesis (F) is in its turn a problem that must be solved. It was solved by Wiles using plausible hypotheses from various mathematics fields. Therefore, what Wiles solved was not Fermat's problem, but rather the problem

---

[62]Ribet (1990, 127).

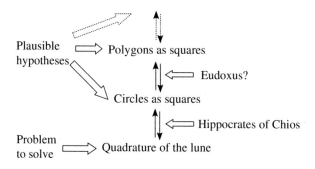

4.10 Basic Features of the Analytic Method

The analytic method has the following basic features.

1) *The hypotheses for solving a problem need not belong to the field of the problem, but may belong to other fields.* Thus the search for a solution to a problem is not carried out in a closed, predetermined space. For example, as we have seen above, to solve a problem of the theory of regular solids, the duplication of the cube, Hippocrates of Chios uses a hypothesis of the theory of ratios and proportions.

2) *The hypotheses for solving a problem are local, not global.* They are not general principles, good for all problems, but are aimed at a specific problem.

3) *Being local, not global, the hypotheses for solving a problem can be efficient.* Being aimed at a specific problem, they can take care of the peculiarities of the problem, which is essential for the feasibility of the solution.

4) *Different problems will generally require different hypotheses.* This follows from the fact that hypotheses are aimed at a specific problem, so they depend on the peculiarities of the problem.

5) *The same problem can be solved using different hypotheses.* A problem has several sides, each of which may suggest different hypotheses, that may lead to different solutions of the problem. When a problem seems to be solvable only by a single hypothesis, one should worry because it might mean that the solution is wrong or that the problem is ill-posed. Different hypotheses may establish different relations between the problem and problems of other fields, thus showing the problem in a new perspective. As Atiyah says, "if you cannot look at a problem from different directions, it is probably not very interesting; the more perspectives, the better!"[13]

6) *Solving a problem is both a process of discovery and a process of justification.* It is a process of discovery, because it involves finding hypotheses by non-deductive rules. It is a process of justification, because it involves comparing the arguments for and against the hypotheses thus found, in order to check their plausibility.

---

[13] Raussen and Skau (2004, 24).

4.9 Origin of the Analytic Method

2) *The quadrature of certain lunules*: Show that, if *PQR* is a right isosceles triangle and *PRQ*, *PTR* are semicircles on *PQ*, *PR*, respectively, then the lunule *PTRU* is equal to the right isosceles triangle *PRS*.

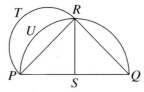

To solve this problem, Hippocrates of Chios states the following hypothesis:

(B) Circles are as the squares on their diameters.

Hypothesis (B) is a sufficient condition for solving the problem. For, by the Pythagorean theorem, the square on *PQ* is twice the square on *PR*. Then, by (B), the semicircle on *PQ*, that is, *PRQ*, is twice the semicircle on *PR*, that is, *PTR*, and hence the quarter of circle *PRS* is equal to the semicircle *PTR*. Subtracting the same circular segment, *PUR*, from both the quarter of circle *PRS* and the semicircle *PTR*, we obtain the lunule *PTRU* and the triangle *PRS*, respectively. Therefore, "the lunule" *PTRU* "is equal to the triangle."[12] This solves the problem.

But hypothesis (B) is in its turn a problem that must be solved. It is solved, presumably by Eudoxus, stating the following hypothesis:

(B′) Similar regular polygons inscribed in circles are as the squares on their diameters.

Hypothesis (B′) is a sufficient condition for solving the problem. For, let P, Q be two circles and R, S the squares on their diameters. We want to show that $P/Q = R/S$. Suppose not. Then either $P/Q > R/S$ or $P/Q < R/S$. If $P/Q > R/S$, then, for some $P' < P$ it will be $P'/Q = R/S$. Let U_n, V_n be the polygons with n sides inscribed in the circles P, Q respectively. For a sufficiently large n it will be $P - U_n < P - P'$, so $U_n > P'$. Since U_n, V_n are similar, by (B′), we have $U_n/V_n = R/S$. From the latter and $P'/Q = R/S$ we obtain $U_n/V_n = P'/Q$, from which, since $U_n > P'$, it follows $V_n > Q$. But, since V_n is inscribed in Q, this is impossible. Similarly if $P/Q < R/S$. We conclude that $P/Q = R/S$, that is, (B). This solves the problem.

But hypothesis (B′) is in its turn a problem that must be solved. And so on, *ad infinitum*.

The process by which the problem of the quadrature of certain lunules has been solved can be schematically represented as follows.

---

[12]Simplicius, *In Aristotelis Physicorum Libros Quattuor Priores Commentaria* (Diels), I 3, 56.18–19.

4.20 Fortune of the Analytic Method

posed by the hypothesis (F). The process through which Fermat's problem was solved can then be schematically represented as follows.

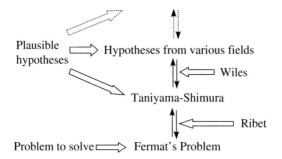

It might be objected that Fermat's problem was not solved by Ribet, because Ribet used a hypothesis, (F), which at the time had not yet been demonstrated. Since the problem posed by hypothesis (F) was solved by Wiles, the solution of Fermat's problem should be credited to him. But this objection has paradoxical consequences. For the solution to the problem posed by hypothesis (F) given by Wiles, uses hypotheses from various fields of mathematics. They, in their turn, depend on other hypotheses, and ultimately on the axioms of set theory, ZFC. Now, the axioms of set theory, ZFC, have still not been demonstrated. Thus, if Ribet did not solve Fermat's problem because his solution used a hypothesis, (F), that at the time had not yet been demonstrated, then Wiles did not solve Fermat's problem because his solution uses a hypothesis, the axioms of set theory, ZFC, that to this very day has still not been demonstrated.

The situation is similar to that of Hippocrates of Chios' solution to the problem of the duplication of the cube. Such solution used a hypothesis, (A), which at the time had not yet been demonstrated. Later on Menaechmus gave a solution to the problem posed by hypothesis (A), using a hypothesis, (A'), which in its turn depended on other hypotheses, and ultimately on the axioms of geometry. Thus, if Ribet did not solve Fermat's problem because his solution used a hypothesis which at the time had not yet been demonstrated, then Hippocrates of Chios did not solve the problem of the duplication of the cube because his solution used a hypothesis which at the time had not yet been demonstrated.

The objection is due to an inadequate notion of what a demonstration is, and specifically to the influence of the Göttingen school and Bourbaki that, as it has been stated in the Introduction, led to the adoption of the top-down approach, and hence of the axiomatic method, as the mathematics paradigm. An adequate notion of demonstration is given only by the analytic notion. For, as it will be argued in Chapters 12 and 17, the axiomatic notion is incompatible with Gödel's incompleteness theorems, only the analytic notion is compatible with them.

Chapter 5
The Analytic-Synthetic Method

5.1 Aristotle's Changes to the Analytic Method

As it has been mentioned in Chapter 4, Aristotle does not completely dismiss the analytic method but replaces it with the analytic-synthetic method. The reason Aristotle gives for this replacement is that the analytic method "does not allow one to know anything in an absolute way, but only on the basis of a hypothesis."[1] The latter is not necessarily true, while "scientific knowledge must proceed from premises that are true."[2] Therefore, scientific knowledge cannot be based on the analytic method.

The replacement of the analytic method with Aristotle's analytic-synthetic method involves two basic changes.

1) The search for a solution to a problem is a finite process, so the ascending sequence of the premises must terminate. If it "did not terminate and there was always something above whatever premise has been taken, then there would be demonstrations of all things."[3] Including falsehoods. Therefore, there would be no scientific knowledge.

2) Once the prime premises have been found, the only role which remains for analysis is to find deductions of given conclusions from prime premises. Therefore, the analytic-synthetic method is primarily a method for finding deductions of given conclusions from given prime premises, that is, a method for finding demonstrations in given axiomatic systems. This explains Geminus' statement, that for Aristotle "analysis is the discovery of demonstration."[4]

In addition to Aristotle's analytic-synthetic method, there is also a variant of it, Pappus' analytic-synthetic method. In this chapter, both versions of the analytic-synthetic method will be considered.

---

[1] Aristotle, *Analytica Posteriora*, A 22, 84 a 5–6.
[2] *Ibid.*, A 2, 71 b 20–21.
[3] *Ibid.*, A 22, 84 a 1–2.
[4] Ammonius, *In Aristotelis Analyticorum Priorum Librum I Commentarium*, (Wallies), 5.28.

5.2 Aristotle's Analytic-Synthetic Method

Aristotle's analytic-synthetic method is the method according to which, to find a deduction of a given conclusion from given prime premises, one looks for premises from which the conclusion can be deduced by syllogism. The premises are obtained from the conclusion either by Aristotle's procedure for finding premises by syllogism, or by induction, both of which will be described in Chapter 7. The premises must be plausible, in the sense already explained in Chapter 4. If the premises thus found are not among the given prime premises or statements already deduced from them, one looks for new premises from which the previous premises can be deduced by syllogism. The new premises are obtained from the previous premises either by Aristotle's procedure for finding premises by syllogism or by induction. The new premises must be plausible. And so on, until one arrives at premises that are among the given prime premises or statements already deduced from them. Then the process terminates. This is analysis. At this point, one tries to invert the direction and obtain a deduction of the conclusion from the given prime premises. This is synthesis.

Aristotle's analytic-synthetic method can be schematically represented as follows.

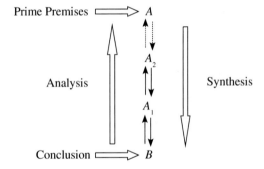

5.3 Original Formulation of Aristotle's Analytic-Synthetic Method

Aristotle's original formulation of the analytic-synthetic method is as follows.

Aristotle states that "by nature the process of knowledge proceeds from what is more knowable and clearer to us to what is clearer and more knowable by nature."[5] Therefore, "we must necessarily proceed in this way, namely, starting from the

---

[5] Aristotle, *Physica*, A 1, 184 a 16–18.

5.3 Original Formulation of Aristotle's Analytic-Synthetic Method

things which are less known by nature but clearer to us, towards those which are clearer and more knowable by nature."[6] Now, what is more knowable and clearer to us is the conclusion we want to establish, while what is clearer and more knowable by nature are the prime premises. They are "most knowable" by nature because "by reason of these, and from these, all other things are known, but these are not known by means of the things subordinate to them."[7] Then, by saying that we must proceed from what is more knowable and clearer to us to what is clearer and more knowable by nature, Aristotle means to say that we must proceed from the conclusion we want to establish to the prime premises.

Indeed, given the conclusion we want to establish, we must find "the necessary premises through which the syllogisms come about."[8] We will find them either by Aristotle's procedure for finding premises by syllogism, or by induction. When they are found, we "should not put these forward right away, but rather should stand off as far above them as possible."[9] That is, by means of the same procedure, we should find other premises from which the previous premises can be deduced. Then we should repeat the process, finding other premises from which the previous premises can be deduced, and so on. This process must go on until we arrive at some premises which are among the given prime premises or statements already deduced from them. Then the process terminates. This is analysis. At this point, we must try to invert the process, deducing the conclusion we want to establish from the prime premises, thus obtaining a demonstration of it and hence scientific knowledge. For "to know scientifically is to know through demonstration."[10] This is synthesis.

For Aristotle, however, the analytic-synthetic method is not only a method for acquiring scientific knowledge, but rather a general method for solving problems in every field – not only theoretical fields, such as mathematics, but also practical fields, such as medicine, oratory and politics, which require deliberation to reach a desired end. Indeed, Aristotle says that doctors, orators, statesmen start from the end, since "the end is the object for which one acts."[11] And, "when the end has been set, they consider how and by what means it is to be attained."[12] Then they consider "by what other means" these "means will be achieved," and so on, "until they arrive at the first cause, which in the order of discovery is last."[13] At that point, they try to invert the process and, starting from the first cause, try to do what contributes to their desired end.

For example, a doctor reasons as follows: "If the subject is to be healthy," there must be "a certain balance" in the functions of the body, and, "if this is to be present,

---

[6] *Ibid.*, A 1, 184 a 18–21.
[7] Aristotle, *Metaphysica*, A 2, 982 b 2–4.
[8] Aristotle, *Topica*, Θ 1, 155 b 29.
[9] *Ibid.*, Θ 1, 155 b 29–30.
[10] Aristotle, *Analytica Posteriora*, A 2, 71 b 18.
[11] Aristotle, *Ethica Eudemea*, B 11, 1227 b 36.
[12] Aristotle, *Ethica Nicomachea*, Γ 3, 1112 b 15–16.
[13] *Ibid.*, Γ 3, 1112 b 18–20.

there must be a certain heat; and the doctor goes on thinking in this way until he reduces the matter to a last thing that he himself can produce."[14] At this point, he tries to invert the process and, starting from this last thing and producing it, tries to do what contributes to healing. The "process from the last thing onward, that is, the process towards healing, is called production."[15]

Thus "he who deliberates seems to carry out an inquiry and an analysis in the way described as though he were carrying out an analysis in a geometrical construction."[16] Once he has carried out the analysis, he tries to invert the process and carry out the synthesis, or construction, again like in the case of a geometrical construction. Since the synthesis starts from the first cause, which is last in the order of discovery, "what is last in the order of analysis is first in the order of construction."[17]

Analysis is not always successful, and "if one comes on an impossibility, one gives up the search," but "if on the contrary the thing appears possible, one tries to do it," where 'possible' is "what can be brought about by one's own efforts."[18]

5.4 An Example of Aristotle's Analytic-Synthetic Method

As an illustration of Aristotle's analytic-synthetic method, let us consider the demonstration of Proposition I.1 of Euclid's *Elements* given in the sixteenth century by Piccolomini, who says to follow Philoponus' commentary to Book I, Chapter 9 of Aristotle's *Posterior Analytics*.[19]

Proposition I.1 states: On a given straight line to construct an equilateral triangle.

Let PQ be a given straight line. With centre P and distance PQ let the circle QRS be described. With centre Q and distance QP let the circle PRT be described. We thus obtain a triangle PQR. We want to establish that PQR is an equilateral triangle.

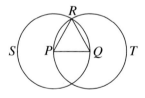

We start from the conclusion we want to establish:

(1) PQR is an equilateral triangle.

---

[14] Aristotle, *Metaphysica* Z, 7, 1032 b 7–9.
[15] *Ibid.*, Z 7, 1032 b 9–10.
[16] Aristotle, *Ethica Nicomachea*, Γ 3, 1112 b 20–21.
[17] *Ibid.*, Γ 3, 1112 b 23–24.
[18] *Ibid.*, Γ 3, 1112 b 24–27.
[19] See Piccolomini (1547, 100r–102r).

5.4 An Example of Aristotle's Analytic-Synthetic Method

Two premises from which (1) can be immediately deduced are:

(2) Every triangle which has its three sides equal is an equilateral triangle.
(3) The triangle *PQR* has its three sides *PQ*, *QR*, *PR* equal.

By Definition 20 of Euclid's *Elements*, (2) is a prime premise. On the other hand, (3) consists of three assertions:

(4) *PR*, *QR* are equal.
(5) *PQ*, *QR* are equal.
(6) *PQ*, *PR* are equal.

Two premises from which (4) can be immediately deduced are:

(7) Things equal to the same thing are equal to one another.
(8) *PR*, *QR* are equal to *PQ*.

By Common Notion 1 of Euclid *Elements*, (7) is a prime premise. On the other hand, (8) consists of two propositions, namely, (5) and (6).

Two premises from which (5) can be immediately deduced are:

(9) Straight lines from the centre of a circle to the circumference are equal to one another.
(10) *PQ*, *QR* are straight lines from the centre of the circle *PRT* to the circumference.

By Definition 15 of Euclid's *Elements*, (9) is a prime premise. On the other hand, (10) is a prime premise since it is true by construction.

Two premises from which (6) can be immediately deduced are:

(11) Straight lines from the centre of a circle to the circumference are equal to one another.
(12) *PQ*, *PR* are straight lines from the centre of the circle *QRS* to the circumference.

Once again, by Definition 15 of Euclid's *Elements*, (11) is a prime premise. On the other hand, (12) is a prime premise since it is true by construction.

Thus we have come upon prime premises.

This is analysis.

Now we try to reverse the analysis in a synthesis. This can be done as follows.

From prime premises (11) and (12) we infer (6). From prime premises (9) and (10) we infer (5). Since (8) consists of (5) and (6), we have thus inferred (8). From prime premise (7) and (8) we infer (4). Since (3) consists of (5), (6) and (4), we have thus inferred (3). From prime premise (2), and (3) we infer (1).

Since, as it will be argued in Chapter 6, Aristotle treats singular assertions as if they were universal ones, all these inferences are syllogisms in Barbara.

This is synthesis.

5.5 The Direction of Analysis in Aristotle's Analytic-Synthetic Method

Clearly, in Aristotle's analytic-synthetic method, analysis is an upward path. Some people, however, maintain that analysis must be a downward path because, if it were an upward path, it would always be trivially convertible into synthesis and hence would be superfluous. For example, Knorr states that Aristotle "portrays analysis as a deductive procedure."[20] If analysis were not a deductive procedure, this would "render superfluous any concern over convertibility" of analysis into synthesis, because "the analysis (of antecedents) would of itself have produced the deductive sequence of the synthesis."[21]

This, however, is unjustified because Aristotle gives two good reasons why analysis as an upward path may not always be convertible into synthesis.

1) "If it were impossible to prove something true from something false, it would be easy to make analyses" – namely, to discover premises from which to deduce the conclusion – "because then the propositions would convert of necessity."[22] But "it is possible to deduce a true conclusion from false premises."[23] Therefore, "sometimes it happens, as in the case of geometrical demonstrations, that, after making the analysis, we are unable to make the synthesis."[24]

2) The premises obtained by analysis may not be the causes of the conclusion. When this occurs, they do not produce scientific knowledge, because "we have scientific knowledge of something only when we know its cause."[25] An example of this will be considered in Chapter 7.

Reasons 1) and 2), which explain why analysis is not always convertible into synthesis, support the interpretation of analysis as an upward path. That, in Aristotle's analytic-synthetic method, analysis is an upward path, is confirmed by Alexander of Aphrodisias who states that, for Aristotle, "analysing is a route from the end up to the principles."[26]

---

[20] Knorr (1993, 75).

[21] *Ibid.*, 95, footnote 65.

[22] Aristotle, *Analytica Posteriora*, A 12, 78 a 6–8.

[23] *Ibid.*, B 2, 53 b 8.

[24] Aristotle, *Sophistici Elenchi*, 16, 175 a 27–28.

[25] Aristotle, *Analytica Posteriora*, A 2, 71 b 30–31.

[26] Alexander of Aphrodisias, *In Aristotelis Analyticorum Priorum Librum Primum Commentarium* (Wallies), 7.14–15.

5.6 Aristotle's Analytic-Synthetic Method and Intuition

Intuition plays an essential role in Aristotle's analytic-synthetic method. In such a method, the prime premises must not only be true but also known to be true, otherwise we could not have scientific knowledge of what follows from them. Then the question arises how the prime premises become known to be true. As we have seen in Chapter 3, according to Aristotle, they become known to be true by intuition. But, while prime premises become known to be true by intuition, it is not by intuition that they are discovered.

It is sometimes claimed that Aristotle "describes a process of discovery of first principles that involves both induction and intuition."[27] This confuses how prime premises are discovered with how they become known to be true. According to Aristotle, prime premises are discovered by the analytic-synthetic method. In fact, in its first application, such method is used to discover prime premises. Once prime premises have been found, the method will be used to discover deductions of given conclusions from given prime premises. On the other hand, prime premises become known to be true only by intuition, because although "the hypotheses are the end" of analysis, it is not "argument that teaches us the prime premises."[28]

Intuition and analysis are essentially different. While intuition belongs to intuitive thinking, analysis belongs to discursive thinking. Moreover, while intuition is supposed to be infallible, analysis is fallible, since hypotheses found by means of it may not be true.

5.7 Plausible Premises and *Endoxa*

In the analytic part of Aristotle's analytic-synthetic method, until one arrives at some prime premise, one proceeds through premises which, for the moment, are only plausible. Plausible premises correspond to what Aristotle calls *endoxa* and are used in the same sense.

It might be objected that, while the plausibility of a hypothesis is defined in terms of the arguments for and against it, Aristotle defines *endoxa* as opinions accepted "by everyone, or by the great majority, or by the wise, and among them either by all of them, or by the great majority, or by the most famous and esteemed."[29] But this cannot be Aristotle's definition of *endoxa*, otherwise *endoxa* would include the superficial or biased opinions of the great majority. In fact, *endoxa* are not opinions on which one agrees on the basis of what one believes right now. They are

---

[27] Witt (1989, 29, footnote 17).
[28] Aristotle, *Ethica Nicomachea*, Z 8, 1151 a 16–18.
[29] Aristotle, *Topica*, A 1, 100 b 21–23.

rather opinions on which one can agree on the basis of a careful examination of the arguments for and against them, thus on the basis of an investigation.

Aristotle's definition of *endoxa* is rather implicit in his assertion that, for each opinion concerning some given subject, we must "examine the arguments for it and the arguments against it."[30] For "going through the difficulties on either side, we shall more readily discern the true as well as the false in any subject."[31] Thus *endoxa* are opinions on which one can agree on the basis of a careful examination of the arguments for and against them, from which the former turn out to be stronger than the latter. This involves comparing the opinion concerned with the existing data, since the arguments for and against it will be based on the existing data. Indeed, Aristotle states that "we must inquire into a premise not only of the basis of a conclusion deduced from premises," but also on the basis of the existing data, "because all the data harmonize with truth, but soon clash with falsity."[32] This justifies the claim that plausible premises correspond to what Aristotle calls *endoxa*.

That *endoxa* are plausible does not exclude that they can be true. Aristotle does not oppose *endoxa* to truths but to *paradoxa*, that is, to opinions "from which absurdities follow."[33] Unlike *endoxa*, *paradoxa* can never be true. That in the analytic method hypotheses must be plausible, only implies that they must be "non-paradoxical."[34]

5.8 The Controversy Between Plato and Aristotle Concerning Method

The analytic method and Aristotle's analytic-synthetic method are essentially different. The analytic method is a method for finding hypotheses to solve problems and is independent of any given axiomatic system. Conversely, once the prime premises have been found, Aristotle's analytic-synthetic method is essentially a method for finding deductions of given conclusions from given prime premises, and hence depends on a given axiomatic system. Therefore, analysis plays only an auxiliary role in Aristotle's analytic-synthetic method, it is simply a heuristic pattern in already axiomatized mathematics.

The distinction between the analytic method and Aristotle's analytic-synthetic method is really an opposition. Plato and Aristotle make this quite clear.

Indeed, as we have seen, on the one hand, Plato criticizes the axiomatic method – the synthesis part of Aristotle's analytic-synthetic method – by the argument that the mathematicians who use it take their prime premises for granted and are

---

[30] *Ibid.*, Θ 14, 163 a 37–b 1.
[31] *Ibid.*, A 2, 101 a 35–6.
[32] Aristotle, *Ethica Nicomachea*, I 8, 1098 b 9–12.
[33] Aristotle, *Topica*, Θ 9, 160 b 18–19.
[34] *Ibid.*, A 10, 104 a 10–11.

unable to give any justification for them. Therefore, their prime premises are mere conventions, and such a fabric of convention could never become a science. On the other hand, Aristotle criticizes the analytic method by the argument that it does not permit one to know anything in an absolute way. For it depends on hypotheses which are not necessarily true, while scientific knowledge must proceed from prime premises that are true and known to be true.

Now, Plato's criticism of the axiomatic method is justified, because mathematicians who use such method are unable to give any justification for prime premises. They assume them to be true, in some sense of 'true', but, as it will be argued in Chapter 12, there is no rational way of knowing whether or not they are true. Conversely, Aristotle's criticism of the analytic method is unjustified, because Aristotle blames the analytic method for starting from premises which are not known to be true, but, as has just been said, there is no rational way of knowing whether or not they are true.

5.9 Pappus' Analytic-Synthetic Method

After considering Aristotle's analytic-synthetic method, let us now consider Pappus' analytic-synthetic method. The two versions of the analytic-synthetic method must not be confused.[35] On the other hand, the analytic method is not to be confused with any of them.[36]

Pappus' analytic-synthetic method is the method according to which, to find a deduction of a given conclusion from given prime premises, one assumes the conclusion and considers a conclusion that can be immediately deduced from it. The conclusion must be plausible. If the conclusion thus obtained is not among the given prime premises or statements already deduced from them, one looks for a new conclusion that can be immediately deduced from it. The new conclusion must be plausible. And so on, until one arrives at a conclusion that is among the given prime premises or statements already deduced from them. Then the process terminates. This is analysis. At this point, one tries to invert the direction and get a deduction of the given conclusion from the given prime premises. This is synthesis

While, in Aristotle's analytic-synthetic method, analysis is an upward path and synthesis a downward path, in Pappus' analytic-synthetic method analysis and synthesis are both downward paths, being both deductive processes.

---

[35]They are often confused. For example, Hintikka and Remes state that "Pappus' description of analysis and synthesis and the Aristotelian passage" in which Aristotle says that he who deliberates seems to carry out an analysis in a geometrical construction "are closely similar" (Hintikka and Remes 1974, 86).

[36]They are often confused. In particular, a whole tradition does not distinguish between the analytic method, as stated by Plato, and Pappus' analytic-synthetic method. See, for example, (Sayre 1969, 15–28); Menn (2002).

Pappus' analytic-synthetic method can be schematically represented as follows.

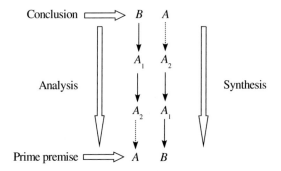

5.10 Original Formulation of Pappus' Analytic-Synthetic Method

Pappus' original formulation of the analytic-synthetic method consists of 1) a general description of analysis and synthesis, and 2) a distinction between two kinds of analysis: theorematic and problematic analysis.

1) Pappus states that "analysis is the way from what is sought [*zetoumenon*], as if it were established, through the things that follow [*akoloutha*], to something that is established in synthesis."[37] That is, to something that is already known or a prime premise. For "in analysis we assume what is sought as if it had been achieved, and look for the thing from which it follows, and again what comes before that thing, until, by proceeding reversely [*anapodizontes*] in this way, we come upon something already known, or ranking as a principle. And we call such a method analysis, as being a reverse solution [*anapalin lusin*]."[38] On the other hand, "in synthesis we assume what was reached last in analysis to have been already achieved, and setting out in natural order as antecedents what before were consequents, and linking them one with another, we in the end arrive at the construction of what was sought. And this we call synthesis."[39]

2) There are "two kinds of analysis; one seeks after the truth, and is called 'theorematic', the other tries to find what was demanded, and is called 'problematic'."[40] In theorematic analysis, "we assume what is sought as a fact and true, and proceed through the things that follow, as if they were true facts according

---

[37] Pappus (1876–1878, II, 634, 11–13).
[38] *Ibid.*, II, 634, 13–18.
[39] *Ibid.*, II, 634, 18–23.
[40] *Ibid.*, II, 634, 24–26.

to the hypothesis, to something established."[41] That is, to something already known or a prime premise. Then, "if the thing that has been established is true, the thing that was sought too will be true, and the demonstration will be the reverse of the analysis; but if we come upon something established to be false, the thing that was sought too will be false."[42] In problematic analysis, "we assume the required thing to be known, and proceed through the things that follow, as if they were true, to something established."[43] That is, to something that is already known or a prime premise. Then, "if the thing that has been established is possible and obtainable," the "required thing too will be possible, and again the demonstration will be the reverse of the analysis; but if we come upon something established to be impossible, the problem too will be impossible."[44]

5.11 An Example of Pappus' Analytic-Synthetic Method

As an illustration of Pappus' analytic-synthetic method, let us consider the demonstration of Proposition XIII.1 of Euclid's *Elements*, given by the unknown author of a scholium to Propositions XIII.1–5.[45]

Proposition XIII.1 states: If a straight line is cut in extreme and mean ratio, the greater segment added to half of the whole is five times greater in square than the square on the half.

Let a straight line PQ be cut in extreme and mean ratio at R, and let the greater segment be PR, and let $PS = \frac{1}{2}QP$. We must show that $RS^2 = 5PS^2$.

We assume the conclusion we want to establish:

(1) $RS^2 = 5PS^2$.

By Proposition II.4 of Euclid's *Elements*, if a straight line is cut at random, then the square on the whole is equal to the squares on the segments and twice the rectangle contained by the segments. Thus:

(i) $RS^2 = RP^2 + PS^2 + 2RP \times PS$.

---

[41] *Ibid.*, II, 636, 1–4.
[42] *Ibid.*, II, 636, 5–7.
[43] *Ibid.*, II, 636, 8–10.
[44] *Ibid.*, II, 636, 10–4.
[45] See Euclid (1883–1916, IV, 366.5–24, 368.1–14); Robinson (1936, 470–471).

From (1) and (i) we obtain:

(2) $RP^2 + PS^2 + 2RP \times PS = 5PS^2$.

From (2) by subtraction we obtain

(3) $RP^2 + 2RP \times PS = 4PS^2$.

Since $PS = \frac{1}{2}QP$, we have $QP = 2PS$, hence:

(ii) $QP \times RP = 2RP \times PS$.

On the other hand, since QP has been cut in extreme and mean ratio, we have:

(iii) $RP^2 = QP \times QR$.

From (3), (ii) and (iii) we obtain:

(4) $QP \times QR + QP \times RP = 4PS^2$.

By Proposition II.2 of Euclid's *Elements*, if a straight line is cut at random, then the rectangle contained by the whole and both of the segments is equal to the square on the whole. Thus we have:

(iv) $QP \times QR + QP \times RP = QP^2$.

From (4) and (iv) we obtain:

(5) $QP^2 = 4PS^2$.

Since $PS = \frac{1}{2}QP$, from (5) we obtain $QP^2 = 4(\frac{1}{2}QP)^2 = QP^2$, therefore (5) is true.

Thus we have come upon something which is true.
This is analysis.
Now we try to reverse the analysis in a synthesis. This can be done as follows.

We start from what we have obtained last in the analysis, namely, (5). By Proposition II.2 of Euclid's *Elements* we have (iv). From (5) and (iv) we obtain (4). Since $PS = \frac{1}{2}QP$, we have $QP = 2PS$, hence (ii). On the other hand, since QP has been cut in extreme and mean ratio, we have (iii). From (4), (ii) and (iii) we obtain (3). From (3) by addition we obtain (2). By Proposition II.4 of Euclid's *Elements* we have (i). From (2) and (i) we obtain (1).

This is synthesis.

The following diagram shows the structure of analysis and synthesis in this demonstration.

$$\text{Analysis:} \quad (1) \Rightarrow (2) \Rightarrow (3) \Rightarrow (4) \Rightarrow (5)$$
$$\uparrow \qquad \quad \uparrow \quad\ \uparrow$$
$$(i) \qquad\ (ii),\ (iv)$$
$$(iii)$$

$$\textit{Synthesis}: \quad (5) \Rightarrow (4) \Rightarrow (3) \Rightarrow (2) \Rightarrow (1)$$
$$\phantom{\textit{Synthesis}: \quad (5) \Rightarrow } \uparrow \uparrow \uparrow$$
$$\phantom{\textit{Synthesis}: \quad (5) \Rightarrow } (\text{iv}) (\text{ii}), (\text{i})$$
$$\phantom{\textit{Synthesis}: \quad (5) \Rightarrow \uparrow \Rightarrow } (\text{iii})$$

In analysis we have a chain from (1) to (5), in synthesis a chain from (5) to (1). Propositions (i)–(iv) are not links in these chains, but are necessary to connect propositions (1)–(5) together. Therefore, synthesis is not really the reverse of analysis.

Since propositions (i)–(iv) are necessary to connect propositions (1)–(5) together, both chains are not really deductions. For example, in the chain from (1) to (5), the link from (1) to (2) is not a deduction of (2) from (1) but rather a deduction of (2) from (1) + (i). In the chain from (5) to (1), the link from (2) to (1) is not a deduction of (1) from (2) but rather a deduction of (1) from (2) + (i).

5.12 The Direction of Analysis in Pappus' Analytic-Synthetic Method

Pappus' original formulation of the analytic-synthetic method is puzzling, because it contains apparently incompatible assertions about the direction of analysis.

In his description of analysis and synthesis, on the one hand, Pappus states that analysis is the way from what is sought, as if it were established, through the things that follow. This suggests that analysis is a downward path. On the other hand, he states that, in analysis, we assume what is sought as if it had been achieved, and look for the thing from which it follows. This suggests that analysis is an upward path.

In his description of theorematic analysis, on the one hand, Pappus states that, in analysis, we assume what is sought as a fact and true, and proceed through the things that follow, to something established. This suggests that analysis is a downward path. On the other hand, he states that, if the thing that has been established is true, the thing that was sought too will be true. If analysis were a downward path, this would be in conflict with the fact that, if something true follows from a given thing, the latter will not necessarily be true because, from a false premise, a true conclusion may follow.

In his description of problematic analysis, on the one hand, Pappus states that, in analysis, we assume the required thing to be known, and proceed through the things that follow, to something established. This suggests that analysis is a downward path. On the other hand, he states that, if the thing that has been established is possible and obtainable, the required thing too will be possible. If analysis were a downward path, this would be in conflict with the fact that, if something possible follows from a given thing, the latter will not necessarily be possible because, from an impossible premise, a possible conclusion may follow.

To solve the puzzle, Leibniz suggests that Pappus tacitly assumes that all links of analysis and synthesis are reciprocal, or convertible. Indeed, Leibniz states that, according to Pappus, analysis "consisted in assuming what is sought and drawing consequences from it, till one comes upon something given or known."[46] Since "the true can be drawn from the false," the "propositions must be reciprocal for the synthetic demonstration to go back retracing analysis."[47] We cannot conclude that what is sought is true "unless, in our reasoning, we make use of pure equations or propositions that are convertible."[48] The "practice of the ancients shows that they were not ignorant of this principle, because they guarded against errors adequately."[49]

But, if one interprets the condition that propositions must be reciprocal, or convertible, in the strict sense that they must be equivalent, Leibniz's suggestion does not account for the practice of the ancients. For, as it is apparent from the demonstration of Proposition XIII.1 of Euclid's *Elements* considered in the previous section, the links of analysis and synthesis need not consist of equivalent propositions. Leibniz's suggestion accounts for the practice of the ancients only if one interprets the condition that propositions must be reciprocal, or convertible, in the weak sense that each of them must be deducible from the other plus some additional true premises. Therefore, synthesis need not consist of the same steps as analysis read in the opposite direction.

That the original formulation of Pappus' analytic-synthetic method contains apparently incompatible assertions about the direction of analysis, may have a simple explanation. Pappus' analytic-synthetic method is not due to Pappus himself but occurs in earlier texts. Pappus draws his statements from different earlier texts which are mutually incompatible. They become compatible only if all links of analysis and synthesis are supposed to be convertible, in the weak sense explained above.

5.13 Fortune of the Analytic-Synthetic Method

As it will be argued in Chapter 8, the originators of the Scientific Revolution of the seventeenth century identify the scientific method with Aristotle's analytic-synthetic method. Nevertheless, in the modern and contemporary periods, Pappus's analytic-synthetic method has had a bigger impact than Aristotle's analytic-synthetic method, especially on mathematicians, starting with Viète. One of the main reasons for this is that, in 1588, Commandino published a Latin translation of Pappus's *Mathematical Collections* [*Mathematike Sunagoge*], which made Pappus's text

---

[46]Leibniz (1965, V, 466).
[47]*Ibid.*
[48]*Ibid.*, I, 195.
[49]*Ibid.*

readily accessible. Another reason is that, unlike Pappus, Aristotle does not present his method in a systematic fashion. As we have seen in Chapter 5, his presentation is scattered among various texts and requires some interpretation.

An example of the lasting influence of Pappus's analytic-synthetic method on mathematicians is Pólya, who states that, in solving a problem, "the most noteworthy step" is "to 'take the problem as solved'."[50] We "imagine that the unknown quantities have values fully satisfying the condition of the problem: this is meant essentially by 'taking the problem as solved'."[51] Similarly, in proving a theorem, the most noteworthy step is to take the theorem "as true," and then "to draw consequences from the theorem" although "we have not yet proved it. People" may "shrink from drawing consequences from an unproved theorem; but such people cannot start an analysis."[52] Taking the problem as solved, or the theorem as true, is the distinctive feature of Pappus' problematic and theorematic analysis, respectively.

5.14 Analytic-Synthetic Method and Axiomatic Method

It has been stated above that analysis plays only an auxiliary role in Aristotle's analytic-synthetic method. The same applies to Pappus' analytic-synthetic method.

This is clear from Pólya, who distinguishes between "finished mathematics," that is, mathematics "presented in a finished form," and "mathematics in the making."[53] Finished mathematics "appears as purely demonstrative."[54] That is, it appears as consisting of demonstrations only. Mathematics in the making "resembles any other human knowledge in the making. You have to guess a mathematical theorem" before you demonstrate it, "you have to guess the idea of the" demonstration "before you carry through the details," so the demonstration "is discovered by plausible reasoning, by guessing."[55]

Pólya's distinction between finished mathematics and mathematics in the making is similar to Aristotle's distinction between finished science and science in the making, which will be considered in Chapter 7. Thus, while Pólya follows Pappus in his formulation of the analytic-synthetic method, he follows Aristotle in his distinction between finished mathematics and mathematics in the making.

Pólya bases such distinction on a distinction between "two kinds of reasoning," that is, "demonstrative reasoning and plausible reasoning."[56] Demonstrative

---

[50]Pólya (1981, 9, footnote 1).
[51]*Ibid.*, 27.
[52]Pólya (1990, 146–147).
[53]Pólya (1954, I, vi).
[54]*Ibid.*
[55]*Ibid.*
[56]*Ibid.*

reasoning is deductive reasoning from given prime premises, plausible reasoning is non-deductive reasoning. Demonstrative reasoning "is safe, beyond controversy, and final," plausible reasoning is "hazardous, controversial and provisional."[57] A demonstration "is discovered by plausible reasoning."[58] But, since the latter is hazardous, we must "secure our mathematical knowledge by demonstrative reasoning."[59] For the mathematician, demonstrative reasoning is "the distinctive mark of his science."[60] Plausible reasoning plays only an auxiliary role. We need it when we build mathematics, much in the same sense in which "we need scaffolding when we erect a building."[61] Once the building is finished, the scaffolding is dismantled and taken away. It would not make sense to keep plausible reasoning in finished mathematics, anymore than it would make sense to keep scaffolding up around a finished building. A mathematical building stands up because of its foundations – the axiomatic method – not because of the scaffolding.

By assigning plausible reasoning only an auxiliary role, Pólya greatly limits the scope of analysis as a way to discovery. He himself seems to be sceptical about this role of analysis, because he states that "the first rule of discovery is to have brains and good luck. The second rule of discovery is to sit tight and wait till you get a bright idea."[62]

5.15 Relations with Reduction to the Impossible

From antiquity it has been widely believed that there is a strict relation between the analytic method, or Aristotle's analytic-synthetic method, on the one hand, and reduction to the impossible, on the other hand. For example, Knorr states that, "by its very name," reduction to the impossible "invites comparison to the method of 'reduction' used, for instance, by Hippocrates" of Chios and "discernible as a precursor of the method of analysis."[63] This is unjustified, because there are some basic differences between the analytic method, or Aristotle's analytic-synthetic method, and reduction to the impossible.

1) The analytic method, or the analytic part of Aristotle's analytic-synthetic method, is an upward path. Conversely, reduction to the impossible is a downward path. For, in order to conclude $\neg A$, one assumes A and deduces a contradiction from it.

---

[57] *Ibid.*, I, v.
[58] *Ibid.*, I, vi.
[59] *Ibid.*, I, v.
[60] *Ibid.*, I, vi.
[61] Pólya (1990, 113).
[62] *Ibid.*, 172.
[63] Knorr (1993, 359).

2) In the analytic method, or in Aristotle's analytic-synthetic method, hypotheses are not known from the beginning, finding them is the goal of the investigation. Conversely, in reduction to the impossible the hypothesis, A, is known from the beginning, because it is the opposite of the conclusion, $\neg A$, which is known from the beginning.

3) In the analytic method, or in Aristotle's analytic-synthetic method, hypotheses must be plausible. Conversely, in reduction to the impossible the hypothesis, A, cannot be plausible, because it is the opposite of the conclusion, $\neg A$, which is intended to be plausible.

A strict relation exists only between Pappus' analytic-synthetic method and reduction to the impossible. Indeed, in Pappus' theorematic analysis, if we come upon something established to be false, the thing that was sought will also be false. Thus reduction to the impossible corresponds to the case of Pappus' theorematic analysis when analysis leads to something established to be false. Similarly, in Pappus' problematic analysis, if we come upon something established to be impossible, the problem will also be impossible. Thus reduction to the impossible corresponds to the case of Pappus' problematic analysis when analysis leads to something established to be impossible.

5.16 The Reason for Use of Reduction to the Impossible

Reduction to the impossible does not do what, according to Aristotle, a demonstration should do, namely, show the causes of the conclusion.

For example, Aristotle states that "the diagonal is incommensurable" with the side of a square "because, if it is assumed to be commensurable, then odd numbers become equal to even ones."[64] According to Alexander of Aphrodisias, the demonstration to which Aristotle alludes is the following.[65] Assume A: The diagonal PR is commensurable with the side PQ of the square $PQRS$.

Let $d{:}s$ be the ratio $PR{:}PQ$ expressed in the smallest possible integers. Then $d > s$ and hence $d > 1$. Now, by the Pythagorean theorem, $PR^2 = 2PQ^2$. Since $PR^2{:}PQ^2 = d^2{:}s^2$, from this it follows $d^2 = 2s^2$. Thus d^2 is even, and hence d is even. Since $d{:}s$ is in its lowest terms, from this it follows B: s is odd. Otherwise

---

[64] Aristotle, *Analytica Priora*, A 23, 41 a 26–27.
[65] See Alexander of Aphrodisias, *In Aristotelis Analyticorum Priorum Librum Primum Commentarium* (Wallies), 260.9–261.28.

both d and s would be divisible by 2, so $d{:}s$ would not be in its lowest terms. Since d is even, $d = 2m$ for some integer m. Then from $d^2 = 2s^2$ it follows $4m^2 = 2s^2$, hence $s^2 = 2m^2$. Thus s^2 is even, and hence s is even. From this it follows $\neg B$: s is not odd. Therefore, A yields a contradiction, B and $\neg B$. Then, by reduction to the impossible, $\neg A$: The diagonal PR is incommensurable with the side PQ of the square $PQRS$.

This demonstration does not show the causes of the fact that the diagonal PR is incommensurable with the side PQ. Nevertheless, it shows that PR cannot be commensurable with PQ. This conclusion is contrary to immediate experience, which suggests that every thing can be measured by some unit. For such reason, Aristotle says that "it seems surprising" that "there is a thing which cannot be measured even by the smallest unit."[66] To establish this conclusion one needs reduction to the impossible.

Generally, one needs reduction to the impossible when one wants to establish something which is contrary to immediate experience. It is not surprising, then, that reduction to the impossible has a central role in the Eleatic philosophy, whose doctrines are contrary to immediate experience.

For example, Parmenides claims that what is is ungenerated. To establish this claim, which is contrary to immediate experience, Parmenides needs reduction to the impossible. For assume A: What is is generated. Now, if what is is generated, then "it is now, all together."[67] Thus B: What is is. On the other hand, if what is is generated, then it came into being. And, "if it came into being, then it is not."[68] Thus $\neg B$: What is is not. Therefore, A yields a contradiction, B and $\neg B$. Then, by reduction to the impossible, $\neg A$: What is is ungenerated.

As another example, Zeno claims that there is no motion. To establish this claim, which is contrary to immediate experience, Zeno needs reduction to the impossible. For assume A: There is motion. Then, since Achilles is faster than the Tortoise, B: Achilles will overtake the Tortoise. On the other hand, "the pursuer must, before he overtakes the pursued, first come to the point from which the pursued started. But in the time which the pursuer takes to reach this point, the pursued advances a certain distance, even if this distance is less than that covered by the pursuer, because the pursued is the slower of the two."[69] And "in the time again which the pursuer takes to cover this distance which the pursuer has advanced, the pursued again advances a certain distance which is proportionately smaller than the last, according as its speed is slower than that of the pursuer."[70] Thus, "in every time in which the pursuer covers the distance which the pursued, being slower, has advanced, the pursued advanced a

---

[66] Aristotle, *Metaphysica*, A 2, 983 a 16–18.
[67] *Ibid.*, 28 B 8.5.
[68] *Ibid.*, 28 B 8.20.
[69] Simplicius, *In Aristotelis Physicorum Libros Quattuor Posteriores Commentaria* (Diels), VI 9, 1014.11–15.
[70] *Ibid.*, VI 9, 1014.15–18.

yet further distance."⁷¹ Thus ¬B: Achilles will not overtake the Tortoise. Therefore, A yields a contradiction, B and ¬B. Then, by reduction to the impossible, ¬A: There is no motion.

5.17 Analytic Method vs. Analytic-Synthetic Method

The analytic method, as stated at the beginning of Chapter 4, has some definite advantages over the analytic-synthetic method, in Aristotle's or Pappus' form.

1) The analytic method accounts for the fact that a solution to a problem is found by a process all of whose steps are explicable. Conversely, the analytic-synthetic method does not account for the fact in question, because a solution to a problem is found using prime premises which are known to be true by a faculty, intuition, which is inexplicable.

2) The analytic method accounts for the fact that a solution to a problem may require hypotheses from fields other than the one to which the problem belongs, because a solution to a problem is sought in an open space. Conversely, the analytic-synthetic method does not account for the fact in question, because a solution to a problem is sought in a closed space. The prime premises are supposed to contain all the knowledge concerning the given field, so the solution must be deduced from them.

3) The analytic method accounts for the fact that the solution to a problem yields something new, because it involves finding hypotheses by means of non-deductive rules, which are ampliative. Conversely, the analytic-synthetic method does not account for the fact in question, because the solution to a problem involves deducing a solution from the prime premises of the field to which the problem belongs, so the solution is already contained in them and hence does not possess novelty with respect to them.

4) The analytic method accounts for the fact that often multiple solutions are found for the same problem. For any problem has several sides, each of which can lead to a distinct hypothesis, and hence to a distinct solution to the problem. Each solution establishes new connections between the problem and the existing knowledge, so it may lead to progress even when other solutions are already known. Conversely, the analytic-synthetic method does not account for the fact in question, because the purpose of demonstration is to give a foundation or justification of a statement. Once a demonstration has been found, and hence a foundation or justification of the statement has been given, there is no point in giving other demonstrations of that statement, even hundreds of them, as in the case of the Pythagorean theorem, for which "over four hundred" demonstrations are "known, and their number is still growing."⁷²

---

[71] *Ibid.*, VI 9, 1014.18–20.
[72] Maor (2007, xi).

5) The analytic method accounts for the fact that the rules for finding a solution to a problem can be changed in the course of the solution. For the rules are not given once for all, new rules may be discovered in the course of the solution, or the existing rules may be changed if they turn out to be inadequate. Conversely, the analytic-synthetic method does not account for the fact in question, because the rules are given once for all and cannot be changed. Changing rules would amount to changing theory.

6) The analytic method accounts for the fact that different solutions to a problem may have different degrees of reliability. Indeed, to solve a problem, one first introduces some hypothesis and checks that it is plausible, then one looks for some other hypothesis to account for the former and checks that it is plausible, and so on. So the solution to a problem is not given once for all but is enriched with time, establishing new connections between the problem and the existing knowledge. Conversely, the analytic-synthetic method does not account for the fact in question, because a solution consists in a deduction from prime premises, and a deduction is either correct or incorrect, so different degrees of reliability are not possible.

Chapter 6
Aristotle's Logic: The Deductivist View

6.1 The Deductivist View of Aristotle's Logic

As we have seen in Chapter 2, Aristotle claims to be the originator of logic as a subject. But what is Aristotle's logic? There are two alternative views, the deductivist view and the heuristic view. This chapter deals with the former, Chapter 7 with the latter.

The deductivist view has been strongly influenced by mathematical logic. According to this view, Aristotle's logic is characterized by the following properties.

1) *Aristotle's logic is essentially concerned with deduction.* Aristotle "shares with modern logicians the notion that central to the study of logic is examining the formal conditions for establishing knowledge of logical consequence."[1] His "principal concern" is "with deduction."[2] He wants "to establish confidence in the deduction process and particularly in his syllogistic deduction system."[3] Indeed, "Aristotle's *Prior Analytics* marks the beginning of formal logic. For Aristotle himself, this meant the discovery of a general theory of valid deductive argument."[4] The first book of *Prior Analytics* is "a fairly coherent presentation of Aristotle's logic as a general theory of deductive argument."[5] Admittedly, at first "the mathematicians and philosophers who developed modern mathematical logic did not have much patience with the old system," so "it was not until the twentieth century that historians of logic realized that Aristotle" had "actually been engaged, though on a very limited scale, in the same project that they were pursuing."[6]

---

[1] Boger (2004, 107).
[2] *Ibid.*, 106.
[3] *Ibid.*, 107.
[4] Striker (2009, xi).
[5] *Ibid.*, xviii.
[6] *Ibid.*, xiv.

2) *Aristotle's logic is an underlying logic, that is, a general schematism with no content of its own but applicable to any content.* Aristotle "intentionally aimed to develop an underlying logic along the lines of modernist thinking."[7] He "modelled his syllogistic as an underlying logic according to the practice of a modern mathematical logician."[8] Syllogistic deductions "employ a topic neutral deduction system to establish knowledge of logical consequence."[9]

3) *Aristotle's logic treats problems as formal objects.* Aristotle "took his logical (formal or artificial) language represented in *Prior Analytics* to be a syntactic object for the purpose of defining an underlying logic."[10] For him, the term 'problem' "does not refer to problems in a given domain" but is meant "to indicate a sentence pattern," thus it "is used purely in reference to a formal object."[11]

4) *Aristotle's logic provides a firm foundation for demonstrative knowledge.* Aristotle shares with modern mathematical logicians the purpose of establishing "a firm theoretical and methodological foundation for *apodeiktike episteme*, or demonstrative knowledge."[12] Specifically, in the *Prior Analytics* his "purpose was to establish a reliable deduction instrument."[13] On the other hand, in the *Posterior Analytics* he "treated the requirements for demonstrative science."[14]

5) *Aristotle's logic is not concerned with the discovery of deductions by analysis.* While "some of Aristotle's contemporaries probably assumed that a deduction could be discovered by a process of 'analysis'," Aristotle did not make this assumption, because the fact that "one cannot infer the falsehood of the conclusion from the falsehood of the premises, or the truth of the premises from the truth of the conclusion, counts decisively against this program."[15]

6) *Aristotle's logic is ampliative because deduction gives new knowledge.* Aristotle defines syllogism to be "a discourse in which, certain things being stated, something other than what is stated follows of necessity because of them."[16] Thus, "in relation to the two premises, the conclusion which arises from their synthesis signifies an advance in knowledge and, as the definition of the syllogism demands, a *heteron ton keimeno* [something other than what is stated]."[17]

---

[7] Boger (2004, 115).
[8] *Ibid.*, 242.
[9] *Ibid.*, 107.
[10] *Ibid.*, 133.
[11] *Ibid.*
[12] *Ibid.*, 107.
[13] *Ibid.*, 242.
[14] *Ibid.*, 108.
[15] Smith (1989, 185).
[16] Aristotle, *Topica*, A 1, 100 a 25–27.
[17] Maier (1896–1900, II.2, 175).

6.2 Assertions

The deductivist view of Aristotle's logic is based on the first 26 chapters of the first book of *Prior Analytics*. There Aristotle describes the morphology of syllogism, explaining "what is a premise, what is a term, and what is a syllogism, and which kind of syllogism is complete and which incomplete."[18]

A premise "is an assertion [*apophansis*] that affirms or denies something of something."[19] Indeed, "not every sentence is an assertion, but only those to which truth or falsity belongs. There is no truth or falsity in all sentences; a prayer is a sentence but is neither true nor false."[20]

Assertions can be distinguished into simple and compound ones.

A "simple [*haple*] assertion" is a statement "capable of signifying if something belongs [*huparchei*] or belongs not to something else."[21] Instead of 'belongs to', sometimes Aristotle uses 'is predicated of' [*kategoreitai*] or 'is a consequent of' [*akolouthei*], with the same meaning. The something that belongs or belongs not to something else is called the 'predicate'. The something else to which it belongs or belongs not is called the 'subject'. Predicates and subjects are called 'terms'. A "term [*horos*]" is "that into which a premise is resolved, namely, what is predicated and that of which it is predicated."[22]

A compound [*sugkeimene*] assertion is an assertion "compounded of simple assertions."[23] Syllogisms only involve simple assertions, so compound assertions are excluded.

There are four kinds of simple assertions: universal, particular, singular, and indeterminate. Each of them is either affirmative or negative.

A universal [*katholou* or *kata pantos*] assertion is "a statement that something belongs to all or to none of something."[24] A universal affirmative assertion is a statement that something belongs to all of something; for example, 'Animal belongs to all men'. A universal negative assertion is a statement that something belongs to none of something; for example, 'Animal belongs to no man'.

A particular [*kata meros*] assertion is a statement that something "belongs to some" or "not to all of something."[25] A particular affirmative assertion is a statement that something belongs to some of something; for example, 'Animal belongs to some man'. A particular negative assertion is a statement that something belongs not to all of something; for example, 'Animal belongs not to all men'.

---

[18] Aristotle, *Analytica Priora*, A 1, 24 a 11–13.
[19] *Ibid.*, A 1, 24 a 16–17.
[20] Aristotle, *De Interpretatione*, 4, 17 a 2–4.
[21] *Ibid.*, 5, 17 a 23–24.
[22] Aristotle, *Analytica Priora*, A 1, 24 b 16–17.
[23] Aristotle, *De Interpretatione*, 5, 17 a 21.
[24] Aristotle, *Analytica Priora*, A 1, 24 a 18.
[25] *Ibid.*, A 1, 24 a 19.

A singular [*kath' hekaston*] assertion is a statement that something either belongs or belongs not to a specific 'this', so it is a statement "about individuals."[26] A singular affirmative assertion is a statement that something belongs to a specific 'this'; for example, 'Animal belongs to Socrates'. A singular negative assertion is a statement that something belongs not to a specific 'this'; for example, 'Animal belongs not to Socrates'.

An indeterminate [*adihoristos*] assertion is a statement that something either belongs or belongs not to something else with no indication of quantity, namely "without the universal or the particular."[27] An indeterminate affirmative assertion is a statement that something belongs to something else with no indication of quantity; for example, 'Animal belongs to man'. An indeterminate negative assertion is a statement that something belongs not to something else with no indication of quantity; for example, 'Animal belongs not to man'.

In what follows, the expressions 'all', 'none', 'some', 'not all' which occur in universal or particular assertions will be called 'quantifiers', although Aristotle does not give any special name to them.

Instead of saying that something belongs not to all of something, it is convenient to say that something belongs to not all of something. This ungrammatical expression allows us to view universal affirmative, universal negative, particular affirmative or particular negative assertions as all having the same pattern, that is:

predicate + belongs to + quantifier + subject

Indeed, universal affirmative assertions are of the form 'A belongs to all B', universal negative assertions of the form 'A belongs to no B', particular affirmative assertions of the form 'A belongs to some B', particular negative assertions of the form 'A belongs to not all B', where the letters A and B are placeholders for terms, specifically for the predicate and the subject, respectively.

These four unnatural 'technical' expressions are supposed to have the same meaning as the idiomatic expressions 'All B are A', 'No B are A', 'Some B are A', 'Not all B are A', respectively, as shown in the following table.

Technical	Idiomatic
A belongs to all B	All B are A
A belongs to no B	No B are A
A belongs to some B	Some B are A
A belongs to not all B	Not all B are A

In standard Greek, it was common to place the subject of an assertion before the predicate. But Aristotle deliberately places the predicate before the subject, because the four technical expressions are supposed to correspond to the four possible ways

---

[26] Aristotle, *De Interpretatione*, 7, 17 b 28.
[27] Aristotle, *Analytica Priora*, A 1, 24 a 20.

in which an essential property may belong to a thing. Thus they are motivated by Aristotle's conception of scientific knowledge.

To denote the four kinds of assertions with which syllogism is concerned, it is customary to use the following letters and abbreviations, although Aristotle has no special notation for them.

Tag	Kind	Assertion Pattern	Abbreviation
A	Universal affirmative	A belongs to all B	AaB
E	Universal negative	A belongs to no B	AeB
I	Particular affirmative	A belongs to some B	AiB
O	Particular negative	A belongs to not all B	AoB

The letters **A, E, I, O** were introduced by Scholastic logicians as a mnemonic aid. In fact, **A** and **I** are the first two vowels of *adfirmo* [I affirm], **E** and **O** the first two vowels of *nego* [I deny]. The abbreviations AaB, AeB, AiB, AoB have come into use more recently.

6.3 Logical Relations Between Assertions

Aristotle considers some basic logical relations between assertions of the four kinds **A, E, I, O**: contraries, subcontraries, contradictories.

Two assertions are said to be 'contraries' [*enantia*] if they "cannot be true together."[28] They, however, can be false together. Assertions **A** and **E** are contraries. Therefore Aristotle states: "I call a universal affirmation and a universal negation contrarily opposed."[29] This is shown in the following table.

Contraries

Assertion Patterns	Abbreviations
A belongs to all B – A belongs to no B	$AaB - AeB$

Two assertions are said to be 'subcontraries' [*antikeimena*] if they cannot be false together. They, however, "can be true together."[30] Assertions **I** and **O** are subcontraries. This is shown in the following table.

---

[28] Aristotle, *De Interpretatione*, 7, 17 b 22–23.
[29] *Ibid.*, 7, 17 b 20–21.
[30] *Ibid.*, 7, 17 b 24.

Subcontraries

Assertion Patterns	Abbreviations
A belongs to some *B* – *A* belongs to not all *B*	*AiB* – *AoB*

Two assertions are said to be 'contradictories' [*antiphaseis*], or that they are a contradiction, if they cannot be true together and cannot be false together, so "it is always necessary for one to be true and the other to be false."[31] Assertions **A** and **O**, as well as assertions **E** and **I**, are contradictories. Therefore Aristotle states: "I call an affirmation and a negation contradictorily opposed when what one signifies universally, the other signifies not universally."[32] This is shown in the following table.

Contradictories

Assertion Patterns	Abbreviations
A belongs to all *B* – *A* belongs to not all *B*	*AaB* – *AoB*
A belongs to no *B* – *A* belongs to some *B*	*AeB* – *AiB*

These basic logical relations between assertions of the four kinds **A, E, I, O** can be schematically represented as follows.

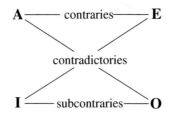

6.4 Syllogisms

A "syllogism [*sullogismos*] is a discourse [*logos*] in which, certain things having been laid down, something other than what was laid down results by necessity because these things are so."[33] Specifically, a syllogism consists of three simple assertions which contain only three terms. The first two assertions are called the 'premises', the last one the 'conclusion'. Since "every syllogism [*sullogismos*] will

---

[31] Aristotle, *Categoriae*, 10, 13 b 2–3.
[32] Aristotle, *De Interpretatione*, 7, 17 b 16–18.
[33] Aristotle, *Analytica Priora*, A 1, 24 b 18–20.

proceed through no more than three terms," it "will be from two premises and no more."[34]

Each of the three simple assertions of which a syllogism consists is either universal or particular. Singular or indeterminate assertions are excluded. This is due to the fact that, as we have seen in Chapter 3, for Aristotle scientific knowledge is always knowledge of universals, so logic can only involve assertions whose terms signify universals.

The premises of a syllogism need not be true, they can be accepted opinions [*endoxa*], in the sense explained in Chapter 5. Syllogisms whose premises are true are called 'scientific', those whose premises are only accepted opinions 'dialectical'. Thus "a dialectical [*dialekticos*] syllogism is one which syllogizes from accepted opinions."[35] A premise of a dialectical syllogism is "the taking of something which is apparent and is an accepted opinion."[36]

6.5 Concerning the Name 'Syllogism'

The notion of deduction is wider than that of syllogism because a deduction may contain more than one syllogism. Nevertheless, Aristotle has no special word to designate deduction, he designates both syllogism and deduction by the same word, *sullogismos*.

Because of this, Smith claims that 'syllogism' is a "bad translation of *sullogismos* in Aristotle."[37] Logicians normally use the word 'syllogism' to mean any valid argument in one of the three figures, but "Aristotle's definition of *sullogismos* comprehends a much wider class: pretty much any valid argument, or at least any argument with a conclusion different from any of its premises."[38] By translating *sullogismos* as 'syllogism', "the broad scope of this definition is obscured."[39] Therefore *sullogismos* should be translated as 'deduction'.

Now, admittedly Aristotle's definition of *sullogismos* given in the previous section does not assume that a *sullogismos* should contain only three terms and two premises, since it says nothing about the number of terms or premises. But, translating *sullogismos* as 'deduction', several of Aristotle's statements would become meaningless. Such is the case of Aristotle's statement in the previous section, that every *sullogismos* will proceed through no more than three terms, so it will be from two premises and no more. This statement does not hold of every deduction.

---

[34] *Ibid.*, A 25, 42 a 31–33.
[35] Aristotle, *Topica*, A 1, 100 a 29–30.
[36] Aristotle, *Analytica Priora*, A 1, 24 b 11–12.
[37] Smith (1995, 30).
[38] *Ibid.*
[39] *Ibid.*

Therefore, it seems preferable to translate *sullogismos* as 'syllogism'. Although this may involve some ambiguity, it will always be clear from the context what is actually meant, whether a syllogism in the sense of the three figures or a deduction.

6.6 Figures and Moods

Since every syllogism will proceed through no more than three terms and will be from two premises and no more, "one must take a middle term [*meson*] between the two that will connect the predications."[40] Thus the middle term is the term that occurs in both premises but not in the conclusion.

On the other hand, the extremes [*akra*] are the terms that occur in the conclusion. In particular, the major [*meizon*] extreme, or the first [*proton*], is the predicate of the conclusion, the minor [*elatton*] extreme, or the last [*eschaton*], the subject of the conclusion.

Since, in a syllogism, "we must take something common in relation to both" premises, that is, the middle term, "this is possible in three ways – for either one predicates A of C and C of B, or C of both, or both of C."[41] These three ways "form the three figures [*schemata*]" and from what has been said "it is evident that every syllogism will necessarily come about in one of these figures."[42]

The three figures in which every syllogism comes about are as shown in the following table, where the letter C is a placeholder for the middle term.

Item	First Figure	Second Figure	Third Figure
Major Premise	A–C	C–A	A–C
Minor Premise	C–B	C–B	B–C
Conclusion	A–B	A–B	A–B

The premise containing the major extreme, namely the predicate of the conclusion, is called the 'major premise', the premise containing the minor extreme, namely the subject of the conclusion, the 'minor premise'.

If, in the above table, we replace each '–' with one of the letters a, e, i, o, we get a triple of assertions as major premise, minor premise, conclusion. Each distinct triple is said to constitute a 'mood'. Thus,

$$\frac{\begin{array}{c} AaC \\ CaB \end{array}}{AaB}$$

---

[40] Aristotle, *Analytica Priora*, A 23, 41 a 11–12.
[41] *Ibid.*, A 23, 41 a 13–16.
[42] *Ibid.*, A 23, 41 a 16–18.

6.6 Figures and Moods

is a mood. The name was introduced by Scholastic logicians as a convenient name for such triples. Since each '–' can be replaced with one of the letters a, e, i, o, in each figure there are 4 possible major premises, 4 possible minor premises and 4 possible conclusions, thus there are $4 \times 4 \times 4 = 64$ moods.

Since each mood may occur in each of the three figures, there are $3 \times 64 = 192$ candidate syllogisms among the various moods and figures. Among the 192 candidate syllogisms, Aristotle identifies 14 which actually result in syllogisms when terms are substituted for the placeholders A, B, C. Of these, 4 are in the first figure, 4 in the second figure and 6 in the third figure.

As a mnemonic aid to designate such 14 candidate syllogisms, Scholastic logicians used the names Barbara, Celarent, Darii, Ferio, Cesare, Camestres, Festino, Baroco, Darapti, Felapton, Disamis, Datisi, Bocardo, Ferison. Each of them contains three vowels, which indicate the form, **A, E, I, O**, of the major premise, the minor premise and the conclusion, respectively. Thus a syllogism in Barbara is one whose premises and conclusion are all of the form **A**.

Syllogisms in Barbara, Celarent, Darii, Ferio are in the first figure, syllogisms in Cesare, Camestres, Festino, Baroco in the second figure, syllogisms in Darapti, Felapton, Disamis, Datisi, Bocardo, Ferison in the third figure.

The 14 candidate syllogisms identified by Aristotle, and the corresponding figures, are shown in the following table.

I

	Barbara	Celarent	Darii	Ferio
Major Premise	AaC	AeC	AaC	AeC
Minor Premise	CaB	CaB	CiB	CiB
Conclusion	AaB	AeB	AiB	AoB

II

	Cesare	Camestres	Festino	Baroco
Major Premise	CeA	CaA	CeA	CaA
Minor Premise	CaB	CeB	CiB	CoB
Conclusion	AeB	AeB	AoB	AoB

III

	Darapti	Felapton	Disamis	Datisi
Major Premise	AaC	AeC	AiC	AaC
Minor Premise	BaC	BaC	BaC	BiC
Conclusion	AiB	AoB	AiB	AiB

	III	
	(continuing)	
	Bocardo	Ferison
Major Premise	AoC	AeC
Minor Premise	<u>BaC</u>	<u>BiC</u>
Conclusion	AoB	AoB

6.7 Singular and Indeterminate Assertions in Syllogisms

It has been stated above that each of the three simple assertions of which a syllogism consists is either universal or particular. In a sense, however, each of these assertions can also be singular or indeterminate if it is rephrased as a universal or particular assertion.

Indeed, Aristotle treats particular assertions as if they were universal ones. For he states that "Pittakos is generous, for the ambitious are generous, and Pittakos is ambitious," is a syllogism "through the first figure."[43] Thus he interprets it as the syllogism: 'Generous belongs to all ambitious', 'Ambitious belongs to all that is Pittakos', therefore 'Generous belongs to all that is Pittakos'.

On the other hand, Aristotle treats indeterminate assertions as if they were particular ones. For he states that "it is then clear that putting an indeterminate premise in place of a positive particular will produce the same syllogism in every figure."[44]

6.8 Complete and Incomplete Syllogisms

To show that the 14 candidate syllogisms actually result in syllogisms, Aristotle assumes, without further justification, that four of them, namely, Barbara, Celarent, Darii, Ferio, are complete, where a candidate syllogism is said to be "complete [*teleios*] if it requires nothing beyond the things posited to make its necessity evident."[45] Indeed, Barbara, Celarent, Darii, Ferio, "are all completed" only "through the premises initially taken."[46]

The remaining ten candidate syllogisms, namely, Cesare, Camestres, Festino, Baroco, Darapti, Felapton, Disamis, Datisi, Bocardo, Ferison, are incomplete, where a candidate syllogism is said to be "incomplete [*ateles*] if it requires one or more additional things which are necessary because of the terms laid down, but that have not been taken among the premises."[47]

---

[43] *Ibid.*, B 27, 70 a 26–27, 29.
[44] *Ibid.*, A 7, 29 a 27–29.
[45] *Ibid.*, A 1, 24 b 22–24.
[46] *Ibid.*, A 4, 26 b 30.
[47] *Ibid.*, A 1, 24 b 24–26.

6.9 Conversion Rules and Strong Reduction to the Impossible

All the incomplete candidate syllogisms "are completed through the first figure."[48] Namely, by means of Barbara, Celarent, Darii, Ferio. They "are all completed either probatively [*deiktikos*] or by a reduction to the impossible [*dia tou adunatou*]."[49]

An incomplete candidate syllogism is said to be "completed probatively" when it is "brought to a conclusion by a conversion [*antistrophe*], and the conversion produces the first figure."[50] Conversions are carried out by certain rules, called 'conversion rules', which will be described below.

An incomplete candidate syllogism is said to be completed by "a reduction to the impossible" if, "once the false assumption is made, the syllogism comes about through the first figure."[51] However, the version of reduction to the impossible needed here is not the one considered in Chapter 2, but a stronger one, which therefore will be called 'strong reduction to the impossible'.

6.9 Conversion Rules and Strong Reduction to the Impossible

As we have seen in the previous section, Aristotle states that, in order to complete the incomplete candidate syllogisms, one needs some conversion rules and a rule of strong reduction to the impossible.

The conversion rules are inference rules, like candidate syllogisms, but unlike them are one-premise rules. Aristotle considers the following three conversion rules CR1–CR3:

CR1. From *AeB* one may infer *BeA*.
CR2. From *AaB* one may infer *BiA*.
CR3. From *AiB* one may infer *BiA*.

Thus the conversion rules concern only assertions of one of the forms *AeB*, *AaB*, *AiB*. There is no conversion rule for assertions of the form *AoB*.

The rule of strong reduction to the impossible is:

SRI: If, from a finite set of assertions Γ and the contradictory of an assertion *L*, we may deduce both an assertion *N* and the contradictory or the contrary of *N*, then from Γ alone we may deduce *L*.

As it has been already mentioned, SRI is stronger than the rule of reduction to the impossible considered in Chapter 2. This will be shown in Chapter 11.

Aristotle gives a justification for the conversion rules, CR1–CR3, by means of strong reduction to the impossible, SRI. The justification is as follows.

---

[48]*Ibid.*, A 7, 29 a 30–31.
[49]*Ibid.*, A 7, 29 a 31–32.
[50]*Ibid.*, A 7, 29 a 33–34.
[51]*Ibid.*, A 7, 29 a 35–36.

CR1: "If A belongs to no B, then B will belong to no A. For if B does belong to some A, say to C, it will not be true that A belongs to no B, since C is one of the B."[52] But A was assumed to belong to no B. Contradiction. Therefore, by SRI, we conclude that B belongs to no A.

CR2: "If A belongs to all B, then B will belong to some A. For if B belongs to no A, then" by CR1 "A will belong to no B; but it was assumed that A belongs to all B."[53] Contradiction. Therefore, by SRI, we conclude that B belongs to some A.

CR3: "If A belongs to some B, then it is necessary that B belong to some A. For if B belongs to no A, then" by CR1 "A will belong to no B."[54] However, A was assumed to belong to some B. Contradiction. Therefore, by SRI, we conclude that B belongs to some A.

Aristotle's justification of CR2 and CR3 depends on his justification of CR1, because it makes use of CR1. On the other hand, Aristotle's justification of CR1 makes use of a rule called *ekthesis* [setting out], which consists in instantiating a particular assertion. Indeed, Aristotle's justification of CR1 runs as follows.

Assume AeB and the contradictory of BeA, that is, BiA. Let C be some A such that B belongs to C [*ekthesis*]. From the fact that C is some A it follows that A belongs to C. From the fact that B belongs to C it follows that C is some B. Since A belong to C and C is some B we conclude that A belongs to some B, namely, AiB. But AiB is the contradictory of AeB. Therefore, by SRI, we conclude BeA.

Scholastic logicians called *conversio simplex* a conversion obtained by CR1 or CR3, thus one which involves interchanging the two terms A and B; *conversio per accidens* a conversion obtained by CR2, thus one which involves interchanging the two terms A and B and replacing a by i.

In terms of CR1–CR3 one may formulate the following direct demonstration procedure for completing an incomplete candidate syllogism. Assume the premises of the incomplete candidate syllogism being considered. By means of one of the conversion rules CR1–CR3, deduce the premises of some complete candidate syllogism whose conclusion is the same as the conclusion of the incomplete candidate syllogism. From such premises, deduce the conclusion by means of such complete candidate syllogism.

In terms of SRI, one may formulate the following indirect demonstration procedure for completing an incomplete candidate syllogism. Assume the premises and the contradictory of the conclusion of the incomplete candidate syllogism in question. From one of the premises and the contradictory of the conclusion of the incomplete candidate syllogism, deduce the contradictory of the other premise. Then infer the conclusion.

Both the direct and the indirect demonstration procedure for completing an incomplete candidate syllogism imply a notion of deduction wider than syllogism.

---

[52] *Ibid.*, A 2, 25 a 15–17.
[53] *Ibid.*, A 2, 25 a 17–19.
[54] *Ibid.*, A 2, 25 a 20–22.

Indeed, a deduction may contain more than one syllogism, obtained by Barbara, Celarent, Darii or Ferio. A deduction may also contain inferences obtained by CR1–CR3 or SRI, thus inferences which are non-syllogistic. Moreover, unlike syllogism, a deduction is not restricted to three terms and two premises. Aristotle makes an allowance for this, since he states that, while every syllogism will proceed through no more than three terms and will be from two premises and no more, in a deduction other things may "be taken in addition to complete the syllogisms."[55]

6.10 The Completion of Syllogisms

To complete Cesare, Camestres, Festino, Darapti, Felapton, Disamis, Datisi, Ferison, the direct demonstration procedure is sufficient. This may be seen as follows.

Cesare: Assume *CeA* and *CaB*. From *CeA* by CR1 we obtain *AeC*. From *AeC* and *CaB* by Celarent we obtain *AeB*.

Camestres: Assume *CaA* and *CeB*. From *CeB* by CR1 we obtain *BeC*. From *BeC* and *CaA* by Celarent we obtain *BeA*, hence by CR1 we get *AeB*. Here a swap [*metathesis*] of the premises has been made: the major premise *CaB* has become the minor premise in Celarent.

Festino: Assume *CeA* and *CiB*. From *CeA* by CR1 we obtain *AeC*. From *AeC* and *CiB* by Ferio we obtain *AoB*.

Darapti: Assume *AaC* and *BaC*. From *BaC* by CR2 we obtain *CiB*. From *AaC* and *CiB* by Darii we obtain *AiB*.

Felapton: Assume *AeC* and *BaC*. From *BaC* by CR2 we obtain *CiB*. From *AeC* and *CiB* by Ferio we obtain *AoB*.

Disamis: Assume *AiC* and *BaC*. From *AiC* by CR3 we obtain *CiA*. From *BaC* and *CiA* by Darii we obtain *BiA*, hence by CR3 we obtain *AiB*. Here a swap of the premises has been made: the minor premise *BaC* becomes the major premise in Darii.

Datisi: Assume *AaC* and *BiC*. From *BiC* by CR3 we obtain *CiB*. From *AaC* and *CiB* by Darii we obtain *AiB*.

Ferison: Assume *AeC* and *BiC*. From *BiC* by CR3 we obtain *CiB*. From *AeC* and *CiB* by Ferio we obtain *AoB*.

On the other hand, to complete Baroco, Bocardo, the indirect demonstration procedure is needed. This can be seen as follows.

Baroco: Assume *CaA* and *CoB* and the contradictory of *AoB*, that is, *AaB*. From *CaA* and *AaB* by Barbara we obtain *CaB*, which is the contradictory of *CoB*. Therefore by SRI we conclude *AoB*.

Bocardo: Assume *AoC* and *BaC* and the contradictory of *AoB*, that is, *AaB*. From *AaB* and *BaC* by Barbara we obtain *AaC*, which is the contradictory of *AoC*. Therefore by SRI we conclude *AoB*.

---

[55]*Ibid.*, A 25, 42 a 34–35.

This establishes Aristotle's claim that all the incomplete candidate syllogisms are completed by means of the first figure. Thus the first figure is basic, since "all the problems [*problemata*] are proved in this figure."[56]

For each of the 14 candidate syllogisms, the following table indicates the completion procedure, the auxiliary syllogism, the conversion rule used, and if a swap of premises is made.

Candidate syllogism	Completion procedure	Auxiliary syllogism	Conversion	Swap of premises
Barbara	through itself	Barbara	no	no
Celarent	through itself	Celarent	no	no
Darii	through itself	Darii	no	no
Ferio	through itself	Ferio	no	no
Cesare	Direct	Celarent	CR1	no
Camestres	Direct	Celarent	CR1	yes
Festino	Direct	Ferio	CR1	no
Baroco	Indirect	Barbara	no	no
Darapti	Direct	Darii	CR2	no
Felapton	Direct	Ferio	CR2	no
Disamis	Direct	Darii	CR3	yes
Datisi	Direct	Darii	CR3	no
Bocardo	Indirect	Barbara	no	no
Ferison	Direct	Ferio	CR3	no

6.11 The Reduction of Syllogisms

As we have seen, Aristotle shows that all the incomplete candidate syllogisms are completed by means of the first figure. Actually, Aristotle does even more. He shows that "it is possible to reduce [*anagein*] all syllogisms to the universal ones in the first figure."[57] Namely, it is possible to reduce all the 14 candidate syllogisms to the syllogisms in Barbara and Celarent. This simplifies the analysis of syllogism.

Specifically, Aristotle proves that it is possible to reduce a syllogism in Darii or Ferio to a syllogism in Celarent. The reduction proceeds as follows.

Darii: Assume *AaC* and *CiB* and the contradictory of *AiB*, that is, *AeB*. From *AeB* by CR1 we obtain *BeA*. From *BeA* and *AaC* by Celarent we obtain *BeC*, hence by CR1 we get *CeB*, which is the contradictory of *CiB*. Therefore, by SRI, we conclude *AiB*.

---

[56]*Ibid.*, A 4, 26 b 31.
[57]*Ibid.*, A 7, 29 b 1–2.

6.11 The Reduction of Syllogisms

Ferio: Assume AeC and CiB and the contradictory of AoB, that is, AaB. From AeC by CR1 we obtain CeA. From CeA and AaB by Celarent we obtain CeB, which is the contradictory of CiB. Therefore, by SRI, we conclude AoB.

Since, as we have just seen, a syllogism in Darii or Ferio can be reduced to one in Celarent and, as we have seen in the previous section, all 14 candidate syllogisms can be completed through Barbara, Celarent, Darii, Ferio, it follows that all 14 candidate syllogisms can be completed and reduced to Barbara and Celarent. Then "it is clear from what has been said that the syllogisms in these figures are both completed [*teleiountai*] through the universal syllogisms in the first figure and reduced [*anagontai*] to these."[58]

On the other hand, it is also clear that the completion and reduction thus obtained – by appealing to the completion of the 14 candidate syllogisms of the previous section – is not a direct completion and reduction of all 14 candidate syllogisms in terms of Barbara and Celarent. For example, Festino is completed through Ferio, which in its turn is reduced via Celarent.

Such detours are unnecessary, because a direct completion of all 14 candidate syllogisms is possible. This is trivial in the case of Barbara and Celarent, it has been shown above for Darii and Ferio, and has been shown in the previous section for Cesare, Camestres, Baroco, Bocardo. Let us now show that this is possible also in the case of the remaining candidate syllogisms, that is, Festino, Darapti, Felapton, Disamis, Datisi, Ferison.

Festino: Assume CeA and CiB and the contradictory of AoB, that is, AaB. From CeA and AaB by Celarent we obtain CeB, which is the contradictory of CiB. Therefore, by SRI, we conclude AoB.

Darapti: Assume AaC and BaC and the contradictory of AiC, that is, AeB. From AeB by CR1 we obtain BeA. From BeA and AaC by Celarent we obtain BeC, which is the contrary of BaC. Therefore, by SRI, we conclude AiC. Here a swap of the premises has been made: the major premise AaC of Darapti becomes the minor premise in Celarent.

Felapton: Assume AeC and BaC and the contradictory of AoB, that is, AaB. From AeC by CR1 we obtain CeA. From CeA and AaB by Celarent we obtain CeB, hence by CR1 we get BeC, which is the contrary of BaC. Therefore, by SRI, we conclude AoB.

Disamis: Assume AiC and BaC and the contradictory of AiB, that is, AeB. From AeB and BaC by Celarent we obtain AeC, which is the contradictory of AiB. Therefore, by SRI, we conclude AiB.

Datisi: Assume AaC and BiC and the contradictory of AiB, that is, AeB. From AeB by CR1 we obtain BeA. From BeA and AaC by Celarent we obtain BeC, which is the contradictory of BiC. Therefore, by SRI, we conclude AiB. Here a swap of the premises has been made: the major premise AaC of Datisi becomes the minor premise in Celarent.

---

[58]*Ibid.*, A 23, 40 b 17–19.

Ferison: Assume *AeC* and *BiC* and the contradictory of *AoB*, that is, *AaB*. From *AeC* by CR1 we obtain *CeA*. From *CeA* and *AaB* by Celarent we obtain *CeB*, hence by CR1 we obtain *BeC*, which is the contradictory of *BiC*. Therefore, by SRI, we conclude *AoB*.

Because of this, Aristotle says that "it is evident that syllogisms in the second figure are all completed through" the universal syllogisms in the first figure, "though not all in the same way."[59] Indeed, "the universal ones are completed by conversion of the negative premise, each of the particular ones is completed through" strong "reduction to the impossible."[60] On the other hand, all syllogisms in the third figure are completed through strong reduction to the impossible.

For each of the 14 candidate syllogisms, the following table indicates the completion procedure, the syllogism, the conversion rule used, and if a swap of premises is made to complete or reduce it.

Candidate syllogism	Completion procedure	Syllogism used	Conversion used	Swap of premises
Barbara	through itself	Barbara	no	no
Celarent	through itself	Celarent	no	no
Darii	indirect	Celarent	CR1	yes
Ferio	indirect	Celarent	CR1	no
Cesare	direct	Celarent	CR1	no
Camestres	direct	Celarent	CR1	yes
Festino	indirect	Celarent	no	no
Baroco	indirect	Barbara	no	no
Darapti	indirect	Celarent	CR1	yes
Felapton	indirect	Celarent	CR1	no
Disamis	indirect	Celarent	no	no
Datisi	indirect	Celarent	CR1	yes
Bocardo	Indirect	Barbara	no	no
Ferison	Indirect	Celarent	CR1	no

6.12 Syllogistic

The first stages of Aristotle's analysis of syllogism outlined above can be presented as a deduction system, which may be called 'syllogistic'.

The 'symbols' of the language of syllogistic include term variables *A*, *B*, *C*, *D*, ... and assertion operators *a*, *e*, *i*, *o*.

---

[59]*Ibid.*, A 7, 29 b 2–4.
[60]*Ibid.*, A 7, 29 b 4–6.

6.12 Syllogistic

'Formulas' are all expressions of one of the forms *AaB*, *AeB*, *AiB*, *AoB*, where *A* and *B* are term variables.

The first term variable in a formula is said to be the 'predicate', the second one the 'subject'.

The intended interpretations of formulas *AaB*, *AeB*, *AiB*, *AoB* are assertions of the form **A, E, I, O**, respectively.

The 'contrary' $Cr(\Theta)$ of a formula Θ is *AeB* if Θ is *AaB*; *AaB* if Θ is *AeB*.

The 'contradictory' $Ct(\Theta)$ of a formula Θ is *AoB* if Θ is *AaB*; *AaB* if Θ is *AoB*; *AiB* if Θ is *AeB*; *AeB* if Θ is *AiB*.

Letters *L, M, N*, ... will denote formulas, letters $\Gamma, \Delta,$ ... will denote finite sets of formulas.

The deductive rules of syllogistic are as follows:

A) Syllogism Rules

(Barbara) $\dfrac{AaC \quad CaB}{AaB}$

(Celarent) $\dfrac{AeC \quad CaB}{AeB}$

(Darii) $\dfrac{AaC \quad CiB}{AiB}$

(Ferio) $\dfrac{AeC \quad CiB}{AoB}$

B) Conversion Rules

(CR1) $\dfrac{AeB}{BeA}$

(CR2) $\dfrac{AaB}{BiA}$

(CR3) $\dfrac{AiB}{BiA}$

C) Rule of Strong Reduction to the Impossible

(SRI) $\dfrac{\begin{array}{cc}[Ct(L)] & [Ct(L)] \\ \vdots & \vdots \\ N & Cr(N)\end{array}}{L} \quad , \quad \dfrac{\begin{array}{cc}[Ct(L)] & [Ct(L)] \\ \vdots & \vdots \\ N & Ct(N)\end{array}}{L}$

A direct deduction is a tree of formulas. The topmost formulas in the tree are arbitrary formulas and are called 'assumptions'. The other formulas in the tree follow from those immediately above by one of the conversion rules or syllogism rules. The downmost formula is called the 'conclusion'.

A direct deduction with conclusion L whose assumptions are included in Γ is called a 'direct deduction of L from Γ'. L is said to be 'directly deducible from Γ' if and only if there is a direct deduction of L from Γ.

An indirect deduction is also a tree of formulas. The topmost formulas in the tree are arbitrary formulas and are called 'assumptions'. The other formulas in the tree, except the downmost one, follow from those immediately above by one of the conversion rules or syllogism rules. The downmost formula is called the 'conclusion', and follows from the formulas immediately above by the rule of strong reduction to the impossible (SRI).

(SRI) may discharge certain assumptions of the form indicated within square brackets, namely $Ct(L)$. A formula L in the tree is said to 'depend' on the assumptions standing above L which have not been discharged in some inference above L. Assumptions, however, may be discharged only in the last step. The undischarged assumptions of an indirect deduction are the assumptions on which the conclusion depends.

An indirect deduction with conclusion L, whose undischarged assumptions are included in Γ, is called an 'indirect deduction of L from Γ'. L is said to be 'indirectly deducible from Γ' if and only if there is an indirect deduction of L from Γ.

From the definitions of direct deduction and indirect deduction it is clear that the notion of deduction is wider than that of syllogism.

In view of what it has been shown in the two previous sections, syllogistic can be simplified by taking (CR1), (Barbara), (Celarent), (SRI) as its only deductive rules. For example, in the simplified syllogistic system, the reduction of Darii established in the previous section is given by the following indirect deduction, where the assumptions are marked by numerals, repeating the numeral on the right side of the (SRI) at which the assumption is discharged:

$$\text{(SRI)}\cfrac{\overset{(2)}{CiB} \qquad \text{(Def.)}\cfrac{\text{(CR1)}\cfrac{\text{(Def.)}\cfrac{\overset{(3)}{Ct(AiB)}}{AeB}}{BeA} \qquad \overset{(1)}{AaC}}{\text{(Celarent)}\cfrac{BeC}{\text{(CR1)}\cfrac{CeB}{Ct(Cib)}}}\ (3)}{AiB}$$

6.13 Limitations of the Deductivist View

That the first stages of Aristotle's analysis of syllogism can be presented as a deduction system might seem to support the deductivist view. This is not so, because the deductivist view has substantial defects.

1) According to the deductivist view, Aristotle's logic is essentially concerned with deduction. This is unjustified, because Aristotle states that the goal of logic is

6.13 Limitations of the Deductivist View

"to find a method by which we shall be able to syllogize from accepted opinions about any problem proposed."[61] As it will be argued in Chapter 7, by this Aristotle means a method by which, for any problem proposed, we shall be able to find premises capable of yielding a solution to the problem. Thus, for Aristotle, the main concern of logic is not how to deduce a given conclusion from given premises, but rather how to find premises for a given conclusion.

2) According to the deductivist view, Aristotle's logic is an underlying logic, that is, a general schematism with no content of its own but applicable to any content. This is unjustified because, as we will see in Chapter 7, Aristotle's method by which, for any problem proposed, we shall be able to find premises capable of yielding a solution to the problem, requires experience specific to the problem, so the method depends on the problem. For this reason, Aristotle states that "we must not on this account expect to find a single method of inquiry which will apply generally to all cases."[62] Indeed, "if a special method of inquiry is laid down for each of the different kinds of problems we have distinguished, then, starting from what is appropriate in each case, it will be easier to make our way right through the task before us."[63]

3) According to the deductivist view, Aristotle's logic treats problems as formal objects. This is unjustified because, for Aristotle, logic is concerned with the essence of things, since "syllogisms start from the essence."[64] And the essence "is manifested through syllogism and through demonstration."[65] For this reason, "inquiring into the principles of syllogism" belongs "to him who studies the nature of all substance."[66] That logic is about the essence of things implies that, as it has been stated above, Aristotle's method depends on the problem. Aristotle takes his logical language represented in *Prior Analytics* to be not a syntactic object for the purpose of defining an underlying logic, but rather a tool for solving problems depending on the problem.

4) According to the deductivist view, Aristotle's logic provides a firm foundation for demonstrative knowledge. This is unjustified because, for Aristotle, logic cannot provide such a foundation. Demonstrative knowledge is based on principles, and "there cannot be scientific knowledge of the principles."[67] Logic gives us means to find premises, not to recognize that principles, or prime premises, are true. Such recognition can be obtained only by intuition. For this reason, Aristotle says that intuition is "the principle of scientific knowledge."[68] Thus it is intuition, rather than logic, that provides a firm foundation for demonstrative knowledge.

---

[61] Aristotle, *Topica*, A 1, 100 a 18–20.
[62] *Ibid.*, A 6, 102 b 35–36.
[63] *Ibid.*, A 6, 102 b 38–103 a 1.
[64] Aristotle, *Metaphysica*, Z 9, 1034 a 32.
[65] Aristotle, *Analytica Posteriora*, B 8, 93 b 17–18.
[66] Aristotle, *Metaphysica*, Γ 3, 1005 b 6–8.
[67] Aristotle, *Analytica Posteriora*, B 19, 100 b 10–11.
[68] *Ibid.*, A 33, 88 b 36.

5) According to the deductivist view, Aristotle's logic is not concerned with the discovery of deductions by analysis. This is unjustified because, as it will be argued in Chapter 7, Aristotle's logic is essentially concerned with the discovery of deductions by analysis. The fact that one cannot infer the falsehood of the conclusion from the falsehood of the premises, or the truth of the premises from the truth of the conclusion, does not count decisively against this programme. It only implies that analysis is not always convertible into synthesis.

6) According to the deductivist view, Aristotle's logic is ampliative because deduction gives new knowledge. This is unjustified. Admittedly, Aristotle defines syllogism to be a discourse in which, certain things being stated, something other than what is stated follows of necessity because of them. Nevertheless, by the expression 'something other than what is stated', Aristotle does not mean 'something new with respect to what is stated', but only 'the conclusion'. The latter is 'something other than what is stated', namely the premises, because it is different from them, but this does not mean that it contains some novelty with respect to them. Indeed, deduction does not give new knowledge.

Chapter 7
Aristotle's Logic: The Heuristic View

7.1 The Ultimate Sources of Aristotle's Logic

In Chapter 2 it has been stated that Aristotle's choice of the title *ta analutika* was intended to suggest a connection of Aristotle's *Analytics* with the analytic method of Hippocrates of Chios and Hippocrates of Cos. In fact the analytic method, as formulated by Plato, and the Greek practice of discussion in the *agora*, in courts or in political debates, are the ultimate sources of Aristotle's logic.

This is apparent from Aristotle's intended uses of logic. He states that logic, or dialectic, is useful in relation to "exercise, encounters, and philosophical sciences."[1] And to "the first premises of any individual science."[2]

1) Logic "is useful in relation to exercise" because, "if we have a method, we shall be more easily able to argue over whatever is proposed."[3] This refers to a propaedeutic value of logic as a mental gymnastics, an exercise in developing argumentative skills. This use of logic is of a personal and private character. Nevertheless, the argumentative skills acquired through it are directed to discuss with other people. Thus this use of logic is propaedeutic to an interpersonal and public use.

2) Logic "is useful in relation to encounters because, once we have reckoned up the opinions held by most people, we shall discuss with them not on the ground of the convictions of other people but of their own convictions, correcting anything they may seem to us not to have stated soundly."[4] This refers to the use of logic in political debates, in deliberative or consultative councils, or in judicial debates in courts. One starts from the opinions held by most people – the audience or the persons taking part in the debate – and tries to convince them that the view of the

---

[1] Aristotle, *Topica*, A 2, 101 a 27–28.
[2] *Ibid.*, A 2, 101 a 37.
[3] *Ibid.*, A 2, 101 a 28–30.
[4] *Ibid.*, A 2, 101 a 30–34.

interlocutor is inadequate. Contrary to use 1), which is of a personal and private character, this use of logic is interpersonal and public.

3) Logic "is useful in relation to the philosophical sciences because, if we are able to go through the difficulties on both sides of a subject, we will more easily discern what is true and what is false in any subject."[5] In fact, "being able to discern the consequences of either hypothesis is no small instrument; for then it only remains to choose one or the other of these rightly."[6] To this end, we will start from accepted opinions [*endoxa*] and will "examine the arguments for and the arguments against."[7] That is, we will "set the different opinions before us and, after first discussing the difficulties, proceed to prove, if possible, the truth of all the accepted opinions about these" things, "or at least the greatest number and the most authoritative. For if the difficulties are solved and the accepted opinions are left standing, we shall have proved the case sufficiently."[8] This is a process of discovery, because "the resolution of a difficulty is a discovery."[9] Like use 2), this use of logic involves determining the merits of different positions. It differs from use 2) in that it is aimed at the discovery of new knowledge.[10]

4) Logic "is useful in relation to the first premises of any individual science" because, "starting from the first premises appropriate to the science in question, it is impossible to say anything about them, since they are the first premises of all."[11] Therefore, "it is necessary to discuss them through the accepted opinions [*endoxa*] about each of them. This task belongs properly, or most appropriately, to dialectic," namely logic, because, "being inquisitive, it possesses the way to the first premises of all inquiries."[12] Like use 3), this use of logic is aimed at the discovery of new knowledge. Specifically, it is aimed at the discovery, including the evaluation, of the first premises of any individual science.

Uses 1) and 2) of logic are related to the Greek practice of discussion in the *agora*, in courts or in political debates. Uses 3) and 4) are related to the analytic method of Hippocrates of Chios and Hippocrates of Cos. This justifies the claim that the analytic method, as formulated by Plato, and the Greek practice of discussion in the *agora*, in courts or in political debates, are the ultimate sources of Aristotle's logic.

---

[5] *Ibid.*, A 2, 101 a 34–36.

[6] *Ibid.*, Θ 14, 163 b 10–13.

[7] *Ibid.*, Θ 14, 163 a 37–b 1.

[8] Aristotle, *Ethica Nicomachea*, H 1, 1145 b 3–7.

[9] *Ibid.*, H 2, 1146 b 7–8.

[10] Aristotle's claim, that in the philosophical science we will start from accepted opinions, corresponds to his own philosophical practice. Indeed, he usually begins his treatment of some topic by reviewing the opinions of his predecessors on that topic, pointing out the difficulties they involve. Then he presents his own position and tries to show that it is not subject to those difficulties, finally concluding that the case is proved sufficiently.

[11] Aristotle, *Topica*, A 2, 101 a 36–101 b 1.

[12] *Ibid.*, A 2, 101 b 1–4.

7.2 The Proximate Source of Aristotle's Logic

While these are the ultimate sources of Aristotle's logic, its proximate source is the philosophical practice of Socrates and Plato's school.[13] The latter has the form of a discussion between two persons, though other persons may also be involved. The discussion concerns a proposed problem, and is carried out "by means of questions and answers."[14] One of the two persons plays the role of the questioner, the other one the role of the respondent.

That the philosophical practice of Socrates and of Plato's school has the form of a discussion between two persons, a questioner and a respondent, externalizes the nature of thinking, which is always "a discourse that the soul has with itself about whatever it is considering."[15] Indeed, "thinking appears to be as nothing else than discussing with itself, itself asking and answering itself, affirming and denying."[16] It is a discourse "not with another person, nor aloud, but in silence, with oneself."[17]

The discussion begins with the questioner setting up a problem and asking the respondent to propose a hypothesis to solve it. For the discussion to continue, the questioner and the respondent must agree on certain things, since the discussion will "start from the thing we have agreed on."[18]

Once the respondent has proposed a hypothesis, the questioner "will not let him go until he has subjected it to a thorough examination, up to the brink of torture."[19] Indeed, "about whatever thing may be hypothesized as being and as not being," it is necessary "to investigate the consequences in relation to that thing itself and in relation to each one of the other things, whichever you may choose."[20] The "other things, again, must be examined both in relation to themselves and in relation to any other thing you may choose, whether you hypothesize it as being or as not being, if you are to be trained thoroughly to discern the truth."[21] This is "a tremendous exercise."[22] But it is necessary because, "without this exploration of all possibilities and in all senses, it is impossible for the mind to attain truth."[23]

This process will go on until some hypothesis will be reached on which the questioner and the respondent will agree. Thus an agreement is necessary not only

---

[13] To speak of 'the philosophical practice of Socrates and Plato's school' is justified insofar as such practices cannot be sharply distinguished.
[14] Plato, *Protagoras*, 336 c 5.
[15] Plato, *Theaetetus*, 189 e 6–7.
[16] *Ibid.*, 189 e 8–190 a 2.
[17] *Ibid.*, 190 a 5–6.
[18] Plato, *Crito*, 48 b 11.
[19] Plato, *Laches*, 188 a 3–4.
[20] Plato, *Parmenides*, 136 b 6–c 2.
[21] *Ibid.*, 136 c 3–6.
[22] *Ibid.*, 136 c 7.
[23] *Ibid.*, 136 e 1–3.

at the beginning of the discussion, but also at the end of it. In fact, an agreement is necessary also at each intermediate step, since the answer of the respondent "must not only be true but must" also "be given in terms with which the questioner admits he agrees."[24]

The final agreement on a hypothesis leads to accept the hypothesis because, "if you agree with me in an argument about any point, that point will have been sufficiently tested by us, and will not require to be submitted to any further test."[25] For "you could not have agreed with me, either from lack of knowledge or from superfluity of modesty, nor yet from a desire to deceive me, because you are my friend, as you yourself claim."[26]

This corresponds to the fact that, in the philosophical practice of Socrates and Plato's school, the questioner and the respondent carry out "a discussion, not a dispute. A discussion is carried out among friends with good will, while a dispute is between rivals and enemies."[27] The discussion has "no other purpose than to investigate those questions which baffle me."[28] That is, it is only meant to carry out an inquiry. In "asking all these questions I have nothing else in view but my desire to know how things stand."[29]

The questioner wants to carry out an inquiry in cooperation with the respondent: "If it is agreeable to you, I am ready to inquire with you."[30] Carrying out an inquiry in cooperation is useful, because "we men together are in a sense better equipped for any action, discourse or thought."[31] For such reason, "if one thinks by himself, he goes off at once looking for someone else to whom he can show his thought and with whom he can confirm it, and will not rest till he finds him."[32]

Nevertheless, the final agreement will not be the end of the inquiry, since the whole truth is never attainable, every cognition which fills a gap will raise new problems. Thus the inquiry is a continuous proceeding from a question, not to a conclusive answer, but to more and more radical questions, which lead to a deepening of the problem.

For such reason, the philosophical practice of Socrates and Plato's school is deliberately inconclusive. Often, at the end of the discussion, the questioner tells the respondent: "I should like to continue our present talk."[33] For "I spend my time on all these matters as a means of taking forethought for my whole life. If you should be willing, you are the one with whom I would most gladly share the inquiry, as I said

---

[24] Plato, *Meno*, 75 d 5–7.
[25] Plato, *Gorgias*, 487 d 7–e 3.
[26] *Ibid.*, 487 e 3–6.
[27] Plato, *Protagoras*, 337 a 8–b 3.
[28] *Ibid.*, 348 c 6–7
[29] *Ibid.*, 360 e 6–8.
[30] Plato, *Charmides*, 158 e 2.
[31] Plato, *Protagoras*, 348 d 2–3.
[32] *Ibid.*, 348 d 3–5.
[33] *Ibid.*, 361 c 4–5.

at the beginning."[34] And the respondent replies: "Well, we will talk of these matters at some future meeting, whenever you like."[35] Mentioning the need to resume the debate at some future meeting is a literary expedient to express that an inquiry is an endless process, an infinite task.

In the discussion, the questioner knows the problem he wants to investigate from the beginning. The problem is usually called the 'conclusion' but, from the point of view of the questioner, it is something that is already there from the start. That the questioner knows the problem from the beginning does not mean, however, that he already knows a solution. Indeed, the questioner tells the respondent: "You are addressing me as though I professed to know the answers to my own questions," but "this is not the case. Rather, I am looking for a solution in your company, because I do not know it."[36] The only thing the questioner knows from the beginning is the problem.

Knowing the problem from the beginning, the questioner looks for suitable questions to ask. The respondent's answers will be hypotheses for solving the problem. Since, when stating a syllogism, the respondent lays down hypotheses first, the hypotheses are called 'premises'. But, in the mind of the questioner, the direction of thinking that leads to setting up the syllogism is opposite to that from the premises to the conclusion. The questioner carries out his thinking reversely: from the conclusion to the premises, rather than from the premises to the conclusion.

It is not obvious how to find the premises for a given conclusion, therefore, it requires a method. Conversely, the transition from the premises to the conclusion is easy: once you have assumed the premises, finding the conclusion is straightforward.

7.3 The Heuristic View of Aristotle's Logic

It is this kind of concrete practice of discussion that Aristotle had in mind in developing his analysis of syllogism. The main feature of that practice was that the conclusion was already given, and the question was how to find premises in order to set up a syllogism. Thus, in developing his analysis of syllogism, Aristotle let himself be guided by the features of the only practice of discussion of which he had first hand knowledge: the one with which he was personally familiar from the philosophical practice of Socrates and Plato's school.

Syllogism can be meant either as a downward process, by which one starts from two given premises and looks for the possible conclusion that can be deduced from them; or as an upward process, by which one starts from a given conclusion and looks for the possible premises from which it can be deduced. Syllogism meant as a

---

[34] *Ibid.*, 361 d 3–6.
[35] *Ibid.*, 361 e 5–6.
[36] Plato, *Charmides*, 165 b 6–10.

downward process is a means of justification, syllogism meant as an upward process is a means of discovery.

Syllogism meant as a downward process is the conception of syllogism the deductivist view attributes to Aristotle. On account of the limitations of that view, however, there seems to be little justification for saying that Aristotle understood syllogism as a downward process. His analysis of syllogism is not so much concerned with how to deduce conclusions from given premises, but rather with how to find premises for a given conclusion, in order to solve the problem expressed by the conclusion. For the main concern of Aristotle's analysis of syllogism is with problem solving.

Aristotle expresses this in the clearest possible terms. After describing the morphology of syllogism in the first 26 chapters of the first book of *Prior Analytic*, he begins Chapter 27 by saying: "Now it is time to tell how we will always find syllogisms on any given subject, and by what method we will find the premises about each thing. For surely one ought not only to investigate how syllogisms are constituted, but also to have the ability to produce them."[37]

Aristotle wants to indicate "how to reach for premises concerning any problem proposed, in the case of any discipline whatever," and, generally, how to find "the way through which we may obtain the principles concerning each subject."[38] Aristotle wants to do this because the main concern of his analysis of syllogism is with problem solving. This explains why he states that, while "arguments are made from premises," the "things with which syllogisms are concerned are problems."[39]

7.4 Aristotle's Procedure for Finding Premises by Syllogism

That the main concern of Aristotle's analysis of syllogism is with problem solving, implies that Aristotle's main purpose is to devise a procedure for finding premises for each problem proposed, and in particular, for finding premises by syllogism.

The procedure Aristotle devises is not an algorithmic one, so it is misleading to say that his procedure "is comparable to a decision procedure for deductive systems."[40] Aristotle's procedure involves knowing how the terms of the problem – predicate and subject – are related to all other terms. This, in its turn, involves knowing essential properties of things, and there is no algorithm for doing that. Aristotle's procedure is rather a heuristic one. This does not diminish its value, because a heuristic procedure essentially reduces the search space, that is, the domain within which the solution is sought.

---

[37] Aristotle, *Analytica Priora*, A 27, 43 a 20–24.
[38] *Ibid.*, B 1, 53 a 1–3.
[39] Aristotle, *Topica*, A 4, 101 b 15–16.
[40] Smith (1989, 150).

7.4 Aristotle's Procedure for Finding Premises by Syllogism

Aristotle's procedure may be described as consisting of the following steps.

STEP 1: Determine the form of the problem proposed.

STEP 2: Determine in what figures of syllogism a problem of that form could possibly be solved and, within that figure, by what kind of syllogism. Since some problems cannot be solved in all three figures and by all kinds of syllogism, this narrows down the range of possible premises.

Thus a problem of the form **A** can be solved only by a syllogism in Barbara; a problem of the form **E** only by a syllogism in Celarent, Cesare or Camestres; a problem of the form **I** only by a syllogism in Darii, Darapti, Disamis or Datisi; a problem of the form **O** only by a syllogism in Ferio, Festino, Baroco, Felapton, Bocardo or Ferison.

STEP 3: "Select the premises about each problem as follows: first, set down the thing itself, its definition, and whatever is peculiar to it; after that, the consequents of the thing, the antecedents of the thing, and whatever cannot belong to the thing."[41]

What Aristotle means to say by this can be explained as follows.

Let $A*E$ be the problem proposed, where $*$ is one of a, e, i, o.

Then, list: $B =$ the consequents of A, namely, those X such that XaA; $C =$ the antecedents of A, namely, those X such that AaX; $D =$ whatever cannot belong to A, namely, those X such that XeA.

Similarly, list: $F =$ the consequents of E, namely, those X such that XaE; $G =$ the antecedents of E, namely, those X such that EaX; $H =$ whatever cannot belong to E, namely, those X such that XeE.

This is shown in the following table.

	$B =$ those X such that XaA		$F =$ those X such that XaE
A	$C =$ those X such that AaX	E	$G =$ those X such that EaX
	$D =$ those X such that XeA		$H =$ those X such that XeE

STEP 4: Find a common X for A and E. We consider four cases, depending on the form of $A*E$.

CASE 1: AaE. By STEP 2 a conclusion of this form can be obtained only by a syllogism in Barbara. Find an X in both C and F such that AaX and XaE. Then the premises will be AaX and XaE, since from them we will obtain AaE by Barbara.

CASE 2: AeE. By STEP 2, a conclusion of this form can be obtained only by a syllogism in Celarent, Cesare or Camestres.

To obtain the conclusion by Celarent, find an X in both D and F such that XeA and XaE. Then the premises will be AeX and XaE. For from XeA, by CR1, we will obtain AeX. Then from AeX and XaE we will obtain AeE by Celarent.

To obtain the conclusion by Cesare, find an X both in D and F such that XeA and XaE. Then the premises will be XeA and XaE, since from them we will obtain AeE by Cesare.

---

[41] Aristotle, *Analytica Priora*, A 27, 43 b 1–5.

To obtain the conclusion by Camestres, find an X both in B and H such that XaA and XeE. Then the premises will be XaA and XeE, since from them we will obtain AeE by Camestres.

CASE 3: AiE. By STEP 2, a conclusion of this form can be obtained only by a syllogism in Darii, Darapti, Disamis or Datisi. However, Aristotle only considers the case when the conclusion is obtained by Darapti.

To obtain the conclusion by Darapti, find an X both in C and G such that AaX and EaX. Then the premises will be AaX and EaX, since from them we will obtain AiE by Darapti.

Alternatively, to produce the conclusion, for example, by Disamis, find an X both in B and G such that XaA and EaX. Then the premises will be AiX and EaX. For from XaA, by CR2, we will obtain AiX. Then from AiX and EaX we will obtain AiE by Disamis.

CASE 4: AoE. By STEP 2, a conclusion of this form can be obtained only by a syllogism in Ferio, Festino, Baroco, Felapton, Bocardo or Ferison. However, Aristotle only considers the case when the conclusion is obtained by Felapton.

To obtain the conclusion by Felapton, find an X both in D and G such that XeA and EaX. Then the premises will be AeX and EaX. For from XeA, by CR1, we will obtain AeX. Then from AeX and EaX we will obtain AoE by Felapton.

From what it has been said, it is apparent that we can select the premises about each problem when we can find a common X for B and G, B and H, C and F, C and G, D and F, or D and G.

As to the remaining three pairs, namely, B and F, C and H, D and H, Aristotle states that finding a common X for such pairs will yield no premises, so in these cases the selection of common terms is "of no use for the production of a syllogism."[42]

For example, if we find an X both in C and H such that AaX and XeE, then from the latter, by CR1, we will obtain EeX, and from the latter and AaX we will obtain EoA by Felapton. But, since assertions of the form EoA are not convertible, in this way we cannot obtain an assertion of the form $A*E$.

This concludes the description of Aristotle's procedure for finding premises by syllogism. Such procedure is, in particular, a procedure for finding the middle term. For this reason, Aristotle says that "the object of our investigation is to discover the middle term."[43] For the same reason, the mediaevals called Aristotle's procedure *inventio medii* [discovery of the middle term].

---

[42]*Ibid.*, A 28. 44 b 26.
[43]*Ibid.*, A 28, 44 b 40.

7.5 Problem Dependence of Aristotle's Procedure

Aristotle's procedure for finding premises by syllogism is the hard core of Aristotle's logic. This sharply contrasts with the deductivist view, according to which syllogism is not a means for discovery but only a means for deduction. Contrary to the deductivist view, for Aristotle, syllogism is primarily a means for discovery.

According to Aristotle, his procedure can be used to solve problems in any area. Indeed, he states that "the method is the same for all subjects, in philosophy as well as in the technical or mathematical disciplines."[44] By means of his procedure "we will be able to find the demonstration and demonstrate anything that admits of demonstration, and, where there cannot be a demonstration, to make this evident."[45]

That, according to Aristotle, his procedure can be used to solve problems in any area, does not mean, however, that it is problem-independent. In order to use the procedure, one must determine the definitions and whatever properties are peculiar to the subject and predicate of the problem proposed, and then the antecedents and consequents of the subject and predicate of the problem proposed. This requires experience specific to the problem, therefore Aristotle's procedure is problem-dependent.

For this reason, Aristotle states that "experience must provide us with the principles about each subject," for example, "experience in astronomy must provide the principles for astronomical science," and "similarly concerning any other art or science whatsoever."[46] Therefore, "we must not on this account expect to find a single method of inquiry which will apply universally in all cases."[47] Rather, "a special method must be laid down for each kind we have distinguished, and then, on the basis of what is appropriate in each case, it will be easier to make our way right through the task before us."[48]

7.6 Finding Premises by Induction

The procedure for finding premises by syllogism is not, however, the only one Aristotle envisages for finding premises. Another procedure is induction. Indeed, Aristotle states that every inquiry "proceeds either by induction or by syllogism."[49] So "one must get the necessary premises either by syllogism or by induction, or

---

[44] Ibid., A 30, 46 a 3–4.
[45] Ibid., A 30, 46 a 25–27.
[46] Ibid., A 30, 46 a 17–22.
[47] Aristotle, *Topica*, A 6, 102 b 36–38.
[48] Ibid., A 6, 102 b 40–103 a 2.
[49] Aristotle, *Ethica Nicomachea*, Z 3, 1139 b 27–28.

some by induction and others by syllogism," except that, "when such premises are absolutely obvious, they may also be put forward right away."[50]

Induction allows one to obtain premises by inferring them from observed facts. The premises thus obtained will be universal, because "induction [*epagoge*] is a passage from particulars to a universal" as it appears from the following example: "If the skilled pilot is the best pilot, and so the skilled charioteer, then generally the skilled man is the best pilot."[51]

While "demonstration starts from universals," induction "starts from particulars."[52] Indeed, "in developing induction we assume a knowledge of the particulars."[53] The number of particulars from which induction starts need not be large, sometimes even a single particular will do.

For example, consider the problem: "Why is there an eclipse, or why is the moon eclipsed?" and the answer: "Because the light leaves it when the earth screens it."[54] Clearly, "if we were on the moon, we would seek neither if there is an eclipse nor why there is, but these things would be immediately clear, since by perceiving" the particular "we would come to know the universal."[55] For then "perception would tell us that the earth is now screening it (since it would be clear that the moon is now eclipsed); from this the universal would come about."[56] Thus, in this case, a single particular suffices to arrive at the universal: every eclipse of the moon is due to the fact that the earth screens the sun's light by occupying a position between the sun and the moon.

Since demonstration starts from universals while induction from particulars, syllogism and induction are different. Nevertheless, they are not opposed, because Aristotle considers induction to be a kind of syllogism. Indeed, he states that "induction, that is, a syllogism from induction, consists in establishing syllogistically one extreme to belong to the middle by means of the other extreme; for example, if C is the middle between A and B, it consists in proving that A belongs to all B by means of C. For this is the manner in which we make inductions."[57] Thus, Aristotle's inductive syllogism looks like this:

AaC (A belongs to all C)
BaC (B belongs to all C)
AaB (A belongs to all B)

---

[50] Aristotle, *Topica*, Θ 1, 155 b 35–38.

[51] *Ibid.*, A 12, 105 a 13–16.

[52] Aristotle, *Analytica Posteriora*, A 2, 81 a 40–81 b 1.

[53] Aristotle, *Analytica Priora*, B 21, 67 a 23–24.

[54] Aristotle, *Analytica Posteriora*, B 2, 90 a 16–18.

[55] *Ibid.*, B 2, 90 a 26–29.

[56] *Ibid.*, B 2, 90 a 29–30.

[57] Aristotle, *Analytica Priora*, B 23, 68 b 15–18.

7.6 Finding Premises by Induction

For example, "let A stand for 'long-lived', B for 'bileless', and C for 'particular long-lived things, such as man, horse, mule'. Now, A belongs to all C (for whatever is C is long-lived). Also B, that is, being bileless, belongs to all C."[58] Then, by induction, A, namely, being long-lived, belongs to all B, the bileless things.

It might be objected that Aristotle's inductive syllogism is not a syllogism in any of the three figures, and hence is not a syllogism at all. Aristotle offers the following answer to this objection: "If C converts with B," and hence B "is not wider in extension" than C, "then necessarily A will belong to all B."[59] Thus Aristotle's inductive syllogism looks like a syllogism in Barbara:

AaC (being long-lived belongs to all C)
$\underline{CaB}$ (being C belongs to all bileless things)
AaB (being long-lived belongs to all bileless things)

The premise CaB states that all bileless things are C, which, together with BaC, entails that the only bileless things are those in C. Thus, in order to affirm CaB, it is necessary that C contains all particular bileless things, namely, that C provides a complete enumeration of all bileless things. For this reason Aristotle states that "one must understand C as composed of all the particular things. For induction is through all of them."[60] Then inductive syllogism requires a complete enumeration of all particular things of a certain kind.

Aristotle, however, is aware that a complete enumeration is not generally possible. Indeed he states that, while "in some cases it is possible for a person performing an induction to put the question in the universal form," in other cases "this is not easy, because there is no common term for all the similar cases."[61] In such cases, "when one has to obtain the universal, one says 'Thus in all cases of this kind'. But to determine which of the cases considered are 'of this kind' is one of the most difficult things."[62] Therefore, the requirement of a complete enumeration of all particular things of a certain kind cannot be generally satisfied. When it cannot be satisfied, induction cannot be said to be a syllogism in the strict sense.

This does not mean that an induction not based on a complete enumeration will not accomplish anything. Although "someone who makes an induction" of this kind "does not demonstrate," he "nevertheless shows something."[63] Even if "there is no syllogism here," the "procedure lets us get to know what the thing is in some other way."[64]

---

[58] Ibid., B 23, 68 b 19–23.
[59] Ibid., B 23, 68 b 23–24.
[60] Ibid., B 23, 68 b 27–29.
[61] Aristotle, Topica, Θ 2, 157 a 21–23.
[62] Ibid., Θ 2, 157 a 23–26.
[63] Aristotle, Analytica Posteriora, B 5, 91 b 34–35.
[64] Ibid., B 5, 91 b 33–34.

On the other hand, an induction not based on a complete enumeration is fallible. Someone who makes an induction of this kind "will not show, thanks to the fact that particulars are manifest, that everything is so because none" of the particulars "is otherwise."[65] For he "does not demonstrate what a thing is," but only "that it is, or is not."[66] This is a significant limitation of induction with respect to syllogism.

7.7 Finding Premises in the Analytic-Synthetic Method

By iterated applications of Aristotle's procedure for finding premises by syllogism or of induction, one may find premises for the premises, premises for the premises of the premises, and so on, until one arrives at prime premises, whose truth is apprehended by intuition. This is the process of analysis in Aristotle's analytic-synthetic method, which then consists in repeated applications of Aristotle's procedure for finding premises by syllogism or of induction, starting from the conclusion.

This process cannot continue infinitely because, "in the demonstrative sciences with which our inquiry is concerned, the terms predicated cannot be infinitely many either in the upward or in the downward direction."[67] An argument that proceeded infinitely would include some hypothesis, thus some assertion that is neither a prime premise nor has been deduced from prime premises. By such an argument one would not "have scientific knowledge properly of any thing, but only on the basis of a hypothesis."[68]

7.8 The Role of Plausibility in the Analytic-Synthetic Method

Aristotle's procedure for finding premises by syllogism or by induction may lead, from the same conclusion, to different premises. Only some of them will produce scientific knowledge, but the two procedures in question provide no means to decide which ones.

This is clear as concerns induction. When a complete enumeration of all particular things of a certain kind is not possible, from the same particulars different conclusions can be drawn by induction, and induction offers no means to decide which of them will produce scientific knowledge.

The same holds of Aristotle's procedure for finding premises by syllogism. In order to produce scientific knowledge, the latter must not merely yield premises, but premises which are the causes of the conclusion – or equivalently a middle term

---

[65] Ibid., B 7, 92 a 37–38.
[66] Ibid., B 7, 92 a 38–b 1.
[67] Ibid., A 22, 84 a 9–10.
[68] Ibid., A22, 84 a 5–6.

7.8 The Role of Plausibility in the Analytic-Synthetic Method

which is the cause of the conclusion, because "the middle term is the cause, and in all cases it is the cause that is sought."[69] But Aristotle's procedure may yield premises which are not the causes of the conclusion, and offers no means to decide which, among alternative premises, or middle terms, are the causes of the conclusion.

For example, by Aristotle's procedure for finding premises by syllogism, from the conclusion, 'Eclipse belongs to the moon', we may obtain both the premises: (A) 'Eclipse belongs to being screened by the earth' and 'Being screened by the earth belongs to the moon'; and the premises: (B) 'Eclipse belongs to not casting a shadow during full moon although nothing visible is between us and the moon' and 'Not casting a shadow during full moon although nothing visible is between us and the moon, belongs to the moon'. The conclusion, 'Eclipse belongs to the moon', follows from either (A) or (B) by Barbara. But the premises (A) produce scientific knowledge, since they are the causes of the conclusion. For "an eclipse is a screening by the earth."[70] Conversely, the premises (B) do not produce scientific knowledge, since they are not the causes of the conclusion. For in this case "it is plain that the moon is eclipsed but not why" and "we know that there is an eclipse but we do not know what it is."[71] In fact, not casting a shadow during full moon although nothing visible is between us and the moon, is not the cause but only an effect of the eclipse. But Aristotle's procedure for finding premises by syllogism offers no means to decide which of (A) and (B) yields scientific knowledge.

To that end, another procedure is needed. This is the plausibility test procedure described in Chapter 4. It might be thought that such procedure could have no part in Aristotle's way to scientific knowledge, because scientific knowledge is concerned with truths, whereas the plausibility test procedure is concerned with accepted opinions [*endoxa*]. But it is not so. Although the plausibility test procedure does not allow one to recognize the premises to be true, it plays an essential role in Aristotle's way to scientific knowledge. Aristotle's procedure for finding premises by syllogism or by induction may lead, from the same conclusion, to alternative premises, only some of which may produce scientific knowledge. To determine which ones, intuition is of no use except when the premises are prime premises. When this is not the case, the only procedure available is the plausibility test procedure. For such reason, the latter plays an essential role in Aristotle's way to scientific knowledge.

Of course, the plausibility test procedure does not ensure truth, so, by Aristotle's procedure for finding premises by syllogism or by induction, one may arrive at prime premises through intermediate premises which are not necessarily true. In Aristotle's analytic-synthetic method the need for synthesis arises exactly from this circumstance. When one has reached the prime premises and recognized them to be true by intuition, one must check if analysis can be inverted so as to obtain a deduction from the prime premises, and this is the task of synthesis.

---

[69] *Ibid.*, B 2, 90 a 6–7.

[70] *Ibid.*, B 8, 93 b 7.

[71] *Ibid.*, B 8, 93 b 2–3.

7.9 Plausibility and Essence

In Chapter 6 it has been stated that, for Aristotle, logic is concerned with the essence of things, since syllogisms start from the essence, and the essence is manifested through syllogism and through demonstration. It might be objected that, while this holds of scientific syllogism – the kind of syllogism involved in demonstration, whose premises are truths – it does not hold of dialectical syllogism, whose premises are only accepted opinions.

This objection, however, is unjustified because, as we have seen above, for Aristotle one of the uses of logic, and hence of dialectical syllogism, is to find the prime premises of any individual science, and in order to find them one must deal with the essence of the objects of that science. Thus also dialectical syllogism may be concerned with the essence of things.

Moreover, as we have seen in the previous section, in order to find premises that produce scientific knowledge, one must decide which – among alternative hypotheses obtained by Aristotle's procedure for finding premises by syllogism or by induction – are the causes of the conclusion, and hence produce scientific knowledge. To that end, one must use the plausibility test procedure. So, until one arrives at prime premises and recognizes them to be true by intuition, scientific syllogism will have premises which are, for the moment, only accepted opinions.

7.10 Finished Science and Science in the Making

For Aristotle, "the goal of theoretical science is truth."[72] But a science is concerned with truth only at the end of the process of analysis-synthesis, that is, when a deduction from the prime premises has been found. When that stage is reached for every known problem of the science in question, the latter becomes a finished science – a science in finished form, consisting entirely of truths and ready to be presented, by means of the axiomatic method, in treatises such as Euclid's *Elements*.

Such treatises have pedagogical purposes. In fact Aristotle calls "didactic arguments" the arguments which "proceed from the proper principles of each subject."[73] Thus, by 'didactic arguments', he means demonstrations by the axiomatic method. In his view, once a science becomes a finished science, the axiomatic method is the proper method for teaching it. The purpose of the axiomatic method is not to acquire new knowledge, but rather to teach already acquired knowledge, because "all teaching and all intellectual learning come from pre-existing knowledge."[74]

For Aristotle, a finished science is purely demonstrative, it consists of demonstrations and truths only. But a finished science is the end of the scientific process.

---

[72] Aristotle, *Metaphysica*, α 1, 993 b 20–21.
[73] Aristotle, *Sophistici Elenchi*, 2, 165 b 1–2.
[74] Aristotle, *Analytica Posteriora*, A 1, 71 a 1–2.

Only at the end of this process a science consists of truths only. A science in the making necessarily involves accepted opinions, so it does not consist of truths only.

A finished science is the end of the scientific process only in the sense in which death is the end of life. It is the last term in the sequence of steps of which the scientific process consists, not the goal for which people engage in the activity of progressing through the steps in this sequence. The goal of the scientific process is not to write treatises such as Euclid's *Elements*, but rather to solve problems arising from previous and current efforts towards knowing what is as it is. Now, solving problems necessarily involves the use of accepted opinions.

7.11 Aristotle's Logic as a Logic of Discovery

According to the heuristic view, Aristotle's logic is primarily a logic of discovery. Indeed, as we have seen, Aristotle states that, by means of it, one can not only know how syllogisms come about, but also have the ability to discover them, and this allows one to acquire scientific knowledge.

Dewey states that in Aristotle "there is no room for any logic of discovery."[75] In his view, for Aristotle knowledge is "immediate rational apprehension, grasp or vision," so it is "of the nature of 'intuition'."[76] Discursive or reflective operations have value only "as processes of personal development (such as might now be called psychological but are merely pedagogical) by means of which individual persons arrived at direct apprehension of essences."[77]

This is unjustified. That, for Aristotle, one may recognize premises to be true only by intuition, does not mean that in Aristotle there is no room for any logic of discovery. One may have intuition of the essence, and hence scientific knowledge, only when one has found the prime premises, and the latter can be found only by the analytic-synthetic method, so by discursive thinking rather than intuitive thinking. Discursive operations have value not merely as psychological or pedagogical processes, but as logical processes for finding prime premises, and, in order to find them, a logic of discovery is necessary.

7.12 Limitations of Aristotle's Logic

Aristotle's logic has several limitations. Here are the main ones.

1) As it has been argued in Chapter 6, for Aristotle logic is concerned with the essence of things. Thus Aristotle's logic is strictly dependent on his conception of

---

[75]Dewey (1938, 87).
[76]*Ibid.*, 88.
[77]*Ibid.*

science, according to which to have scientific knowledge is to have knowledge of the essence of things. But the fact that Aristotle's logic is concerned with the essence of things makes it inadequate to the needs of modern science because, as it will be argued in Chapter 8, the latter is not concerned with the essence of things.

2) If, as Aristotle claims, there existed a faculty such as intuition, capable of recognizing premises to be true, this would trivialize the process of discovering prime premises. For prime premises can be expressed by finite strings of symbols of a given alphabet, and there is an algorithm for enumerating all such strings. So, if there existed a faculty such as intuition, capable of recognizing premises to be true when one meets them, then, when in such an enumeration one would reach a prime premise, one would be able to recognize it to be true by intuition. This would provide a procedure for discovering prime premises.

3) Aristotle's analysis of assertions is incapable of dealing with relations, so Aristotle's logic cannot account for inferences involving them. For example, Aristotle's logic cannot account for an inference such as 'All horses are animals, therefore all heads of horses are heads of animals'. This inference is of the form:

$$\frac{AaB}{CaD}$$

and no syllogism rule or conversion rule justifies it. There is no doubt that Aristotle would have recognized inferences of this kind to be valid. For he uses inferences of a related form, such as, "If knowledge is judgment, then also an object of knowledge is an object of judgment;" or, "If sight is sensation, then also an object of sight is an object of sensation."[78] But Aristotle's logic cannot account for them, because it is intended to be a means for scientific knowledge. According to Aristotle, the latter is concerned with essence, thus with essential properties, not with relations between individuals, which are not part of the essence.

4) Aristotle's analysis of assertions is incapable of dealing with singular assertions *qua* singular assertions. As we have seen in Chapter 6, it treats them as if they were universal assertions. This is due to the fact that, as we have seen in Chapter 3, for Aristotle there is no scientific knowledge of individuals *qua* individuals, but only of their essential properties, which are universals, because all scientific knowledge is always knowledge of universals.

5) Aristotle's logic is incapable of accounting for inferences involving compound assertions, such as, 'If it is day, then it is light, but it is not light, therefore, it is not day'. There is no doubt that Aristotle would have recognized inferences of this kind to be valid. For he states that, "when two" assertions "are so related to each other that if one is, then the other necessarily is, then, if the second is not, the first will not be either."[79] Such inferences are part of what Aristotle calls syllogisms "from a

---

[78] Aristotle, *Topica*, B 9, 114 a 18–19.
[79] Aristotle, *Analytica Priora*, B 4, 57 b 1–2.

7.12 Limitations of Aristotle's Logic 131

hypothesis [*ex upotheseos*]."[80] Also strong "reduction to the impossible" SRI "is a part of syllogisms from a hypothesis."[81]

In a syllogism from a hypothesis, "the syllogism is for the substituted assertion," namely for the assertion which is taken as a substitute for the original thing to be demonstrated, "while the original thing" to be demonstrated "is reached through an agreement or some other kind of hypothesis."[82] That is, in a syllogism from a hypothesis, the original thing to be demonstrated is not directly the conclusion of a demonstrative syllogism, and hence is not properly inferred by a syllogism. It is inferred indirectly via an agreed hypothesis, which connects the original thing to be demonstrated with another assertion that is properly inferred by a demonstrative syllogism.

Despite his attention to syllogisms from a hypothesis, however, Aristotle does not develop the theory of such syllogisms, because they play only an auxiliary role in the use of logic as a means for scientific knowledge – intended as concerned with essence. Developing their theory would be irrelevant for that use of logic.

6) Aristotle's logic is subject to the problem that there are terms which, when substituted for A and B in the conversion rule CR2, result in inferences with true premises and false conclusion. For example, from the true premise, 'To be even belongs to all things that are even and odd', by CR2 we may infer the false conclusion, 'To be even and odd belongs to some even thing'. The premise is true because all things that were even and odd in particular would be even, while the conclusion is false, because no even thing can be even and odd.

This problem also affects Darapti and Felapton because, as we have seen in Chapter 6, CR2 is necessary to obtain a completion of Darapti or Felapton candidate syllogisms. In fact, there are terms that, when substituted for A, B and C in a Darapti or Felapton candidate syllogism, do not result in a syllogism. For example, from the true premises, 'To have head and wings of a gryphon belongs to all hippogriffs' and 'To be an animal with the back of a horse belongs to all hippogriffs', by Darapti we may infer the false conclusion, 'To have head and wings of a gryphon belongs to some animal with the back of a horse'. The conclusion is false because there are no animals with the back of a horse which have head and wings of a gryphon. Similarly in the case of a Felapton candidate syllogism.

At the origin of the problem there is the fact that CR2 entails that assertions of the form **A** have existential import. Such assertions imply that something exists because from them, by CR2, one may infer assertions of the form **I**, which obviously have existential import. Indeed, if one translates CR2 into the predicate calculus, it becomes the invalid rule: From $\forall x(B(x) \to A(x))$ one may infer $\exists x(A(x) \wedge B(x))$.

One might think of solving this problem by stipulating that Aristotle's logic is to be used only with non-empty terms, namely, that in each of the assertions **A**, **E**, **I**, **O** only non-empty terms can be substituted for the letters A and B. This would be

---

[80]*Ibid.*, A 23, 41 a 21.
[81]*Ibid.*, A 44, 50 a 39.
[82]*Ibid.*, A 23, 41 a 38–41 b 1.

justified by the fact that, according to Aristotle, every assertion affirming something of a non-existent subject is false, because it asserts what is not, and "asserting what is not is false."[83] This would solve the problem of the existential import because, in CR2, the only way in which AaB could be true and BiA false is if there were no B. This would exclude the inference from the premise, 'To be even belongs to all numbers which are even and odd', to the conclusion, 'To be numbers which are even and odd belongs to some even numbers', since there are no numbers which are even and odd.

The snag with this solution is that the emptiness of a term, for example 'hippogriff', can be a factual matter, which would make logic depend on factual matters. Without bringing the latter into logic, one may only discover the emptiness of terms by reasoning with them, namely, by means of syllogisms and conversions. But the non-emptiness assumption prevents one from doing so.

The limitations listed above are basic drawbacks of Aristotle's logic. By and large, they are overcome by mathematical logic. On the other hand, Aristotle's logic is capable of dealing with questions, such as discovery, that mathematical logic cannot handle. In view of this, it seems improper to say, as Tarski does, that "the old traditional logic forms only a fragment of the new, moreover a fragment which is entirely insignificant from the standpoint of requirements of other sciences, and of mathematics in particular."[84] Of course, Aristotle's logic is capable of dealing with the question of discovery only in a restricted framework, but that is another matter.

7.13 The Stoics' Deductivist Turn

Contrary to Aristotle, for whom logic is primarily a logic of discovery, the Stoics make a deductivist turn, limiting logic to the study of deduction. Thus Cicero states that "every careful doctrine of arguing involves two arts, one of discovering" new arguments, "one of judging" the correctness of arguments already found, and "Aristotle came first in both."[85] On the contrary, the Stoics "diligently pursued the ways of judging by means of that science which they call *dialektike*, but wholly disregarded the art of discovering, which is called *topike*, and which was more serviceable for use and certainly prior in the order of nature"[86]

This sweeping change with respect to Aristotle was deeply influenced by the Stoics' view of the universe. According to the Stoics, "everything happens according to fate."[87] The latter is "the eternal cause of things, why past things happened,

---

[83] Aristotle, *Metaphysica*, Γ 7, 1011 b 26–27.
[84] Tarski (1994, 17–18).
[85] Cicero, *Topica*, 6.
[86] *Ibid.*
[87] Cicero, *De Divinatione*, I.125.

present things are happening, and future things will happen."[88] Fate is identical with God, the mind on which the order of things is based, since "God is one and the same with mind and fate and Zeus."[89] Being based on God, who is a mind, the order of things is a rational one. Specifically, it is "a perpetual and immutable succession of things, and a chain that develops and is implicated through an eternal order of consequence, to which it is associated and connected."[90] Thus the order of things is based on the relation of logical consequence.

Since fate is the eternal cause of things, it would be foolish to oppose it. The wise man will try to live in conformity with it, seeking "life in accordance with nature."[91] This "is the same as virtuous life. For virtue is the goal towards which nature guides us."[92] Now, in order to live in conformity with fate and nature, the wise man must know the course of future events, so as to harmonize the conduct of his life with them. But, since the order of things is based on the relation of logical consequence, the course of future events can be deduced from the past and present ones. Therefore, the wise man can know the course of future events through deduction.

For this reason, according to the Stoics, the task of logic is the study of deduction. Since deduction is all that is necessary to discover the course of future events, there is no need for a logic of discovery. The "end and purpose" of logic is "to show that, when premises are compounded with one another in certain ways, something may be deduced by necessity from what is posited or conceded."[93] Then logic is the science of deduction – science because, while, for Aristotle, logic "is not a part but an instrument of philosophy," for the Stoics logic is "a part of philosophy."[94]

---

[88] *Ibid.*, I.126.

[89] Diogenes Laertius, VII.135.

[90] Gellius, *Noctes Atticae*, VII 2.1.

[91] Diogenes Laertius, *Vitae Philosophorum*, VII.87.

[92] *Ibid.*

[93] Alexander of Aphrodisias, *In Aristotelis Analyticorum Priorum Librum Primum Commentarium* (Wallies), 1.19–2.2.

[94] *Ibid.*, 1.8–9.

Part II
Modern Perspectives

Chapter 8
The Method of Modern Science

8.1 Galileo's Method

It is widely held that the core of the Scientific Revolution of the seventeenth century was a revolutionary change in the scientific method which involved a break with Aristotle. Thus Cohen states that Galileo earns the title of "founder of the scientific method of inquiry."[1] This is unjustified, because Galileo's method is really Aristotle's analytic-synthetic method.

Contemporary Aristotelians claimed that "Aristotle founded himself mainly on the *a priori* discourse," establishing a conclusion "by means of natural, manifest and clear principles."[2] Only "afterwards he established the same" conclusion "*a posteriori*, by means of sense."[3] To this Galileo objects: "This, to which you refer, is the method by which" Aristotle "has written his doctrine," that is, the one by which he gave a presentation of it, not "the one by which he investigated it."[4] Indeed, Aristotle "first procured, by way of senses, experiments and observations, to assure himself as much as possible of the conclusion."[5] Only "afterwards he sought the means to demonstrate it."[6] That is, Aristotle first assured himself as much as possible of the conclusion *a posteriori*, and only afterwards established the same conclusion *a priori*.

The terms *a priori* and *a posteriori* first occur in the Scholastic tradition with reference to demonstration. For example, Albert of Saxony says that "demonstration is twofold," namely, "that which proceeds from causes to effects, and is called *a priori* demonstration," and that "which proceeds from effects to causes," and "is

---

[1] Cohen (1985, 142).
[2] Galilei (1968, VII, 75).
[3] *Ibid.*
[4] *Ibid.*
[5] *Ibid.*
[6] *Ibid.*

called *a posteriori* demonstration."[7] Thus *a posteriori* demonstration corresponds to analysis, *a priori* demonstration corresponds to synthesis, and hence the terms *a posteriori* and *a priori* refer to the two parts of Aristotle's analytic-synthetic method.

Then, by saying that Aristotle first assured himself as much as possible of the conclusion *a posteriori*, and only afterwards established the same conclusion *a priori*, Galileo actually states that Aristotle proceeded by means of Aristotle's analytic-synthetic method. This is also the method by which Galileo proceeds. Indeed, Galileo says that in his work he follows what "Aristotle teaches us in his Dialectic."[8]

8.2 Galileo and Pappus' Method

It might be objected that the method by which Galileo proceeds is rather Pappus' analytic-synthetic method, on account of the following two facts.

1) A reply to Galileo's critics written jointly by Galileo and Benedetto Castelli, though published only under Castelli's name, states that "the resolutive method," namely analysis, consists in taking "the conclusion as true," and "going on deducing this, and then that, and then that other consequence from it, until one comes across a consequence which is manifest, either by itself or because it has been demonstrated."[9] From the latter "one reaches the intended conclusion by the compositive method," namely synthesis, "deducing the reason of a conclusion from its true and known principles."[10]

2) Galileo states that, "when the conclusion is true, by making use of the resolutive method one may easily hit upon some proposition that has been previously demonstrated, or arrive at some principle known by itself."[11] Conversely, "if the conclusion is false, one may go on to infinity without ever hitting upon any known truth, unless someone hits upon some manifest impossibility or absurdity."[12] Then "the certainty of a conclusion helps not a little in the discovery of its demonstration, again, I mean, in the demonstrative sciences."[13]

The objection, however, is unjustified, for the following reasons.

1) The passage concerning the resolutive and compositive method quoted above does "not occur in the manuscript" and we lack "any criterion for deciding who

---

[7] Albert of Saxony (1986, Book I, Question IX, f. 8 r.).
[8] Galilei (1968, XVIII, 248).
[9] *Ibid.*, IV, 521.
[10] *Ibid.*
[11] *Ibid.*, VII, 75.
[12] *Ibid.*
[13] *Ibid.*, VII, 76.

could be its author."[14] It can be argued, however, that its author is Castelli because, being a mathematician, he was more likely to refer to Pappus' analytic-synthetic method than to Aristotle's analytic-synthetic method. For as it has been said in Chapter 5, in the modern and contemporary periods, Pappus' analytic-synthetic method has had a bigger impact than Aristotle's analytic-synthetic method, especially on mathematicians.

2) When saying that the certainty of a conclusion helps not a little in the discovery of its demonstration, Galileo adds: in the demonstrative sciences, thus in mathematics. Now, Pappus' analytic method, while useful in mathematics, is of little or no use in the physical sciences, with which Galileo is mainly concerned. For, as it has been stated in Chapter 5, in Pappus's analytic-synthetic method propositions must be reciprocal, or convertible, at least in the weak sense that each of them must be deducible from the other one plus some additional true premises. But, as Aristotle pointed out, in the physical sciences, "convertible propositions rarely occur in actual demonstrations."[15] This explains why Galileo specifies that his statement refers to demonstrative sciences, that is, to mathematics, rather than to physical sciences. Evidence for this is provided by what Galileo says about the invention of the telescope. While the Hollander, first inventor of the telescope, observed "the resulting effect" only "casually handling lenses of various sorts," Galileo himself "discovered the same thing by means of reasoning."[16] In this he was not helped by the "knowledge and certainty of the telescope having already been made."[17] The "received opinion of the truth of the conclusion was of no help to me."[18] For, in the physical sciences, convertible propositions rarely occur in actual demonstrations.

8.3 An Example of Galileo's Method

That the method by which Galileo proceeds is Aristotle's analytic-synthetic method is apparent, for example, from his solution to the problem: Show that a heavy movable body, for example, a bronze sphere, dropped from the top of the mast of a ship moving at uniform speed, will hit the deck of the ship at the foot of the mast, and its trajectory will be semi-parabolic.

According to contemporary Aristotelians, the sphere will fall "to the foot of the mast when the ship is standing still," and "as far as from that same point as the ship has advanced during the time of the fall" of the sphere "when the ship is sailing."[19] The man dropping the sphere is supposed to give no "impetus with his arm" but

---

[14] Favaro (1968, 14).

[15] Aristotle, *Analytica Posteriora*, A 3, 73 a 17–18.

[16] Galilei (1968, VI, 259).

[17] *Ibid.*, VI, 258.

[18] *Ibid.*, VI, 259.

[19] *Ibid.*, VII, 167.

"only to open his hand and let it go: so" the sphere "will not be able to follow the motion of the boat" through "any force impressed upon it by its thrower," and "therefore will remain behind."[20]

This view seems so natural that several people hold it even today.[21] Nevertheless, it is wrong. As Galileo points out, an "experiment will show" that the sphere "always falls in the same place on the ship, whether the ship is standing still or moving with any speed you please."[22] This raises the question of how this comes about and what the trajectory of the sphere will be. To answer this question, Galileo formulates the following hypothesis:

(A) (i) If a heavy movable body is "launched along a horizontal plane, all impediments having been removed," its "motion will be uniform and perpetual in along this same plane, if the latter extends to infinity."[23]

    (ii) If the plane is "terminated and in an elevated position," the movable body, "arriving at the edge of the plane and continuing its course, will add, to the previous uniform and perpetual motion, that downward propensity which is due to its own weight."[24]

    (iii) This "will result in a motion compounded of a horizontal uniform motion and a downward" uniformly "accelerated motion."[25]

Clearly, hypothesis (A) is a sufficient condition for solving the problem. Indeed, a ship which moves over a calm sea, or a bronze sphere on top of its mast, is like a heavy movable body launched along a horizontal plane, all impediments having been removed. Therefore, by (A) (i), the sphere will continue to move forward at the same speed as the ship.

On the other hand, a bronze sphere which is dropped from the top of the mast of a ship, is like a heavy movable body, arriving at the edge of a plane terminated and in an elevated position, and continuing its course. Therefore, by (A) (ii), the sphere will add, to the previous uniform and perpetual motion, that downward propensity which is due to its own weight.

By (A) (iii), this will result in a motion compounded of a horizontal uniform motion and a downward uniformly accelerated motion. Now, as we will see in Chapter 21, Galileo shows that such a motion describes a semi-parabolic line. Therefore, the trajectory of the sphere will be semi-parabolic. We may then conclude that the sphere will fall to the foot of the mast, and its trajectory will be semi-parabolic.

---

[20] *Ibid.*, VII, 176.
[21] See, for example, Song et al. (1997).
[22] Galilei (1968, VII, 170).
[23] *Ibid.*, VIII, 268.
[24] *Ibid.*
[25] *Ibid.*

8.3 An Example of Galileo's Method

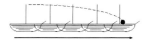

The same will hold if a bronze sphere is dropped from the top of a tower, "the same cause holding good on the Earth as on the ship."[26] Then the motion of the sphere will be compounded of the horizontal uniform motion of the Earth and a downward uniformly accelerated motion.

Galileo arrives at hypothesis (A) by making experiments and observations and drawing conclusions from them by induction, therefore, by analysis.

For example, Galileo arrives at (A) (i) by making experiments with a bronze sphere rolling down or up on an inclined plane. The experiments show that, "on an inclined plane," the sphere "spontaneously descends and is continuously accelerated, and requires the use of force to keep it at rest."[27] On the other hand, "on an ascending path, a force is needed to make it move that way" and "the motion impressed on it is continuously diminishing, so that eventually it is annihilated."[28] From this Galileo concludes that, if the plane is not inclined, then, "since there is no downward slope, there cannot be a natural tendency to move," and, "since there is no upward slope, there cannot be a resistance to being moved."[29] Then the sphere "would be indifferent between the propensity to motion and the resistance to it."[30] Therefore, if the sphere "were given an impetus in some direction," it "would move in that direction," and would remain in motion "as long as the extension of that surface," so that, "if such a surface were endless, the motion on it would likewise be endless."[31]

Similarly, Galileo arrives at (A) (ii), (iii). This is analysis. On the other hand, the above argument, that the sphere will fall at the foot of the mast or tower and its trajectory will be semi-parabolic, deduces this fact from (A). This is synthesis. Therefore Galileo's solution to the problem is an instance of Aristotle's analytic-synthetic method.

Notice that (A) (i) is a formulation of the law of inertia, but a flawed one because, by a horizontal plane, Galileo means a segment of the spherical surface of the Earth. Indeed, he says that the sphere which is on top of the mast moves "carried by the

---

[26] *Ibid.*, VII, 170.
[27] *Ibid.*, VII, 172.
[28] *Ibid.*, VII, 172–173.
[29] *Ibid.*, VII, 173.
[30] *Ibid.*
[31] *Ibid.*

ship, it too going along the circumference of a circle about its centre."[32] Thus, in (A)(i), the expression 'along this same plane' means 'along a segment of the spherical surface of the Earth' rather than 'along a straight line'. The flaw is rectified by Newton: "Every body persists in its state of being at rest or of moving uniformly along a straight line, unless it is compelled to change that state by forces impressed upon it."[33]

8.4 Newton's Method

Newton's account of the scientific method is similar to Galileo's, but more detailed. He states that "as in mathematicks, so in natural philosophy, the inquiry of difficult things by the method of analysis, ought ever to precede the method" of synthesis, or "composition."[34]

Now, "analysis consists in making experiments and observations, and in drawing general conclusions from them by induction, and admitting of no objections against the conclusions, but such as are taken from experiments, or other certain truths."[35] Of course, "the arguing from experiments and observations by induction" is "no demonstration of general conclusions; yet it is the best way of arguing which the nature of things admits of."[36] Moreover, it "may be looked upon as so much the stronger, by how much the induction is more general."[37]

Once a general conclusion has been reached, "if no exception occur from phenomena, the conclusion may be pronounced generally."[38] But if "any exception shall occur from experiments," the conclusion will "then begin to be pronounced with such exceptions as occur."[39] For "in experimental philosophy, propositions gathered from phenomena by induction, when no contrary hypotheses are opposed, must be considered to be true either exactly or very nearly, until other phenomena occur by which" such propositions "are made either more exact or liable to exceptions."[40] Then the propositions will be pronounced with the exceptions.

By this way of inquiry one may proceed "from effects to their causes, and from particular causes to more general ones, till the argument end in the most general. This is the method of analysis."[41] On the other hand, "synthesis consists in assuming

---

[32] *Ibid.*, VII, 174.
[33] Newton (1972, I, 54).
[34] Newton (1952, 404).
[35] *Ibid.*
[36] *Ibid.*
[37] *Ibid.*
[38] *Ibid.*
[39] *Ibid.*
[40] Newton (1972, II, 555).
[41] Newton (1952, 404).

8.4 Newton's Method

the causes discovered, and established as principles, and by them explaining the phenomena proceeding from them, and proving the explanations."[42]

Thus, according to Newton, premises are obtained from experiments and observations by induction. The latter is not demonstration, and yet is the best way of dealing with the objects of nature, as distinguished from mathematical objects. Moreover, induction is so much stronger by how much it is more general. Premises obtained by means of it are accepted as long as no counterexample occurs. This is analysis. From the premises, which give the causes, one then deduces the phenomena. This is synthesis.

This is Aristotle's analytic-synthetic method, and is also the method by which Newton proceeds. Indeed, Newton states that ancient mathematicians had two methods, which "they called synthesis and analysis, or composition and resolution. By the method of analysis they found their inventions," that is, they made their discoveries, and "by the method of synthesis they composed them," that is, they demonstrated them, "for the publick."[43] On the other hand, "the mathematicians of the last age have much improved analysis, but stop there and think they have solved a problem when they have only resolved it."[44] Thus "the method of synthesis is almost laid aside."[45] The "synthetic style of writing is less pleasing" to them, "because it is less revealing of the manner of discovery."[46]

As to Newton himself, his own propositions "were invented by analysis. But, considering" that ancient mathematicians "admitted nothing into geometry before it was demonstrated by composition," he composed, that is, he wrote synthetically, what he "invented by analysis to make it geometrically authentic and fit for the publick."[47] Of course, "he could have written analytically" what he "had found out analytically," but he "was writing for scientists steeped in the elements of geometry, and putting down geometrically demonstrated bases for physical science."[48] Therefore, he wrote "in words at length after the manner of the ancients."[49] That is, synthetically.

Admittedly, "if any man who understands analysis will reduce the demonstrations of the propositions from their composition back into analysis," he "will see by what method of analysis they were invented."[50] But this will require considerable skill, because synthesis tends to hide analysis. This "makes it now difficult for unskilful men to see the analysis by which those propositions were found out."[51]

---

[42] *Ibid.*, 404–405.
[43] Cohen (1971, 294).
[44] *Ibid.*
[45] *Ibid.*
[46] Newton (1967–1981, VIII, 451).
[47] Cohen (1971, 294).
[48] Newton (1967–1981, VIII, 451).
[49] Cohen (1971, 294).
[50] *Ibid.*
[51] *Ibid.*, 295.

8.5 Newton and Pappus' Method

It might be objected that the method by which Newton proceeds is rather Pappus' analytic-synthetic method, on account of the following two facts.

1) Newton states that "the main business of natural philosophy is to argue from phenomena" and "to deduce causes from effects."[52]

2) Newton states: "I derive from the celestial phenomena the forces of gravity, with which bodies tend to the Sun and the several planets. Then from these forces" I "deduce the motions of the planets, the comets, the Moon, and the sea."[53]

This objection, however, is unjustified, for the following reasons.

1) When Newton states that the main business of natural philosophy is to argue from phenomena and to deduce causes from effects, he means to say that, in natural philosophy, "propositions are deduced from the phenomena and rendered general by induction," and this is the way in which the "laws of motion and of gravitation were discovered."[54] Thus, what is deduced from the phenomena are singular propositions, which are then made general by induction. Therefore, it is induction, rather than deduction, that yields the hypotheses.

2) Newton's derivation of the forces of gravity from the celestial phenomena is not really a deduction, but rather a mixture of induction and deduction.

8.6 Galileo vs. Idealization

It is sometimes claimed that, rather than a revolutionary change in the scientific method, the core of the Scientific Revolution of the seventeenth century was the use of idealization. For example, Nowak states that "Galileo systematically applied the method of idealization. And that was the real meaning of the revolution in the natural sciences which was named after him."[55]

This is unjustified, because Galileo actually opposes idealization. This is clear, for example, from his answer to the objection of contemporary Aristotelians, that mathematicians "may well demonstrate with their principles that *sphaera tangit planum in puncto* [a sphere touches a plane at a single point]" but, "when we deal with matter, things are otherwise."[56] For "material spheres are subject to many contingencies to which immaterial ones are not subjected."[57] Thus, if we place a bronze "sphere upon a plane, its weight" may "press down in such a way that the

---

[52] Newton (1952, 369).
[53] Newton (1972, I, 16).
[54] *Ibid.*, II, 764.
[55] Nowak (2000, 21).
[56] Galilei (1968, VII, 229).
[57] *Ibid.*, VII, 233.

8.6 Galileo vs. Idealization

plane yields a little, or that the sphere itself" is "indented at the point of contact."[58] Then the sphere will not touch the plane at a single point, but with a part of its surface. This shows that "mathematical subtleties," when "applied to sensible and physical matter, do not work out."[59]

Galileo's answer is that the objection assumes that the application of mathematical subtleties to sensible and physical matter is based on idealization. Idealization consists in treating a situation as having features that it does not really have. Thus, it is an idealization to treat an imperfect material sphere as being a perfect sphere, and an imperfect material plane as being a perfect plane. But the application of mathematics to physical matter must not be based on idealization, it must make allowance for the fact that the situation concerns "a sphere that is not a sphere and a plane that is not a plane."[60]

We must "find and demonstrate conclusions abstracted from the impediments" of matter, so as "to make use of them in practice under those limitations that experience will teach us."[61] When a tradesman in the marketplace wants to calculate the weight of the goods sold, he must subtract the weight of "containers, straps, and other packing items."[62] Similarly, "when the geometrical philosopher wants to find in the concrete the effects which he has demonstrated in the abstract, he must deduct the impediments of matter."[63] If he will do so, "things will agree no less exactly than with arithmetical computations."[64]

Even "in the abstract an immaterial sphere which is not a perfect sphere can touch an immaterial plane which is not a perfect plane not at a single point but with a part of its surface."[65] Therefore, "what happens in the concrete happens in the same manner in the abstract."[66] In fact, "errors consist neither in the abstract nor in the concrete, neither in geometry nor in physics, but in the calculator, who does not know how to do the accounting correctly."[67] Errors consist in idealization, which does not make allowance for the fact that the situation concerns a sphere that is not a sphere and a plane that is not a plane.

---

[58] *Ibid.*
[59] *Ibid.*, VII, 229.
[60] *Ibid.*, VII, 233.
[61] *Ibid.*, VIII, 276.
[62] *Ibid.*, VII, 234.
[63] *Ibid.*
[64] *Ibid.*
[65] *Ibid.*, VII, 233.
[66] *Ibid.*
[67] *Ibid.*, VII, 234.

8.7 Galileo's Philosophical Revolution

The core of the Scientific Revolution of the seventeenth century was neither a revolutionary change in the scientific method nor the use of idealization, but rather a change in the goal of science. While, for Aristotle, the goal of science was to penetrate the true and intrinsic essence of natural substances, for Galileo it was only to know certain properties of natural substances, mathematical in character. This is Galileo's philosophical revolution.

Indeed, Galileo states: "Either, by speculating, we seek to penetrate the true and intrinsic essence of natural substances, or we content ourselves with coming to know some of their properties [*affezioni*]."[68] Trying to penetrate the essence of natural substances is "a not less impossible and vain undertaking with regard to the closest elemental substances than with the remotest celestial things."[69] Therefore, we will content ourselves with coming to know "some properties of them, such as location, motion, shape, size, opacity, mutability, generation, and dissolution."[70] All these properties are mathematical in character, including mutability, generation, and dissolution, since they are changes in size and shape. While we cannot know the essence of natural substances, "we need not despair of our ability" to come to know such properties "even with respect to the remotest bodies, just as those close at hand."[71]

For example, we will not try to penetrate the essence of the sunspots, since it "could be a thousand things unknown and inconceivable to us."[72] Rather, we will content ourselves with coming to know whether the rotation of the sunspots about the Sun "happens because the body of the Sun itself rotates and turns on itself carrying them with it, or rather because" the "revolution is that of the ambient, which contains them and carries them with itself."[73] Thus, the question of the essence of the sunspots is replaced with a question concerning their motion, which is mathematical in character.

8.8 Galileo's Philosophical Revolution and Mathematics

With Galileo's philosophical revolution, and only with it, a mathematical treatment of nature became possible. The latter was impossible with Aristotle's science, which aimed at penetrating the essence of natural substances, since essence is

---

[68] *Ibid.*, V, 187.
[69] *Ibid.*
[70] *Ibid.*, V, 188.
[71] *Ibid.*
[72] *Ibid.*, V, 105.
[73] *Ibid.*, V, 133.

not mathematical in character. For this reason, Aristotle states that "the method of mathematics is not well suited to physics."[74] Only if one contents oneself with coming to know certain properties of natural substances, mathematical in character, the method of mathematics may be well suited to physics.

Actually, with Galileo's philosophical revolution, a mathematical treatment of nature became not only possible but also necessary, because treating properties mathematical in character essentially requires mathematics. For such reason, Galileo states that "trying to deal with natural questions without geometry is attempting to do what is impossible to be done."[75]

8.9 Galileo's Great Book of the World vs. Aristotle's Books

That, with Galileo's philosophical revolution, a mathematical treatment of nature became not only possible but also necessary, does not mean, as Husserl says, that for Galileo "nature is, in its 'true being-in-itself', mathematical."[76]

Admittedly, Galileo states that natural "philosophy is written in this very great book that is continually open to us before our eyes (I say the universe)."[77] It "is written in mathematical language, and the characters are triangles, circles, and other geometrical figures, without the use of which it is impossible to humanly understand any word of it."[78] This was meant to be polemic with contemporary Aristotelians, who thought that natural philosophy was written in Aristotle's books. According to them, "philosophizing is and can be nothing but to work Aristotle's texts over and over."[79] They never want to lift their eyes from Aristotle's texts, "as if this great book of the world had been written by nature to be read by nobody but Aristotle, and his eyes had been destined to see for all posterity."[80] Conversely, for Galileo, philosophy is written in the great book of the world, it is written in mathematical language, and everybody can read it.

But this does not mean, as Husserl says, that for Galileo nature is, in its true being-in-itself, mathematical. Otherwise, Galileo would contradict the basic assumption of his philosophical revolution, that we must content ourselves with coming to know certain properties of natural substances, mathematical in character. If nature were, in its true being-in-itself, mathematical, then, by knowing those properties, we would know the essence of natural substances, contrary to Galileo's warning that penetrating their essence is an impossible and vain undertaking.

---

[74] Aristotle, *Metaphysica*, α 3, 995 a 16–17.
[75] Galilei (1968, VII, 229).
[76] Husserl (1970, 54).
[77] Galilei (1968, VI, 232).
[78] *Ibid.*
[79] *Ibid.*, V, 190.
[80] *Ibid.*

8.10 Galileo's Distinction Between Primary and Secondary Qualities

What Galileo actually means by saying that philosophy is written in the great book of the world and is written in mathematical language, is clear from his distinction between primary and secondary qualities.

Primary qualities are properties which cannot be separated from matter or corporeal substance, such as location, motion, shape, size. They are such that, "as soon as I conceive a matter or corporeal substance, I feel compelled by the need to conceive along with it" that it has such qualities, and "I cannot separate it from these conditions by any stretch of imagination."[81] Primary qualities are mathematical in character.

On the other hand, secondary qualities are properties which can be separated from matter or corporeal substance, such as colour, odour, taste and sound. They are such that, when I conceive a matter or corporeal substance, "I do not feel my mind forced to apprehend it as necessarily accompanied by such conditions."[82] Secondary qualities are not mathematical in character.

Since primary qualities are properties which cannot be separated from matter or corporeal substance, for Galileo they exist in the external world, though only as phenomenal properties of natural substances, not as their true and intrinsic essence. Conversely, secondary qualities do not exist in the external world. Indeed, "nothing is required in external bodies except size, shape, number, and slow or quick motion, to excite in us tastes, smells, and sounds."[83] In fact, "if ears, tongues, and noses were taken away, shapes, numbers, and motions would certainly remain, but not odours, tastes, sounds, which, outside the living animal," are "nothing but mere names."[84] Thus secondary qualities exist only in the mind.

Then, when Galileo says that natural philosophy is written in the great book of the world and is written in mathematical language, he means to say that scientific knowledge is not about secondary qualities but about primary qualities – properties which are mathematical in character and exist in the external world, although not as the true and intrinsic essence of natural substances but only as their phenomenal properties.

---

[81] *Ibid.*, VI, 347.
[82] *Ibid.*, VI, 347–348.
[83] *Ibid.*, VI, 350.
[84] *Ibid.*

8.11 Limitations of Galileo's Distinction

Galileo's distinction between primary and secondary qualities is, however, somewhat problematic. As we have seen, according to Galileo, while primary qualities exist in the external world, secondary qualities exist only in the mind. But, as Berkeley argues, "let anyone consider those arguments, which are thought manifestly to prove that colours and tastes exist only in the mind, and he shall find they may with equal force, be brought to prove the same thing of extension, figure, and motion."[85] Then if, as Galileo argues, secondary qualities exist only in the mind, primary qualities too "exist only in the mind."[86] Indeed, "great and small, swift and slow, are allowed to exist no where without the mind."[87]

Like secondary qualities, primary qualities do not exist in the external world. They are simply our ways of categorizing the world, by means of which we make it comprehensible to ourselves. The world is not written in mathematical language, the latter is only the language in which we express the properties in terms of which we categorize the world and acquire knowledge about it. On the other hand, the only knowledge we can have about the world is through our ways of categorizing it. Therefore, mathematics is a basic means for our acquiring knowledge about the world.

8.12 The Need for a New Kind of Mathematics

Consistently with his claim that, trying to deal with natural questions without geometry is attempting to do what is impossible to be done, in his work Galileo basically relies on geometry and the Eudoxian theory of proportions. While sufficient in some cases, this, however, was not the kind of mathematics the Scientific Revolution required.

Up to the sixteenth century, mathematics had almost exclusively dealt with static items: numbers and figures. Such was the case of geometry. But the Scientific Revolution required dealing with dynamic items: motion and change. This was alien to Greek mathematics, for a reason that is apparent from Aristotle's definition of motion: "Motion is the actualization of the potential as such."[88] This is a purely qualitative definition which resists mathematization. Moreover, for Aristotle, "there is no motion in an instant."[89]

---

[85] Berkeley (1948–1957, II, 47).
[86] *Ibid.*, II, 45.
[87] *Ibid.*
[88] Aristotle, *Physica*, Γ 2, 202 a 7–8.
[89] *Ibid.*, Z 3, 234 a 31.

To deal with motion and change, a new kind of mathematics was needed. Mathematical objects had to be brought nearer to physics, subjected to motion and viewed not as static things but as dynamic things, as things in flux. Such new kind of mathematics was introduced by Newton through his calculus of fluxions. An example of the latter will be considered in Chapter 21.

8.13 The Effectiveness of Mathematics in the Natural Sciences

Although Galileo did not provide the new kind of mathematics the Scientific Revolution required, his philosophical revolution laid down the basis for an explanation of the effectiveness of mathematics in dealing with the world. Before Galileo, such explanation was given in terms of the assumption that the universe is an order because it is governed by a divine mind, and is a mathematical order, so the universe is, in its true being-in-itself, mathematical. Thus Plato states that, "when the God undertook ordering the universe," he modelled "fire and water and earth and air" by means "of forms and numbers."[90] Such explanation has remained popular until today. For example, Dirac states that "God is a mathematician of a very high order, and he used very advanced mathematics in constructing the universe."[91]

This explanation, however, is unsatisfactory, because it is based on the unproven assumption that God exists and is a mathematician. Therefore an alternative explanation is necessary. In the last century, several people have despaired that such an explanation could be given. Thus they have concluded that the effectiveness of mathematics in dealing with the world "is something bordering on the mysterious, and there is no rational explanation for it."[92]

This is unjustified. To explain the effectiveness of mathematics in dealing with the world one need only ask: Why was mathematics not very effective in dealing with the world from antiquity to the seventeenth century, and has become so effective ever since then? Clearly, its effectiveness must be related to Galileo's philosophical revolution. As long as Aristotle's science aimed at penetrating the essence of natural substances, mathematics had no chance of being effective in dealing with the natural world. For essence is not mathematical in character, so it was impossible to use mathematics to deal with it. Conversely, with Galileo's philosophical revolution, it became possible to use mathematics to deal with the natural world.

As it has been pointed out above, however, Galileo's philosophical revolution must not be interpreted in terms of the view that primary qualities exist in the external world. It must rather be interpreted in terms of the view that such properties

---

[90]Plato, *Timaeus*, 53 b 1–5.
[91]Dirac (1963, 53).
[92]Wigner (1960, 2).

are only our ways of categorizing the world. Mathematics is effective in dealing with the world not because the world is written in mathematical language but rather because, as a result of Galileo's philosophical revolution, we content ourselves with coming to know certain properties of natural substances which are mathematical in character, in the sense that we are able to deal with them in terms of our mathematics.

With this proviso, Galileo's philosophical revolution provides an explanation of the effectiveness of mathematics in dealing with the world. Or, at least, it provides the proximate explanation of its effectiveness. The ultimate explanation is to be found in two capacities human beings have as a result of both biological and cultural evolution: the capacity to conceptualize regularities in the observation data, and the capacity to formulate a variety of mathematical models, some of which may be sufficient approximations to the conceptualizations of regularities in the observation data. Then there is nothing mysterious in the usefulness of mathematics in dealing with the world, it is simply an outcome of Galileo's philosophical revolution and, ultimately, of biological and cultural evolution.[93]

8.14 Modern Science and Truth

What is the goal of science according to the originators of the Scientific Revolution? Being still heavily influenced by Aristotle, they identify it with truth. Thus Galileo states that the goal of science is to know "the true constitution of the universe, for such a constitution exists, and is unique, true, real and could not possibly be otherwise."[94] This might have been written by Aristotle, except that, presumably, by 'the true constitution of the universe', Galileo only means a unique arrangement of parts, with no commitment as to the essential nature of true being-in-itself.

After Galileo, many people have continued to assert that the goal of science is truth. For example, Popper states that "science is the search for truth," and "truth is therefore the aim of science."[95] But, if the goal of science is truth, then science must involve some concept of truth. Which one? It cannot involve Aristotle's concept of truth as intuition of the essence, because modern science is based on Galileo's philosophical revolution, the renunciation to penetrate the essence of natural substances. Popper claims that science must involve the concept of truth as correspondence, because "science aims at truth in the sense of correspondence to the facts or to reality."[96] But this is unjustified, because such concept of truth does not provide a criterion of truth – it does not allow one to decide whether particular statements are true or false.

---

[93] For more on this, see Cellucci (2013a).
[94] Galilei (1968, V, 102).
[95] Popper (1996, 39).
[96] Popper (1972, 59).

As we have seen in Chapter 3, this is the substance of Aristotle's criticism of the concept of truth as correspondence. In addition, it is also the substance of Kant's argument about such a concept of truth. Indeed, Kant states that the concept of truth as correspondence does not provide a criterion of truth because "I can compare the object with my cognition" only "by cognizing it."[97] But, "since the object is outside me, the cognition in me, all I can ever pass judgment on is whether my cognition of the object agrees with my cognition of the object."[98] I cannot pass judgment on whether my cognition of the object agrees with the object itself. With this concept of truth, "it is just as when someone makes a statement before a court" and "appeals to a witness with whom no one is acquainted, but who wants to establish his credibility by maintaining that the one who called him as witness is an honest man."[99]

On the other hand, no other known concept of truth provides a criterion of truth. Thus no known concept of truth allows one to decide whether particular statements are true or false. Therefore, if the goal of science is truth, such goal cannot be generally achieved because it transcends human capacities.

8.15 Concept of Truth and Criterion of Truth

It might be objected that a concept of truth need not provide a criterion of truth. For example, Tarski states that there is no point in complaining that the concept of truth as correspondence – as made mathematically precise by his own definition of truth – does not provide "a workable criterion for deciding whether particular sentences" are "true or false."[100] Such concept of truth "is not designed at all for this purpose."[101] Indeed, a "criterion" of truth "will never be found."[102] We can only find "partial criteria of truth" and "develop procedures that may enable us to ascertain or negate the truth" of "as many sentences as possible."[103] The notion of demonstration "refers just to a procedure of ascertaining the truth of sentences which is used primarily in deductive sciences."[104]

This objection, however, is unjustified. If the goal of science is truth and, on the other hand, a concept of truth does not provide a criterion of truth, we will generally be unable to determine whether a given sentence is true or false. Then, as it has been pointed out in the previous section, the goal of science cannot be generally achieved because it transcends human capacities. But, as Dummett states, "the notion of

---

[97] Kant (1992, 557).
[98] *Ibid.*, 557–558.
[99] *Ibid.*, 558. For more about Kant on truth, see Capozzi (2002), Chapter 12.
[100] Tarski (1969, 69).
[101] *Ibid.*
[102] Tarski (1944, 363–364).
[103] Tarski (1969, 70).
[104] *Ibid.*

truth" must be explained "in terms of our capacity to recognize statements as true, and not in terms of a condition which transcends human capacities."[105]

Appealing to partial criteria of truth, in particular to procedures that may enable us to ascertain or negate the truth of as many sentences as possible, will not do. For example if, as Tarski suggests, we take demonstration to be such a procedure, then, by Gödel's second incompleteness theorem, it will be impossible to demonstrate by any absolutely reliable means that the axioms are true, and hence that so are the theorems proved from them. Thus demonstration is not a viable procedure of ascertaining the truth of sentences. Therefore, there is a basic difficulty in the view that the goal of science is truth.

8.16 Mathematics and Truth

A similar difficulty arises with mathematics. Several mathematicians hold that the goal of mathematics is truth. For example, Byers states that "mathematics is about truth."[106] It "is a way of using the mind with the goal of knowing the truth, that is, of obtaining certainty."[107] For "truth is normally seen as knowledge that is certain."[108] But "the certainty of mathematics is different from the certainty one finds in other fields."[109] It is absolute certainty. Mathematics has this kind of "certainty, this quality of inexorability. This is its essence."[110]

This contrasts with the fact that, as it has been argued in the Introduction, by Gödel's second incompleteness theorem, mathematics cannot be said to be absolutely certain. Then, if the goal of mathematics is truth, such goal cannot be generally achieved and hence will be generally inaccessible. Thus there is a basic difficulty in the view that the goal of mathematics is truth.

Actually, by 'absolute certainty' Byers means "the 'immediate certainty' that accompanies flashes of mathematical insight."[111] He admits that this kind of certainty "is subjective," but claims that this "does not necessarily disqualify it as an object of study."[112] This is fair enough, but it is one thing to say that such subjective feeling of immediate certainty is worth studying, and another thing to say that it shows that mathematics is a way of using the mind with the goal of knowing the truth, that is, of obtaining certainty.

---

[105] Dummett (1993, 75).
[106] Byers (2007, 327).
[107] *Ibid.*
[108] *Ibid.*, 330.
[109] *Ibid.*, 328.
[110] *Ibid.*
[111] *Ibid.*, 334.
[112] *Ibid.*

8.17 Plausibility in Place of Truth

Rather than truth, the goal of science is plausibility. Scientific theories do not deal with the essence of natural substances, but only with some of their phenomenal properties, and deal with them on the basis of plausible hypotheses. Then a scientific theory is not a set of truths but rather a set of plausible hypotheses. Thus the goal of science is plausibility rather than truth.

The idea that the goal of science is truth has its root in Parmenides', Plato's and Aristotle's distinction between appearance and essence, which is the basis of their distinction between belief and knowledge. According to them, belief concerns the appearance, knowledge concerns the essence, and truth is to intuit the essence. Therefore, the concept of truth is crucial for their conceptions of science. But modern science originated from Galileo's renunciation to know the essence of natural substances, it is inherently a system of provisional, rather than final, knowledge which is acquired on the basis of plausible hypotheses, so the concept of truth is irrelevant to it. All that modern science needs is the concept of plausibility. Therefore, the concept of truth, which is proper to Aristotle's science, must be replaced with that of plausibility.

The same applies to mathematics. Hume states that no mathematician places "entire confidence in any truth immediately upon his discovery of it."[113] Every time "he runs over his proofs, his confidence encreases" and "is rais'd to its utmost perfection by the universal assent and applauses of the learned world," but "this gradual encrease of assurance is nothing but the addition of new probabilities."[114] Therefore, "all knowledge resolves itself into probability."[115]

Hume's statement is a perfectly reasonable one if 'probability' is replaced with 'plausibility'. If the goal of mathematics is plausibility, then one need not assume that intuition exists and is infallible. Such assumption is problematic, because there is quite a lot of evidence that intuition, if it exists at all, is highly fallible.

Comparing the concepts of truth and plausibility, two important differences emerge.

1) A criterion of truth does not exist. Even Tarski states that such a criterion will never be found. Conversely, a criterion of plausibility exists. It is given by the plausibility test procedure described in Chapter 4.

2) The concept of truth, at least, truth as correspondence, can be made mathematically precise through Tarski's definition of truth. But it does not allow us to decide whether particular sentences are true or false. Therefore, it does not satisfy Frege's condition on a concept, "that we should be able to decide definitely

---

[113] Hume (1978, 180).
[114] *Ibid.*
[115] *Ibid.*, 181.

8.17 Plausibility in Place of Truth

about every object whether it falls under that concept or not."[116] Conversely, the concept of plausibility cannot be made mathematically precise, since it refers to the judgment of a given community at a given moment. But it allows us to decide whether particular sentences are plausible or not plausible, relative to that judgment. Therefore, it satisfies Frege's condition on a concept.

---

[116]Frege (1959, 87).

Chapter 9
The Quest for a Logic of Discovery

9.1 Logic and the Scientific Revolution

While not involving a break with Aristotle as regards the scientific method, the Scientific Revolution of the seventeenth century gave rise to a considerable debate over the nature of logic. In particular, it led to a quest for a logic of discovery. The most important thinkers of the age took part in such a debate. Some of them considered a logic of discovery to be opposed to Scholastic logic, others to be just an improvement over it.

This chapter discusses Bacon's, Descartes', Leibniz's and Kant's views concerning the nature of logic, with special reference to their attitude towards the character and feasibility of a logic of discovery.

9.2 Bacon's Quest for a Logic of Discovery

According to Bacon, progress in science requires an adequate method. This is not provided by Scholastic logic, where "one flies immediately" to "the most general propositions," the axioms, and then "one derives everything else from them by means of middle terms."[1] On the contrary, the true way "to investigate and discover truth" is that which derives "axioms from the senses and particulars," not flying immediately to them but "ascending continuously and gradually, so that it arrives at the most general axioms last of all; this is the true way, but as yet untried."[2]

A logic of discovery must be based on this true way. Bacon's choice of the title *Novum Organum* for his main work makes quite clear his ambition to replace Aristotle's organon with an entirely new logical instrument, a logic of discovery.

---

[1] Bacon (1961–1986, I, 136).
[2] *Ibid.*

Indeed he states that "in this Organon of ours we are dealing with logic".[3] Unlike Scholastic logic, the new "logic instructs the understanding and trains it" to "dissect the nature truly, and to discover the powers and actions of bodies and their laws limned in matter."[4]

The new logic differs from Scholastic logic "in its end, in its order of demonstration, and in the starting point of its inquiry."[5] The end of the new logic is "the discovery of arts," and "not of inferences from principles."[6] The order of demonstration in the new logic is not determined by syllogism, which is "quite divorced from practice and completely irrelevant to the active part of the sciences."[7] Instead "we consider induction to be the form of demonstration which respects the senses, stays close to nature, fosters results and is almost involved in them itself."[8] Specifically, "the directions for the interpretation of nature comprehend in general terms two parts: the first one is about how to educe and form axioms from experience."[9] This is the concern of induction. The "second part is about how to deduce or derive new experiments from axioms."[10] The starting point of the inquiry in the new logic is set "further back than men have done so far," since "true logic should enter the provinces of the individual sciences," and compel their "supposed principles themselves to give an account as to what extent they are firmly established."[11] Indeed, "none of the things the intellect has accumulated by itself escapes our suspicion, and we do not confirm them without submitting them to a new trial."[12] In particular, we must scrutinize the information of the senses themselves, since "the senses often deceive."[13]

9.3 Bacon's Induction

By induction Bacon does not mean Aristotle's induction by simple enumeration. According to him, "the induction which proceeds by simple enumeration is a childish thing, its conclusions are precarious, and it is exposed to the danger of the contrary instance, it normally bases its judgment on fewer instances than is

---

[3] *Ibid.*, I, 363.
[4] *Ibid.*
[5] *Ibid.*, I, 135.
[6] *Ibid.*
[7] *Ibid.*, I, 136.
[8] *Ibid.*
[9] *Ibid.*, I, 235.
[10] *Ibid.*
[11] *Ibid.*, I, 137.
[12] *Ibid.*, I, 138.
[13] *Ibid.*

9.3 Bacon's Induction

appropriate, and merely on available instances."[14] On the contrary, "the induction which will be useful for the discovery and demonstrations of sciences and arts ought to separate out a nature, by appropriate rejections and exclusions; and then, after as many negatives as are required, conclude on the affirmatives."[15]

To carry out an investigation, "first, for any given nature, one must make a presentation to the intellect of all known instances which meet in the same nature."[16] For example, to investigate the nature of heat, one must list all known instances of the presence of heat, such as the rays of the sun. We call the resulting list "the table of existence and presence."[17]

Secondly, "one must make a presentation to the intellect of instances which are devoid of a given nature."[18] For example, in the case of heat, one must list all instances of absence of heat in related instances, such as the rays of the moon. We call the resulting list "the table of divergence, or of closely related absences."[19]

Thirdly, "one must make a presentation to the intellect of instances in which the nature under investigation exists more or less; this may be done by comparing the increase and decrease in the same subject, or by comparing it in different subjects."[20] For example, in the case of heat, one must list different planets which have different temperatures, and compare the latter. We call this "the table of degrees or table of comparison."[21]

After these three tables have been built, "induction itself has to be put to work."[22] Now, "the first task of true induction" is "the rejection or exclusion of singular natures which are not found in an instance in which the given nature is present, or which are found in an instance where the given nature is missing, or are found to increase in an instance where the given nature decreases, or to decrease when the given nature increases."[23] For example, in the case of heat, one will exclude light and brightness as the causes of heat, because the rays of the moon are light and bright without being hot.

---

[14] *Ibid.*, I, 205.
[15] *Ibid.*
[16] *Ibid.*, I, 236.
[17] *Ibid.*, I, 238.
[18] *Ibid.*
[19] *Ibid.*
[20] *Ibid.*, I, 247–248.
[21] *Ibid.*, I, 248.
[22] *Ibid.*, I, 256.
[23] *Ibid.*, I, 257.

9.4 Limitations of Bacon's Attempt

Bacon says that, "by a due process of exclusion and rejection," true induction will lead "to a necessary conclusion."[24] This contrasts with the fact that a process of exclusion and rejection might either leave open too many possibilities, or none at all. Therefore, it might not lead to a necessary conclusion.

Here is a first weakness of Bacon's method. To remedy this weakness, Bacon makes a plea for giving "the intellect permission" at this point to "try an interpretation of nature in the affirmative; on the basis of both the instances in the tables and the instances occurring elsewhere."[25] That is, Bacon makes a plea for giving the intellect permission to formulate a first hypothesis. He calls "such a first attempt an authorization of the intellect, or a first approach to an interpretation, or a first harvest."[26] In the case of heat, the hypothesis will concern the essence of heat. The hypothesis Bacon formulates is that the essence, or "the quiddity of heat, is motion and nothing else."[27] The consequences of this hypothesis will then be tested against new data, and the hypothesis will be modified if it does not stand the test.

Here, however, is another weakness of Bacon's method. For he does not really derive his hypothesis from an examination of the tables. Rather he borrows it from one of the views on heat which were discussed at the time. Indeed, the view that the quiddity of heat is motion was already in evidence in the thirteenth century. Actually, Bacon's method provides no means to positively formulate hypotheses.

Moreover, Bacon claims that his method is one by which "the mind is from the very outset not left to itself, but constantly guided, so that everything proceeds, as it were, mechanically."[28] That is, his method is a mechanical one. Being mechanical, his method is such as "not to leave much to the acuteness and strength of talents, but more or less to equalise talents and intellects."[29]

Here is a further weakness of Bacon's method. For, if his method is, as he claims, really mechanical, then it is inadequate for discovery in the sciences. Since the laws of Nature contain something more than what is given by mere observation, discovery requires inferences whose conclusion is not uniquely and mechanically determined by their premises. In fact Bacon's mechanical induction is an extremely limited one and in a sense can be reduced to deduction, so it is not really ampliative and hence is generally inadequate for discovery.

From the above weaknesses of Bacon's method it is apparent that Bacon does not really provide a logic of discovery.

---

[24] *Ibid.*, I, 137.
[25] *Ibid.*, I, 261.
[26] *Ibid.*
[27] *Ibid.*, I, 262.
[28] *Ibid.*, I, 152.
[29] *Ibid.*, I, 172.

9.5 Descartes' Quest for a Logic of Discovery

According to Descartes, the new science originated by the Scientific Revolution requires a method for acquiring knowledge. Such a method is not provided by Scholastic logic, whose syllogistic forms "serve rather to explain to someone else the things one already knows" than "to discover them."[30] They are fetters, "the truth often fails to be held fast by these fetters," and "those who make use of them are left behind in bondage."[31]

Since syllogistic forms are of no use in discovering things, it will be better "to reject them altogether."[32] A new logic is necessary that will teach "one to direct his reason to discover the truths of which one is ignorant."[33] It will permit to solve "all problems which can be proposed concerning any sort of quantity, whether continuous or discrete."[34] It will "demonstrate which problems can be solved in this or that way and not in another one, so that almost nothing" will "remain to be discovered."[35]

Traces of this new logic "appear in Pappus and Diophantus."[36] But Greek mathematicians generally presented their results by the synthetic, that is, the axiomatic method, hiding their way to discovery. They did so "not because they were utterly ignorant" of a method of discovery, but rather "because they had such a high regard for it that they wished to keep it to themselves as a secret."[37] Fearing that, if their method of discovery "were divulged," their discoveries "would be depreciated," in order to "gain our admiration" they exposed "some barren truths, skilfully demonstrated deductively, as if they were the fruits of their method," rather than "teaching us the method itself, which would have dispelled our admiration."[38] Thus they concealed their method of discovery "with a sort of pernicious cunning."[39]

Nevertheless, "there have been certain very gifted men who in this century have attempted to revive it."[40] The new logic will be based on this method. We "shall comply with it exactly if we will gradually reduce convoluted and obscure propositions to simpler ones."[41] Thus we will eventually arrive at the simplest of all propositions, "which can be intuited first and per se, independently of any other one."[42]

---

[30] Descartes (1996, VI, 17).
[31] *Ibid.*, X, 406.
[32] *Ibid.*, X, 439–440.
[33] *Ibid.*, IX-2, 13–14.
[34] *Ibid.*, X, 156–157.
[35] *Ibid.*, X, 157.
[36] *Ibid.*, X, 376.
[37] *Ibid.*, VII, 156.
[38] *Ibid.*, X, 376–377.
[39] *Ibid.*, X, 376.
[40] *Ibid.*, X, 377.
[41] *Ibid.*, X, 379.
[42] *Ibid.*, X, 383.

This is analysis. Then, "from the intuition of the simplest of all" propositions, "we will try to ascend through the same steps to a knowledge of all the others."[43] For "all the others can be perceived only by deducing them from those."[44] This is synthesis. Thus the method "is twofold, one by analysis, the other by synthesis."[45]

The simplest of all propositions at which we will eventually arrive in analysis will be the causes of the convoluted and obscure ones which are their effects in synthesis. Thus the new logic will allow us "to see how the effects depend on the causes."[46] In the new logic "the reasons follow one another in such a way that, as the last ones are demonstrated by the first ones, which are their causes, these first ones are conversely demonstrated by the last ones which are their effects."[47] Thus the effects are demonstrated from the causes, and the causes by the same effects.

It might be objected that "it is a logical circle to demonstrate effects from a cause, and then to demonstrate this cause by the same effects."[48] For "the things which are put forward first must be known without any help from the things that follow, and all the remaining ones must be arranged in such a way that they are demonstrated only from the things that precede them."[49] But the circle is only apparent. For the effects are known not through the causes, but rather by experience, since "experience makes the greater part of these effects most certain."[50] There is "nothing circular in demonstrating a cause by several effects which are known independently" by experience "and then demonstrating certain other effects from this cause."[51]

That, for Descartes, the effects are known independently by experience is apparent, for example, from what he says about the magnet. If one wants to investigate the nature of the magnet, "first he diligently collects all the experiences he can have concerning this stone, from which he then tries to deduce what mixture of simple natures is necessary for producing all the effects he has experienced in the magnet."[52] This example shows that Descartes' problem solving procedure is similar to Galileo's and Newton's. One first makes experiences, namely experiments or observations, and tries to deduce some simple natures from them as their causes. This is analysis. Then, by taking such simple natures as causes, one tries to deduce all the effects which have been independently experienced. This is synthesis. Notice

---

[43] *Ibid.*, X, 379.
[44] *Ibid.*, X, 383.
[45] *Ibid.*, VII, 155.
[46] *Ibid.*, IX–1, 121.
[47] *Ibid.*, VI, 76.
[48] *Ibid.*, II, 197–198.
[49] *Ibid.*, VII, 155.
[50] *Ibid.*, VI, 76.
[51] *Ibid.*, II, 198.
[52] *Ibid.*, X, 427.

that Descartes uses 'to deduce' not in the restricted sense of 'to draw as conclusion by syllogism', but in the more general sense of 'to infer'. More on this will be said later in this chapter.

9.6 Descartes' Opposition of Analysis to Synthesis

While Descartes' problem solving procedure involves both analysis and synthesis, for him analysis plays a more basic role than synthesis.

Indeed, Descartes states that "analysis shows the true way by which a thing was discovered methodically."[53] If "the reader will be willing to follow it and give sufficient attention to everything, he will understand the thing thus demonstrated not less perfectly, and will make it not less his own, than if he had himself discovered it."[54] Admittedly, analysis "contains nothing to compel belief in an inattentive or reluctant reader; for if he fails to attend even to the very least thing, the necessity of the conclusion will not appear."[55] Conversely, synthesis "demonstrates the conclusion clearly," through "a long series of definitions, postulates, axioms, theorems and problems, so that, if anyone denies one of the conclusions, it can be shown at once that it is contained in what has gone before."[56] Thus synthesis "extorts the approval of the reader, however reluctant and obstinate."[57] Indeed, in synthesis "there is no difficulty, except in deducing the consequences properly; which" however "can be done even by the less attentive people, provided only that they remember what has gone before."[58] For such reasons, synthesis "may be very properly put after analysis."[59]

Nevertheless, synthesis is "not as satisfying" as analysis, "nor appeases the minds of those who are eager to learn, for it does not show how the thing in question was discovered."[60] Thus things seem to be "discovered more by chance than by skill."[61] Then, by using synthesis, "we get out of the habit of using our reason."[62] Accordingly, in his *Geometry* Descartes does not use synthesis but only analysis. This is motivated by the fact that analysis involves reduction of geometrical

---

[53] *Ibid.*, VII, 155.
[54] *Ibid.*
[55] *Ibid.* VII, 155–156.
[56] *Ibid.*, VII, 156.
[57] *Ibid.*
[58] *Ibid.*, VII, 156–157.
[59] *Ibid.*, VII, 156.
[60] *Ibid.*
[61] *Ibid.* X, 375.
[62] *Ibid.*

problems to simultaneous equations for which solution procedures are known or discoverable, and, being equalities, all equations, are convertible. Then there is no need for synthesis, because synthesis will automatically be the reverse of analysis.

9.7 Descartes' Appeal to Intuition

One would have thought that, after fixing the general features of method, Descartes would have set up rules for a logic of discovery. He, however, does nothing of the kind. This is because he assumes that "all science consists in certain and evident knowledge."[63] In science one must "reject all merely probable cognitions," resolving "to believe only that which is perfectly known, and in respect of which no doubt is possible."[64] Then a logic of discovery should guarantee absolute certainty.

To this end, Descartes bases method on intuition and deduction. He states that, if we review "all the actions of the intellect by means of which we are able to arrive at a knowledge of things without any fear of being deceived," we "recognize only two: intuition and deduction."[65] For "no other ways to certain knowledge of the truth are open to men but evident intuition and necessary deduction."[66] Intuition serves to apprehend the simplest of all propositions, which "are known only by intuition."[67] Deduction serves to apprehend convoluted propositions starting from the simplest ones, since "we can apprehend" convoluted propositions "only by deducing them from those."[68]

Intuition is "the conception of a clear and attentive mind which is so easy and distinct that there can be no room for doubt about what we are understanding," and "proceeds from the light" of nature "alone."[69] What is intuited is "comprehended, obviously, clearly and distinctly" and "all at once, and not in successive moments."[70] It is also comprehended infallibly, because "I would not be able to cast doubt upon anything that the light of nature makes me see to be true."[71] Clearness, distinction, immediateness and infallibility are the basic characters of intuition. On the other hand, deduction is "everything that is necessarily concluded from other things which are known with certainty."[72] We "can deduce" either "the cause from the

---

[63] *Ibid.*, X, 362.
[64] *Ibid.*
[65] *Ibid.*, X, 368.
[66] *Ibid.*, X, 425.
[67] *Ibid.*, X, 370.
[68] *Ibid.*, X, 383.
[69] *Ibid.*, X, 368.
[70] *Ibid.*, X, 407.
[71] *Ibid.*, IX–1, 30.
[72] *Ibid.*, X, 369.

9.7 Descartes' Appeal to Intuition

effect, or the effect from the cause."[73] From this it is clear that, as it has been mentioned above, Descartes uses 'to deduce' not in the restricted sense of 'to draw as conclusion by syllogism', but in the more general sense of 'to infer'.

This use of the terms 'intuition' and 'deduction' differs from the usual one but, according to Descartes, it corresponds to "what the individual words signify in Latin."[74] For 'intuition' comes from the Latin *intuitus*, which derives from *intueri*, that means 'to look inside attentively by means of the intellect'. So, by 'intuition', Descartes means 'intellectual intuition', that is, the immediate apprehension of intellectual objects. On the other hand, 'deduction' comes from the Latin *deductio*, which derives from *deducere*, that means 'to lead from'. So, by 'deduction', Descartes means 'the leading from one proposition to another'.

While distinct from intuition, deduction is based on it. For, according to Descartes, a deduction consists of a number of simple inferences or simple deductions, and "a simple deduction of one thing from another is performed by intuition."[75] Thus "the self-evidence and certainty of intuition is required not only for apprehending single propositions, but also for any train of reasoning whatsoever."[76] Therefore, deduction is based on intuition.

Not only deduction is based on intuition, but, in a sense, reduces to it. For, when a deduction is very long, in order to apprehend it, "we survey the links one after the other, and remember that each link from first to last is attached to its neighbour."[77] Thus "we know that the last link in a long chain is connected to the first" by memory, "even if we do not contemplate all the intermediate links on which the connection depends by a single intuition of the eyes."[78] Memory, however, only allows us to remember a few links at once, while a deduction can be so long that, when we arrive at the conclusion, "we do not readily remember the whole route that has led us to it."[79] Therefore, we "must aid the weakness of memory by a continuous motion of thinking."[80] That is, we must run through all the links of the deduction "several times in a continuous motion of the imagination, simultaneously intuiting single things and passing on to the others," until we learn "to pass from the first to the last so quickly" that, "leaving hardly any part to memory," we seem "to intuit the whole thing at once."[81] In this sense, deduction reduces to intuition. Therefore, Descartes states: "I have only the light of nature," namely, intuition, "as my rule of truth."[82]

---

[73] *Ibid.*, X, 428.
[74] *Ibid.*, X, 369.
[75] *Ibid.*, X, 407.
[76] *Ibid.*, X, 369.
[77] *Ibid.*, X, 370.
[78] *Ibid.*, X, 369–370.
[79] *Ibid.*, X, 387.
[80] *Ibid.*
[81] *Ibid.*, X, 388.
[82] *Ibid.*, II, 597.

This explains why Descartes does not set up rules for a logic of discovery. He ultimately bases method on intuition, for which there are no rules. Therefore, he says that "method cannot go so far as to teach us how to perform the actual operations of intuition and deduction, because these are the simplest and most primitive of all."[83] Thus, "if our intellect were not already able to perform them, it would not comprehend any of the rules of the method."[84]

That Descartes ultimately bases method on intuition depends on his assumption that a logic of discovery should guarantee absolute certainty. This assumption is motivated by his view that all science consists in certain and evident knowledge. To show that this kind of knowledge is possible, one must dispel doubts about our cognitive faculties, which could be misled by "some evil genius, supremely powerful and cunning" who "has devoted all his efforts to deceiving me."[85]

To dispel the evil genius doubt, Descartes argues that, if some evil genius is deceiving me, then "I also undoubtedly exist," so "this proposition, 'I am, I exist', whenever it is put forward by me, or conceived in my mind, is necessarily true."[86] Therefore "this knowledge, 'I think, therefore I am', is the first and most certain of all."[87] Now, this knowledge is based on intuition, because "when someone says, 'I think, therefore I am, or I exist', he does not deduce existence from thought by means of a syllogism, but recognizes it as something known per se by a simple intuition of the mind."[88] The cognition in question "is not the work of your reasoning," it is something that "your mind sees, feels and handles," and shows "the capacity of our soul for receiving intuitive knowledge."[89]

Thus Descartes dispels the evil genius doubt, and hence the doubts about our cognitive faculties and the possibility of certain and evident knowledge, by appealing to intuition. Intuition appears to him to be the ultimate source of certainty. Therefore, in order to achieve absolute certainty, he ultimately bases method on it.

9.8 Limitations of Descartes' Attempt

That Descartes ultimately bases method on intuition prevents him from developing a logic of discovery. Descartes himself says that his method proceeds "with no logic, no rule, no pattern of argument, only by the light" of nature and "good sense."[90] He cannot "teach the method which everyone must follow to direct his reason

---

[83] *Ibid.*, X, 372.
[84] *Ibid.*
[85] *Ibid.*, VII, 22.
[86] *Ibid.*, VII, 25.
[87] *Ibid.*, VIII–1, 7.
[88] *Ibid.*, VII, 140.
[89] *Ibid.*, V, 138.
[90] *Ibid.*, X, 521.

9.8 Limitations of Descartes' Attempt

correctly."[91] He can only describe how he himself has directed his own reason, but this description is to be taken "only as a history or, if you prefer, a fable."[92] His choice of the title, *Discourse on the method*, is intended to stress that he does not want "to teach the method but only to speak about it."[93] His method "consists much more in practice than in theory."[94]

Thus Descartes virtually renounces to develop a logic of discovery. In fact he merely gives some very general precepts which are of no help in specific cases. His failure to develop a logic of discovery is due to the fact that he ultimately bases method on intuition. As it has been already pointed out, this depends on his assumption that a logic of discovery should guarantee absolute certainty. This assumption is incompatible with a logic of discovery. The latter must necessarily be based on non-deductive rules, because only such rules are ampliative. Now, rules of this kind will not generally lead from true premises to a true conclusion, and hence will not guarantee absolute certainty.

The assumption that a logic of discovery should guarantee absolute certainty is also faced with another problem. While Descartes thinks he can dispel the evil genius doubt by appealing to intuition, there is no guarantee that an evil genius, supremely powerful and cunning, who has devoted all his efforts to deceiving him, would not mislead his intuition. So, basing method on intuition, Descartes exposes himself to the deceptions of the evil genius.

To avoid them, Descartes must appeal to the existence of a truthful God. Indeed he states that, "until I know that God exists, and is a truthful God who will curb that evil genius, I can and should always continue to fear that" the evil genius "is tricking me and is forcing what is false on me under the guise of truth."[95] Only if "I have gained a thorough understanding that God exists" I can know that "he will necessarily prevent" the evil "genius imposing on me concerning things which I clearly and distinctly understand."[96] Thus "I plainly see that the certainty and truth of every science depends uniquely on the knowledge of the true God."[97] In particular, even if an atheist mathematician can be "clearly aware that the three angles of a triangle are equal to two right angles," he "cannot be certain that he is not being deceived on matters that seem to him to be very evident," and "will never be free of this doubt until he acknowledges that God exists."[98]

Thus Descartes ultimately relies on the assumption that there exists a truthful God. Since this assumption is unproven, this jeopardizes his attempt to develop a new logic, capable of coping with the needs of the new science.

---

[91] *Ibid.*, VI, 4.
[92] *Ibid.*
[93] *Ibid.*, I, 349.
[94] *Ibid.*
[95] *Ibid.*, VII, 455.
[96] *Ibid.*, VII, 455–456.
[97] *Ibid.*, VII, 71.
[98] *Ibid.*, VII, 141.

9.9 Leibniz's Attempt to Keep a Foot in Two Shoes

While Descartes rejects Scholastic logic and sets himself the task of developing a new logic, Leibniz tries to keep a foot in two shoes. On the one hand, he does not reject Scholastic logic, and only wants to extend it so as to make it capable of dealing with inferences it is unable to account for. On the other hand, he wants logic to be a logic of discovery.

Indeed, on the one hand, Leibniz states that he finds "much that is good and useful in the logic until now."[99] Those "who despise it do not understand it."[100] In fact, "if syllogisms are rejected, all reasons are rejected: for all reasons are always syllogisms."[101] Undeniably, there are valid inferences that "cannot be rigorously demonstrated by any syllogism," such as, "If Jesus Christ is God, then the mother of Jesus Christ is the mother of God."[102] But this limitation can be easily overcome extending Scholastic logic so as to obtain "a texture of reasoning which will represent any argument."[103]

On the other hand, Leibniz states that logic must be "the art of using the intellect, not only to judge what is proposed, but also to discover what is hidden."[104] Such an art "should be sought by all means and valued highly, and even considered as the key to all arts and sciences."[105] Therefore, logic should be not only an art of justification but also an art of discovery.

Descartes failed to provide such an art. His rules were "nearly like the precept of I do not know which chemist: Take what you should and do what you should, and you will get what you want."[106]

The art of discovery must be based on the axiomatic method rather than on the analytic method, because "certain things are discovered more successfully by means of synthesis."[107] Analysis "is more necessary in practice to solve problems that are given to us; but whoever is capable of more theoretical pursuits" will "practice synthesis," since "thus he will always progress pleasantly and easily."[108] Those "who think that the analytic description consists in revealing the origin of a discovery, the synthetic description in keeping such origin concealed, are in error."[109]

---

[99] Leibniz (1965, VII, 516).
[100] *Ibid.*, VII, 481.
[101] Leibniz (1948, 22).
[102] Leibniz (1965, V, 461).
[103] *Ibid.*, V, 463.
[104] *Ibid.*, VII, 516.
[105] *Ibid.*
[106] *Ibid.*, IV, 329.
[107] Leibniz (1971, VII, 206).
[108] Leibniz (1965, VII, 297).
[109] *Ibid.*

The axiomatic method is not only a method of justification but also a method of discovery. For the starting point of any inquiry is to make an inventory of the truths already known, to examine them and to arrange them in a certain order. Then "one can survey and measure them, and with the help of the order that is produced in them, one can all the more readily discover something new."[110] Now, the axiomatic method is essential to make an inventory of the truths already known, to examine them and to arrange them in a certain order. By means of it, "propositions are arranged according to their simplest demonstrations, in the manner in which they arise from each other."[111] One starts from "the simplest and most general notions and truths which first present themselves to the intellect, and then descends to special and composite notions."[112] Thus one may discover new truths.

9.10 Leibniz's Universal Language and Calculus of Reasoning

According to Leibniz, however, in order to be an effective method of discovery, the axiomatic method must be converted into a formal axiomatic method. This involves setting up a formal language capable of expressing all thoughts, and a system of formal deductive rules capable of representing all human reasoning.

Leibniz calls the formal language capable of expressing all thoughts 'universal language' [*lingua universalis*], or 'rational language' [*lingua rationalis*], or 'universal characteristic' [*characteristica universalis*]. Such language will be based on the fact that "all human ideas can be resolved into a few ones as primitive ideas."[113] The latter are ideas "which are conceived per se, and from whose combination all other our ideas arise."[114] They are like "a sort of alphabet of human thought."[115] All other ideas will "arise from a combination of the primitive ones, and the more composite" ideas will arise "from the combination of the less composite ones."[116] One will then be able to assign characters to the primitive ideas and form new characters for all other ideas by means of combinations of such characters, which will "have among themselves the relation that the ideas have among themselves."[117] The resulting characters will form the universal language, which will provide "a mechanical

---

[110] *Ibid.*, VII, 523.
[111] *Ibid.*, VII, 180.
[112] Leibniz (1988, 159).
[113] Leibniz (1965, VII, 205).
[114] Leibniz (1988, 430).
[115] Leibniz (1965, VII, 292).
[116] *Ibid.*, VII, 293.
[117] Leibniz (1966, 80).

thread of meditation, as it were, with whose aid we can most easily resolve any idea whatever into those of which it is composed."[118]

On the other hand, Leibniz calls the system of formal deductive rules, capable of representing all human reasoning, 'calculus of reasoning' [*calculus ratiocinator*]. Such a calculus is necessary because, to "avoid being left wandering in a labyrinth," the "mind must be guided by some (as it were) sensible thread."[119] The mind is "unable to embrace distinctly many things at the same time," only by means of a calculus of reasoning it will be able to "do without imagination, using signs in place of things."[120] The calculus of reasoning will be "like a sort of general algebra" that will "give the means to perform reasoning by calculation."[121] With it, human beings will "possess a new kind of organon" which will "enhance the capacities of the mind to a far greater extent than optical instruments strengthen the eyes," and will be "as much superior to microscopes and telescopes, as reason is finer than eyesight."[122] Therefore, the calculus of reasoning will truly deserve "the name of organon of the mind."[123]

Leibniz makes the following claims for the projected universal language and calculus of reasoning.

1) *They are feasible.* Indeed, "a few selected persons might be able to do the whole thing in five years."[124]

2) *They will permit to avoid the problem Descartes had with intuition.* For they will only involve "a dull thought, as in algebra, where one thinks of symbols in place of things."[125] Thus they will relieve the imagination. By means of them, the mind will be "exempted from distinctly thinking of things themselves, and yet everything comes out correctly."[126] For "letters or signs relieve memory, and there is no evil genius who might deceive us tampering with them."[127]

3) *They will permit to avoid the problem Descartes had with deduction.* For a deduction will consist of purely mechanical steps, which will not require us to stop and think about the meaning of propositions, and yet will force our assent. Thus the calculus of reasoning will provide a "mechanical direction of the mind which even the most stupid person could recognize."[128] By means of the calculus of reasoning,

---

[118] Leibniz (1971, IV, 461).
[119] *Ibid.*, VII, 17.
[120] *Ibid.*
[121] Leibniz (1965, VII, 26).
[122] *Ibid.*, VII, 187.
[123] *Ibid.*, VII, 32.
[124] Leibniz (1971, VII, 187).
[125] *Ibid.*, VII, 555.
[126] Leibniz (1988, 256).
[127] Leibniz (1966, 58).
[128] Leibniz (1965, VII, 14).

"everything that can be obtained from the data by a great and highly trained wit in virtue of reasoning," will be "established with an unmistakable method."[129]

4) *They will give a mechanical method of discovery*. The calculus of reasoning will provide a universal decision procedure. By means of this procedure, human beings will "always be able to know whether it is possible to decide the question on the basis of the knowledge which is already given to them."[130] This will be useful even when the question is decided negatively, because "it is important at least to know that what is sought cannot be found by the means available to us."[131] By providing a universal decision procedure, the calculus of reasoning will dispose of the problem of discovery altogether, since it will reduce discovery to a purely mechanical business. This is necessary, because "a method of discovery is perfect if we can foresee from the start, and even demonstrate before dealing with the thing, that following this method we shall attain our goal."[132] Only a universal decision procedure can provide a method of discovery with this feature. Such a procedure will make theoretically irrelevant the question of "the history of our discoveries," that is, the question of how they are actually discovered, "which is different in different men."[133] Indeed, the application of the mechanical method will require no intelligence, since it will offer "a thread of meditation," namely, "a sensible and mechanical direction for the mind, as it were, that even the most stupid will acknowledge."[134]

Since the calculus of reasoning will reduce discovery to a purely mechanical business, Leibniz's programme of setting up a calculus of reasoning is really a programme of mechanizing discovery.

9.11 Limitation of Leibniz's Attempt

Leibniz's claims for the projected universal language and calculus of reasoning, however, are unjustified.

1) The claim that they are feasible is unjustified for reasons that will be clear in Chapter 12.

2) The claim that they will permit to avoid the problem Descartes had with intuition is unjustified, because Leibniz ultimately bases the calculus of reasoning on intuition. Indeed, he states that, "of a distinct, primitive notion there is no other than an intuitive cognition."[135] The same can be said about "primitive truths, which

---

[129] *Ibid.*, VII, 202.
[130] *Ibid.*, VII, 25.
[131] *Ibid.*
[132] Couturat (1961, 161).
[133] Leibniz (1965, V, 392).
[134] *Ibid.*, VII, 14.
[135] *Ibid.*, IV, 423.

are known by intuition."[136] Then, like Descartes, Leibniz is faced with the problem that an evil genius might mislead our intuition.

3) The claim that they will permit to avoid the problem Descartes had with deduction is unjustified, because deductions in the calculus of reasoning will consist of characters which are sensible objects, and hence depend on perception. Now perception can be subject to the deceptions of the evil genius who, of course, can deceive not only our memory but also our senses. The evil genius can deceive us even in the preliminary step of translating thoughts into expressions, and deductions into formal deductions. Then, like Descartes, Leibniz is faced with the problem that an evil genius might deceive us tampering with our perceptions.

4) The claim that they will give a mechanical method of discovery is unjustified for reasons that will be clear in Chapter 12.

To overcome the problem that an evil genius might mislead our intuition and deceive us tampering with our perceptions, Leibniz appeals to the action of God upon us. Indeed he states that "we have in our soul the ideas of all things only by virtue of the continual action of God upon us."[137] And the ideas in our soul are "the ground of our certitude in regard to universal and eternal truth."[138] Thus Leibniz's attempt to set up a universal language and a calculus of reasoning ultimately depends on the assumption of the existence of God. Since this assumption is unproven, this jeopardizes his attempt. The latter is an impossible compromise between Scholastic logic and a logic of discovery, because Scholastic logic is a deductive logic, while a logic of discovery is necessarily non-deductive.

Scholz says that, with Leibniz, "a 'new life' began for Aristotelian logic," more precisely, for Scholastic logic, "whose most beautiful manifestation nowadays is modern exact logic."[139] This is a double-edged praise. For it means, on the one hand, that Leibniz did not introduce any new logic paradigm but simply tried to revitalize and expand Scholastic logic, and, on the other hand, that mathematical logic is nowadays the most beautiful manifestation of Scholastic logic.

9.12 Kant's View of Logic as a Canon

Leibniz's denial that Descartes developed a logic of discovery has a counterpart in Kant's denial that Leibniz developed such a logic.

Kant states that, after "Leibniz had advertised the merits of his discovery" of a logic of discovery, "men of learning all complained" that his discovery could not be found in his writings, and hence must have "been buried along with the great man

---

[136] *Ibid.*, V, 434.
[137] *Ibid.*, IV, 453.
[138] *Ibid.*, V, 373.
[139] Scholz (1961, 50).

9.12 Kant's View of Logic as a Canon

himself."[140] One may say about Leibniz what is said about the alchemists, that they "eventually came to suppose that there would no longer be anything which was not in their power, provided only they put their hands to it."[141] They "talked of those things as achieved which they inferred might, indeed, 'must' happen provided only that they addressed their minds to the realisation of these things."[142] Both Leibniz's and the alchemists' claims are unwarranted.

But, if Leibniz did not develop a logic of discovery, this is not because of his limitations, but rather because of the nature of logic itself. Logic is "the science of the necessary laws of the understanding and reason in general."[143] Such laws are necessary, "because without them we would not think at all."[144] Thus "logic is a canon for understanding and reason in general," where a canon is "the sum of the total *a priori* principles of the correct use of certain cognitive faculties in general."[145]

Logic, however, "is a canon but not an organon."[146] An organon "is a directive as to how a certain cognition is to be brought about."[147] But logic is only a "universal propaedeutic to all use of the understanding and of reason in general," so "it may not go into the sciences and anticipate their matter."[148] It "teaches us nothing at all about the content of cognition, but only the formal conditions of agreement with the understanding."[149] Therefore, using logic "as a tool (organon) for an expansion and extension of its information, or at least the pretension of so doing, comes down to nothing but idle chatter."[150]

Some people "believe that logic is a heuristic (art of discovery), that is, an organon of new knowledge, with which one makes new discoveries," but "logic cannot be a heuristic, because it abstracts from any content of knowledge."[151] If logic were a heuristic, it would serve for expanding our cognition, whereas it can serve "merely for passing judgment and for correcting our cognition, but not for expanding it."[152] Therefore, logic is "not a universal art of discovery, to be sure, and not an organon of truth" with "whose help hidden truths can be discovered."[153]

---

[140] Kant (2003, 8).
[141] *Ibid.*
[142] *Ibid.*, 8–9.
[143] Kant (1992, 528).
[144] *Ibid.*
[145] Kant (1997a, 672, B 824).
[146] Kant (2005, 32).
[147] Kant (1992, 528).
[148] *Ibid.*, 529.
[149] Kant (1997a, 199, B 86).
[150] *Ibid.*
[151] Kant (1998, II, 279).
[152] Kant (1992, 529).
[153] *Ibid.*, 534. This does not mean that Kant did not think of a methodology of discovery, although not as a part of logic as a canon but as a part of the doctrine of method; see Capozzi (2006).

9.13 Kant's Opposition of Artificial Logic to Natural Logic

Since, for Kant, logic is a canon, it "must contain nothing but laws *a priori*, which are necessary," so it cannot be concerned with "how thinking does take place and how it is under various subjective obstacles and conditions."[154] Therefore, the so-called 'natural logic' cannot be logic.

It is "customary to divide logic" into "'natural' or 'popular' logic and 'artificial' or 'scientific' logic ('*logica naturalis*', '*log. scholastica s. artificialis*')."[155] Natural logic consists of the "rules for how we think."[156] These are the rules of the uses of the understanding "'*in concreto*', that is, under the contingent conditions of the subject, which can hinder or promote this use, and which can be given only empirically."[157] On the other hand, artificial logic consists of the "rules for how we ought to think."[158]

This division, however, "is inadmissible. For natural logic" is "not really logic but an anthropological science that has only empirical principles, in that it deals with the rules of the natural use of the understanding and of reason."[159] Only "artificial or scientific logic deserves this name" as "a science of the necessary and universal rules of thought, which can and must be cognized *a priori*, independently of the natural use of the understanding and of reason."[160] Then "basically there is only an artificial logic, for basically there is no natural logic."[161]

Since there is no natural logic, logic "draws nothing from psychology," which "therefore has no influence at all on the canon of the understanding."[162] Psychology "is the doctrine of the phenomena of human mind, or it deals with the general rules of the actual behaviour of human mind."[163] Thus, "if we were to take" logical "principles from psychology," we "would merely see how thinking does take place."[164] But in logic "we do not want to know how the understanding is and does think and how it has previously proceeded in thought, but rather how it ought to proceed in thought. Logic is to teach us the correct use of the understanding."[165] Then logic is not descriptive but normative, like pure morals, "which contains merely the necessary moral laws of a free will in general," without bringing

---

[154] Kant (1992, 529).
[155] *Ibid.*, 532.
[156] *Ibid.*, 252.
[157] Kant (1997a, 195, B 78–79).
[158] Kant (1992, 252).
[159] *Ibid.*, 532.
[160] *Ibid.*
[161] *Ibid.*, 434.
[162] Kant (1997a, 195, B 78).
[163] Kant (1900–, XXIV, 611).
[164] Kant (1992, 529).
[165] *Ibid.*

in "empirical and psychological principles."¹⁶⁶ To bring psychological principles "into logic is just as absurd as to derive morals from life."¹⁶⁷ Therefore, "every psychological observation must be left out of logic."¹⁶⁸

9.14 Kant's Divisions of Logic

When Kant says that logic is a canon, by 'logic' he means 'pure logic', namely, a logic which "has to do with strictly *a priori* principles."¹⁶⁹ Such a logic abstracts "from all empirical conditions under which our understanding is exercised," thus "from the influence of the senses, from the play of imagination, the laws of memory, the power of habit, inclination, etc."¹⁷⁰

Pure logic must be distinguished from applied logic, which "considers the understanding insofar as it is mixed with the other powers of the mind."¹⁷¹ Contrary to pure logic, applied logic "is directed to the rules of the use of the understanding under the subjective empirical conditions that psychology teaches us."¹⁷² Namely, under the contingent conditions of the subject which can be given only empirically. Only pure logic is properly logic, since it alone "is properly science, although brief and dry."¹⁷³ Applied logic is merely "a psychology in which we consider how things customarily go on in our thought, not how they ought to go on."¹⁷⁴ Therefore, applied logic "should not properly be called logic. It is a psychology."¹⁷⁵

Some people claim that "technique, or the way of building a science, ought to be expounded in applied logic."¹⁷⁶ But this is wrong because, if one does so, then one "begins to build before one has materials, and one gives form, but content is lacking. Technique must be expounded within each science."¹⁷⁷ Therefore, applied logic is "neither a canon of the understanding in general nor an organon of particular sciences."¹⁷⁸

---

[166] Kant (1997a, 195, B 79).
[167] Kant (1992, 529).
[168] Kant (1900–, XXIV, 694).
[169] Kant (1997a, 194, B 77).
[170] *Ibid.*
[171] Kant (1992, 532–533).
[172] Kant (1997a, 194, B 77).
[173] *Ibid.*, 195, B 78.
[174] Kant (1992, 533).
[175] *Ibid.*
[176] *Ibid.*
[177] *Ibid.*
[178] Kant (1997a, 195, B 77–78).

9.15 Kant on the Nature of the Scientific Method

That, for Kant, logic cannot be an organon, does not mean that for him logic has nothing to do with the scientific method. According to Kant, the scientific method merely arranges cognition already given according to the relation of ground and consequence, so that each consequence "is related to grounds" and "the form of this science shines forth distinctly."[179] Therefore, the scientific method cannot serve to acquire new cognition. It can only be used "when a science has already been discovered and brought to a certain level."[180] Thus it can only serve when "the science is already long complete, and requires only the final touch for its improvement and perfection."[181]

The scientific method "is divided into synthetic and analytic method."[182] The synthetic method proceeds "from grounds to consequences," the analytic method "from consequences to grounds."[183] With the "synthetic method one begins with principles of reason and proceeds toward things that rest on principles," with the "analytic method one proceeds toward principles from things that rest on principles."[184] Thus "synthesis proceeds '*descendendo*'," while "analysis proceeds '*ascendendo*'."[185]

The analytic method is usually called "the method of invention."[186] But, like the synthetic method, it is merely a manner of organizing cognition, which "is more appropriate for the end of popularity."[187] Namely, it is more appropriate for adjusting "a science to the power of comprehension and the taste of the common world."[188] For it proceeds "from common cognition to the determination of its supreme principle."[189]

Conversely, the synthetic or axiomatic method is more appropriate "for the end of scientific and systematic preparation of cognition."[190] Even "if I have thought the thing analytically, the synthetic method is what makes it a system."[191] For "a system is a unity in cognition that can be derived from a *principium*."[192] The synthetic

---

[179] Kant (1992, 418).
[180] Kant (1900–, XXIV, 610).
[181] Kant (1997a, 194, B 76).
[182] Kant (1992, 418).
[183] *Ibid.*, 511.
[184] *Ibid.*, 418.
[185] *Ibid.*, 85.
[186] *Ibid.* 639.
[187] *Ibid.*
[188] *Ibid.*, 278.
[189] Kant (1999a, 47).
[190] Kant (1992, 639).
[191] *Ibid.*, 419.
[192] *Ibid.*, 327.

method "seeks to bring the greatest manifold of cognition" to "the smallest number of principles (universal conditions), and thereby to effect the highest unity of that manifold."[193]

The method of mathematics is "the synthetic method, which proceeds from the first grounds of a cognition and stops at the last consequences."[194] It "differs from all others in that it presents through intuition."[195]

9.16 Kant's Closed World View of Science

According to Kant, by making a manifold of cognition a system, the synthetic or axiomatic method constitutes a science, since "a science is a whole of cognition as a system."[196] If, in addition, "the connection of cognition in this system is an interconnection of grounds and consequence," a science is a "rational science."[197] Thus a rational science is a science which starts from principles, because "rational knowledge is *cognitio ex principiis*."[198]

In a rational science, principles must be *a priori* because, if "the grounds or principles themselves are still in the end merely empirical," then "the whole of cognition does not deserve the name of a science in the strict sense."[199] A "rational doctrine of nature" deserves "the name of a natural science only in the case the fundamental natural laws therein are cognized *a priori*."[200]

Since a rational science is a science which starts from principles, to develop a rational science is to deduce conclusions from principles. A science is all contained in its principles. They are "like a seed [*Keim*], all of whose parts still lie very involuted and are hardly recognizable even under microscopic observation."[201] The development of a science is like the growth of a plant from a seed. It is also like the growth of an animal body from an embryo. For a science "can grow internally (*per intussusceptionem*)" by growth from within, "not externally (*per appositionem*)" by external addition, so it is "like an animal body, whose growth does not add a limb but rather makes each limb stronger and fitter."[202]

This means that, for Kant, a science is a closed system, namely, a system based on principles that are given once for all and cannot change, and whose development

---

[193] Kant (1997a, 390, B 361).
[194] Kant (1992, 515).
[195] *Ibid.*, 511.
[196] *Ibid.*, 630.
[197] Kant (2002, 184).
[198] Kant (1997a, 693, B 864).
[199] Kant (2002, 184).
[200] *Ibid.*
[201] Kant (1997a, 692, B 862).
[202] *Ibid.*, 691, B 861.

9.17 Kant on the Solvability of All Mathematical Problems

Against the claim that Kant's view of science is a closed world view, it might be objected that mathematics is a counterexample to it. For Kant believes that answers can be given to all mathematical questions. Answers can be given to them not because they can be deduced from given principles, but rather because our "intuitive grasp" does give "the promise of answers to all our questions about the grasped object or domain."[203] There is more to a mathematical object or domain than can be described by any given principles, and the extra content can be captured by our intuitive grasp. Therefore, mathematics is not a closed system.

This objection, however, is unjustified, because Kant claims that answers can be given not only to all mathematical questions, but also to all questions of transcendental philosophy and pure morals. Indeed, Kant states that "there are sciences whose nature entails that every question occurring in them must absolutely be answerable from what one knows."[204] It must absolutely be answerable in the sense that, either a solution to the question can be given, or "at least the impossibility of such a solution can be known with certainty."[205] The sciences in questions include "transcendental philosophy" and two other "pure sciences of reason," namely, "pure mathematics and pure morals."[206] Each of them "can demand and expect clear and certain solutions to all the questions belonging within it (*quaestiones domesticae*), even if up to this time they still have not been found."[207]

Now, if answers can be given not only to all mathematical questions, but also to all questions of transcendental philosophy and pure morals, this cannot be due to our intuitive grasp of their objects. For if "mathematical knowledge is intuitive," conversely "philosophical knowledge is only discursive."[208] Therefore, we do not have any intuitive grasp of the objects of transcendental philosophy and pure morals. According to Kant, transcendental philosophy, pure mathematics and pure morals can demand and expect clear and certain solutions to all the questions belonging within them, not because we have an intuitive grasp of their objects, but rather because they are pure sciences of reason. Indeed, Kant states that "there is no

---

[203] Posy (2000, 214).
[204] Kant (1997a, 503, B 504).
[205] *Ibid.*, 505, B 508.
[206] *Ibid.*
[207] *Ibid.*
[208] Kant (1998, II, 292).

question at all dealing with an object given by pure reason that is insoluble by this very same human reason."[209]

Other is the case of natural science, since "natural appearances are objects that are given to us independently of our concepts, to which, therefore, the key lies not in us and in our pure thinking, but outside us, and for this reason in many cases it is not found."[210] Therefore, "in the explanation of the appearances of nature," and hence in natural science, "much must remain uncertain and many questions insoluble."[211]

Moreover, as we have seen above, for Kant every question occurring in mathematics, transcendental philosophy or pure morals must absolutely be answerable 'from what one knows'. Since the sciences in question are rational sciences, thus knowledge from principles, 'what one knows' are principles or conclusions already deduced from them. Then what Kant actually says when he states that every question occurring in these sciences must absolutely be answerable from what one knows, is that it must absolutely be answerable from principles or conclusions already deduced from them. Therefore, the sciences in question, including mathematics, are closed systems.

9.18 Kant on Induction and Analogy

As we have seen, Kant claims that logic cannot be a heuristic. Nevertheless, he eventually accepts that logic must include induction and analogy, which are basic means for a logic of discovery.

For a long time, Kant does not assign induction and analogy any definite logical status. He admits that they are useful to produce empirical generalizations, even indispensable, since "there is no other way that we can determine our universal judgments through experience."[212] Therefore, "we cannot at all dispense with" induction and "analogy."[213] But he holds that they "do not belong to logic," even if "really they have no other place."[214] However, in the later years of his teaching of logic, Kant assigns induction and analogy to logic, even to pure logic, since he places them in his 'Doctrine of Elements', among the "inferences of the power of judgment."[215]

Kant assigns induction and analogy to pure logic because they are regular inferences, being subject to strict principles.

---

[209] Kant (1997a, 504, B 505).
[210] Ibid., 505, B 508.
[211] Ibid., 503–504, B 504–505.
[212] Kant (1992, 408).
[213] Kant (1997b, 279).
[214] Kant (1992, 408).
[215] Ibid., 627.

Indeed, induction is subject to "the principle of universalization: What belongs to many things of a genus belongs to the remaining ones too."[216] Here the emphasis is on the fact that the things on which an inductive inference is carried out belong to the same genus, so they are homogeneous with respect to the genus. Therefore, one may say that "what belongs to many things of a genus belongs to the remaining ones too."[217] For example, from the fact that "Mercury, Venus, Earth, Mars, Jupiter, Saturn, Uranus are dark planets," we infer "through induction that the remaining planets, which perhaps can still be discovered, might also be dark."[218] For the remaining planets will be homogeneous to those of which we already have experience.

On the other hand, analogy is subject to "the principle of specification: Things of one genus, which we know to agree in much, also agree in what remains, with which we are familiar in some things of this genus but we do not perceive in others."[219] Once again, the emphasis is on the fact that things with respect to which an analogical inference is carried out are homogeneous with respect to the genus.

Homogeneity with respect to the genus justifies considering induction and analogy to be regular inferences. Undeniably, induction and analogy "give only empirical certainty," so "we must make use of them with caution and care."[220] But judgments obtained by means of them, however provisional, are "quite necessary, indeed, indispensable, for the use of the understanding," since "they serve to guide the understanding in its inquiries and to provide various means thereto."[221] Moreover, although induction and analogy give only empirical certainty, this is certainty of a kind: the propositions obtained by induction or analogy are valid for the time being.

Of course, induction and analogy are different from syllogism, because they proceed "from the particular to the universal in order to draw from experience (empirically) universal – hence not *a priori* – judgments."[222] Moreover, "no logician has yet developed analogy and induction properly. This field still lies open."[223] Nevertheless, it is a part of logic which deserves to be developed.[224]

---

[216] *Ibid.*, 626.
[217] *Ibid.*
[218] *Ibid.*, 508.
[219] *Ibid.*, 625.
[220] *Ibid.*
[221] *Ibid.*, 578.
[222] *Ibid.*, 626.
[223] *Ibid.*, 504.
[224] On the development of Kant's views concerning induction and analogy, see Capozzi (2011).

9.19 The Twilight of the Quest for a Logic of Discovery

Although, in the later years of his teaching, Kant assigns induction and analogy to logic, even to pure logic, he does not develop a logic of discovery. This task is apparently taken over by Mill, because he states that he intends to provide a logic of "the process itself of advancing from known truth to unknown."[225] Thus a "logic of the pursuit of truth."[226]

By 'logic of the pursuit of truth', however, Mill only means a logic which "furnishes the principles and rules of the estimation of evidence."[227] According to him, "logic neither observes, nor invents, nor discovers; but judges."[228] Mill only wants "to bring together or frame a set of rules or canons for testing the sufficiency of any given evidence to prove any given proposition."[229] Thus his purpose is to provide a set of rules or canons for a logic of justification rather than for a logic of discovery.

The second half of the nineteenth century marks the swan song of the view that logic must provide means to acquire knowledge. With the rise of mathematical logic such view is abandoned and logic makes a deductivist turn, akin to that of the Stoics in the ancient world, considered in Chapter 7. Frege is the key factor in this turn.

---

[225] Mill (1963–1986, VII, 12).
[226] Ibid., VII, 182.
[227] Ibid., VII, 10, footnote b.
[228] Ibid., VII, 10.
[229] Ibid., VII, 12.

Chapter 10
Frege's Approach to Logic

10.1 Frege's Restriction of Logic to the Study of Deduction

While, throughout the seventeenth and eighteenth century, the quest for a logic of discovery is a live question, the situation essentially changes with Frege. Although strongly influenced by Kant, Frege excludes induction and analogy from the domain of logic. For him, there cannot be a logic of discovery but only a logic of justification based on deduction, and the goal of logic is the study of deduction.

Indeed, Frege states that "the question of how we arrive at the content of a judgment, should be kept distinct from the other question, Whence do we derive the justification for its assertion?"[1] Logic cannot be concerned with the former, the question of discovery, because it is a psychological question, "not a logical one."[2] It can be concerned only with the latter, the question of justification. For one cannot "count the grasping of the thought as knowledge, but only the recognition of its truth."[3]

Now, in order to give a justification of a judgment, we must determine "upon what primitive laws it is based."[4] The primitive laws must be true, because a justification can be given only by "those grounds of judgment which are truths."[5] After determining the primitive laws upon which the judgment is based and ascertaining that they are true, we must deduce the judgment from them. This will provide the required justification, because to deduce is "to make a judgment because

---

[1] Frege (1959, 3).
[2] Frege (1979, 146).
[3] *Ibid.*, 267.
[4] Frege (1984, 235).
[5] Frege (1979, 3).

we are cognisant of other truths as providing a justification for it."[6] There are "laws governing this kind of justification," the laws of deduction, and "the goal of logic" is to study these laws, since they are the "laws of valid inference."[7]

10.2 Frege's Assumptions Concerning the Nature of Logic

That there cannot be a logic of discovery but only be a logic of justification based on deduction, and that the goal of logic is the study of deduction, must be seen on the background of Frege's general views about the nature of logic, which can be summarized as follows.

1) Logic "is concerned with the laws of truth."[8] More precisely, it is concerned with "the most general laws of truth."[9] For "we do not demand" of logic "that it should go into what is peculiar to each branch of knowledge and its subject-matter," but rather that it should say "what holds with the utmost generality for all thinking, whatever its subject-matter."[10]

2) In particular, logic is concerned with the laws of deduction, because to deduce is to "recognize a truth on the basis of other previously recognized truths according to a logical law."[11]

3) Logic is objective and independent of us, because "what is true is something objective and independent of the judging subject."[12] It is "true independently of whether anyone takes it to be true."[13] It is true even independently of whether anyone thinks them, so it is "independent of our thinking as such."[14]

4) Being objective and independent of us, logic has nothing to do with psychology. Indeed, it is necessary "always to separate the psychological from the logical, the subjective from the objective."[15]

5) Since logic has nothing to do with psychology, it cannot be concerned with discovery. The processes of discovery are subjective and psychological, because they are inner acts of a mind, and an inner act "of one person's mind is not that

---

[6] Ibid.
[7] Ibid.
[8] Ibid., 149.
[9] Ibid., 128.
[10] Ibid.
[11] Frege (1980, 17).
[12] Frege (1964, 15).
[13] Frege (1984, 363).
[14] Frege (1979, 133).
[15] Frege (1959, x).

of another's" and "we are unable to unite the inner states experienced by different people in one consciousness and so compare them."[16]

6) Logic is "a normative science."[17] It is not concerned "with the question of how men think, but with the question of how they must think."[18] The laws of logic are "prescriptions to which our judgments must conform."[19]

10.3 Frege's Ideal of Atomizing Deduction

The goal Frege assigns to logic, the study of deduction, is faced with the problem that, "if we try to list all the laws governing inference which occur when arguments are conducted in the usual way, we find an almost unsurveyable multitude which apparently has no precise limits," so "it is easy for something to intrude which is not logical in nature."[20] At closer scrutiny, however, it appears that "these inferences are composed of simpler ones."[21] Then, in order to avoid that something which is not logical in nature might intrude, we "must split" a deduction "into the logically simple steps of which it is composed."[22] This is "essential if our trains of thought are to be relied on," because the simpler the modes of inference, "the more perfect a mastery can we have of them."[23]

This is Frege's ideal of atomizing deduction. Its purpose is not to make deduction efficient, obtaining the conclusion in the speediest way, because "such a resolution of composite modes of inference into their simple components has as a necessary consequence the lengthening of proofs."[24] Its purpose is rather to "attain to the necessary certainty."[25] Atomizing deduction is indispensable to this purpose because, only when deduction is based on logically simple steps, we can "have accurate knowledge of the grounds upon which each individual theorem is based."[26] In this way "no presupposition can pass unnoticed."[27]

---

[16]Frege (1979, 3–4).
[17]*Ibid.*, 128.
[18]*Ibid.*, 149.
[19]*Ibid.*, 145.
[20]Frege (1984, 235).
[21]*Ibid.*
[22]Frege (1964, 29).
[23]Frege (1979, 39).
[24]Frege (1984, 235).
[25]Frege (1959, ix).
[26]Frege (1964, 3).
[27]*Ibid.*, 29.

10.4 Frege's View of Mathematical Practice and Mathematics

Frege's restriction of logic to the study of deduction is instrumental to his view of mathematical practice and mathematics, according to which the method of mathematics is the axiomatic method.

According to Frege, what we do in mathematics is that we form chains of deductive "inferences starting from known theorems, axioms, postulates or definitions and terminating with the theorem in question."[28] In "any step forward we take" from the known theorems, axioms, postulates or definitions to the theorem, we are "aware of the logical" deductive "inferences involved."[29] Then, if any error will arise, we will be able to state precisely where "the error lies: in the basic laws, in the definitions, in the rules, or in the application of the rules at a definite point."[30] Now, "since they are intended as premises," the axioms "have to be true."[31] Therefore, mathematics is "a system of truths that are connected with one another by" deductive "inference."[32]

That, for Frege, mathematics is a system of truths has two important consequences for mathematical practice. First, "if Euclidean geometry is true, then non-Euclidean geometry is false," and "whoever acknowledges Euclidean geometry to be true must reject non-Euclidean geometry as false."[33] Now, unless we want to consider Euclid's axioms as false, "we can put Euclid's axioms forward as propositions that are neither false nor doubtful. In that case non-Euclidean geometry will have to be counted amongst the pseudo-sciences" and "made to line-up as a museum piece alongside alchemy and astrology."[34] Secondly, "what is to serve as the premise of an inference must be true."[35] Therefore, if from the premises '$2 < 1$' and 'If something is smaller than 1, then it is greater than 2' we derived the conclusion '$2 > 2$', "this would not be an inference because the truth of the premises is lacking."[36] This means that "mere hypotheses cannot be used as premises."[37] Thus Frege would not allow for anything like Gentzen's natural deduction rules, which will be considered in Chapter 11.

---

[28] Frege (1984, 204).
[29] *Ibid.*, 205.
[30] Frege (1964, 3).
[31] Frege (1979, 244).
[32] Frege (1984, 205).
[33] Frege (1979, 169).
[34] *Ibid.*
[35] Frege (1980, 79).
[36] *Ibid.*, 17.
[37] *Ibid.*, 182.

10.5 Frege's Closed World View of Mathematics

Frege's view of mathematics is a closed world view, similar to that of Kant. According to Frege, a mathematical theory is a closed system, that is, a system based on primitive truths that are given once for all and cannot change, whose development consists entirely in deducing conclusions from them. Therefore, the whole of a mathematical theory is contained in its primitive truths. Frege expresses this using Kant's metaphor of seed. He states that "the whole of mathematics is contained" in the "primitive truths as in a seed [*Keim*]."[38] It is not contained in them "as beams are contained in a house," but rather "as plants are contained in their seeds."[39] The "essence of mathematics has to be defined by this seed of truths."[40] Once we have established it, "our only concern is to generate the whole of mathematics from this seed."[41] Namely, to deduce mathematics from the primitive truths.

This, for Frege, is the normal mode of development of mathematics. The latter then consists in deducing conclusions from the primitive truths of some closed system. If the system turns out to be inadequate, it must be abandoned and replaced with a new one. For a closed system is incapable of evolving, it is either accepted as a whole or rejected as a whole. Indeed, Frege states that "what is once standing must remain, or else the whole system must be dismantled in order that a new one may be constructed."[42] In "mathematics we must always strive after a system that is complete in itself," so if the system "that has been acknowledged until now proves inadequate, it must be demolished and replaced by a new structure."[43]

Frege acknowledges that the closed world view is in conflict with the real development of mathematics, because "in history we have development; a system is static," therefore "we must always distinguish between history and system."[44] But he claims that "the progress of the history of the sciences runs counter to the demands of logic."[45] The "striving after" a closed "system is a justified one," because "order can only be created by" a closed "system."[46] Science "only comes to fruition in" a closed "system. We shall never be able to do without" closed "systems. Only through" a closed "system can we achieve complete clarity and order."[47]

---

[38] Frege (1979, 204–205). Frege's translation quoted in the text uses 'kernel' in place of 'seed'. The translation has been modified to emphasize that Frege uses the same term as Kant, that is, 'Keim', which in Kant's translation quoted in Chapter 9 is rendered as 'seed'.

[39] Frege (1959, 101).

[40] Frege (1979, 205).

[41] *Ibid*.

[42] *Ibid*., 242.

[43] *Ibid*., 279.

[44] *Ibid*., 241–242.

[45] *Ibid*., 241.

[46] *Ibid*., 205.

[47] *Ibid*., 242

Thus Frege's attitude towards mathematics is static. He does not consider mathematics as a living and growing enterprise, but rather as a closed system of knowledge. This depends on his belief that only through a closed system it is possible to achieve that complete clarity and order which is essential for the absolute certainty of mathematics. According to Frege, to get absolute certainty, "in mathematics we must never rest content with the fact that something is obvious or that we are convinced of something, but we must strive to obtain a clear insight into the network of inferences that support our conviction."[48] This means that "we must know what its premises are" and must "be aware of the logical inferences involved."[49] Only "in this way can" a closed "system be constructed."[50] Moreover, the logical inferences must be as simple as possible, for only in this way can we achieve complete clarity in deduction.

10.6 Frege's Analysis of Assertions

Since Frege's restriction of logic to the study of deduction is instrumental to his view of mathematical practice and mathematics, he cannot be satisfied with Aristotle's logic. For the latter is incapable of dealing with certain deductive inferences that are necessary in mathematics.

In order to deal with them, Frege replaces Aristotle's analysis of assertions and deduction with a different one, based on "what is called a function in mathematics."[51] By 'function', however, Frege does not mean the current notion of function as an arbitrary correspondence between two sets satisfying a uniqueness condition. He rather means the eighteenth century notion of function as a mathematical expression containing variables. Indeed, he says that "we must go back to the time when higher Analysis was discovered," when "a function of x was taken to be a mathematical expression containing x, a formula containing the letter x."[52] For example, the mathematical expression x^2 is a function of x.

Actually, Frege extends the eighteenth century notion of function by including expressions such as "$x^2 = 1$, where x takes the place of the argument as before."[53] He also includes ordinary language expressions, such as 'x is the twin of Pollux'. The value of these functions "is a truth-value."[54] For example, the value of the function 'x is the twin of Pollux' is the truth-value 'true' when x is assigned the value 'Castor', the truth-value 'false' when x is assigned, say, the value 'Helen'.

---

[48] *Ibid.*, 205.
[49] *Ibid.*
[50] *Ibid.*
[51] Frege (1984, 137).
[52] *Ibid.*, 138.
[53] *Ibid.*, 144.
[54] *Ibid.*

A function of two or more arguments "whose value is always a truth-value" is called "a relation."[55] Then $x^2 = y$ and 'x is the twin of y' are relations.

Thus, contrary to Aristotle's analysis of assertions, Frege's analysis can deal with singular assertions and relations. By using connectives and quantifiers, it can also account for inferences involving compound assertions, such as: "If from the circumstance that" a man "is alive his breathing can be inferred, then from the circumstance that he does not breathe his death can be inferred."[56]

10.7 Shortcomings of Frege's Concept of Function

The eighteenth century notion of function that Frege uses has two serious shortcomings.

1) It may lead to incoherences, because the same function can be represented by different expressions.

2) It is restrictive, because it accounts only for the so-called 'analytic functions', a subclass of the class of continuous functions.

Nevertheless, these shortcomings do not convince Frege to adopt the current notion of function. For him, the latter "has no sense, unless it is completed by mentioning the law of correlation."[57] This law must be expressed by "an equation," such as $y = x^2 + 3x$, "in which the letter y stands on the left side whereas on the right there appears a mathematical expression consisting of numerals, mathematical signs, and the letter x."[58] This means that, for Frege, the current notion of function has no sense unless it is reduced to the eighteenth century notion of function.

Frege acknowledges that the eighteenth century notion of function is subject to the above two shortcomings, but he believes that 1) can be avoided by identifying a function with the denotation of an expression, thus not with an expression but with "what is designated thereby."[59] On the other hand, 2) can "be avoided by introducing new signs into the symbolic language of arithmetic."[60]

Frege's solution, however, is inadequate. Identifying a function with the denotation of an expression does not overcome 1), because this does not really make the definition of a function independent of its representation, and leaves indefinite how an expression determines a function. On the other hand, introducing new signs does not overcome 2), because not all functions can be defined in this way.

---

[55] Frege (1979, 244).
[56] Frege (1967, 44).
[57] Frege (1984, 289).
[58] Ibid., 289–290.
[59] Frege (1964, 33).
[60] Frege (1984, 290).

10.8 Frege's Analysis of Deduction

Frege's analysis of deduction agrees with his view that the method of mathematics is the axiomatic method. Indeed, his analysis of deduction is given in terms of that method, and consists of nine logical axioms and a single logical deductive rule.[61]

The nine logical axioms are:

(A1) $A \rightarrow (B \rightarrow A)$
(A2) $(A \rightarrow (B \rightarrow C)) \rightarrow ((A \rightarrow B) \rightarrow (A \rightarrow C))$
(A3) $(A \rightarrow (B \rightarrow C)) \rightarrow (B \rightarrow (A \rightarrow C))$
(A4) $(A \rightarrow B) \rightarrow (\neg B \rightarrow \neg A)$
(A5) $\neg \neg A \rightarrow A$
(A6) $A \rightarrow \neg \neg A$
(A7) $x = y \rightarrow (F(x) \rightarrow F(y))$
(A8) $x = x$
(A9) $\forall x F(x) \rightarrow F(y)$.

The only logical deductive rule is *modus ponens*:

(MP) $\dfrac{A \quad A \rightarrow B}{B}$.

A 'deduction', or 'deductive derivation', or simply 'derivation', of a formula A from a set of formulas Γ, is a finite sequence of formulas each of which is either a member of Γ, or a logical axiom, or is obtained from two earlier formulas in the sequence by means of (MP), and whose last formula is A. A deduction of A from $\Gamma = \emptyset$ is called a 'demonstration of A'.

10.9 Limitations of Frege's Analysis of Assertions and Deduction

Frege's analysis of assertions and deduction has several limitations. Here are the main ones.

1) Frege's analysis of assertions describes things in terms of a set of homogeneous individuals, that is, individuals of the same kind; and in terms of a set of homogeneous relations between the individuals in such a set, that is, relations of the same kind. Therefore, his analysis of assertions can only give a low level unstructured representation of things. This is inadequate when one has to represent complex things. The latter may require a structured representation in which data are organized in more complex knowledge structures.

---

[61] See Frege (1967).

2) Frege's analysis of deduction makes deductions unnecessarily complicated. For example, a demonstration of $A \to A$ will run as follows:

(1)	$A \to ((A \to A) \to A)$	A1
(2)	$(A \to ((A \to A) \to A)) \to ((A \to (A \to A)) \to (A \to A))$	A2
(3)	$A \to (A \to A)$	A1
(4)	$(A \to (A \to A)) \to (A \to A)$	1,2 MP
(5)	$A \to A$	3,4 MP

It is difficult to understand why one would need anything as complicated as (2) to demonstrate such a simple logical law as $A \to A$.

3) Frege's analysis of deduction does not provide adequate rules for $\forall$. This depends on the fact that Frege assumes letters $x, y, z, \ldots$ to express generality, so that $F(y)$ has the same meaning as $\forall x F(x)$. Thus, for him, rules such as

$$\frac{F(y)}{\forall x F(x)} \quad \text{or} \quad \frac{G \to F(y)}{G \to \forall x F(x)} \quad \text{where } y \text{ does not occur in } G,$$

are implicitly assumed. This is a source of confusion, and Frege himself sometimes makes inferences which are not obviously legitimate.

4) Frege's analysis of deduction does not really achieve his ideal of atomizing deduction. Indeed (A4)–(A6), which are axioms for $\neg$, contain not only $\neg$ but also $\to$; (A7), which is an axiom for $=$, contains not only $=$ but also $\to$; (A9), which is an axiom for $\forall$, contains not only $\forall$ but also $\to$. Thus Frege's analysis of deduction does not separate the roles of $\neg, =, \forall$ in deduction from the role of $\to$.

10.10 Frege's Logicist Programme

In the Introduction it has been stated that, according to Frege, mathematical logic can actually give a secure foundation for mathematics because, by means of it, every gap in the chain of deductions is eliminated, so we can say with certainty upon what primitive truths a demonstration depends. Then intuition will permit us to acknowledge that the primitive truths are actually truths.

As regards intuition, however, Frege makes a "difference between geometry and arithmetic in the way in which their fundamental principles are grounded."[62] According to Frege, "the elements of all geometrical constructions are intuitions, and geometry refers to intuition as the source of its axioms."[63] The axioms of

---

[62] Frege (1984, 56).
[63] Ibid., 56–57.

geometry "derive their validity from the nature of our intuitive faculty."[64] They are "propositions that are true but are not proved because our knowledge of them flows from a source very different from the logical source, a source which might be called spatial intuition."[65] Namely, Kant's pure sensible intuition. By 'source' of knowledge Frege means "what justifies the recognition of truth."[66] Then, by stating that our knowledge of the axioms of geometry flows from spatial intuition, Frege asserts that Kant's pure sensible intuition permits us to acknowledge that the axioms of geometry are true.

Unlike the axioms of geometry, "the basic propositions on which arithmetic is based cannot apply merely to a limited area whose peculiarities they express in the way in which the axioms of geometry express the peculiarities of what is spatial," they "must extend to everything that can be thought."[67] For "we can count just about everything that can be an object of thought: the ideal as well as the real, concepts as well as objects."[68] Therefore, "the object of arithmetic does not have an intuitive character," and the basic propositions on which arithmetic is based "cannot stem from intuition either. And how could intuition guarantee propositions which hold for all such heterogeneous quantities, some species of which may still be unknown to us?"[69] Rather, "we are justified in ascribing such extremely general propositions to logic."[70] Then "Kant was wrong about arithmetic."[71] Kant's pure sensible intuition does not permit us to acknowledge that the basic propositions on which arithmetic is based are true.

Nevertheless, another kind of intuition permits us to acknowledge that they are true: intellectual intuition. Indeed, as we will see in the next section, according to Frege, intellectual intuition permits us to acknowledge that the primitive laws of logic are true. Then, if we are justified in ascribing the basic propositions on which arithmetic is based to logic, intellectual intuition will permit us to acknowledge that such propositions are true.

Of course, this depends on the claim that we can ascribe the basic propositions on which arithmetic is based to logic, and hence that arithmetic is merely "a further

---

[64] *Ibid.*, 1.
[65] Frege (1980, 37).
[66] Frege (1979, 267).
[67] Frege (1984, 112).
[68] *Ibid.*
[69] *Ibid.*, 57.
[70] *Ibid.*, 112.
[71] Frege (1959, 102). Kant had already dealt with Schultz's "contention that there are no synthetic a priori cognitions in arithmetic, only analytic ones" (Kant 1999b, 283). According to Kant, a sum such as $3 + 4$ is "the setting of a problem," that is, "conjoin 3 and 4 in one number" (*Ibid.*, 284). The solution of the problem, namely the number 7, must not have arisen "by means of an analysis. Rather, it must have arisen by means of a construction, that is, synthetically. This construction presents the concept of the composition of two numbers in an a priori intuition, namely a single counting up" (*Ibid.*).

development of logic."[72] In order to establish this claim, one must show that "a more rigorous establishment of arithmetical laws reduces them to purely logical laws and to such laws alone."[73] That is, one must show that all arithmetical laws are derivable from the primitive laws of logic. This is Frege's logicist programme.[74] Frege's ideal of atomizing deduction is instrumental to this programme, because only if demonstrations "are split up into logically simple steps can we be persuaded that the root of the matter is logic alone."[75]

If such a programme could be carried out, this would give a secure foundation for arithmetic, because it would show that "arithmetic is merely a more highly developed logic."[76] That is, it would show that logic is the foundation of arithmetic.

10.11 Frege's Foundation of Logic

Frege's emphasis on logic as the foundation for arithmetic raises the question: What is, according to him, the foundation of logic itself? Frege is somewhat elusive on this point, therefore it has been said that, for Frege, "the primitive laws of logic cannot be justified."[77] And that "the father of modern logic had no opinions on the ground of logical truth."[78] But it is not so. According to Frege, the primitive laws of logic can be justified, and the ground of logical truth is intuition, intellectual intuition. The latter is then the foundation of logic.

Indeed, Frege states that "the question why and with what right we acknowledge a law of logic to be true, logic can answer only by reducing it to another law of logic."[79] But, with regard to the primitive laws of logic, "logic can give no answer."[80] An answer can be given only "if we step away from logic."[81] Frege seeks such an answer in intuition.

Admittedly, Frege does not say in so many words that he seeks an answer in intuition. The reason for his reticence is that he fears that intuition, intellectual intuition, might be confused with Kant's pure sensible intuition, which does not permit us to acknowledge that the basic proposition on which arithmetic is based are true. For this reason, Frege avoids speaking of intuition altogether. Rather, he

---

[72] Frege (1984, 145).

[73] *Ibid.*

[74] Notice that Frege does not limit his programme to the arithmetic of the numbers which are used for counting purposes, namely natural numbers. He extends it to the arithmetic of the numbers which are used for measuring magnitudes, namely real numbers.

[75] Frege (1964, 3).

[76] *Ibid.*

[77] Weiner (1990, 72).

[78] Coffa (1991, 124).

[79] Frege (1964, 15).

[80] *Ibid.*

[81] *Ibid.*

speaks "of grasping a thought, of conceiving, laying hold of, seizing, understanding, of *capere, percipere, comprehendere, intelligere*."[82] Later on, he speaks of "the logical source of knowledge."[83] But, as Dummett points out, although "Frege does not use the word 'intuition', but speaks only of the logical source of knowledge," he "evidently means to refer to some faculty by which we are assured of certain truths, and so the use of the word 'intuition' seems appropriate."[84]

10.12 Frege's Logicist Programme and Leibniz's Logicist View

In some respects, Frege's logicist programme is akin to Leibniz's logicist view of mathematics. Indeed, Leibniz states that the laws of arithmetic are propositions "whose truth depends on axioms which I am accustomed to call identical, as for instance, that two contradictories cannot exist, that a thing at one and the same time is what it is, for instance, that it is as big as it is, or equal to itself, that it is similar to itself, etc."[85] That is, the laws of arithmetic are propositions whose truth depends on the primitive laws of logic. As to the primitive laws of logic, Leibniz states that they are known by – intellectual – intuition, because the propositions "which I call by the general name 'identicals'" are among "the primitive truths that we know by intuition."[86]

In another respect, however, Frege's logicist programme diverges from Leibniz's view of mathematics. Leibniz makes no difference between geometry and arithmetic with respect to intuition. According to him, arithmetic and geometry have the same source, intellectual intuition, because the primitive laws of logic suffice "for demonstrating all arithmetic and all geometry, that is, all mathematical principles."[87] On the other hand, as we have seen, Frege's logicist programme makes a difference between geometry and arithmetic. This is somewhat incongruous because, since Descartes, we know that Euclidean geometry can be mapped into the theory of real numbers and hence into arithmetic, the arithmetic of real numbers. Then, if all arithmetical laws are derivable from the primitive laws of logic, all geometrical truths too will be derivable from them.

This limitation of Frege's logicist programme is addressed by Russell, who follows Leibniz in saying that "all pure mathematics – arithmetic, analysis, geometry – is built up by combinations of the primitive ideas of logic, and its propositions are

---

[82]Frege (1979, 137).
[83]*Ibid.*, 267.
[84]Dummett (1981, 663).
[85]Leibniz (1965, I, 369).
[86]*Ibid.*, V, 343.
[87]*Ibid.*, VII, 355.

deduced from the general axioms of logic."[88] Showing this is Russell's logicist programme.

10.13 Frege's Primitive Laws of Logic

To carry out his logicist programme, Frege must indicate the primitive laws of logic from which all arithmetical laws are to be derived. His crucial primitive law of logic is the following:

$$\{x : F(x)\} = \{x : G(x)\} \leftrightarrow \forall x(F(x) \leftrightarrow G(x)).$$

This law – which is known as the Basic Law (V) because it occurs fifth in Frege's list of primitive laws of logic – states that, for any functions F, G, the extension of F is identical to the extension of G if and only if, for every x, $F(x)$ if and only if $G(x)$.

For the reason explained above, Frege does not say that intellectual intuition permits us to acknowledge that the Basic Law (V) is true, he only says that the Basic Law (V) is "what people have in mind, for example, where they speak of the extensions of concepts."[89] For $\forall x(F(x) \leftrightarrow G(x))$ "expresses the same sense" as $\{x : F(x)\} = \{x : G(x)\}$, although "in a different way."[90] But Frege is so confident in intellectual intuition that he states that "it is prima facie improbable" that his logic "could be erected on a base that was uncertain or defective."[91] And he adds: "As a refutation in this I can only recognize someone's actually demonstrating either that a better, more durable edifice can be erected" on another base, "or else that my principles lead to manifestly false conclusions. But no one will be able to do that."[92]

10.14 Failure of Frege's Foundation of Mathematics

This, however, is just what Russell was able to do, deducing a contradiction from the Basic Law (V). The contradiction – Russell's paradox – can be deduced as follows. Let $x \in y$ be an abbreviation for $\exists G(G(x) \land y = \{z : G(z)\})$. First we show:

(1) $\forall x(x \in \{y : F(y)\} \leftrightarrow F(x))$.

Assume $x \in \{y : F(y)\}$. Then, by the definition of $\in$, we have $\exists G(G(x) \land \{y : F(y)\} = \{y : G(y)\})$. From the latter, by the Basic Law (V), we obtain $\exists G(G(x) \land \forall y(F(y)$

---

[88] Russell (1994, 76).
[89] Frege (1964, 4).
[90] Frege (1984, 143).
[91] Frege (1964, 25).
[92] Ibid.

$\leftrightarrow G(y)))$. Let G be such that $G(x) \wedge \forall y(F(y) \leftrightarrow G(y))$. Then $G(x)$ and $F(x) \leftrightarrow G(x)$, hence $F(x)$.

Conversely, assume $F(x)$. Now $\{y : F(y)\} = \{y : F(y)\}$. Then $F(x) \wedge \{y : F(y)\} = \{y : F(y)\}$, hence $\exists G(G(x) \wedge \{y : F(y)\} = \{y : G(y)\})$. From the latter, by the definition of $\in$, we obtain $x \in \{y : F(y)\}$.

From (1) it follows $\exists z \forall x (x \in z \leftrightarrow F(x))$, from which we obtain the 'unrestricted comprehension principle':

(2) $\forall F \exists z \forall x (x \in z \leftrightarrow F(x))$.

Now, let $F(x)$ be $x \notin x$. By the unrestricted comprehension principle (2) we have $\exists z \forall x (x \in z \leftrightarrow x \notin x)$. Let z be such that $\forall x (x \in z \leftrightarrow x \notin x)$. Then in particular $z \in z \leftrightarrow z \notin z$. Contradiction. This is Russell's paradox.

Russell's paradox shows that Frege's intuition behind the Basic Law (V) was wrong. In fact, the Basic Law (V) contrasts with the concept of set involved in mathematical practice, according to which a set is an arbitrary subcollection of a given collection. Indeed, in mathematical practice one considers "sets of integers, or of rational numbers (i.e., of pairs of integers), or of real numbers (i.e., of sets of rational numbers), or of functions of real numbers (i.e., of sets of pairs of real numbers), etc."[93] The unrestricted comprehension principle (2) is not true of this concept of set, because it allows one to form sets z as extensions of arbitrary functions $F(x)$.

10.15 Failure of Frege's Foundation of Logic

In addition to showing that intuition is an inadequate foundation for arithmetic, Russell's paradox also shows that intuition is an inadequate foundation for logic. This follows from the fact that Frege considers the Basic Law (V) to be a primitive law of logic.

After the discovery of Russell's paradox, Frege tries to modify his formulation of the primitive laws of logic, without success. He acknowledges: "My efforts to become clear about what is meant by number have resulted in failure."[94] Thus, "I have had to abandon the view that arithmetic is a branch of logic and that, therefore, in arithmetic everything must be proven in purely logical terms."[95] Then, in the final year of his life, Frege proposes a new foundation. Arithmetic "does not have to flow from purely logical principles, as I originally assumed. There is the further possibility that it has a geometrical source."[96] Arithmetic flows from the geometrical source of knowledge, spatial intuition, that is, Kant's pure sensible intuition. Thus

---

[93] Gödel (1986–2002, II, 258).

[94] Frege (1979, 263).

[95] Frege (1969, 298). Oddly, this passage is missing from Frege (1979), English translation of Frege (1969).

[96] Frege (1979, 277).

10.15 Failure of Frege's Foundation of Logic

"arithmetic and geometry, and hence the whole of mathematics flows from one and the same source of knowledge – that is the geometrical one. This is thus elevated to the status of the true source of mathematical knowledge."[97] In this way, Frege cancels his previous distinction between geometry and arithmetic with respect to intuition. In addition to abandoning the view that arithmetic is a branch of logic, he abandons "the view that arithmetic does not need to appeal to intuition either in its proofs, understanding by intuition the geometrical source of knowledge."[98] Earlier, he had claimed that the basis of arithmetic "cannot be spatial intuition, because thereby the discipline would be reduced to geometry."[99] Now he states that geometry and arithmetic "have developed on the same basis," spatial intuition, "so that mathematics in its entirety is really geometry" and hence presents itself "as completely homogenous."[100]

Thus Frege denies his previous statement that Kant was wrong about arithmetic. The neo-Kantian philosopher Hönigswald welcomes this change: "The spirit that informs your paper and the methodical results you reach correspond exactly to our endeavours and wishes."[101] Actually, by assuming that spatial intuition is the source of all mathematical knowledge, Frege even goes beyond Kant because, according to Kant, arithmetic involves not only spatial intuition but also temporal intuition. Admittedly, Frege acknowledges that "besides the spatial, the temporal must also be recognized. A source of knowledge corresponds to this too."[102] But, in his new foundation for mathematics, he assigns no role to the temporal source of knowledge – temporal intuition. The notions he takes "as basic are 'line' and 'point'," and the relation which he takes as basic is: "The point A is 'symmetric' with the point B with respect to the line l."[103] He shows that every ratio between intervals in the plane is represented by a unique point in the plane. A complex number can then be identified with this point. Thus, in his new foundation for arithmetic, "right at the outset" Frege goes "straight to the final goal, the general complex numbers."[104] Starting from the latter, Frege thinks of introducing all other kinds of numbers.

Frege's new foundation is too briefly outlined to be properly assessed. Nevertheless, something can be said about logic. Frege states that, in the new foundation, "the logical source of knowledge" is also "involved at every turn."[105] He, however, indicates no new foundation for logic. Since intuition is an inadequate foundation for it, this means that he leaves logic without foundation.

---

[97] Ibid., 279.
[98] Ibid., 278.
[99] Frege (1984, 113).
[100] Frege (1979, 277).
[101] Hönigswald (1980, 53).
[102] Frege (1979, 274).
[103] Ibid., 280.
[104] Ibid., 279.
[105] Ibid., 280.

Chapter 11
Gentzen's Approach to Logic

11.1 Formal Languages

In Chapter 10 it has been argued that Frege's analysis of deduction does not achieve his ideal of atomizing deduction. A better approximation to this ideal is provided by Gentzen's analysis of deduction. In order to describe it, we need to fix some terminology and notation about first-order languages.

First-order languages consist of symbols, terms and formulas.

'Symbols' include infinitely many individual variables $x, y, z, \ldots$; any number of individual constants; for each $n > 0$, any number of n-ary function constants; for each $n > 0$, any number of n-ary relation constants; logical constants, consisting of connectives $\neg, \wedge, \vee, \rightarrow$ and quantifiers $\forall, \exists$; auxiliary symbols (parentheses and comma).

Individual constants, function constants and relation constants are called 'non-logical constants'.

'Terms' are individual variable; individual constants; all expressions of the form $f(t_1, \ldots, t_n)$, where f is an n-ary function constant and $t_1, \ldots, t_n$ are terms.

'Atomic formulas' are all expressions of the form $P(t_1, \ldots, t_n)$, where P is an n-ary relation constant and $t_1, \ldots, t_n$ are terms.

'Formulas' are atomic formulas; all expressions of one of the forms $\neg A, (A \wedge B), (A \vee B), (A \rightarrow B)$ where A and B are formulas; all expressions of one of the forms $\forall xA, \exists xA$ where x is an individual variable and A is a formula.

An occurrence of an individual variable x in a formula A is said to be 'bound' or 'free' according as the occurrence is or is not in the scope of a quantifier that is immediately followed by x.

For any formula A and term t, A_t^x denotes the result of replacing all free occurrences of x in A by t. The term t might contain some occurrence of an individual variable which becomes bound in A_t^x. When this is not the case, x is said to be 'replaceable' by t in A. In what follows, when the notation A_t^x is used, x is supposed to be replaceable by t in A.

The 'subformulas' of a formula A are A itself; B and C if $(B \wedge C)$, $(B \vee C)$, or $(B \rightarrow C)$ is a subformula of A; B_t^x if $\forall x B$ or $\exists x B$ is a subformula of A.

11.2 Gentzen's Analysis of Deduction

Gentzen's analysis of deduction is in terms of his natural deduction rules.[1] Each such rule introduces or eliminates a logical constant in the conclusion. There are introduction (I) and elimination (E) rules for each logical constant. The introduction and elimination rules for $\wedge, \vee, \rightarrow, \forall, \exists$ are the following.[2] The rules for $\neg$ will be discussed in a later section.

$$(\wedge I) \frac{A \quad B}{A \wedge B} \qquad (\wedge E) \frac{A \wedge B}{A}, \frac{A \wedge B}{B}$$

$$(\vee I) \frac{A}{A \vee B}, \frac{B}{A \vee B} \qquad (\vee E) \frac{A \vee B \quad \overset{[A]}{C} \quad \overset{[B]}{C}}{C}$$

$$(\rightarrow I) \frac{\overset{[A]}{B}}{A \rightarrow B} \qquad (\rightarrow E) \frac{A \rightarrow B \quad A}{B}$$

$$(\forall I) \frac{A_y^x}{\forall x A} \qquad (\forall E) \frac{\forall x A}{A_t^x}$$

$$(\exists E) \frac{A_t^x}{\exists x A} \qquad (\exists E) \frac{\exists x A \quad \overset{[A_y^x]}{C}}{C}.$$

A 'deduction', or 'deductive derivation', or simply 'derivation', is a tree of formulas. The topmost formulas can be arbitrary and are called 'assumptions'. The other formulas are obtained from those immediately above them by means of an introduction or an elimination rule. The downmost formula is called the 'conclusion' of the deduction.

An 'introduction' is an application of an introduction rule, an 'elimination' is an application of an elimination rule.

In an elimination, the premise containing the logical constant being eliminated is said to be the 'major premise', the other premises, if any, the 'minor premises'. Thus A is the minor premise of $(\rightarrow E)$, C a minor premise of $(\vee E)$ or $(\exists E)$.

---

[1] Gentzen sequent calculus rules give an analysis of deducibility rather than deduction.
[2] See Gentzen (1969, 77).

When an assumption A is made, the formulas in the deduction below A are said to 'depend' on that assumption. However, one or more assumptions of the same form A may be discharged by one of the rules ($\vee$E), ($\rightarrow$I), ($\exists$E) at a later step in the deduction. This means that the conclusion of the rule will no longer depend on those assumptions.

Assumptions of the form A which are discharged by one of the rules ($\vee$E), ($\rightarrow$I), ($\exists$E) at the same step in a deduction, are said to 'belong to the same assumption class', $[A]$. In rules ($\vee$E), ($\rightarrow$I), ($\exists$E), an assumption class $[A]$ written above a premise indicates that assumptions belonging to that class may occur above that premise and may be discharged by the rule.

The 'undischarged' assumptions of a deduction are those on which the conclusion of the deduction depends. A deduction whose conclusion is A and all of whose undischarged assumptions are in a set of formulas Γ is called a 'deduction of A from Γ'. A deduction of A from $\Gamma = \emptyset$ is called a 'demonstration of A'.

Rules ($\forall$I), ($\exists$E) are subject to restrictions. The restriction on ($\forall$I) is that the individual variable y must have no free occurrence in any assumption on which the premise A_y^x depends. The restriction on ($\exists$E) is that the individual variable y must have no free occurrence in C or in any assumption on which the premise C depends, except A_y^x.

Assumptions are marked by numerals, and the numeral is repeated on the right side of the introduction or elimination at which the assumption is discharged. Assumptions belonging to the same assumption class are marked by the same numeral. For example, the following is a demonstration of $A \rightarrow A$:

$$(\rightarrow \text{I}) \frac{\overset{(1)}{A}}{A \rightarrow A} (1).$$

Gentzen's analysis of deduction is a better approximation to Frege's ideal of atomizing deduction than Frege's own analysis, because each introduction or elimination concerns a single logical constant. Moreover, it is not subject to the drawback of Frege's analysis that it makes deductions unnecessarily complicated. Just compare the above demonstration of $A \rightarrow A$ with the demonstration of the same formula by Frege's rules, considered in Chapter 10.

11.3 The Significance of Gentzen's Analysis

For Gentzen, the fact that there are introduction and elimination rules for each logical constant is not merely a technical feature, but has a deeper significance. According to him, "the introductions represent, as it were, the 'definitions' of the" logical constants "concerned, and the eliminations are no more, in the final analysis, than the consequences of these definitions."[3] This means that, in eliminating a logical constant, one may use it only in the sense afforded it by the introduction of that logical constant. By "making these ideas more precise it should be possible to display the E-inferences as unique functions of their corresponding I-inferences, on the basis of certain requirements."[4]

Prawitz explains this by saying that "an introduction rule" for a logical constant "states a sufficient condition for introducing a formula with this constant as outermost symbol," and "this condition may now be taken as the 'meaning' of the logical constant."[5] The eliminations "are 'justified' by this very meaning given to the constants by the introductions."[6]

The "corresponding introductions and eliminations are inverses of each other," in the sense that "the conclusion obtained by an elimination does not state anything more than what must have already been obtained if the major premise of the elimination was inferred by an introduction."[7] Thus "nothing new is obtained by an elimination immediately following an introduction (of the major premise of the elimination)."[8]

Prawitz expresses this by saying that "the pairs of corresponding introductions and eliminations satisfy the inversion principle."[9] Thus "the inversion principle states that each particular elimination following an introduction is justified since, by a reduction, the conclusion can also be obtained directly without this detour."[10]

11.4 Inferentialism

Gentzen's statement about the role of introductions and eliminations is at the origin of inferentialism, the view that "the meaning of expressions" is "determined by inference rules that govern their use."[11] The latter are supposed to be meaning-constitutive and self-justifying, that is, not in need of any outside justification. In particular, for Gentzen, the introduction rules are meaning-constitutive and self-justifying. The elimination rules are justified by the meanings constituted by the introduction rules.

As we have seen in Chapter 6, Aristotle assumes that the rules for syllogisms in the first figure, Barbara, Celarent, Darii, Ferio, are self-justifying, because

---

[3] *Ibid.*, 80.
[4] *Ibid.*, 81.
[5] Prawitz (1971, 247).
[6] *Ibid.*
[7] *Ibid.*, 246.
[8] *Ibid.*, 247.
[9] *Ibid.*
[10] *Ibid.*, 259.
[11] Prawitz (2011, 393).

such syllogisms require nothing beyond the things posited to make their necessity evident. Then he justifies the rules for all other kinds of syllogisms in terms of them. Thus, for Aristotle, the rules for syllogisms in the first figure "were a basis for the reasoning by which he established that certain figures represent syllogisms."[12] The status Gentzen assigns to the introduction rules is similar to the one Aristotle assigns to the rules for syllogisms in the first figure.

The ultimate purpose of inferentialism is to show that the whole of logic is self-justifying, that is, in need of no outside justification. Inferentialism wants to achieve this purpose by assigning a special status to certain inference rules – for Gentzen, the introduction rules – that is, the status of rules which draw their justification from themselves.

11.5 Detour Contractions

By Prawitz's inversion principle, an elimination immediately following an introduction of the major premise of the elimination is "an unnecessary detour" in a deduction, which "can be removed."[13] It can be removed by means of certain transformations of deductions, called 'detour contractions'. There are detour contractions for each logical constant. Those for $\wedge, \vee, \rightarrow, \forall, \exists$ are the following:[14]

$\wedge$-contraction

$$(\wedge\text{I}) \ (\wedge\text{E}) \frac{\frac{\vdots \quad \vdots}{A \quad B}}{\frac{A \wedge B}{A}} \quad \Rightarrow \quad \begin{array}{c} \vdots \\ A \end{array}$$

Similarly with B in place of A.

$\vee$-contraction

$$(\vee\text{I}) \ (\vee\text{E}) \frac{\frac{\vdots}{A} \quad [A] \quad [B]}{\frac{A \vee B \quad \vdots \quad \vdots}{C}} \quad \Rightarrow \quad \begin{array}{c} [A] \\ \vdots \\ C \end{array}$$

Similarly with B in place of A.

---

[12]Ibid., 387.
[13]Prawitz (1971, 248).
[14]See Prawitz (2006, 35–38); Prawitz (1971, 252–253).

→-contraction

$$(\to I)\ \dfrac{\begin{array}{c}[A]\\ \vdots\\ B\end{array}}{A\to B}\quad \begin{array}{c}\vdots\\ A\end{array}$$
$$(\to E)\ \dfrac{A\to B\quad A}{B}\quad \Rightarrow\quad \begin{array}{c}[A]\\ \vdots\\ B\end{array}$$

∀-contraction

$$(\forall I)\ \dfrac{\begin{array}{c}\vdots\\ A\end{array}}{\forall y A_y^x}$$
$$(\forall E)\ \dfrac{\forall y A_y^x}{A_t^x}\quad \Rightarrow\quad \begin{array}{c}\vdots^{\,x}_{\,t}\\ A_t^x\end{array}$$

Here $\vdots^{\,x}_{\,t}$ denotes the result of replacing each free occurrence of x in the deduction $\vdots$ by t.

∃-contraction

$$(\exists I)\ \dfrac{\begin{array}{c}\vdots\\ A_t^y\end{array}}{\exists x A_x^y}\quad \begin{array}{c}[A]\\ \vdots\\ C\end{array}$$
$$(\exists E)\ \dfrac{\exists x A_x^y\quad C}{C}\quad \Rightarrow\quad \begin{array}{c}[A_t^y]\\ \vdots^{\,y}_{\,t}\\ C\end{array}$$

Here $\vdots^{\,y}_{\,t}$ denotes the result of substituting every free occurrence of y in the deduction $\vdots$ by t.

11.6 Permutation Contractions

Another kind of unnecessary detour in a deduction occurs when, at applications of (∨E) or (∃E), an introduction is followed by an elimination without giving rise to a detour contraction. For example, consider the deduction:

$$(\vee E)\ \dfrac{A\vee A\quad (\wedge I)\dfrac{A\quad A}{A\wedge A}\quad (\wedge I)\dfrac{A\quad A}{A\wedge A}}{(\wedge E)\dfrac{A\wedge A}{A}}.$$

11.6 Permutation Contractions

It contains two ($\wedge$I) followed two steps later by an ($\wedge$E). But one cannot apply $\wedge$-contraction, because of the repetition of $A \wedge A$ that occurs owing to ($\vee$E). To avoid this problem, the order of the rule applications must be changed, moving ($\wedge$E) upwards over the minor premises of ($\vee$E), as follows:

$$(\vee E) \frac{A \vee A \quad (\wedge I) \dfrac{A \quad A}{A \wedge A} \quad (\wedge I) \dfrac{A \quad A}{A \wedge A}}{A} \frac{(\wedge E) \dfrac{A \wedge A}{A} \quad (\wedge E) \dfrac{A \wedge A}{A}}{A}$$

Then one may apply $\wedge$-contraction, obtaining:

$$(\vee E) \frac{A \vee A \quad A \quad A}{A}.$$

Generally, to avoid the problem that, at applications of ($\vee$E) or ($\exists$E), an introduction may be followed by an elimination without giving rise to a detour contraction, the order of the rule applications must be changed by means of deduction transformations, called 'permutation contractions', which move the eliminations upwards over minor premises of ($\vee$E) or ($\exists$E). The permutation contractions are the following, where $\vdots^*$ denotes a deduction of a minor premise, which may be empty if the E-rule is ($\wedge$E) or ($\forall$E):[15]

$\vee$-permutation contraction

$$\text{(E-rule)} \dfrac{(\vee E) \dfrac{A \vee B \quad \begin{matrix}[A] & [B]\\ \vdots & \vdots\\ C & C\end{matrix}}{C} \quad \vdots^*}{D} \quad \Rightarrow \quad (\vee E) \dfrac{A \vee B \quad \text{(E-rule)} \dfrac{\begin{matrix}[A]\\ \vdots\\ C\end{matrix} \quad \vdots^*}{D} \quad \text{(E-rule)} \dfrac{\begin{matrix}[B]\\ \vdots\\ C\end{matrix} \quad \vdots^*}{D}}{D}$$

---

[15] See Prawitz (2006, 51); Prawitz (1971, 253).

∃-permutation contraction

$$(\exists E)\dfrac{\exists x A \quad \begin{matrix}[A_y^x]\\ \vdots\\ C\end{matrix}}{(E\text{-rule})\dfrac{C \quad \vdots *}{D}} \quad \Rightarrow \quad (\exists E)\dfrac{\exists x A \quad (E\text{-rule})\dfrac{\begin{matrix}[A_y^x]\\ \vdots\\ C\end{matrix} \quad \vdots *}{D}}{D}$$

11.7 Simplification Contractions

Another kind of unnecessary detour in a deduction occurs when, at applications of $(\vee E)$, one of the two assumption classes $[A]$ or $[B]$ is empty, or, at applications of $(\exists E)$, the assumption class $[A_y^x]$ is empty. This detour can be removed by means of certain transformations of deductions, called 'simplification contractions'. The simplification contractions are the following:

$\vee$-simplification contraction

$$(\vee E)\dfrac{\begin{matrix}\vdots\\ A\vee B\end{matrix} \quad \begin{matrix}:1\\ \vdots\\ C\end{matrix} \quad \begin{matrix}:2\\ \vdots\\ C\end{matrix}}{C} \quad \Rightarrow \quad \begin{matrix}:i\\ \vdots\\ C\end{matrix}$$

Here no assumption in $\overset{:i}{\underset{C}{\vdots}}$ ($i = 1$ or 2) is discharged by $(\vee E)$.

$\exists$-simplification contraction

$$(\exists E)\dfrac{\begin{matrix}\vdots\\ \exists x A\end{matrix} \quad \begin{matrix}\vdots\\ C\end{matrix}}{C} \quad \Rightarrow \quad \begin{matrix}\vdots\\ C\end{matrix}$$

Here no assumption in $\overset{\vdots}{\underset{C}{}}$ is discharged by $(\exists E)$.

11.8 Normal Deductions

A deduction which contains none of the three kinds of detour stated above is said to be a 'normal deduction'.

The following 'normalization theorem' holds: Every deduction can be transformed into a normal deduction by a finite number of detour contractions, permutation contractions or simplification contractions.[16] This means that all detours can be removed from a deduction, which "justifies the logical system as a whole."[17]

Normal deductions have the 'subformula property': Each formula occurring in a normal deduction of A from a set of assumptions Γ is a subformula of A or of some formula of Γ.[18] Gentzen expresses this by saying that a normal deduction "is not roundabout," in the sense that no concepts enter into the deduction "other than those contained in its final result" or in its assumptions, and "their use was therefore essential to the achievement of that result."[19]

By inspection of the natural deduction rules, from the subformula property one obtains the separation property: The only rules used in a normal deduction of A from a set of assumptions Γ are introduction and elimination rules for the logical constants occurring in A or in some formula of Γ.

The separation property is essential to the tenets of inferentialism. For if the introduction and elimination rules for the logical constants occurring in A or in some formula of Γ were not enough to deduce A from Γ, this would mean that there is more to the meaning of such logical constants than what is stated by the introduction rules. Therefore, the latter would not really be meaning-constitutive.

11.9 The Case of Negation

The normalization theorem, the subformula property and the separation property hold for the fragment of logic containing only the logical constants $\wedge, \vee, \rightarrow, \forall, \exists$. Things change when the logical constant $\neg$ is added. Unlike the introduction and elimination rules for $\wedge, \vee, \rightarrow, \forall, \exists$, those for $\neg$ are problematic. As Gentzen states, for $\neg$ "there exist several distinct forms of inference and these cannot be divided clearly into $\neg$-introductions and $\neg$-eliminations."[20] Therefore, "the choice of elementary forms of inference" for $\neg$ is "more arbitrary than in the case of the other logical connectives."[21]

---

[16] See Prawitz (2006, 50–51).
[17] Prawitz (1971, 259).
[18] See Prawitz (2006, 53).
[19] Gentzen (1969, 69).
[20] *Ibid.*, 149.
[21] *Ibid.*, 154.

Gentzen adopts the following two rules for $\neg$:[22]

$$(\neg I)\dfrac{\overset{[A]}{B} \quad \overset{[A]}{\neg B}}{\neg A} \qquad (\neg E)\dfrac{\neg\neg A}{A}$$

Actually, Gentzen does not present them as introduction and elimination rules for $\neg$, but Prawitz calls them $(\neg I)$ and $(\neg E)$.[23]

Rule $(\neg I)$ corresponds to the rule of reduction to the impossible, as stated in Chapter 2 with reference to Parmenides. Aristotle's rule of strong reduction to the impossible, (SRI), stated in Chapter 6, is a combination of $(\neg I)$ and $(\neg E)$. For if, assuming $\neg A$, we may deduce a contradiction, then by (SRI) we may conclude A, while by $(\neg I)$ we may only conclude $\neg\neg A$. To conclude A we need $(\neg E)$.

Rules $(\neg I)$ and $(\neg E)$ are not of the same kind as the introduction and elimination rules for the other logical constants. For example, in $(\neg E)$, the logical constant $\neg$ eliminated in the conclusion must occur in a formula of the form $\neg\neg A$, so $(\neg E)$ does not apply to formulas of the form $\neg A$ for arbitrary A.

Moreover, $(\neg I)$ and $(\neg E)$ do not satisfy the inversion principle. For example, a demonstration of the excluded middle law, $A \vee \neg A$, will necessarily contain a formula which is both the conclusion of an introduction and the major premise of an elimination, as in the following demonstration:

$$(\neg I)\dfrac{(\vee I)\dfrac{\overset{(1)}{A}}{A \vee \neg A} \quad \overset{(2)}{\neg(A \vee \neg A)}}{\dfrac{(\neg I)\dfrac{(\vee I)\dfrac{\neg A}{A \vee \neg A} \quad \overset{(2)}{\neg(A \vee \neg A)}}{(\neg E)\dfrac{\neg\neg(A \vee \neg A)}{A \vee \neg A}}(2)}{}}(1)$$

11.10 Limitations of Gentzen's Analysis of Deduction

That the rules for $\neg$ are problematic is a first indication that Gentzen's analysis of deduction has substantial limitations. The main ones are the following.

1) The rules $(\neg I)$ and $(\neg E)$ make it impossible to establish a normalization theorem because, as it has been stated above, they do not satisfy the inversion principle.

---

[22] Ibid., 153.
[23] Prawitz (2006, 35).

11.10 Limitations of Gentzen's Analysis of Deduction

To avoid this problem, Prawitz replaces the logical constant $\neg$ with a logical constant $\bot$ for falsity, then he writes $\neg A$ as an abbreviation for $(A \to \bot)$, and states the following deductive rule for $\bot$:

$$(\bot) \frac{\begin{array}{c}[\neg A]\\ \vdots \\ \bot\end{array}}{A}$$

For the resulting rules one can establish a normalization theorem. This, however, involves eliminating $\vee$, $\exists$ as primitive logical constants, writing $(A \vee B)$, $\exists x A$ as abbreviations for $(\neg A \to B)$, $\neg \forall x \neg A$ respectively, and restricting the rule $(\bot)$ to the case where A is an atomic formula different from $\bot$.[24]

The resulting rules permit to deduce the same formulas from the same assumptions as Gentzen's deductive rules, but only in a very roundabout way. As a result, the deduction of formulas involving $\neg$ can be very complicated, so that one could hardly say that the rules come "as close as possible to actual reasoning."[25]

2) The rules ($\vee$E) and ($\exists$E) contain a formula C having no structural connection with the major premise. This raises two problems.

(i) Because of ($\vee$E) and ($\exists$E), deductions are only apparently trees of formulas, since the relevant relations between formulas are not those between the nodes of the tree arrangement of formulas. Gentzen himself acknowledges that, because of ($\vee$E) and ($\exists$E), "the tree form" does "not bring out the fact that it is after the enunciation" of the major premise "that we distinguish the cases."[26]

(ii) The lack of a structural connection of C with the major premise makes it necessary to use permutation contractions, and to identify the two deductions on the left and the right of $\Rightarrow$ in the permutation contractions. Such two deductions are essentially different, so identifying them changes the character of the deduction.

To overcome the problems concerning ($\vee$E), Gentzen suggests to reformulate it as a multiple-conclusion deductive rule: From $A \vee B$ infer that "one of the two possibilities, A or B, holds."[27] That is:

$$(\vee\text{E}') \frac{A \vee B}{A \quad B}.$$

This, however, leads to several complications because then deductions are no longer trees, and makes it necessary to introduce certain unnatural restrictions on

---

[24] Ibid., 39–41.
[25] Gentzen (1969, 68).
[26] Ibid., 79.
[27] Ibid., 255.

the other rules.[28] Gentzen himself admits that ($\vee$E′) "constitutes a departure from the 'natural'."[29]

An apparently more manageable alternative is to consider sequent-conclusion rules, that is, rules involving finite sequences of formulas as premises and conclusion. Then one can reformulate ($\vee$E) as follows:

$$(\vee E'') \frac{\Gamma, A \vee B}{\Gamma, A, B}.$$

But, while ($\vee$E″) solves the problem concerning ($\vee$E), it leaves open the problem concerning ($\exists$E). On the other hand, a sequent-conclusion formulation of ($\exists$E), while solving this problem, raises other problems.[30] Moreover, if one admits sequent-conclusion deductive rules, one must add structural rules, such as weakening:

$$(W) \frac{\Gamma}{\Gamma, A}.$$

Now, (W) permits to introduce an arbitrary formula A in the conclusion, so it has the same effect as an introduction rule. For example, it permits to infer B, A from B, which has the same effect as ($\vee$I) because B, A has the same meaning as $B \vee A$. This contrasts with Gentzen's claim that the meaning of a logical constant is given by the introduction rule for that constant.

3) Rules ($\rightarrow$I) and ($\rightarrow$E) are not sufficient to prove all logical truths containing $\rightarrow$ as their sole logical constant. Such is the case of Peirce's Law:

$$((A \rightarrow B) \rightarrow A) \rightarrow A.$$

If A and B are atomic formulas, Peirce's Law contains $\rightarrow$ as its sole logical constant, but it can be shown that it has no demonstration containing ($\rightarrow$I) and ($\rightarrow$E) alone. To obtain a demonstration, one may add the rule:

$$(PR) \frac{\begin{array}{c} [A \rightarrow B] \\ \vdots \\ A \end{array}}{A}$$

Then one may give a demonstration of Peirce's Law as follows:

$$(\rightarrow I) \frac{(\rightarrow E) \frac{\overset{(1)}{A \rightarrow B} \quad \overset{(2)}{(A \rightarrow B) \rightarrow A}}{(PR) \frac{A}{A}(1)}}{((A \rightarrow B) \rightarrow A) \rightarrow A}(2)$$

---

[28] See Shoesmith and Smiley (1978); Ungar (1992).
[29] Gentzen (1969, 255).
[30] See Cellucci (1992).

11.10 Limitations of Gentzen's Analysis of Deduction

Alternatively, one may give a demonstration of Peirce's Law using $(\neg I)$ and $(\neg E)$, as follows:

$$
(\neg I)\cfrac{\cfrac{\cfrac{\cfrac{\overset{(1)}{A}\quad \overset{(2)}{\neg A}}{\neg\neg B}}{B}}{A\to B}\;{\scriptstyle (1)}\quad \overset{(3)}{(A\to B)\to A}}{(\to E)\cfrac{\cfrac{A \qquad\qquad\qquad\qquad\qquad \neg A}{(\neg E)\cfrac{\neg\neg A}{A}}\;{\scriptstyle (2)}}{(\to I)\cfrac{}{((A\to B)\to A)\to A}\;{\scriptstyle (3)}}}
$$

Thus one is faced with the alternative: Either one must add (PR), or one must admit that the theory of $\to$ has to rely on the theory of $\neg$.

Zimmermann claims that adding (PR) as an $\to$-elimination rule is adequate, because then a demonstration of the normalization theorem "can be given."[31] But this is unjustified because, in order to obtain a normalization theorem, one needs permutation contractions and also other kinds of contractions. This involves identifying deductions that are essentially different. Thus one runs into a problem similar to the one discussed in 2) above.

On the other hand, to admit that the theory of $\to$ has to rely on the theory of $\neg$ is also unsatisfactory, because then no normalization theorem is possible. Indeed, the above demonstration of Peirce's Law using $(\neg I)$ and $(\neg E)$ contains formulas that are both a conclusion of $(\neg I)$ and a major premise of $(\neg E)$ and that cannot be removed. Therefore, one cannot say that the introductions represent the definitions of the logical constants concerned and the eliminations are the consequences of these definitions.

4) The problem with Peirce's Rule is a special case of a more general problem: introduction and elimination rules do not generally have the separation property. In order to deduce a formula A from a set of assumptions Γ, it is not generally sufficient to use introduction and elimination rules for the logical constants occurring in A or in some formula in Γ. Now, as it has been pointed out above, the separation property is essential to the tenets of inferentialism. Then, the fact that introduction and elimination rules do not generally have such a property refutes such tenets.

5) The claim of inferentialism, that the meaning of logical constants is given by certain deductive rules which are self-justifying, can also be refuted more directly, considering counterexamples to Gentzen's view about the role of introductions and eliminations.

One of these counterexamples is given by Prawitz. Let us consider a formal language whose only non-logical constant is the binary relation constant $\in$ for membership. Let $t\in u$ be an abbreviation for $\in(t,u)$. Let us add a logical constant λ

---

[31] Zimmermann (2002, 562).

for set abstraction. The terms of the resulting language will be individual variables and all expressions of the form λxA, where A is a formula. A term of the form λxA expresses the set of all sets such that A. The introduction and elimination rules for the symbol λ are the following:

$$(\lambda \text{I}) \; \frac{A_t^x}{t \in \lambda xA} \qquad\qquad (\lambda \text{E}) \; \frac{t \in \lambda xA}{A_t^x}$$

A sequence consisting of a (λE) immediately following a (λI) is a detour which can be removed by means of the following contraction:

λ-contraction:

$$(\lambda \text{I}) \; \frac{A_t^x}{t \in \lambda xA} \\ (\lambda \text{E}) \; \frac{}{A_t^x} \quad\Rightarrow\quad A_t^x$$

Therefore (λI) and (λE) satisfy the inversion principle. Nevertheless, by means of (λI) and (λE), we can obtain Russell's paradox. For let t be $\lambda x \neg (x \in x)$. Then we have the following demonstration of Russell's paradox:

$$(\wedge \text{I}) \frac{(\neg \text{I}) \dfrac{t \in t^{(1)} \quad (\lambda \text{E}) \dfrac{t \in t^{(1)}}{\neg(t \in t)}}{\neg(t \in t)}^{(1)} \quad (\lambda \text{I}) \dfrac{}{t \in t} \qquad (\neg \text{I}) \dfrac{t \in t^{(1)} \quad (\lambda \text{E}) \dfrac{t \in t^{(1)}}{\neg(t \in t)}}{\neg(t \in t)}^{(1)}}{t \in t \wedge \neg(t \in t)}$$

Thus, while satisfying the inversion principle, these rules "are nevertheless inconsistent."[32]

In addition to (λI) and (λE), other examples can be given of introduction and elimination rules which, while satisfying the inversion principle, are nevertheless inconsistent.[33] These rules are a serious problem for inferentialism, because the meaning they constitute is a contradictory one.

A solution would be to accept inconsistent rules as meaning-constitutive, thus with the same status as the introduction rules. This solution, however, is inadequate because, as Prawitz states, it would lead to taking "too many inference rules as meaning constitutive."[34] Indeed, if inconsistent rules were accepted as meaning-constitutive, there would be no reason for not taking any inference rule whatsoever

---

[32]Prawitz (2011, 394, footnote 6).
[33]See Read (2010); Wansing (2006).
[34]Prawitz (2011, 395).

as meaning-constitutive. This would lead to a Babel Tower of meanings, which would make inferentialism of no use.

Another solution, proposed by Belnap, would be to require that, when meaning-constitutive rules for a new logical constant are added, "the extension must be conservative," in the sense that it must not permit to deduce any statement containing only old logical constants "unless the statement is already" deducible "in the absence of" the new meaning-constitutive "rules."[35] This solution, however, is inadequate, because then the justification of the meaning-constitutive rules for the new logical constant would depend on the meaning of the old logical constants, and hence would require an outside guarantee. Thus the rules for the new logical constant would not be self-justifying.

A further problem for inferentialism arises from the strong incompleteness theorem for second-order logic. This question will be discussed in Chapter 12.

11.11 Failure of the Ideal of Atomizing Deduction

Because of the limitations considered above, Gentzen's analysis of deduction fails to achieve Frege's ideal of atomizing deduction.

On the other hand, as we have seen in Chapter 10, this ideal is essential for the purpose of mathematical logic of giving a secure foundation for mathematics. For, as Frege says, only when deductions are split up into logically simple steps can we be persuaded that the root of the matter is logic alone and hence can attain to the necessary certainty.

Frege's ideal of atomizing deduction is also essential for the purpose of inferentialism of showing that logic is self-justifying since so are its meaning-constitutive rules. Its failure means that inferentialism falls short of giving logic a foundation.

Moreover, the failure of Frege's and Gentzen's attempts to achieve the ideal of atomizing deduction leaves logic without justification, if by justification one means the kind of absolute justification that Frege and Gentzen sought. Another kind of justification is required. This question will be discussed in Chapter 18.

---

[35]Belnap (1962, 1932).

Chapter 12
The Limitations of Mathematical Logic

12.1 The Claims Concerning Mathematical Logic

Despite the limitations of Frege's and Gentzen's analysis of deduction, throughout the twentieth century mathematical logic has been extolled, and the importance of Aristotle's logic downplayed. For example, Russell states that mathematical logic gives thought "wings. It has, in my opinion, introduced the same kind of advance into philosophy as Galileo introduced into physics."[1] On the contrary, Aristotle's "logic put thought in fetters."[2] Thus "any person in the present day who wishes to learn logic will be wasting his time if he reads Aristotle."[3]

These claims are unjustified. Of course, unlike Aristotle's analysis, Frege's analysis of assertions and deduction accounts for inferences involving relations and singular assertions. Nevertheless, as it has been argued in Chapters 10 and 11, Frege's analysis is inadequate and so is Gentzen's analysis of deduction. What is worse, by confining logic to the study of deduction, Frege neglects important questions Aristotle's logic took care of, starting with discovery.

12.2 The Abandonment of Aristotle's Broad Conception of Logic

The confinement of logic to the study of deduction is a sharp change with respect to a tradition, starting with Plato and Aristotle, according to which logic must be a logic of discovery. Despite the importance of this tradition, in the past one and a

---

[1] Russell (1999, 68–69).
[2] *Ibid.*, 68.
[3] Russell (2004, 194).

half century the view that logic must be a logic of discovery has been put aside. The prevailing view has been that there can only be a logic of justification.

This has led to abandon Aristotle's broad conception of logic, in particular, the assumption that logic must be concerned with the question of how to discover premises for a given conclusion. It has also led to abandon the view that there is a very strict relation of logic with the scientific method. The abandonment of Aristotle's broad conception of logic has been influenced by Kant's view that logic cannot be an organon of the sciences. Nevertheless, as we have seen in Chapter 9, in the later years of his teaching of logic, Kant assigned induction and analogy – two basic tools of a logic of discovery – to logic, even to pure logic. Thus the decisive factor in the abandonment of Aristotle's broad conception of logic must have been Frege rather than Kant.

12.3 The Abandonment of the Analytic-Synthetic Method

The abandonment of Aristotle's broad conception of logic has meant the abandonment of Aristotle's analytic-synthetic method. The analytic part of Aristotle's analytic-synthetic method has been put aside, only the synthetic part, namely the axiomatic method, has been retained.

The basis for this change has been the replacement of Aristotle's concrete view of the axiomatic method with the abstract one, especially due to the influence of Hilbert. According to the abstract view, axioms are not true of given concepts but are arbitrarily chosen, subject only to the requirement of consistency. Thus Hilbert states that "the axioms can be taken quite arbitrarily."[4] They are only subject to the condition that "the application of the given axioms can never lead to contradictions."[5] Indeed, "if these axioms contradict each other, then no logical consequences can be drawn from them; the system defined then does not exist for the mathematician."[6]

With the replacement of Aristotle's concrete view of the axiomatic method with the abstract one, the question of the discovery of axioms becomes empty. Being arbitrarily chosen, subject only to the requirement of consistency, axioms are no longer discovered but only stipulated. Thus the analytic part of Aristotle's analytic-synthetic method becomes redundant.

The abandonment of Aristotle's broad conception of logic, in particular, of the analytic part of Aristotle's analytic-synthetic method, has greatly restricted the scope of logic. Mathematical logic is a result of this restriction. Indeed, as Barnes states, "the discipline which the ancients called logic comprehended more than the

---

[4]Hilbert (2004b, 563).
[5]Hilbert (1996a, 1093).
[6]Hilbert (2004b, 563).

modern discipline of the same name."[7] Because of its restricted scope, mathematical logic has had little impact on scientific research. This, however, is not the only problem with it. An even more serious problem is that all of its basic tenets have been refuted by Gödel's incompleteness theorems and other limitative results. This is the subject of the remaining part of this chapter.

12.4 Failure of the Ideal of a Universal Language

According to Frege, mathematical logic gives a universal language for mathematics, that is, a language capable of expressing all mathematical concepts. Indeed, Frege states that mathematical logic gives "a *lingua characterica* in the first instance for mathematics."[8]

This is unjustified. The possibility of a universal language for mathematics is ruled out by Tarski's undefinability theorem.[9] By the latter, there cannot be any consistent, sufficiently strong, deductive theory T capable of expressing all mathematical concepts. Specifically, the property of being a true sentence of T cannot be expressed in T. This also implies that Leibniz's claim, considered in Chapter 9, that a universal language is feasible, is unjustified.

12.5 Failure of the Ideal of a Calculus of Reasoning

According to Frege, mathematical logic gives a calculus of reasoning, that is, a system of rules capable of representing all mathematical reasoning. Indeed, Frege states that mathematical logic gives, not only a *lingua characterica*, but also "a *calculus ratiocinator*."[10] Hilbert even claims that mathematical logic gives a calculus of reasoning capable of representing all mathematical reasoning faithfully, since the axioms and theorems of formal systems are "copies of the thoughts constituting customary mathematics as it has developed till now."[11] In particular, Gentzen claims that such a calculus of reasoning is given by his natural deduction rules, since they reflect "as accurately as possible the actual logical reasoning involved in mathematical proofs."[12]

These claims are unjustified. The possibility of a calculus of reasoning is ruled out by the strong incompleteness theorem for second-order logic, by which there

---

[7]Barnes (2003, 21).
[8]Frege (1979, 12).
[9]See, for example, Cellucci (2007, 188–191).
[10]Frege (1984, 242).
[11]Hilbert (1967, 465).
[12]Gentzen (1969, 74).

is no consistent set of rules for second-order logic capable of deducing all second-order logical consequences of any given set of formulas.

This follows from Gödel's first incompleteness theorem for second-order Peano arithmetic *2P* and the categoricity of *2P*. For suppose there is a consistent set R of rules capable of deducing all second-order logical consequences of any given set of formulas. By Gödel's first incompleteness theorem for *2P*, there is a statement *G* which is true in the intended interpretation of *2P* but cannot be deduced from *2P* by means of R. By our hypothesis, from this it follows that *G* cannot be a second-order logical consequence of *2P*. Then there must be some interpretation in which the axioms *2P* are true and *G* false.[13] Now, by the categoricity of *2P*, any interpretation in which the axioms *2P* are true is isomorphic to the intended interpretation of *2P*. Then *G* must be false in the intended interpretation of *2P*. But *G* is true in such interpretation. Contradiction. Therefore, we conclude that there cannot be any such set R of rules.[14]

Then Scholz's claim, cited in the Introduction, that mathematical logic gives us the complete inferential rules which the development of the tremendously exacting modern mathematics requires, is unjustified. For the same reason Leibniz's claim, considered in Chapter 9, that a calculus of reasoning is feasible, is unjustified.

12.6 Inadequacy of the Closed World View

As we have seen in Chapter 9, Frege supports a closed world view of mathematics. According to him, a mathematical theory is a closed system, that is, a system based on primitive truths that are given once for all and cannot change, and whose development consists entirely in deducing conclusions from them. Therefore, the whole of a mathematical theory is contained in its primitive truths.

This view is unjustified. By Gödel's first incompleteness theorem, for any consistent, sufficiently strong, deductive theory *T*, there is a sentence *G* of *T* which is true but cannot be deduced from the axioms of *T*. Therefore, mathematical theories cannot be closed systems. This also implies that Kant's closed world view of science, considered in Chapter 9, is unjustified.

12.7 Inadequacy of the Analytic-Synthetic Method

That Aristotle's conception of logic is essentially broader than Frege's, does not mean that his conception is satisfactory in all respects. Indeed, Aristotle's analytic-synthetic, method, on which Aristotle's conception of logic is based, has serious

---

[13] 'Interpretation' here means 'full interpretation', namely, interpretation where the domain of n-ary relations is set of all n-ary relations on the domain of individuals.

[14] For details, see, for example, Cellucci (2007, 202–208).

limitations. A first limitation arises from the fact that, as we have seen in Chapter 3, for Aristotle, a thing of a given kind must be demonstrated from principles of that kind.

Now, by Gödel's first incompleteness theorem, for any consistent, sufficiently strong, principles of a given kind, there are truths of that kind which cannot be demonstrated from those principles. Their demonstration may require principles of another kind.

Then Aristotle's analytic-synthetic method is incompatible with Gödel's first incompleteness theorem, and hence the scientific method cannot be identified with it. The same applies to Pappus' analytic-synthetic method and the axiomatic method.

12.8 The Unknowability of the Truth of Principles

Another limitation of Aristotle's analytic-synthetic method arises from the fact that, while, as we have seen in Chapter 3, for Aristotle, principles must be true and known to be true, they cannot actually be known to be true, even in Hilbert's weak sense that they must be consistent.

Indeed, by Gödel's second incompleteness theorem, for any consistent, sufficiently strong principles, the statement, 'The principles in question are consistent', cannot be proved by absolutely reliable means. Therefore, principles cannot be known to be true, even in Hilbert's weak sense that they must be consistent.

Then Aristotle's analytic-synthetic method is incompatible with Gödel's second incompleteness theorem.

12.9 Failure of the Logicist Programme

As we have seen in Chapter 10, Frege's logicist programme requires showing that all arithmetical laws are derivable from the primitive laws of logic. As we have also seen, Frege's choice of primitive laws of logic leads to contradiction. But this leaves open the possibility that all arithmetical laws be derivable from some other choice of primitive laws of logic.

Such possibility, however, is ruled out by Gödel's first incompleteness theorem. Suppose that all arithmetical laws are derivable from some primitive laws of logic L. This means that all truths of arithmetic can be deduced from L. But, by Gödel's first incompleteness theorem, there are truths of arithmetic which cannot be deduced from L. Contradiction. This is the end of Frege's logicist programme. For the same reason, Russell's logicist programme cannot be carried out, and Leibniz's logicism is untenable.

12.10 Failure of Hilbert's Conservation Programme

An alternative to Frege's project of giving a secure foundation for mathematics is put forward by Hilbert. He distinguishes mathematics into two parts, finitary and infinitary mathematics. Finitary mathematics is the concrete part of mathematics, which is based on Kant's pure sensible intuition. Infinitary mathematics also involves abstract concepts, such as that of actual infinity. Thus finitary mathematics is a proper part of infinitary mathematics.

Being based on Kant's pure sensible intuition, finitary mathematics is absolutely reliable. So, if a statement of finitary mathematics is demonstrable in finitary mathematics, this will guarantee that it is true. On the contrary, if a statement of finitary mathematics is demonstrable in infinitary mathematics, this will not guarantee that it is true, because its demonstration may use abstract concepts, which are problematic. On the other hand, the use of abstract concepts is advantageous, because it permits to simplify the demonstrations of statements of finitary mathematics. In particular, "just as $i = \sqrt{-1}$ was introduced to preserve in simplest form the laws of algebra," abstract concepts were introduced "to preserve the simple formal rules of ordinary Aristotelian logic."[15]

Since the use of abstract concepts is advantageous, the question is how to guarantee that it will not lead to falsities. To that purpose one must show, in finitary mathematics, that every statement of finitary mathematics which is demonstrable in infinitary mathematics is also demonstrable in finitary mathematics. This requires showing that every statement containing abstract concepts can be eliminated from a demonstration of a statement of finitary mathematics. That is, "the arrays formed by means of" abstract concepts can be replaced with arrays formed by means of concrete concepts, "in such a way that the formulas resulting" go "over into 'true' formulas by virtue of those replacements."[16] This is Hilbert's conservation programme.[17]

If such a programme could be carried out, this would give a secure foundation for mathematics, because it would show that every statement of finitary mathematics which is demonstrable in infinitary mathematics is true. For, as it has been stated above, according to Hilbert, if a statement of finitary mathematics is demonstrable in finitary mathematics, this will guarantee that it is true. Therefore, if Hilbert's conservation programme could be carried out, one could trust that the use of the axioms of infinitary mathematics in proving statements of finitary mathematics could "never lead to a provably false result."[18]

---

[15] Hilbert (1983, 195).
[16] Hilbert (1967, 477).
[17] For further details on Hilbert's conservation programme see, for example, Cellucci (2007, 43–47).
[18] Hilbert and Bernays (1968–1970, I, 44).

However, the possibility of carrying out Hilbert's conservation programme is ruled out by Gödel's third incompleteness theorem.[19] By the latter, it is impossible to show in finitary mathematics that, if a statement of finitary mathematics is demonstrable in infinitary mathematics, it is also demonstrable in finitary mathematics. This is the end of Hilbert's conservation programme.

12.11 Failure of Hilbert's Consistency Programme

Hilbert also formulates a variant of the conservation programme, which is equivalent to it. According to this variant, in order to guarantee that the use of the abstract concepts of infinitary mathematics does not lead to falsities, it is sufficient to prove, in finitary mathematics, that infinitary mathematics is consistent, that is, no contradiction can be deduced from its axioms. For "wherever the axiomatic method is used it is incumbent upon us to prove the consistency of the axioms."[20] This is Hilbert's consistency programme.[21]

If such a programme could be carried out, this would give a secure foundation for mathematics, because it would show that, when the abstract concepts of infinitary mathematics "are introduced, it is impossible for us to obtain two logically contradictory propositions, A and $\neg A$."[22]

However, the possibility of carrying out Hilbert's consistency programme is ruled out by Gödel's second incompleteness theorem, by which it is impossible to prove, in finitary mathematics, that infinitary mathematics is consistent. This is the end of Hilbert's consistency programme.

12.12 Inadequacy of Consistency as a Criterion of Truth

Hilbert's consistency programme is based on the assumption that consistency is an adequate criterion of truth. Indeed, Hilbert states that, if "arbitrarily given axioms do not contradict one another with all their consequences, then they are true" and this "is for me the criterion of truth."[23]

---

[19]See, for example, Cellucci (2007, 185–187). For Gödel's original formulation, see Gödel (1986–2002, II, 305).

[20]Hilbert (1967, 472).

[21]For further details on Hilbert's consistency programme see, for example, Cellucci (2007, 47–48). On the equivalence between Hilbert's conservation programme and consistency programme, see ibid., 48–49.

[22]Hilbert (1967, 471).

[23]Hilbert (1980, 39–40).

The view that consistency is an adequate criterion of truth goes back at least to Spinoza, who states that, "if an architect conceives a building in proper fashion, although such a building has never existed nor is ever likely to exist, his thought is nevertheless a true thought, and the thought is the same whether the building exists or not."[24] Thus, consistent thoughts are true, and "that which constitutes the specific character of a true thought" must not be sought in the correspondence of that thought to some "external object" but "must be sought in that very same thought."[25]

As a criterion of truth, however, consistency is not viable because, by Gödel's second incompleteness theorem, even when an axiom system is consistent, it is generally impossible to demonstrate by absolutely reliable means, and hence to know, that it is consistent.

As a criterion of truth, consistency is also inadequate because, by a corollary of Gödel's first incompleteness theorem, for any consistent, sufficiently strong, deductive theory S, there is a consistent extension T of S in which some false sentence is demonstrable. Thus the axioms of T, though consistent, cannot be said to be true. For if they could be said to be true, only true sentences should be deducible from them.

The corollary easily follows from Gödel's first incompleteness theorem. By the latter, for any consistent, sufficiently strong, deductive theory S, there is a sentence G of S which is true but undemonstrable in S. Then let T be the deductive theory which is obtained from S by adding $\neg G$ as a new axiom. Since G is undemonstrable in S, the theory T is consistent. Trivially $\neg G$, being an axiom of T, is demonstrable in T. On the other hand, since G is true, $\neg G$ is false. Thus, T is a consistent extension of S in which the false sentence $\neg G$ is demonstrable.

12.13 Failure of Hilbert's Programme of Mechanizing Discovery

Contrary to Frege, who considers the problem of discovery to be a psychological question, Hilbert tries to trivialize that problem, by showing "the decidability of a mathematical question in a finite number of operations."[26] That is, by showing that there is an algorithm for determining whether or not a mathematical statement is true. Then discovery would reduce to a purely mechanical business. In order to know whether or not a mathematical statement is true, one would simply need to apply the algorithm. This is Hilbert's programme of mechanizing discovery.

If such a programme could be carried out, this would dispose of the problem of discovery altogether. Mathematics would be replaced by an algorithm by means

---

[24]Spinoza (2002, 19).
[25]*Ibid.*, 20.
[26]Hilbert (1996b, 1113).

of which everybody could decide the provability or unprovability of any given statement. The publication of demonstrations of theorems would no longer be necessary. Mathematicians would simply publish the statements of theorems, the reader would then find a demonstration simply by applying the algorithm. Also Leibniz's programme of mechanizing discovery could be carried out.

The programme in question is alive even today. Some people still believe that "the ultimate goal of mathematics is to eliminate all need for intelligent thought."[27] According to this view, progress in mathematics is achieved by turning mathematical thought into algorithms that make discovery unnecessary.

The possibility of carrying out Hilbert's programme of mechanizing discovery, however, is ruled out by the undecidability theorem. By the latter, for any consistent, sufficiently strong, deductive theory, there is no algorithm for deciding whether or not a mathematical statement can be deduced from the axioms of the theory.[28] This is the end of Hilbert's programme of mechanizing discovery. It is also the end of Leibniz's programme of mechanizing discovery.

12.14 Inadequacy of Logic as the Study of Deduction

As we have seen, according to Frege, the goal of logic is the study of deduction. For logic to be adequate to that study, there should be a consistent set of deductive rules capable of deducing all logical consequences of any given set of formulas. But, as it has been stated above, by the strong incompleteness theorem for second-order logic, there is no such set of deductive rules for second-order logical consequences. Therefore if, as Frege claims, the goal of logic is the study of deduction, then logic is inadequate to that study.

The reason for Frege's claim is his assumption that the method of mathematics is the axiomatic method. This assumption is refuted by Gödel's first incompleteness theorem.

Hintikka objects that this conclusion is unwarranted, because there are second-order deductive theories, such as second-order Peano arithmetic, which are descriptively complete, that is their models comprise only the intended models. A "descriptively complete mathematical theory does not force us to search for new axioms, for the old ones already imply everything."[29] The strong incompleteness theorem for second-order logic only implies that we must search for "stronger and stronger formal rules of" deductive "inference."[30] This vindicates "the idea

---

[27]Graham et al. (1994, 56).
[28]For details see, for example, Cellucci (2007, 192).
[29]Hintikka (2000, 44).
[30]*Ibid.*

of mathematics as being concerned primarily with" deducing "theorems from axioms."[31] That is, it vindicates the idea that the method of mathematics is the axiomatic method.

This objection, however, is unjustified, because the process of discovering stronger and stronger formal rules of deductive inference cannot be accounted for by the axiomatic method, but only by the analytic method. Therefore, the method of mathematics is not the axiomatic method. Hintikka himself states that, "contrary to the oversimplified picture that most philosophers have of mathematical practice, much of what a mathematician actually does is not to derive theorems from axioms."[32]

12.15 Failure of Inferentialism

Some shortcomings of inferentialism were considered in Chapter 11. A further shortcoming follows from the strong incompleteness theorem for second-order logic. By the latter, for any consistent set R of deductive rules for second-order logic, there is a statement of the form $\forall X(A(X) \to G(X))$, containing a binary relation variable X but no non-logical constant, which is a logical truth but cannot be proved by means of the deductive rules in R.[33] This implies that the meaning of second-order logical constants cannot be fully determined by any consistent set of deductive rules. This is the end of inferentialism.

It would be no use to replace inferentialism with weak inferentialism – the view that "following certain inferential rules is constitutive of our grasp of the primitive logical constants;" and, "if certain inferential rules are constitutive of our grasp of certain concepts, then we are *eo ipso* entitled to them, even in the absence of any reflectively appreciable support."[34] Following the inferential rule which leads from $\{x: F(x)\} = \{x: G(x)\}$ to $\forall x(F(x) \leftrightarrow G(x))$ was constitutive of Frege's grasp of the primitive logical constant $\{\ldots : \ldots\}$. And yet, by Russell's paradox, Frege was not *eo ipso* entitled to that rule. This refutes the tenet of weak inferentialism.

12.16 High Expectations, Modest Returns

There is a gross disproportion between the original high expectations on logic and the modest returns of mathematical logic.

---

[31] *Ibid.*

[32] Hintikka (1996, 95).

[33] 'Logical truth' here means 'statement true in all full interpretations'. For this version of the strong incompleteness theorem for second-order logic, see Robbin (2006, 163).

[34] Boghossian (2003, 248).

12.16 High Expectations, Modest Returns

1) Parmenides, Plato, Aristotle thought that logic would provide means to acquire knowledge of the universe. But mathematical logic provides nothing of the kind, because it furnishes us with no means of discovery.

2) Frege thought that mathematical logic would provide a universal language for mathematics. But, by Tarski's undefinability theorem, this is impossible.

3) Frege, Hilbert and Gentzen thought that mathematical logic would provide a calculus of reasoning capable of representing all mathematical reasoning, and representing it faithfully. But, by the strong incompleteness theorem for second-order logic, this is impossible.

4) Frege and Hilbert thought that mathematical logic would give a secure foundation for mathematics. But, by Gödel's first, second and third incompleteness theorems, this is impossible.

5) Hilbert thought that mathematical logic would trivialize the problem of discovery. But, by the undecidability theorem, this is impossible.

6) Frege thought that mathematical logic would be the study of deduction. But, by the strong incompleteness theorem for second-order logic, this is impossible.

7) Gentzen thought that mathematical logic would be self-justifying. But, by the strong incompleteness theorem for second-order logic, and for other reasons, this is impossible.

Chapter 13
Logic, Method and Psychology of Discovery

13.1 The Divorce of Logic from Method

Frege's view, that there cannot be a logic of discovery but only a logic of justification based on deduction, and that the goal of logic is the study of deduction, has had a deep impact on the relation of logic to method. Such relation was a very strict one at the origin of logic and from the sixteenth to the first half of the nineteenth century. But, with Frege, it ended up in a divorce, and the subsequent developments of mathematical logic consolidated the divorce.

An example of this are the Kneales and Blanché who, as we have seen in the Introduction, consider the copious and passionate discussions on the scientific method in the Scientific Revolution to be extrinsic to logic and even opposed to it. Another example is Tarski who states that there is "little rational justification for combining the discussion of logic and that of the methodology of empirical sciences."[1] This contrasts with the originators of the Scientific Revolution who, as we have seen in Chapter 8, identify the scientific method with Aristotle's analytic-synthetic method.

A further step in the divorce of logic from method is analytic philosophy, according to which there is an "analogy between" the scientific method "and metamathematics."[2] Metamathematics "is concerned not with a descriptive account of mathematical research but rather with the formal characterization of correct proof."[3] Similarly, the scientific method is concerned not with a descriptive account of scientific research but rather with the formal characterization of correct scientific argument. This makes method irrelevant to scientific practice.

---

[1] Tarski (1994, xiii).
[2] Hempel (2000, 200).
[3] *Ibid.*

13.2 The Collapse of the Discussion on Method

An extreme form of the divorce of logic from method is the view that there is no scientific method at all. A prominent representative of this view is Popper. His position, however, is incongruous because, on the one hand, he states that there is no method of discovery, only a method of justification, consisting in the deductive method of testing, and, on the other hand, he states that there is no method of justification.

Indeed, on the one hand, Popper states that "there is no method of discovering a scientific theory."[4] The "initial stage, the act of conceiving or inventing a theory seems" neither "to call for logical analysis not to be susceptible of it."[5] Every "discovery contains 'an irrational element', or 'a creative intuition', in Bergson's sense."[6] The "processes involved in the stimulation and release of an inspiration" are "the concern of empirical psychology but hardly of logic."[7] The logical analysis of scientific knowledge is concerned only "with questions of justification."[8] From a new idea, or theory, discovered by creative intuition, "conclusions are drawn by means of logical deduction."[9] The theory is then tested "by way of empirical applications of the conclusion which can be derived from it."[10] This is the scientific method, which then consists in "the deductive method of testing."[11] On the other hand, Popper states that "there is no justification, including, of course, no final justification of a refutation."[12] Holding that there is no method of discovery and no method of justification, Popper concludes that the "scientific method does not exist."[13]

This is unjustified, because claiming that every discovery contains an irrational element, or a creative intuition in Bergson's sense, overlooks that an unrestrained creative intuition might generate so many ideas, or theories, or hypotheses, that it would be impossible to test all of them. There must be some criterion for picking up some hypothesis among all the possible ones and for judging it worth testing. This criterion will act as a rule of discovery, so, at least in this sense, there must be a method of discovery. On the other hand, testing may involve some research, thus some discovery task, therefore justification is not independent of discovery.

---

[4] Popper (2000, 6).
[5] Popper (2002, 7).
[6] *Ibid.*, 8.
[7] *Ibid.*
[8] *Ibid.*, 7.
[9] *Ibid.*, 9.
[10] *Ibid.*
[11] *Ibid.*, 7.
[12] Popper (2000, xxxv).
[13] *Ibid.*, 5.

Popper's incongruous position is due to the fact that he makes two tacit assumptions: 1) Only deduction is rational; 2) A procedure of justification must be algorithmic. Since deduction, being non-ampliative, cannot yield new knowledge, and hence there can be no deductive procedure of discovery, from 1) Popper infers that discovery must contain an irrational element. On the other hand, since, by the undecidability theorem, there is no algorithm for determining whether a given statement is true or false, from 2) Popper infers that there is no method of justification. But assumptions 1) and 2) are unwarranted. Assumption 1) is unwarranted, because the non-deductive rules on which the analytic method is based, though not yielding absolutely certain hypotheses, are absolutely rational. Assumption 2) is unwarranted, because the plausibility test procedure described in Chapter 4 is a non-algorithmic method of justification.

Popper claims that, by stating that induction "is a biologically useful mechanism" but "has no rational basis whatsoever," Hume makes "man an irrational animal," and human knowledge "utterly irrational."[14] On the contrary, Popper makes man an animal who not only reasons "rationally, and therefore contrary to the principle of induction, established as invalid by Hume," but also acts "rationally: in accordance with reason rather than with induction."[15] But this is unjustified. Popper too makes man an irrational animal since, by claiming that the scientific method does not exist, he is bound to conclude that the success of science is "miraculously improbable, and therefore inexplicable."[16] Human knowledge has "its basis in an irrational decision," therefore one must admit "a certain priority of irrationalism."[17]

Contrary to Popper's claim, human knowledge is rational at any stage, including the most important one, discovery. The latter is obtained by the analytic method, which is completely rational. It may be objected that the analytic method is only a heuristic method, so it does not guarantee to yield hypotheses that are sufficient conditions for solving a problem. But this objection overlooks that, as Pólya states, "if you take a heuristic conclusion as certain, you may be fooled and disappointed; but if you neglect heuristic conclusions altogether you will make no progress at all."[18]

13.3 The Psychology of Discovery

Another outcome of the divorce of logic from method is the replacement of the logic of discovery with the psychology of discovery, which was implicit in Frege's view of the problem of discovery as a psychological question. Poincaré played an important role in this replacement.

---

[14] Popper (1972, 90).
[15] Ibid., 95.
[16] Ibid., 23.
[17] Popper (1945, II, 218).
[18] Pólya (1990, 181).

According to Poincaré, "mathematical discovery" consists "in making new combinations" with ideas "that are already known" and in selecting "those that are useful," because "discovery is discernment, selection."[19] This is the work partly of the conscious mind, partly of the unconscious mind. Specifically, mathematical discovery consists of the following four successive stages.

1) When "the mind is in complete repose," ideas, which can be compared to "Epicurus' hooked atoms," are "immovable; they are, so to speak, attached to the wall."[20] But, when the conscious mind concentrates upon the problem to be solved by some voluntary effort, this has the effect "to liberate some of these atoms, to detach them from the wall and set them in motion."[21] This period of conscious work may be called the 'preparation' stage.

2) The liberated atoms will "experience collisions, either with each other, or with the atoms that have remained stationary."[22] Such collisions may "produce new combinations."[23] This can only be the work of the unconscious mind, although "the only combinations that have any chance of being formed are those in which one at least of the elements is one of the atoms deliberately selected" in the preparation stage "by our will."[24] This period of unconscious work may be called the 'incubation' stage.

3) Among the combinations thus formed, the unconscious mind must select those which are useful. Now, "the useful combinations are precisely the most beautiful," those "that can most charm that special sensibility that all mathematicians know."[25] The unconscious mind selects them on the basis of the "feeling of mathematical beauty."[26] This period of unconscious work may be called the 'illumination' stage.

4) The selections made by the unconscious mind, however, are not invariably sound. Therefore, "it is necessary to work out the results of the inspiration, to deduce the immediate consequences and put them in order and to set out the demonstrations; but, above all, it is necessary to verify them."[27] This is the work of the conscious mind. This period of conscious work may be called the 'verification' stage.[28]

---

[19]Poincaré (1914, 50–51).
[20]*Ibid.*, 61.
[21]*Ibid.*
[22]*Ibid.*, 62.
[23]*Ibid.*, 61.
[24]*Ibid.*, 62.
[25]*Ibid.*, 59.
[26]*Ibid.*
[27]*Ibid.*, 56.
[28]The names 'preparation', 'incubation', 'illumination', 'verification' for the four stages were introduced in (Wallas 1926).

13.4 Psychology of Discovery, Logic and Intuition

According to Poincaré, the process of mathematical discovery thus described involves two different faculties of the mind: intuition and logic. Each of them "is indispensable," because "intuition is the instrument of invention" while "logic, which alone can give certainty, is the instrument of demonstration."[29] Intuition is the instrument of invention, because it allows us to find axioms, each of which "is a new act of intuition."[30] It also allows us to find deductions from axioms, because intuition "is necessary to the explorer for choosing his route."[31] On the other hand, logic is the instrument of demonstration, because it "teaches us that on such and such a road we are sure of not meeting an obstacle."[32]

The reason why Poincaré considers intuition to be the instrument of invention is that he rejects the analytic method. In his view, "analysis means division, dissection. It can have, therefore, no tool other than the scalpel and the microscope."[33] On the contrary, discovery requires "a faculty which makes us see the end from afar, and intuition is this faculty."[34]

13.5 Limitations of Psychology of Discovery

Poincaré's views are still popular today. Nevertheless, they are based on some dubious assumptions.

1) *Discovery consists in making new combinations with ideas that are already known*. If so, there would be some primitive ideas out of which all combinations of ideas would be made. Then, as Leibniz suggests, it would be possible to assign characters to primitive ideas, and form new characters for all other ideas by means of combinations of such characters. The resulting characters would be a universal language for mathematics, because it would be possible to express all mathematics ideas in terms of them. This conflicts with Tarski's undefinability theorem, by which, as we have seen in Chapter 12, there cannot be such a universal language. Actually, rather than merely making new combinations with ideas that are already known, discovery involves introducing new ideas.

2) *Only the unconscious mind can make the new combinations on which discovery is based*. Therefore, the unconscious mind must be capable of – unconscious – processes not available to the conscious mind. Now, as it will be argued in Chapter

---

[29] Poincaré (1958, 23).
[30] Poincaré (1914, 163).
[31] Poincaré (1958, 22).
[32] Poincaré (1914, 129).
[33] Poincaré (1958, 23).
[34] *Ibid.*, 22.

14, unconscious processes are either native or acquired. The native unconscious processes are a result of biological evolution, and hence are too rudimentary to account for the sophisticated constructs of mathematics as a subject. The acquired unconscious processes are a result of repeated use of operations performed by the conscious mind, and hence cannot go beyond the capacities of the latter. Therefore, the unconscious mind cannot be capable of processes not available to the conscious mind.

3) *The unconscious mind selects, among the new combinations, the useful ones on the basis of the feeling of beauty.* This conflicts with the fact that such feeling is often an obstacle to selecting useful hypotheses. For example, the feeling of beauty led Galileo to stick to Copernicus' circular orbits for planets, which contrasted with observations, rejecting Kepler's elliptical orbits, which agreed with them. To Galileo, who opposed mannerism in favour of Raphael's classicism, Kepler's compressed elliptic orbits appeared unbearable aesthetic deformations. This led him to state that, "for the maintenance of perfect order among the parts of the world, it is necessary to say that movable bodies are movable only circularly."[35] Similarly, the feeling of beauty led Dirac to stick to his own version of quantum electrodynamics, which made predictions that were often infinite and hence unacceptable, rejecting renormalization which led to accurate predictions. According to Dirac, although renormalization "has been very successful in setting up rules for handling the infinities and subtracting them away," the "resulting theory is an ugly and incomplete one," and hence "cannot be considered as a satisfactory solution of the problem of the electron."[36] Admittedly, as it will be argued in Chapter 15, the aesthetic emotion often motivates and effectively guides the mathematician in his work. But this does not mean that the feeling of beauty is the deciding factor in discovery.

4) *Logic cannot be the instrument of invention, intuition alone can be such an instrument.* This conflicts with the fact that the analytic method is an instrument of invention and, as it has been argued in Chapter 4, in that method intuition plays no role. Peirce states that "we have no power of intuition, but every cognition is determined logically by previous cognitions."[37] This is perfectly fine if 'logically' is intended in the sense of 'non-deductively'.

5) *Logic is the instrument of demonstration, because it teaches us that on such and such a road we are sure of not meeting an obstacle.* This conflicts with Gödel's second incompleteness theorem, by which it is impossible to demonstrate by absolutely reliable means that on such and such a road we are sure of not meeting a contradiction.

---

[35]Galilei (1968, VII, 56).
[36]Dirac (1951, 291).
[37]Peirce (1931–1958, 5.265).

13.6 Limitations of Self-Reports

As evidence for his views, Poincaré offers self-reports of some of his own mathematical discoveries.

1) After a typically unsuccessful day, one night he "took some black coffee" and "was unable to sleep."[38] Then "a host of ideas kept surging" in his head, "until two of them coalesced" to form "a stable combination. When morning came," he "had established the existence of one class of Fuchsian functions."[39]

2) When getting "into a break to go for a drive," just as he put his "foot on the step, the idea" of the equivalence of Fuchsian functions and the transformations of non-Euclidean geometry came to him, "though nothing in" his "former thoughts seemed to have prepared" him "for it."[40]

3) While spending "a few days at the seaside" thinking of different things, as he "was walking on the cliff, the idea came" to him that "arithmetical transformations of indefinite ternary quadratic forms are identical with those of non-Euclidean geometry."[41]

4) After unsuccessful efforts to form all "Fuchsian functions other than those which are derived from the hypergeometric series," as he "was crossing the street, the solution of the difficulty which had brought" him "to a standstill came" to him "all at once."[42]

Poincaré's self-reports, however, are unconvincing in several respects. They were made some thirty years after the events occurred, which raises questions about their accuracy. Although Poincaré was eminent as a mathematician and theoretical physicist, he had no specific training and experience as a behavioural scientist, which may have limited his ability to provide valuable data about his own experiences. His self-reports give us only qualitative descriptions of his experiences, which cannot serve in a rigorous analysis. The only information they give us is that taking some black coffee at night, or getting into a break to go for a drive, or walking on a cliff, or crossing a street, may prompt mathematical discovery, which is not very helpful.[43]

---

[38]Poincaré (1914, 52).
[39]*Ibid.*, 52–53.
[40]*Ibid.*, 53.
[41]*Ibid.*, 54.
[42]*Ibid.*
[43]For other critical remarks on Poincaré views, see Weisberg (2006), Chapter 8.

13.7 The Romantic Myth of Genius

The view of the psychology of discovery, that intuition is the instrument of invention, is a remnant of the Romantic myth of genius: mathematical discovery is based on leaps of intuition and is the result of extraordinary thought processes.

Such myth goes back to Novalis, according to whom the mathematician's constructions "are leaps – (intuitions, resolutions)" and products "of the genius – of the leaper *par excellence*."[44] The "mathematical method consists in the construction of intuitions," in "the nonsensible, immediate presentation of intuitions," and "in the fixing of intuitions (reflections) by means of thoughts."[45] Poincaré shares this myth since he states that "this feeling, this intuition of mathematical order, which enables us to guess hidden harmonies and relations, cannot belong to every one."[46] Only those who possess it can "become creators, and seek to make discovery with more or less chance of success, according as their intuition is more or less developed."[47] The Romantic myth of genius seems to be popular among mathematicians even today. For example, Byers states that there are "people who find a way to transcend their limitations" and "dare to do what appears to be impossible."[48] The "impossible is rendered possible through acts of genius," and "mathematics boasts genius in abundance."[49] Genius is a matter of insight, and "insight often reveals itself in a flash."[50] Thus "mathematics transcends logic."[51]

Like all myths, however, the Romantic myth of genius is at odds with facts. Mathematical discovery is not based on leaps of intuition, but on rational processes that can be analysed in terms of rules. Even Hilbert states that "our understanding does not practice any secret arts, but rather always proceeds according to well-determined and presentable [*aufstellbar*] rules."[52] Indeed, it proceeds according to the rules of the analytic method. Moreover, mathematical discovery is not the result of extraordinary thought processes, but of ordinary thought processes that produce an extraordinary outcome.

Rather than genius, the discoverer must have a prepared mind. Specifically, he must have enough knowledge to go to the edge of the field, while being flexible enough to go over the border. Moreover, he must be able to undergo long periods of total absorption in the problem – as witnessed by Newton's cat that grew very fat by eating the food which his master left untouched on his plate when absorbed

---

[44] Novalis (2007, 28).
[45] *Ibid.*, 205.
[46] Poincaré (1914, 50).
[47] *Ibid.*
[48] Byers (2007, 16).
[49] *Ibid.*
[50] *Ibid.*, 329.
[51] *Ibid.*, 26.
[52] Hilbert (1998, 233).

in a problem. Newton himself stated: "If I have seen further, it is by standing on the shoulders of giants."[53] Indeed, his discoveries had been made possible by the assimilation of the achievements of his predecessors. And, when asked how he made his discoveries, he replied: *Nocte dieque incubando* [by thinking about it night and day]. His achievements in mathematics and natural philosophy were due "more to patient attention than to any other talent."[54] Newton knew what he was talking about.

13.8 Analytic Method vs. Intuition

Supporters of the Romantic myth of genius might object that, while many people may have enough knowledge to go to the edge of the field and undergo long periods of full immersion in the problem, only few of them make great accomplishments. And while many people may attempt to follow the analytic method, only a few of them produce important results. Therefore, there must be something special about mathematical discovery, and this is intuition. This objection, however, overlooks some basic facts.

1) The view that mathematical discovery is based on leaps of intuition, leaves it unexplained why intuition only occurs to people who have a prepared mind.

2) The view that mathematical discovery is based on leaps of intuition, depends on the argument that mathematical discovery cannot be based on inference because inference must be conscious. Since some discoveries are apparently instantaneous, it only remains that discovery be the result of leaps of intuition. This argument is based on the assumption that inference must be conscious. This is unjustified because, in the analytic method, some non-deductive inferences by which hypotheses are obtained may be unconscious. These are inferences which were originally conscious and have become automatic and unconscious as a result of repeated use, so they are acquired unconscious processes. Being inferences, they have nothing to do with intuition.

3) Mathematicians often say that they have intuitions and that this is a real phenomenon. But their self-reports are not evidence. After all, a lot of people say that they have extra-sensory perceptions or mystical experiences and that this is a real phenomenon. And indeed it is real to them. The question is to investigate this phenomenon and to explain it in rational terms. So far no such explanation has been given for intuition, and, until it is given, appealing to intuition is problematic.

4) By 'intuition', mathematicians often simply mean that feeling of immediate certainty that is "part of what is often called the 'aha' or 'eureka' experience," by which "one is absolutely certain that the solution that has just sprung into one's

---

[53]Newton (1959–1977, I, 416).
[54]Reid (1863, II, 537).

mind is the correct one."[55] One is absolutely certain of it, although one has not consciously gone through a step-by-step reasoning process to get to the solution. But there is no need to speak of intuition here. The feeling of immediate certainty can be easily explained in terms of the fact that mathematicians arrived at the hypothesis through some unconscious non-deductive inferences, which leads them to trust that the hypothesis may be plausible. As it has been stated above, such non-deductive inferences are originally conscious, and become unconscious only as a result of repeated use.

5) The analytic method is not an algorithmic method but rather a heuristic method. While an algorithmic method guarantees to achieve the solution, a heuristic method does not guarantee that, and yet it may greatly reduce the search space, that is, the domain within which the solution is sought, thus making the solution feasible.

6) The analytic method is a tool and, as such, different people may use it with different success, depending on their individual training, culture, working environment etc.. This is similar to the fact that different artisans may use the same physical tool with different success. In the case of a physical tool, we would not speak of intuition to explain the differences in success. Why should we speak of intuition in the case of a non-physical tool? Learning to use a physical tool effectively is a practical skill which is acquired by imitation and practice. The same can be said about learning to use the analytic method effectively.

7) The same person may use the analytic method effectively in dealing with one problem, and ineffectively in dealing with another problem. This is due to the fact that the effectiveness of the analytic method depends not only on the person using it, but also on the problem and the existing data.

8) The non-deductive rules on which the analytic method is based may lead from the same premises to different conclusions, hence to different hypotheses, therefore one must choose among them. This can be done by means of the plausibility test procedure described in Chapter 4, but may involve a lot of hard work. Moreover, one may feel frustrated by the failure of several hypotheses before arriving at a plausible one. Failures may be very discouraging and, if one is not obsessed enough with the problem, one may easily give up.

9) The non-deductive rules on which the analytic method is based are not a closed set, given once for all, but rather an open set that can always be expanded as research develops. In several cases, discovery does not occur until proper non-deductive procedures are found. This is inexplicable if discovery is based on leaps of intuition.

---

[55]Byers (2007, 329).

Part III
An Alternative Perspective

Chapter 14
Reason and Knowledge

14.1 The Need to Reconsider the Nature of Logic

The limitations of mathematical logic and the divorce of logic from method suggest that a different approach to logic is necessary, based on an alternative logic paradigm.

As anticipated in the Introduction, with respect to mathematical logic, the alternative logic paradigm will involve a new view of the relation of logic to evolution, language, reason, method and knowledge, and a new view of the relation of philosophy to knowledge.

In order to formulate such new views, we must first examine the nature of reason and knowledge, and the relation of reason and knowledge to emotion. This chapter will examine the former, Chapter 15 the latter.

14.2 The Origin of Logic and Reason

As we have seen in Chapter 2, Parmenides, Plato and Aristotle provide an explanation of the origin of logic, meant as that rational faculty which all human beings have. According to them, logic originates from the fact that the human mind mirrors the divine mind which governs the universe. As a result, all human beings have a rational faculty, and logic is that faculty.

This explanation of the origin of the rational faculty and logic has survived until today. For example, Wittgenstein states that "how things stand, is God. God is, how things stand."[1] Thus God is "the world – which is independent of our will."[2] On the

---
[1] Wittgenstein (1979, 1.8.16).
[2] *Ibid.*, 8.7.16.

other hand, "logic is not a body of doctrine but a mirror-image of the world."[3] It forms "a great mirror."[4] Therefore, "logic fills the world: the limits of the world are also its limits."[5] And "to give the essence of proposition means to give" the "essence of the world."[6]

Such an explanation, however, is unsatisfactory because it is based on the assumption that there is a divine mind that governs the universe and the human mind mirrors, but there is no evidence for this assumption. The mediaevals warned: *Non est philosophi recurrere ad Deum* [a philosopher should not make explanatory recourse to God]. The explanation in question contravenes this warning. Towards an alternative explanation of the origin of the rational faculty and logic, we must consider the concept of reason. For logic has been traditionally viewed as a part of reason, being an attempt to describe the rules by which reason, at least discursive reason, operates.

14.3 The Concept of Reason

What is reason? According to the common concept, "reason is the ability of the human mind to form and operate on concepts in abstraction," a "type or aspect of mental thought which has traditionally been claimed as distinctly human, and not to be found elsewhere in the animal world."[7] This concept of reason, however, is unsatisfactory because it implies that no non-human animal possesses reason. This overlooks that non-human animals, even animals without a brain, have behaviours that, in human beings, would be said to be rational. As Peirce points out, "thought is not necessarily connected with a brain."[8] This casts doubts on the view that reason is a kind of mental thought that is distinctly human and is not to be found elsewhere in the animal world.

Towards a more adequate concept of reason, it may be useful to remember that, like the strictly related term 'rationality', the term 'reason' derives from the Greek *logos*, or more directly from the Latin *ratio*, one of whose meanings is 'relation'. In fact, reason is a matter of the relation of means to given ends. It can be defined as the capacity to choose appropriate means to given ends. It has nothing to do with the choice of ends. On the other hand, rationality is the exercise of reason. This concept of reason is not limited to human beings but extends to all organisms, because all organisms are capable of choosing appropriate means to certain given ends, starting with that of survival.

---

[3] Wittgenstein (1922, 6.13).
[4] *Ibid.*, 5.511.
[5] *Ibid.*, 5.61.
[6] *Ibid.*, 5.4711.
[7] Ivancevic and Ivancevic (2008, 13).
[8] Peirce (1931–1958, 4.551).

That this is the proper concept of reason has been acknowledged by a number of people. Thus Dewey states that "rationality is an affair of the relation of means and consequences," that is, the relation of "means (methods) employed and conclusions attained as their consequence."[9] Russell states that reason "signifies the choice of the right means to an end that you wish to achieve. It has nothing whatever to do with the choice of ends."[10]

Against this concept of reason, Rescher objects that "reason at large must care for ends as well as means."[11] It hinges critically "on the appropriateness of our ends."[12] For "the pursuit of what we want is rational only in so far as we have sound reasons for deeming this to be want-deserving."[13]

But this objection overlooks that one cannot assert of any ends that they are appropriate. For suppose that one asserts that certain ends are appropriate. Then the question arises: Why are such ends appropriate? If one answers that they are appropriate because there are good reasons for deeming them to be appropriate, then the question arises: Why are such reasons good reasons? If one answers that they are good reasons because there are good reasons for deeming them to be good reasons, then the question arises: Why are such reasons good reasons? And so on, *ad infinitum*.

Since one cannot assert of any ends that they are appropriate, reason cannot have anything to do with the choice of ends, but only with the choice of appropriate means to given ends. Already Aristotle observed that "we deliberate not about ends, but about means to ends."[14] For example, "a doctor does not deliberate about whether he shall heal, nor an orator whether he shall persuade, nor a statesman whether he shall produce good order, nor does anyone else deliberate about his end."[15] Rather, when the end has been set, they consider how and by what means it is to be attained.

One could assert that certain ends are appropriate only if there were an ultimate purpose of the world. Some religions claim that an ultimate purpose exists, but this is an unproven claim, so it all boils down to a matter of faith.

14.4 The Metaphor of Choosing

It might be objected that, while extending to all organisms, the above definition of reason appeals to a capacity, the capacity to choose, which is distinctly human. This objection, however, is invalid because, in such definition, the expression 'capacity

---

[9] Dewey (1938, 9).
[10] Russell (1954, viii).
[11] Rescher (1988, 96).
[12] *Ibid.*, 100.
[13] *Ibid.*, 99.
[14] Aristotle, *Ethica Nicomachea*, Γ 3, 1112 b 11–12.
[15] *Ibid.*, Γ 3, 1112 b 12–15.

to choose' is only a metaphor. One of the uses of metaphor is to extend familiar properties to unfamiliar contexts. Here metaphor is used to extend the expression 'capacity to choose', which usually applies to human beings, to the unfamiliar context of non-human organisms.

Metaphor is ubiquitous in science, including biology, where one often finds expressions such as, 'the brain believes', or 'the cell decides', or 'the enzyme recognizes', or 'natural selection prefers'. Such expressions help to understand the unfamiliar in terms of the familiar. They make complicated processes intelligible, by highlighting their functional components in a human reference frame. The use of such metaphors is justified by the complexity of the phenomena involved. Metaphors are harmful only if one considers them as referring to actually existing entities or acts, otherwise they are harmless.

14.5 Human Nature

Since one cannot assert of any ends that they are appropriate, the above concept of reason is not an absolute but only a relative one, relative to given ends. One may wonder whether, with respect to human beings, such concept of reason might be made less relative by defining reason as the capacity to choose appropriate means to ends which are conformable to human nature. To give an answer to this question we must consider what human nature is.

Now, human nature is the result of two factors: biological and cultural evolution. In explaining what human nature is, biological evolution plays an essential role, because our biological makeup has a basic importance in determining what we are.

This view is fiercely opposed by those who think that cultural evolution has nothing to do with biological evolution because our biological makeup has no importance in determining what we are. According to them, there is no biological basis of our most important behaviours, they are only a result of cultural evolution. In particular, human beings have made a qualitative leap through language, which is the key factor in their superiority upon non-human animals. Through it, human beings have access to culture, which is a separate world of its own. Only human beings have access to it, since only they can think.

For example, Heidegger states that "the fact that physiology and physiological chemistry can scientifically investigate the human being as an organism is no proof" that "the essence of the human being consists" in "this 'organic' thing, that is, in the body scientifically explained."[16] There is a basic difference between the human being and non-human animals, which makes the latter "separated from our ek-sistent essence by an abyss," that is, the fact that they "lack language."[17] Language "is not the utterance of an organism; nor is it the expression of a living thing," rather it is the

---

[16]Heidegger (1998, 247).
[17]*Ibid.*, 248

"advent of being itself."[18] Only the human being, possessing language, has access to thinking, because "thinking builds upon the house of being."[19]

This, however, is unjustified. The claim that language is the key factor in the superiority of human beings upon non-human animals overlooks that, as Pinker states, language is only "a distinct piece of the biological makeup of our brains."[20] As non-human animals can do things human beings cannot do, human beings can do things non-human animals cannot do. The superiority of human beings upon non-human animals is only an anthropocentric prejudice.

Moreover, the claim that culture is a separate world of its own, and that only human beings have access to it since only they can think, overlooks that human beings can only think the thoughts their biological makeup permits them to think. Pinker says that "spiders spin spider webs because they have spider brains, which give them the urge to spin and the competence to succeed."[21] Similarly, we can say that human beings think human thoughts because they have human brains, which give them the urge to think and the competence to succeed. Thus, culture depends on the biological makeup of human beings, and hence is not a separate world of its own.

Rather, culture is a shared system of cognitions, beliefs and behaviours that human beings develop or acquire from other human beings, and transmit to succeeding generations non-genetically. Such a system has a biological basis, because it depends on the biological makeup of human beings.[22]

14.6 Cultural and Biological Evolution

Cultural evolution too depends on the biological makeup of human beings. It consists in the modifications or expansions that shared systems of cognitions, beliefs or behaviours undergo in the succeeding generations, and all such modifications and expansions depend on the biological makeup of human beings.

Admittedly, cultural and biological evolution are distinct. The former does not reduce to the latter for at least the following reasons.

1) Biological evolution is slow, it takes thousands of unfavourable mutations before a favourable one emerges. Cultural evolution is much faster, being a result of non-genetic interactions between billions of human beings.

2) Human beings are able to do things which are not strictly necessary for survival. In the course of biological evolution they have been faced with situations that had not occurred in their evolutionary past. The world changes continually and

---

[18] *Ibid.*, 248–249.
[19] *Ibid.*, 272.
[20] Pinker (1995, 18).
[21] *Ibid.*
[22] In addition to human culture there are also non-human cultures, but this will not be pursued here.

irregularly, so human beings have to deal all the time with new situations. If their problem-solving resources were always strained to the limit, they might easily fail when certain critical situations occur, and if these failures had frequently occurred in their evolutionary past, we would not be here to tell. To be able to cope with critical situations during times of peak demand, human beings must have excess capacity to spare for other issues at slack times. Thanks to this, in normal circumstances they may engage in activities that are not immediately necessary for survival. Such activities are a result of cultural evolution.

3) Cultural evolution makes a significant difference between human beings and the simplest organisms. While the latter have little control upon the environment, human beings may exert a considerable control upon it due to cultural evolution. Of course, for most part of their history, they have been in a condition not too dissimilar from that of the simplest organisms, and hence have had to devote most of their efforts to survival. Due to cultural evolution, however, the situation changed, and today a substantial number of human beings may devote only a comparatively limited part of their efforts to survival.

But, even if cultural and biological evolution are distinct and the former does not reduce to the latter, cultural evolution depends on the biological makeup of human beings, and hence on biological evolution. Thus between cultural and biological evolution there is no opposition, but rather continuity. In fact, between them there could be no long-term conflict. It would be an unequal conflict, one in which biological evolution would always win and cultural evolution would always lose.

14.7 Essential Relativity of the Concept of Reason

Since human nature is the result of biological and cultural evolution, and the latter depends on the biological makeup of human beings, thus on biological evolution, there is no fixed invariable human nature. The latter has a contingent character, owing to the contingent status of the present stage of evolution. Biological evolution does not proceed according to a preconceived design, and has no ends. Already some early Greek philosopher asked: "What forbids that nature should work with no end, and not for the sake of the better"?[23]

Since there is no fixed invariable human nature, we must give a negative answer to the question whether the above concept of reason might be made less relative by defining reason as the capacity to choose appropriate means to ends which are conformable to human nature. Ends conformable to human nature are relative to human nature, which has a contingent character. Therefore, the above concept of reason is relative to the contingent character of human nature, which is a contingent result of biological and cultural evolution.

---

[23] Aristotle, *Physica*, B 8, 198 b 17.

14.8 Natural and Artificial Reason

Since human nature is the result of biological and cultural evolution, two kinds of reason must be distinguished: natural and artificial reason. Natural reason is that capacity to choose appropriate means to given ends which virtually all kinds of organisms have as a result of biological evolution, thanks to which they may survive. The name 'natural reason' is intended to stress that it is a result of biological evolution. Artificial reason is that capacity to choose appropriate means to given ends which human beings have as a result of cultural evolution. The name 'artificial reason' is intended to stress that it is not a result of biological evolution but rather of cultural evolution.

This explains the relation of reason to evolution: natural reason is a result of biological evolution, artificial reason a result of cultural evolution.

Natural and artificial reason are distinct, nevertheless between them there is no opposition but rather continuity. For they are a result of biological and cultural evolution, respectively, and, as it has been stated above, between cultural and biological evolution there is no opposition but rather continuity. While artificial reason is a comparatively recent thing, by their natural reason human beings were capable of choosing appropriate means to given ends perhaps as much as 200,000 years ago, otherwise they would not have survived. Even artificial reason ultimately depends on that capacity, which is a result of biological evolution.

A special case of the distinction between natural and artificial reason is that between natural and artificial logic. This will be discussed in Chapter 16.

A remark about the expressions 'natural' and 'artificial'. Using 'artificial' with respect to reason may sound odd, but the antonym for 'natural' is 'unnatural', and using it in place of 'artificial' would sound even odder. Moreover, the first dictionary meaning of 'artificial' is 'produced by human art or effort rather than originating naturally', which is exactly what is meant here.

14.9 Reason and Mind

Reason is traditionally regarded as a faculty of mind, distinct from other faculties, such as emotion. Then, since the above concept of reason is not limited to human beings but extends to all organisms, the mind too is not limited to human beings but extends to all organisms.

This conclusion may appear odd but is not so. For the mind does not really exist, it is only a way of saying, it merely denotes certain capacities of the body. The capacities of the body which make up the mind are present to a certain extent in all organisms. One may speak of the mind only as consisting in such capacities, not as an entity per se. Therefore, it is not odd to say that mind extends to all organisms.

In the case of the human mind, to assume that it is an entity per se is to neglect the basic role the body plays in human thinking and in knowledge. Several central aspects of human thinking and knowledge depend on the kind of body we have, and can be explained only in terms of it. Therefore, the view that the mind is an entity per se is untenable.[24] The human mind merely consists of certain capacities of the human body. We do not merely have a body, we are a body.

14.10 The Sapient Paradox

The capacities of the body which make up the human mind have not been always the same. The features of our 'sapient' status started emerging only some 10,000 years ago. This leads to the so-called "sapient paradox: that the biological basis of our species has been established" perhaps "for as much as 200,000 years," while "the novel behavioural aspects of our 'sapient' status have taken so long to emerge."[25]

Towards solving this paradox, it is important to notice that the features of our 'sapient' status started emerging roughly simultaneously with the inception of the sedentary revolution – the transition from nomadic to permanent, year-round settlement which ensued from the end of the last ice age. This is not accidental, because the sedentary revolution radically changed the way of life of several human beings, setting them new challenging tasks.

Coping with them required new capacities to choose appropriate means to given ends. For example, the rise of agriculture, one of the features of the sedentary revolution, required the capacity to choose appropriate means to foresee recurring changes and regularities in natural events, and to direct natural events to human ends. Requiring such new capacities, the sedentary revolution involved that extension of reason which characterizes our 'sapient' status.

14.11 The Extended Mind

That the sedentary revolution involved an extension of reason means that, if reason is a faculty of the mind, then the sedentary revolution involved an extension of the mind. The mind of our remotest ancestors was mostly confined to the body, in particular to the brain. The sedentary revolution changed all this. It led to new situations and changes in the environment, which gave rise to new material conditions, cultural practices and interpersonal relationships, setting human beings new challenging tasks.

The mind could cope with them only by acquiring new capacities. It acquired them by spreading out across the body-world boundary, through processes external to the body, from material to symbolic ones, such as pictures, models, maps, and

---

[24]Other reasons why this view is untenable are presented in Cellucci (2008a), Chapter 11.
[25]Renfrew (2008, 2041).

symbol systems.[26] Such external processes formed an integrated whole with those internal to the body, which essentially changed the nature of the mind making it an 'extended mind'.

The concept of extended mind goes back at least to Dewey, who states that "thinking, or knowledge-getting," is "not an event going on exclusively within the cortex."[27] For "hands and feet, apparatus and appliances of all kinds are as much a part of it as changes in the brain."[28] Then "thinking is mental, not because of a peculiar stuff which enters into it or of the peculiar non-natural activities which constitute it, but because of what physical acts and appliances do."[29]

Of course, as the mind does not exist, the extended mind does not exist, it is only a way of saying. It merely denotes certain capacities of the body expanded with processes external to it. One may speak of the extended mind only in this sense.

The extended mind provides an answer to the sapient paradox. The novel behavioural aspects of our 'sapient' status started emerging only some 10,000 years ago because the sedentary revolution set human beings new challenging tasks. Human beings could cope with them only because the mind acquired new capacities by spreading out across the body-world boundary, thus becoming an extended mind. This is, indeed, an ongoing process. Even today we are finding new ways in which to expand certain capacities of the body with processes external to it, from material to symbolic ones.

14.12 Extended Mind and World

The rise of the extended mind involved a change in the subject of knowledge. Objects in the environment came to play a role in knowledge similar to that of neural states, so the subject of knowledge was no longer the body alone, but the body plus certain processes external to it. Such processes were a constituent part of the way human beings acquired knowledge of the world, so knowledge became distributed knowledge – distributed between the body and external processes. The mind became only a piece of the world that was looking at another piece of the world, using processes occurring in the world.

As Calvino's Mr. Palomar says, usually "you think of the ego as one who is peering out of your own eyes as if leaning on a window sill, looking at the world stretching out before him in all its immensity."[30] The "world is out there; and in here, what do we have? The world still – what else could there be?"[31] Simply, "for

---

[26]For more on this, see Cellucci (2008a), Chapter 21.

[27]Dewey (1916, 13–14).

[28]*Ibid.*, 14.

[29]*Ibid.*

[30]Calvino (1985, 114).

[31]*Ibid.*

the occasion" the world "has been split into a looking world and a world looked at."[32] The ego of Mr. Palomar is only "a piece of the world that is looking at another piece of the world," and "through which the world looks at the world. To look at itself the world needs the eyes (and the eyeglasses) of Mr. Palomar."[33]

14.13 Extended Mind and Brain Plasticity

The concept of extended mind contrasts with a tradition according to which "how the world is makes no difference to one's mental states."[34] Contrary to such tradition, how the world is makes all the difference to one's mental states, because the interactions with external processes produce modifications in the structure of the brain that enhance its capacities.

The extended mind required new capacities of the human brain not available earlier. They cannot be attributed to biological evolution, because the sedentary revolution is too recent to have exerted any evolutionary pressure on brain evolution. They must rather be attributed to brain plasticity, the ability of the human brain to partially rewire itself as a result of experience, through interactions with external processes. Through biological evolution, the nervous system has inherited changes that do not depend on the whims of individual experience, so the architecture of the human brain is laid down under tight genetic constraints. Nevertheless, it has a certain variability range, so the nervous system can rewire itself to a certain extent as the result of experiences that occur during an individual lifetime.

Specifically, when the human brain is faced with tasks for which it was not prepared by biological evolution, it partially reconverts some cerebral circuits initially selected to support evolutionary relevant functions, but sufficiently plastic for acquiring new functions. Therefore, "cultural inventions invade evolutionary older braid circuits."[35] Thus cognitive abilities evolved for evolutionary purposes are co-opted for new tasks.

Saying that the human brain partially reconverts a limited number of cerebral circuits, means that the human brain is not a blank slate but is highly structured. Biological evolution has built up specialized cerebral circuits that carry out specific mental functions. Nevertheless, the structure of the human brain is sufficiently modifiable through experience, especially in young children, so as to make it capable of functions different from those for which it was prepared by biological evolution. As a result, although we are born with the same brain as our hunter-gatherer ancestors, our extended mind is not the same as their mind.

---

[32] Ibid.
[33] Ibid.
[34] Fodor (1981, 228).
[35] Dehaene and Cohen (2007, 384).

On the other hand, the modifications of the human brain can never totally overturn the structure resulting from biological evolution. The reconversion of a limited number of cerebral circuits is possible only insofar as it remains within a certain variability range. Thus the new capacities reflect the intrinsic constraints of the underlying architecture of the human brain. Therefore, the cultural inventions which invade evolutionary older braid circuits "inherit many of their structural constraints."[36] The modifications in question are not genetically but only culturally heritable, so they need to be reiterated by each child since birth. Each child can participate into the phylogenetic acquisition of culture only through that personal (ontogenetic) acquisition of skills and experience which gives rise to the extended mind.

14.14 Biological Role of Knowledge

It has been said earlier that the above concept of reason is not limited to human beings but extends to all organisms, since all organisms are capable of choosing appropriate means to certain given ends, starting with the end of survival. But how do they implement such capacity? In particular, how do they manage to choose appropriate means to the end of survival?

In order to survive, all organisms must use energy sources present in the environment, and avoid dangers that could destroy them. To that end, they must acquire knowledge about the environment. All organisms acquire such knowledge, thanks to which they assume behaviours that, when successful, ensure their survival.

'All organisms' includes the most elementary ones, such as the prokaryotes, the unicellular organisms which were the first form of life on the Earth. While not having a nervous system, they have molecules on their cell membrane which act as sensors. On the basis of the information encoded in their genoma, they interpret the data about the environment they receive through sensors, and react to them with flagellar movements. This results in behaviours which have permitted prokaryotes to be the only form of life on Earth for at least two billion years, and the toughest one, capable of surviving in the coldest, hottest, most acidic and most highly pressurized environments.

'All organisms' even includes plants. Some of them, when attacked by herbivores, implement sophisticated defence strategies. They produce complex polymers that reduce plant digestibility, or produce toxins that repel and even kill the herbivores. They even use other insects against the herbivores, emitting volatile organic compounds which attract other carnivorous insects that kill the attacking herbivores. These volatile organic compounds may be perceived by neighbouring yet-undamaged plants, and alert them to adjust their defensive phenotype to the risk of attack. Thus they function as external signals for within-plant communication.

---

[36] *Ibid.*

Since, in order to survive, all organisms must acquire knowledge about the environment, knowledge is a natural phenomenon that occurs in all organisms. All organisms are cognitive systems, and life itself owes its existence and development to cognitive processes. Therefore, knowledge has a biological role, just like other capacities which ensure the survival of organisms. To know something is an act which is as biological as digesting, because knowledge is essential for life. That to know something is such a biological act is an important issue to which, rather surprisingly, not enough attention has been paid.

The knowledge about the world that organisms have consists first of all of knowledge encoded in the genome. Such knowledge concerns facts of the evolutionary past of organisms, but new facts may occur not encountered in the past. To cope with them, organisms must acquire new knowledge about the world. They are, as it were, knowledge which calls for new knowledge.

Organisms acquire knowledge about the world through their cognitive faculties, which permit them to categorize things and facts of the world into a relatively small set of classes which are meaningful from an evolutionary point of view. Categorization is vital for survival, because it permits organisms to make fast decisions based on limited sensory information. Even organisms with tiny brains, such as insects, are able to perceive the world in terms of high-level categories, because cognitive capabilities found in insects, such as categorisation-like processes, may require a limited number of neurons.

14.15 The Consciousness Argument

Against the claim that knowledge is a natural phenomenon which occurs in all organisms, it might be objected that knowledge requires consciousness, which only human beings can have, therefore only they can have knowledge. For example, Descartes states that "there can be no knowledge except in a mind."[37] But "there can be nothing in the mind, in so far as it is a thinking thing, of which" the mind "is not conscious."[38] Therefore, only human beings can have knowledge, since "animals do not see as we do when we are conscious that we see; but only as we do when our mind is elsewhere."[39]

This objection is unjustified, because consciousness is neither necessary nor sufficient for knowledge. It is not necessary, because a significant part of human knowledge is arrived at through processes which are unconscious, in the sense explained in the next section. It is not sufficient, because beliefs arrived at consciously need not be knowledge. For example, Frege arrived at his Basic Law

---

[37] Descartes (1996, VII, 442).
[38] *Ibid.*, VII, 246.
[39] *Ibid.*, I, 413.

(V) consciously, but this did not prevent it from leading to a contradiction. Thus his belief that the Basic Law (V) was true was not knowledge.

The objection is an expression of human conceit. It is human conceit to think that knowledge is something which is unique to human beings, and that such uniqueness is due to the fact that knowledge requires consciousness, which only human beings can have.

14.16 Unconscious Processes

In the previous section it has been stated that a significant part of human knowledge is arrived at through processes which are unconscious. They are unconscious not because they are repressed in Freud's sense, but rather because they occur too fast and at too low a level in the mind to be accessible to direct inspection. An example of knowledge of this kind is perceptive knowledge. As it will be argued in Chapter 16, perception is the result of unconscious inferences.

As it has been already mentioned in Chapter 13, unconscious processes are of two kinds: native or acquired. Native unconscious processes are those which are performed by the unconscious mind by itself alone, without training. They are based on capacities which the unconscious mind has as a result of biological evolution, and hence are innate. Acquired unconscious processes are those which are performed by the unconscious mind automatically, as a result of repeated use of operations learned through experience and training, such as artisanry or ballet. Therefore, they are the automatization of operations performed by the conscious mind. Because of their origin, these processes are not innate, but rather a result of cultural evolution. Thus, artisanry is a cultural product originating in the first urban societies, ballet a cultural product originating in the Italian Renaissance courts of the fifteenth and sixteenth centuries.

The processes of natural reason are native unconscious processes. Those of artificial reason are partly conscious processes, partly acquired unconscious processes.

14.17 Knowledge and the Unknowability of Things in Themselves

In acquiring knowledge, the cognitive system of organisms plays an essential role, because it permits them to get data about the world and elaborate them. In particular, this applies to the human cognitive system. Having evolved in response to certain challenges of the world, it is fit to handle those aspects of the world from which such challenges arise. This, however, does not mean that the human cognitive system is fit to handle all aspects of the world. Clearly, the human perceptual system is subject to limitations. For example, it cannot pick up ultraviolet light, since the latter played no role in the evolution of the human species, say, in food or sexual selection. On the other hand, there is no reason to believe that the human conceptual system is exempt from limitations, inasmuch as "the human conceptual system was derived in large measure from the long preexisting primate perceptual apparatus."[40]

The world exists independently of us, or rather, including us, because we are part of it. But what we can know about it depends on our experience, which in its turn depends on our perceptual and conceptual systems and their limitations.[41] Of course, we can expand the capacities of our cognitive system by building new machinery, such as microscopes, telescopes, etc.. But we could have knowledge of all aspects of the world only if we could expand such capacities beyond all limits, and there is no evidence that this is at all possible. Therefore, we cannot claim that our cognitive system is fit to handle all aspects of the world.

Saying this is not a form of mysterianism, but only a version of Kant's view that we cannot know things in themselves, where 'thing in itself' is "merely a boundary concept," and "therefore only of negative use."[42] Such concept "serves for nothing but to designate the boundaries of our sensible cognition."[43] 'Thing in itself' and 'phenomenon' do not designate two different realms of being, but only two different ways of considering the same thing, as a thing in itself or as phenomenon. That we cannot know things in themselves is just another way of saying that we can only know that "which can be brought into connection with our actual perceptions."[44] Thus, with our cognitive system.

Kant's view has been variously criticized. For example, Plotkin states that, "if living things could never know the things in themselves, then life would never survive for any time at all beyond that given by chance matching."[45] Then "Kant must be wrong," because "we and the myriad other forms of life do survive."[46] This is based on the assumption that survival depends on knowledge of the things in themselves. But such an assumption is unwarranted. Survival only depends on knowledge of certain phenomenal aspects of the world, otherwise the first unicellular organisms out of which life evolved would not have survived.

As another example, Nagel states that Kant is wrong in assuming that, like secondary qualities, "primary qualities, too, describe the world only as it appears to us."[47] For "our conception of primary qualities is a partial conception of things as they are in themselves."[48] This disregards the nature of Galileo's philosophical

---

[40]Sullivan (2009, 66).

[41]Concerning the dependence of what we can know on our perceptual and conceptual systems, see also the remarks in Rescher (2009), Chapter 3.

[42]Kant (1997a, 350, B 310–311).

[43]*Ibid.*, 381, B 345.

[44]Kant (2002, 143).

[45]Plotkin (1997, 241).

[46]*Ibid.*

[47]Nagel (1986, 101).

[48]*Ibid.*, 104.

revolution, according to which, as it has been argued in Chapter 8, primary qualities are only phenomenal properties of natural substances, not their true and intrinsic essence.

14.18 The Purpose of Knowledge

That we cannot claim that our cognitive system is fit to handle all aspects of the world, implies that the purpose of knowledge cannot be to give us a complete picture of the world. As Suppes states, "the collection of past, present, and future scientific theories is not converging to some bounded fixed result that will in the limit give us complete knowledge of the universe."[49] Rather than to give us a complete picture of the world, the purpose of knowledge is to find hypotheses that work in solving the problems with which we are confronted, starting with that of survival. In particular, since some of such hypotheses work in solving the problem of survival, knowledge is essential for life.

This sharply contrasts with the view of those Greek philosophers according to whom knowledge is an end in itself, and nothing derives from it apart from contemplation. For example, Aristotle states that human beings "pursue knowledge only for the sake of knowing, and not for any utilitarian end."[50] From knowledge "nothing results apart from contemplation."[51] The remote origin of this view can perhaps be traced back to Ajax's prayer to Zeus: "Father Zeus, deliver from the darkness the sons of the Acheans, | make heaven serene, let us see: | and since you want us to perish, at least let us perish in the light."[52] For Ajax, even dying is acceptable if one is in the light of knowledge, since knowledge is an end in itself.

Such a view was quite natural in ancient Greece, where there was a sharp division between doing and knowing, reflecting an economic and social organization in which useful work was done mainly by slaves. This relieved free men from labour, permitting them to devote themselves to "those sciences which do not aim" at "the necessities of life."[53] Conversely, the view in question is incongruous with modern science, in which scientific knowledge is not pursued only for the sake of knowing, but also to improve man's lot.

According to Aristotle, the view that human beings pursue knowledge only for the sake of knowing, and not for any utilitarian end, "is confirmed by the facts: when almost all the necessities of life and the things that make for comfort and recreation had been secured, only then knowledge began to be sought."[54] But it is not so. Knowledge did not begin to be sought only then, it was sought from the very

---

[49] Suppes (1984, 10).

[50] Aristotle, *Metaphysica*, A 2, 982 b 20–21.

[51] Aristotle, *Ethica Nicomachea*, K 7, 1177 b 2.

[52] Homer, *Ilias*, XVII.645–648.

[53] Aristotle, *Metaphysica*, A 1, 981 b 21–22.

[54] *Ibid.*, A 2, 982 b 22–24.

beginning because it plays a vital role in human life, and generally in the life of all organisms – literally vital because, without knowledge, life could not have existed nor could continue to exist.

It is through knowledge that life, from the prokaryotes to human beings, has been able to exist and preserve itself. The resources whose scarcity is an obstacle to the preservation of life are not only food and other material things, but also knowledge. The prokaryotes who solved their survival problem using knowledge obtained through their rudimentary sense organs, were the first to discover that knowledge is essential for life, and indeed a precondition of it.

14.19 Cultural Role of Knowledge

It has been said above that knowledge has a biological role. In addition, of course, it has a cultural role. This is implicit in the very concept of culture. As it has been said earlier, the latter is a shared system of cognitions, beliefs and behaviours that human beings develop or acquire from other human beings, and transmit to succeeding generations non-genetically. Therefore, a culture is a system of knowledge.

The origin of the cultural role of knowledge can be traced back to the rise of the extended mind, and hence to the sedentary revolution of some 10,000 years ago. This led to a drastic acceleration in the rate of innovation. Survival was no longer dependent on the capacity to find and exploit wild resources, but became increasingly dependent on the capacity to control the environment. Rather than moving to new locations, solving problems became the crucial factor for survival. Problems prompted the search for hypotheses to solve them, which led to further problems and hypotheses, and so on. This yielded a continued growth of knowledge, which greatly increased the means by which to face the challenges posed by the world, enabling human beings to meet more and more complex challenges in shorter and shorter time. Once that stage was reached, biology became only part of the story. Cultural evolution took over from biological evolution in the development of the means by which human beings could face and modify their physical and social environment.

This does not mean that the cultural role of knowledge is opposed to the biological one. Rather, it is a development of it and could not exist without it. The continuity between the cultural and the biological role of knowledge is apparent, for example, from the fact that, even in its cultural role, knowledge may affect biological evolution, either positively or negatively. The system of cognitions, beliefs and behaviours in which a culture consists, may enable human beings to develop means for survival, and to modify the environment by making it more suitable to them. But it may also enable them to modify the environment in ways that might endanger the survival of human beings. In both cases, the changes in the environment may determine changes in biological evolution.

Generally, both in its biological and cultural role, knowledge develops in sustained interaction between human beings and their environment. This depends on the fact that knowledge is oriented towards solving problems, starting from that of survival.

14.20 Scientific Knowledge

Of course, when saying that the cultural role of knowledge is not opposed to the biological one but rather a development of it, knowledge includes scientific knowledge.

Sometimes people speak as if scientific knowledge referred to a world other than the one to which our ordinary everyday knowledge refers. This is not so. There is just one world, scientific knowledge and ordinary everyday knowledge refer to the same world. The only difference between them is that we do not need much apparatus or professional expertise to discover the facts of our ordinary everyday knowledge. Conversely, we need a good deal of apparatus and professional expertise to discover the facts of scientific knowledge. And yet, the latter are by no means separated from the facts of our ordinary everyday experience, because they refer to the same world.

It is for this reason that, as it has been already mentioned, scientific knowledge can improve man's lot. In particular, scientific knowledge can affect biological evolution. As Mach says, "we can hardly doubt that" science "has developed into the factor that is biologically and culturally most beneficial."[55] Science "has taken over the task of replacing tentative and unconscious adaptation by a faster variety that is fully conscious and methodical."[56]

In this respect, scientific knowledge can be viewed as an extension of the activities by which our remotest ancestors solved their survival problem. Such activities, and those underlying scientific knowledge, are based on essentially similar cognitive processes. Our hunter-gatherer ancestors solved their survival problem by making hypotheses about the location of predators or prey on the basis of hints they found in the environment – crushed or bent grass and vegetation, bent or broken branches or twigs, mud displaced from streams, and so on. Much in the same way, scientists solve problems by making hypotheses on the basis of hints they find in nature.

14.21 Mathematical Knowledge

Even mathematical knowledge can affect biological evolution. In order to survive, human beings must have cognitive systems capable of capturing some basic information about number and space. In fact, current research in cognitive science indicates that, as a result of biological evolution, human beings have "systems of core knowledge" that are "phylogenetically ancient, innate, and universal across

---

[55] Mach (1976, 361).
[56] *Ibid.*

humans" and capture "the primary information in the system of positive integers" and "the primary information in the system of Euclidean plane geometry."[57]

Such systems reside in the biological makeup of human beings and have a biological function. Biological evolution has hardwired organisms to perform certain mathematical operations, building mathematics in several features of their biological set up, such as locomotion and vision, which require some sophisticated embodied mathematics. Such mathematical operations are essential for survival, because only through them organisms can escape from danger, or search for food, or seek out a mate. This explains why these systems of core knowledge are not unique to the human species but are present also in other species.[58]

On the other hand, the development of pictures, models, maps, and symbol systems permitted human beings to go beyond the systems of core knowledge, giving rise to mathematics as a subject. Unlike natural mathematics, which is innate, mathematics as a subject is acquired. Therefore, two kinds of mathematics must be distinguished: natural and artificial mathematics. Natural mathematics is the mathematics based upon the systems of core knowledge. The name 'natural mathematics' is intended to stress that it is embodied in organisms as a result of biological evolution. Artificial mathematics is mathematics as a subject. The name 'artificial mathematics' is intended to stress that it is not a direct natural product, not being a direct result of biological evolution, but rather a human product, thus only an indirect natural product.

Artificial mathematics is a product of the extended mind. It goes beyond the systems of core knowledge, because it makes use of cultural artifacts such as pictures, models, maps, and symbol systems. Thus artificial mathematics is a result of cultural evolution. The relation between natural and artificial mathematics is similar to that between natural and artificial reason: they are distinct, and yet between them there is no opposition, but rather continuity. For they are a result of biological and cultural evolution and, as it has been stated above, between cultural and biological evolution there is no opposition, but rather continuity.

Like natural mathematics, artificial mathematics has a biological function, since it permits human beings to cope with situations dissimilar from those that occurred in their evolutionary past. It develops tools that allow us to see and think about the world in our own terms, namely, in terms compatible with our biological makeup. For tools are always constrained by the nature of the organisms which make them.

---

[57] Spelke (2011, 287).
[58] For some examples, see Devlin (2005).

Chapter 15
Reason, Knowledge and Emotion

15.1 Reason and Emotion

After considering the nature of reason and knowledge, this chapter examines the relation of reason and knowledge to emotion.

According to a view widespread since antiquity, emotion is opposite to reason and an obstacle to knowledge acquisition. For example, the Stoics state that emotion is "a vehement opinion, inherent and deeply implanted," which is an obstacle to knowledge since it is the "belief that one knows what one does not know."[1] Russell states that, although "the emotions are what makes life interesting, and what makes us feel it important," when "we are trying to understand the world, they appear rather as a hindrance. They generate irrational opinions" which "cause us to view the universe in the mirror of our moods."[2]

This view, however, is unjustified because emotion plays an important role in evaluating knowledge about the environment, taking advantage of favourable occasion and avoiding danger. Only organisms which perceive a favorable occasion as a positive emotion, and danger as a negative one, can manage to survive. Therefore, emotion helps to choose appropriate means to the end of survival. Evolution has provided all organisms, from the most complex to the most elementary ones, with means to regulate and preserve life automatically, without having to resort to elaborate forms of thought. Emotion is one of them. Indeed, "there is abundant evidence of 'emotional' reactions" even "in simple organisms," including "a lone paramecium."[3] The reactions of such unicellular organisms contain the core of the process of emotion of human beings.

---

[1] Cicero, *Tusculanae Disputationes*, IV.26.
[2] Russell (1995a, 175–176).
[3] Damasio (2003, 40).

Of course, in human beings, emotion helps to choose appropriate means also to ends different from survival. For example, it helps to choose an appropriate means to the end of continuation of the species: falling in love. Thus emotion helps to choose appropriate means to certain given ends.

15.2 Emotion as a Compensation for the Limitations of Reason

Helping to choose appropriate means to certain given ends, emotion is not opposite to reason but complementary to it. Emotion is complementary to reason also in another respect: it can compensate for the limitations of reason. As it has been argued in Chapter 14, reason does not concern the choice of ends, but rather the choice of appropriate means to given ends. Emotion can do what reason cannot, it can help to choose ends. Each of our actions is accompanied by an emotional colouring, which has a relevant role in our choice not only of means but also of ends. Such colouring is a result of our emotional side, which never leaves us and silently guides us in each moment of our day.

Of course, the ends emotion can help to choose cannot be said to be appropriate because, as it has been argued in Chapter 14, one cannot assert of any ends that they are appropriate. Moreover, emotion is a result of biological evolution, which has no ends. Nevertheless, emotion can help to choose ends.

That emotion is not opposite to reason but complementary to it is the relation of reason to emotion.

15.3 Knowledge and Emotion

In human beings, emotion helps to choose appropriate means not only to practical ends such as survival, but also to a theoretical end such as knowledge acquisition. Of course, sometimes emotion may negatively affect knowledge acquisition, because it may lead us to disregard data that might serve as evidence for a hypothesis we are interested in. At other times, however, emotion may positively affect knowledge acquisition because, avoiding us from assigning a conclusive refutation role to data that might count as contrary evidence, it may save us from prematurely dropping hypotheses which might be fruitful. This may favour the advancement of knowledge. Indeed, prematurely abandoning hypotheses, for example, abandoning them as soon as an anomaly occurs, may be self-defeating.

This is already pointed out by Galileo, who criticizes the claim that "*ad destruendum sufficit unum* [a single instance is sufficient for refutation]."[4] Those

---

[4]Galilei (1968 VII, 222).

who make this claim are like "the man who wanted to tear down his house to the foundations, saying that it was uninhabitable and architecturally flawed, only because the chimney made too much smoke."[5] And he would have done so if a friend of his "had not pointed out that it was enough to fix the chimney without tearing down the rest."[6] Indeed "if, because of any particular new accident which is discovered in some part of the heavens, one had to change the whole structure of the world, one would never get anywhere."[7] In fact, "the motions, sizes, distances, and arrangements of spheres and stars are never observed to be so correct that they do not need constant corrections."[8] Thus Galileo warns from prematurely abandoning hypotheses.

15.4 Solving Problems and Emotion

Emotion may positively affect knowledge acquisition not only because, avoiding us from assigning a conclusive refutation role to data that might count as contrary evidence, it may save us from prematurely abandoning hypotheses that might be fruitful, but also because there can be no knowledge without emotion. If emotion is missing, one will lack the drive to seek knowledge, or will not focus attention on the means to achieve it. Emotion provides the drive for a bout of action and helps focusing attention on the features of the required action.

Knowledge is acquired by solving problems. But to solve a problem we must first have a problem, and we have a problem when we desire to achieve a given end. Therefore, to have a problem involves a certain amount of emotional commitment. It is the latter that drives us to invest efforts in solving a problem and promotes its solution. Interest, curiosity, wonder and surprise are aspects of an emotional commitment. We do not involve ourselves in things which do not interest us, or make us curious, or make us wonder, or surprise us.

Anxiety and stress are indications that we have a problem. When something worries us, this causes a tension that leads us to concentrate on it. At times we may have a hazy feeling that something is wrong but we do not know what it is, and such feeling is an indication that we have a problem. Conversely, poor emotional control may disrupt attention to a problem and hinder the solution. Therefore, our emotional commitment may precede our recognition that we have a problem. Moreover, it may lead us to focus attention on certain aspects of the problem, thus increasing our capacity to solve it.

Of course, emotion is not reasoning, but may play an auxiliary role in it, because it may contribute to increase the effectiveness of reasoning by making it quicker.

---

[5] *Ibid.*, VI, 533.
[6] *Ibid.*
[7] *Ibid.*, VI, 534.
[8] *Ibid.*

Sometimes emotion may even act as a surrogate for reasoning. This occurs, for example, when, under the impulse of emotion, we avoid choices which might turn out to be harmful, or seize opportunities which might turn out to be advantageous.

Our response to emotion may even give rise to some sort of thinking. When we start reflecting on a problem or hypothesis, some thoughts may trigger certain bodily feelings in us. If the feelings are unpleasant, this may lead us to focus on those thoughts and may alert us that the problem or hypothesis might have undesirable consequences. If the feelings are pleasant, this may encourage us to continue in that way. This response to our bodily feelings is a sort of thinking that occurs through the sensations and awareness of muscle, sinew and skin. This sort of thinking is often at the very origin of an inquiry, since something may become a problem for us when we feel physically uncomfortable. This feeling of discomfort may urge us to seek a solution for the problem, and may act as a springboard for conscious thought.

Even Russell acknowledges this function of emotion since he says: "In all creative work that I have done, what has come first is a problem, a puzzle involving discomfort. Then comes concentrated voluntary thought entailing great effort."[9]

15.5 Choice of Problems or Hypotheses and Emotion

What has been said in the previous section suggests that emotion may affect knowledge acquisition both in the choice of problems and in the choice of hypotheses for solving problems.

That emotion may affect knowledge acquisition in the choice of problems, is apparent from the fact that we seek solutions only for a small part of the problems that arise. Emotion may serve as a guide in choosing which problems to consider and which to disregard. Only if we feel strongly involved in a problem we may have the drive to get involved in it and face the hard work that finding a solution may involve. The drive arises from our needs and desires, and from the ends we want to achieve.

On the other hand, that emotion may affect knowledge acquisition in the choice of hypotheses for solving problems, is apparent from the fact that, if the search for a solution to a problem is not guided by emotion, it eventually decays. The absence of emotion may even exert a paralyzing effect because, in solving a problem, we may be faced with so many alternative hypotheses that it would be unfeasible to consider all of them. Confronted with the task of choosing between them, we might fall into a Buridan's ass situation. Emotion may guide us in choosing which hypothesis to consider and which to disregard, thus it may act as a shortcut.

With respect to knowledge acquisition, what is good to ignore may be as important as what is good to consider. Indecision must come to an end. Through our bodily feelings, emotion may put an end to it, directing us in choosing between

---

[9]Russell (1949, 112).

alternative hypotheses. That emotion has a significant impact on our choices and decisions is apparent from the results of the neurosciences, which show that patients suffering a damage to the ventromedial prefrontal cortex "have an abnormality in their processes of emotion and feeling" so severe that they are "unable to decide advantageously on matters pertaining to their own lives."[10]

In particular, emotion may save us from getting lost in an endless examination of the potentially infinite hypotheses produced by non-deductive rules. It may help us to stop at an appropriate place. Of course, emotion may also affect us negatively. For example, if we are in a great rage, our decision may not be that wise. But this does not cancel the positive role emotion may have in knowledge acquisition.

That emotion may affect knowledge acquisition in the choice of both problems and hypotheses for solving problems, is the relation of knowledge to emotion.

15.6 Scientific Knowledge and Emotion

Since emotion may affect knowledge acquisition both in the choice of problems and in the choice of hypotheses for solving problems, it plays a significant role in scientific knowledge. Indeed, eliminating emotions from science would amount to cancelling one of science's most vital sustaining forces. A scientist must have a deep interest in what he does. A non-interested and bored scientist will do little and often not very well. Scientists themselves sometimes acknowledge that emotion may affect their work. Thus Rubbia states: "We are essentially driven not" by "the success, but by a sort of passion, namely the desire of understanding better, to possess, if you like, a bigger part of the truth."[11]

In particular, among the emotions that affect scientific knowledge acquisition, several scientists assign a prominent role to the aesthetic emotion. Thus Dirac states that "it is more important to have beauty in one's equations that to have them fit experiment."[12] For, "if one is working from the point of view of getting beauty in one's equations, and if one has really a sound insight, one is on a sure line of progress."[13] It may be risky to rely on the aesthetic emotion as a basis for accepting or rejecting scientific hypotheses, because this may easily lead one astray. For example, as it has been mentioned in Chapter 13, relying on the feeling of beauty led Galileo to stick to circular orbits for planets, rejecting Kepler's elliptical orbits, and led Dirac himself to stick to his own version of quantum electrodynamics, rejecting renormalization. And yet, the aesthetic emotion often motivates and effectively guides several scientists in their work.

---

[10]Bechara et al. (2000, 295).
[11]Rubbia (1997, 197).
[12]Dirac (1963, 47).
[13]*Ibid.*

15.7 Mathematical Knowledge and Emotion

Emotion plays a significant role even in mathematical knowledge. Mathematicians themselves sometimes acknowledge this. For example, Rota states that "it is a frequent experience among mathematicians" that "they cannot solve a problem unless they like it."[14] In fact, "motivation and desire are essential components of mathematical reasoning."[15] Even the initial acceptance of a demonstration may depend, not on a thorough scrutiny of detail, but rather, as it were, on gut feeling, which suggests that there is something basically right about it.[16] For example, several mathematicians came to believe that Wiles' original demonstration of the Conjecture of Taniyama-Shimura was basically right long before the details could be checked.

Among the emotions that affect mathematical knowledge acquisition, several mathematicians too assign a prominent role to aesthetic emotion. For example, as we have seen in Chapter 13, Poincaré considers the feeling of beauty as the basis for selecting useful combinations of ideas which lead to mathematical discovery. Penrose states that "the strong conviction of the validity of a flash of inspiration" is "very closely bound up with its aesthetic qualities. A beautiful idea has a much greater chance of being a correct idea than an ugly one."[17] The "importance of aesthetic criteria applies not only to the instantaneous judgments of inspiration, but also to the much more frequent judgments that we make all the time in mathematical (or scientific) work."[18] Hrbacek and Jech state that the theory of large cardinals has such an "aesthetic appeal" that it is "difficult not to believe that it describes true aspects of the universe of set theory."[19] Once again, it may be risky to rely on the aesthetic emotion as a basis for accepting or rejecting mathematical hypotheses, because this may easily lead one astray. And yet, the aesthetic emotion often motivates and effectively guides mathematicians in their work.

15.8 Error and Emotion

An argument which is often used to support the claim that emotion is an obstacle to knowledge acquisition is that emotion may cause error. This argument is based on the assumption that error is intrinsically heterogeneous with respect to knowledge since it is non-knowledge, absence of knowledge. According to this view, either

---

[14] Rota (1991, 262).
[15] Rota (1997, 160).
[16] Gershon (1998) refers to the gut as the second brain.
[17] Penrose (1991, 421).
[18] *Ibid.*, 422.
[19] Hrbacek and Jech (1999, 270).

there is knowledge or there is error, thus, if there is error, then there cannot be knowledge. Therefore, knowledge must be always true.

This assumption, however, only applies to knowledge in the sense of Aristotle's science, where truth is to intuit and state the essence of things, and not to intuit is not to know them and hence to be in error. As we have seen in Chapter 3, for Aristotle everyone is in error on matters about which he has no knowledge. Thus error is simply non-knowledge, absence of knowledge. Other is the case of knowledge in the sense of modern science, which does not consist in intuiting and stating the essence of things, but rather in finding plausible hypotheses to solve problems. An error arises when the hypothesis at hand is not plausible. Then an analysis of the causes of error may give indications as to how to revise the hypothesis or formulate a new one.

One can err in many ways, but learn only from some of them. And yet, there are ways of erring from which one can learn. Since the analysis of the causes of error can lead to new knowledge, error can play a positive role in knowledge. Of course, this involves that hypotheses be obtained through a rational procedure, such as the analytic method. For those who deny that hypotheses can be so obtained, an analysis of the causes of error cannot yield new knowledge.

Such is the case of Popper. While agreeing that error can play a positive role in knowledge, he claims that an analysis of the causes of error cannot give indications as to how to revise an existing hypothesis or formulate a new one, simply because hypotheses are not obtained through a rational procedure but are "the result of an almost poetic intuition."[20] The "refutation of a theory" is "a step forward that takes us nearer to the truth. And this is how we can learn from our mistakes."[21] Thus, according to Popper, the positive role of error does not consist in the fact that an analysis of its causes can yield new knowledge, but rather in the refutation of the theory as such.

Popper's view, however, is unjustified. Error can play a positive role because the analysis of the causes of error can provide indications as to how to revise an existing hypothesis or formulate a new one. But if error can play a positive role in knowledge acquisition, then it is not intrinsically heterogeneous with respect to knowledge, on the contrary, it is homogeneous to it. In fact, knowledge and error have the same origin, since they both arise from formulating hypotheses by non-deductive rules. That they yield knowledge or error does not depend on the non-deductive rules by means of which hypotheses are obtained, but rather on the compatibility of the hypotheses with the existing data, so on experience, thus on something which is external to inference. Therefore knowledge and error arise from the same sources and can be distinguished only by experience.

---

[20]Popper (1974, 192).
[21]*Ibid.*, vii.

15.9 Doubt and Emotion

Also doubt, which is one of the main sources of knowledge, is connected with emotion. For doubt is a kind of fear, the fear that a hypotheses on which we have invested could turn out to be unfounded. When we start doubting a hypothesis that we considered plausible, we become anxious about its reliability, fearing that it might turn out to be unjustified. Doubt indicates that the present evidence does not seem to us to be adequate to the hypothesis.

Our emotional response to a hypothesis, namely, the hope that the present evidence will turn out to be adequate or the fear that it may turn out to be inadequate, provides a sort of preliminary evaluation of the hypothesis, and hence an indication of the rationality of our trust in it. Because of this, knowledge can be positively affected by the emotion connected with doubt. For doubt leads us to reflect on the plausibility of the hypothesis and to seek new evidence for it. This clarifies in what sense doubt is one of the main sources of knowledge.

Chapter 16
Logic, Evolution, Language and Reason

16.1 Natural and Artificial Logic

On the basis of what has been said in the previous two chapters, this chapter examines the relation of logic to evolution, language and reason, Chapter 17 the relation of logic to method and knowledge, and Chapter 19 the relation of philosophy to knowledge.

As it has been mentioned in Chapter 14, logic has been traditionally viewed as a part of reason, being an attempt to describe the rules by which reason, at least discursive reason, operates. But if logic is a part of reason, then, as a special case of the distinction made in Chapter 14 between natural and artificial reason, two kinds of logic must be distinguished: natural and artificial logic. Natural logic is that problem solving capacity that virtually all organisms have as a result of biological evolution, thanks to which they may survive. The name 'natural logic' is intended to stress that it is a result of biological evolution. Artificial logic is that problem solving capacity that human beings have as a result of cultural evolution. The name 'artificial logic' is intended to stress that it is not a result of biological evolution but rather of cultural evolution.

This explains the relation of logic to evolution: natural logic is a result of biological evolution, artificial logic a result of cultural evolution.

Natural and artificial logic are distinct, nevertheless between them there is no opposition, but rather continuity. This follows from the fact that the relation between natural and artificial logic is a special case of that between natural and artificial reason. Such distinction revises and extends the distinction between the three different senses of logic, (A)–(C), considered in Chapter 2. Natural logic revises and extends sense (A), logic as that rational faculty which all human beings have. For it is a faculty that not only human beings, but virtually all organisms have. Moreover, it is not based, as Parmenides, Plato and Aristotle assume, on the fact that the human mind mirrors the divine mind which governs the universe, but rather is a result of biological evolution, being essential for the survival of all organisms. Artificial logic revises and extends sense (B), logic as the development of procedures for acquiring knowledge, as well as sense (C), logic as the systematic study of procedures for acquiring knowledge. For such procedures include not only syllogism and induction but also others, such as the ones that will be considered in the last part of this book. The procedures in question are a result of cultural evolution.

16.2 Remarks on the Distinction Between Natural and Artificial Logic

Some remarks about the distinction between natural and artificial logic may be useful.

1) That problem solving capacity in which natural logic consists is not the same in all organisms. Different kinds of organisms are capable of solving different problems, and solve them in different ways. The capacity in question is based on native unconscious processes, in the sense explained in Chapter 14.

2) That problem solving capacity in which artificial logic consists is based either on conscious processes or on acquired unconscious processes, once again in the sense explained in Chapter 14.

3) That problem solving capacity in which artificial logic consists, when based on acquired unconscious processes, is not to be confused with that problem solving capacity in which natural logic consists. The former, being based on acquired unconscious processes, is a result of cultural evolution, the latter, being based on native unconscious processes, is a result of biological evolution.

16.3 Origin of the Distinction Between Natural and Artificial Logic

As we have seen in Chapter 9, the distinction between natural and artificial logic is discussed by Kant. But a version of the distinction already occurs in some late-mediaeval and early-modern philosophers. According to them, natural logic is that innate capacity to make syllogisms that all human beings have, artificial logic is the logic that Aristotle developed modelling it on natural logic.

For example, Zabarella states that natural logic "is a certain innate power, inherent in the minds of men, by means of which even wholly untaught people make syllogisms and arguments, having acquired it with no study, no amount of exertion."[1] On the other hand, "artificial logic was discovered and composed by

---

[1] Zabarella (1608, col. 106).

Aristotle."² He "generated artificial logic from natural logic," observing "methods and procedures by which others argued by natural logic."³

With respect to late-mediaeval and early-modern philosophers, however, the distinction between natural and artificial logic stated above involves three changes.

1) Natural logic is that problem solving capacity that, not only human beings, but virtually all organisms have as a result of biological evolution, thanks to which they may survive.

2) Artificial logic comprises not only syllogism and induction, but also other kinds of procedures, such as those considered in the last part of this book.

3) Artificial logic cannot be simply modelled on natural logic because, as it will be argued below, it goes essentially beyond natural logic.

16.4 Anti-evolutionism in Logic

The distinction between natural and artificial logic made by some late-mediaeval and early-modern philosophers, is reaffirmed until the eighteenth-century. With Kant, however, things begin to change because, as we have seen in Chapter 9, he claims that natural logic is not really logic. The change becomes complete with Frege, who denies the possibility of a natural logic, using anti-evolutionary arguments.

According to Frege, if there were a natural logic, this would imply that, since "man, like all other living creatures, has undergone a continuous process of evolution," the "laws of his thinking" might have not "always been valid" and might not "always retain their validity."⁴ This is absurd, the laws of logic are "true and will continue to be so even if, as a result of Darwinian evolution, human beings were to come" to deny them, since such laws are "eternal and independent of being thought by anyone and of the psychological makeup of anyone."⁵ If something were "true only for us and through being recognized by us as such," there "would be no science" since then, "properly speaking, there would be nothing true in the normal sense of the word."⁶

This view has several followers within contemporary analytic philosophy. For example, Nagel states that a law of logic "would be true even if I were not in existence or were unable to think it."⁷ If "our rational capacity was the product

---

²*Ibid.*
³*Ibid.*
⁴Frege (1979, 4).
⁵*Ibid.*, 174.
⁶*Ibid.*, 133.
⁷Nagel (1997, 66).

of natural selection," there "would be no reason to trust its results in mathematics and science, for example."[8]

The view in question, however, is unjustified, because there is no evidence that the laws of logic are eternal and independent of being thought by anyone and of the psychological makeup of anyone. On the contrary, there is evidence that they are a product of organisms which are the outcome of biological evolution, and hence depend on their biological makeup as well as on the constitution of the world. Moreover, there is no evidence that, if something were true only for us and through being recognized by us as such, there would be no science. Science is only a way in which human beings make the world comprehensible to themselves. Scientific knowledge is not true but only plausible, and plausibility is relative to human beings, so it depends on being recognized by them.

16.5 The Reducibility Thesis

Being extreme, Frege's denial of the possibility of a natural logic using anti-evolutionary arguments was likely to raise extreme reactions. An understandable extreme reaction is the view that artificial logic is reducible to natural logic, and specifically to evolutionary theory.

A significant representative of this view is Cooper, who states that the whole of "logic is reducible to evolutionary theory."[9] Indeed, "from general evolutionary theory one can derive a special branch of population biology known as life-history strategy theory," from the latter one can derive "decision theory," from the latter one can derive "inductive logic or probability theory," and finally from the latter one can derive "deductive logic."[10] Then "the laws of logic emerge naturally as corollaries of the evolutionary laws."[11]

The view that artificial logic is reducible to evolutionary theory, however, is based on the assumption that "inductive logic is another name for probability theory" or, at least, that "probability theory" is "an adequate formalization of inductive reasoning."[12] This assumption is unjustified, because inductive logic is concerned with plausibility rather than with probability and, as we have seen in Chapter 4, already Kant pointed out that plausibility is different from probability. Further arguments for their distinction will be given in Chapter 20. Since plausibility is different from probability, being concerned with plausibility rather than with probability, inductive logic is not another name for probability theory. Thus the reducibility of artificial logic to evolutionary theory breaks down.

---

[8]*Ibid.*, 135.
[9]Cooper (2001, 2).
[10]*Ibid.*, 21.
[11]*Ibid.*, 5.
[12]*Ibid.*, 89.

16.6 The Need for Artificial Logic

Although the reducibility of artificial logic to evolutionary theory breaks down, the need for an artificial logic distinct from natural logic requires further justification. Indeed, most human beings do not solve problems by artificial logic. They do not proceed on the basis of learned logical cognitions but use logical means, such as induction, the cause-effect relation or the identity principle, and generally make inferences, without having attended any logic course. They can do so because biological evolution has designed them to do so by endowing them with a natural logic. Of course, 'designed' not in the sense of 'directed towards a goal'. While a toaster is directed towards the goal of producing toast since it has been designed for that goal, biological evolution is not directed towards the goal of survival, in fact it is not directed towards any goal at all.

On the other hand, that most human beings do not solve problems by artificial logic, does not mean that there is no need for an artificial logic distinct from natural logic. The natural logic with which biological evolution has endowed human beings enables them to cope only with situations similar to those that occurred in their evolutionary past. And it enables them to do so automatically, with no need for each single human being to reinvent the means to cope with them. But the world changes continually and irregularly, thus it faces human beings all the time with situations dissimilar from those that already occurred in their evolutionary past. To cope with them, natural logic is not enough and must be supplemented with an essentially richer logic: artificial logic.

16.7 Logic and Language

In Chapter 14 we have seen that opponents of the view that our biological makeup has a basic importance in determining what we are think that language is the key factor in the superiority of human beings upon non-human animals. In addition, they think that logic is bound to language, and only human beings possess it. Thus Heidegger states that "logic is the science of *logos*, strictly taken, of language."[13] Only human beings possess it, not animals, because they "are never placed freely into the clearing of being."[14] But thinking that logic is bound to language and only human beings possess it, is unjustified because both human beings and non-human animals have logical capacities that do not depend on language. Specifically:

1) Pre-verbal human beings and non-human animals have logical capacities that do not depend on language. For example, they possess the systems of core

---

[13] Heidegger (2009, 11).
[14] Heidegger (1998, 248).

knowledge mentioned in Chapter 14. This contradicts the claim that "neither an infant one week old nor a snail is a rational creature."[15]

2) Adult human beings have logical capacities that do not depend on language. For example, Einstein states: "The words or the language, as they are written or spoken, do not seem to play any role in my mechanism of thought."[16] Similarly, Hadamard states: "Words are totally absent from my mind when I really think," and "do not reappear in my consciousness before I have accomplished or given up the research."[17]

3) Human beings and non-human animals have logical capacities that do not depend on language also because, as it will be argued in the next section, perception is the result of inference.

Therefore logic is not necessarily bound to language, and hence need not be restricted to discursive logic. That logic is not necessarily bound to language is the relation of logic to language.

16.8 Perception as Inference

In Chapter 14 and in the previous section it has been said that perception is the result of inference. This needs explanation. Perception is often viewed as a passive recording, but it is not so. It is rather an active process which elaborates sensory inputs on the basis of endogenous knowledge derived from prior experience. This applies in particular to visual perception, which has an important place within perception. It is significant that a greater part of our cerebral cortex is devoted to visual processing than to any other perceptive processing.

The eye is often viewed as a camera. According to the eye-as-a-camera view, light is projected onto the retina by the lense, a retinal image is created, and our visual experience is built up from it. This view, however, does not explain, for example, why we see the world around us as three-dimensional, while the image on the retina is two-dimensional. Actually, the structure and working of the eye is quite different from the structure and working of a camera. In the eye, photoreceptors are not evenly distributed throughout the retina. Only a very restricted region of the latter, of a diameter of about half a millimetre, the fovea, has high visual acuity. The latter rapidly decreases outside the fovea. The same can be said about sensitivity to colours. In addition, the focal length is different for red and blue, so one of the two extremes of the colour spectrum is always out of focus. Moreover, in the region where the optic nerve is bundled and leaves the retina, there are no photoreceptors, so there is a blind spot. To compensate for these limitations, our visual system makes

---

[15] Davidson (2001, 90).
[16] Hadamard (1954, 142).
[17] *Ibid.*, 75.

very fast movements of the eye, called saccades, which direct the fovea to points of interest.

Therefore, the eye-as-a-camera view is inadequate. Our visual system does not simply record a visual scene passively, as a camera does. Seeing is not direct apprehension of the world in front of us, it is inference from incomplete information. It involves making hypotheses about the world out there, by means of inferences from the data. Thus our visual system is a hypothesis generator.

The same applies to our whole perceptual system. Built into brain circuitry there are complex inference rules, which enable the brain to make hypotheses about the world out there by means of inferences from the data. Therefore, perception is the result of inference. The belief that perception is direct is an illusion. That perception is the result of inference implies that logic need not be only discursive, it can also be perceptual. Thus the traditional view that logic is only discursive is inadequate.

The inferences involved in perception are non-propositional, non-deductive and unconscious. They are non-propositional, because they yield hypotheses which are not encoded by propositions and are obtained from data which are not encoded by propositions. They are non-deductive, because they yield hypotheses which go beyond the poor quality data provided by our sense organs. They are unconscious, because they yield hypotheses by processes which occur too fast and at too low a level in the mind to be accessible to direct inspection. Specifically, such processes are partly native unconscious, partly acquired unconscious. For example, newborn babies need experience and training in order to make sense of the image of what is in front of them.

16.9 Non-propositional Inferences

That inferences involved in perception are non-propositional requires extending the traditional concept of inference, according to which inferences are transitions from propositions to propositions. The traditional concept does not account for inferences involved in perception, nor for inferences involved in processes concerning mental images. In order to account for them, inferences must rather be conceived as transitions from data to data. Propositional inferences are then the special case when the data are expressed propositionally.

Of course, there are several kinds of transitions from data to data, as there are several kinds of transitions from propositions to propositions. Which of them may be considered to be inferences depends on the ends of the inference rules. Such ends will be discussed in Chapter 18.

16.10 The Origin of Perception as Inference

The idea that perception is the result of inference goes back to Ptolemy and Alhazen, but in the modern age von Helmholtz resumed it. According to von Helmholtz, although inferences involved in perception "lack the purifying and checking work of conscious thinking," they "may be classed as inferences, inductive inferences unconsciously formed."[18] Thus the inferences involved in perception are non-deductive and unconscious. Moreover, while "the 'conclusions' of logicians" are "capable of expression in words," the conclusions of such inferences "are not; because, instead of words, they only deal with sensations."[19] Thus, the inferences involved in perception are non-propositional.

As it has been stated in the previous section, this requires extending the traditional concept of inference according to which inferences are transitions from propositions to propositions. This was promptly noted by Dilthey, who stated that "logic is capable of complying with the demands of critical consciousness only by extending its province beyond the analysis of discursive thought."[20] The "achievement by which the perceptual process transcends what is given to it is an equivalent of discursive thought. The profound notion of unconscious inferences as developed by Helmholtz implies such an extension of logic."[21]

16.11 The Irresistibility of Inferences Involved in Perception

Being unconscious, the inferences involved in perception are irresistible, in the sense that we cannot unperceive what we perceive even when we know that it is an illusion.

An example is provided by the Hering illusion. When we look at the following image, the two vertical lines look like they are bowing out. But it is not so, they are perfectly straight, as it can be checked by a ruler. Once we have checked it, we know that the two vertical lines are perfectly straight, our conscious experience tells us that they are such, and yet we cannot unsee what we see.

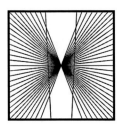

---

[18] von Helmholtz (1867, 449).
[19] von Helmholtz (1995, 198).
[20] Dilthey (1989, 166).
[21] *Ibid.*, 167.

Another example is provided by the Adelson illusion. When we look at the following image on the left, square A seems to be a different shade of grey than square B. But it is not so, they are the same shade of grey, as it can be checked by looking at the image on the right. Once we have checked it, we know that the two squares are the same shade of gray, our conscious experience tells us that they are such, and yet we cannot unsee what we see.

Inferences involved in perception are irresistible because, as a result of biological evolution, the human brain embodies neural circuits that make inferences through which the human brain categorizes data without our being aware of them.

The two examples above also illustrate the claim, made in Chapter 8, that, like secondary qualities, primary qualities are simply our ways of categorizing the world. Although shape, which is involved in the Hering illusion, is a primary quality, and colour, which is involved in the Adelson illusion, is a secondary quality, they give rise to essentially similar situations.

16.12 Objections to Perception as Inference

The view that perception is the result of inference is subject to a number of objections.

1) *Intuition*. Perception is intuition, though "the lowest level of possible intuition."[22] In "sense perception, the 'external' thing appears 'in one blow', as soon as our glance falls upon it. The manner in which it makes the thing appear present is straightforward."[23] This objection is unjustified because an object given by perception does not appear 'in one blow', as soon as our glance falls upon it. For example, as it has been already mentioned, newborn babies need experience and training in order to make sense of the image of what they see. As another example, the born blind who recover sight after an operation, at first have little idea of shape, no idea of distance, no idea of depth and very little idea of solidity.

---

[22]Husserl (2001, II, 282).
[23]*Ibid.*, II, 283.

Therefore, they do not have normal sight, and their previous tactual and auditory experience is not easily correlated with their newly acquired visual experience. This is inexplicable if perception is based on intuition. Contrary to intuition, the manner in which sense perception makes the thing appear present is not straightforward. This can be explained only if perception is the result of inference.

2) *Propositional Inferences.* Inferences are "transformations of propositions in accordance with a rule, derivations of propositions from premises in conformity with a pattern of derivation."[24] On the contrary, "perceiving something involves no transformation of propositions."[25] One must not be misled "by the incoherent assertion that perceptions are conclusions of unconscious inferences. One may form hypotheses about what one sees, but to see is not to form a hypothesis."[26] This objection is unjustified, because inferences involved in perception are not transformations of propositions, but rather transformations of data. The objection depends on the unwarranted assumption that all inferences must be propositional, but data need not be expressed in propositions.

3) *Invariants.* Perception is not mediated by "inference."[27] It is the direct "pickup of invariants."[28] The perceptual system simply "resonates to the invariant structure or is attuned to it."[29] This objection is unjustified, because it overlooks that, as Fodor and Pylyshyn point out, saying that perception is the direct pickup of invariants "is empty unless the notions of 'direct pickup' and of 'invariant' are suitably constrained," and there is "no workable way of imposing the required constraints consonant" with the "assumption that perception is direct."[30] The two notions in question "can be appropriately constrained only on the assumption that perception is inferentially mediated."[31] But then it is not a direct pickup. Moreover, the view that perception is the direct pickup of invariants is unable to explain sensory illusions. It is no use to say that "the illusion of reality is a myth" since illusions occur only in situations with an artificially impoverished ambient light, such as those produced in "the psychological laboratory."[32] Illusions also occur naturally. For example, if you stare for some time at something that moves steadily in one direction, such as a waterfall, and then transfer your gaze to a stationary scene, you will experience movement in the opposite direction.

4) *Constraints.* Perception is based on the fact that our perceptual system embodies "certain very general constraints on the interpretations that it is allowed

---

[24] Bennett and Hacker (2003, 137).
[25] *Ibid.*
[26] *Ibid.*
[27] Gibson (1986, 238).
[28] *Ibid.*, 254.
[29] *Ibid.*, 249.
[30] Fodor and Pylyshyn (1981, 141).
[31] *Ibid.*
[32] Gibson (1986, 281).

to make."[33] Such constraints "lead to the correct interpretation" of stimuli, thus they yield perception "without 'unconscious inference'."[34] This objection is unjustified, because saying that our perceptual system embodies certain very general constraints which lead to the correct interpretation of stimuli, amounts to saying that the human brain embodies specialized circuits that make inferences by which the human brain categorizes data.

16.13 Discursive and Visual Logic

Since, as it has been stated earlier, visual perception has an important place within perception, visual logic, that is, the logic underlying visual perception, has an important place within perceptual logic. Visual logic is essentially different from discursive logic. The main differences are the following.

1) Discursive logic uses linguistic representations, which mirror relations between objects and events but have no likeness to them. Conversely, visual logic uses iconic representations, which mirror relations between objects and events and have some likeness to them.

2) Discursive logic uses representations which are static since they are fixed, discrete since the characters of which they consist are discrete, and unidimensional since so are linguistic expressions. Conversely, visual logic uses representations which are dynamic since they are capable of evolving, continuous and multidimensional since so is space.

3) Discursive logic focuses on the representation of objects or events by propositions, which leads one to concentrate on the form of propositions rather than on their content. Conversely, visual logic focuses on the representation of objects or events by icons, which leads one to concentrate on the content of icons.

4) Discursive logic depends on the recognition of patterns in linguistic representations, which is generally very slow. Conversely, visual logic depends on the recognition of patterns in iconic representations, which can be very fast.

5) Discursive logic permits disjunctive reasoning, namely, reasoning involving disjunction. Conversely, visual logic does not permit disjunctive reasoning, because icons *qua* icons cannot express: Either individual x or individual y has property A. The closest one may come to this is to have two icons, one showing that individual x has property A, the other showing that individual y has property A, together with the implicit assumption that at least one of them is the case.

6) Discursive logic permits negative reasoning, that is, reasoning involving negation. Conversely, visual logic does not permit negative reasoning, because icons

---

[33] Pylyshyn (2003, 96).
[34] *Ibid.*

qua icons cannot express: No individual *x* has property *A*. The closest one can come to this is to have an icon in which there is no thing *x* having property *A*, together with the implicit assumption that all the relevant things occur in the icon.

7) Discursive logic permits quantificational reasoning, that is, reasoning involving quantifiers. Conversely, visual logic does not permit quantificational reasoning, because icons *qua* icons cannot express: All things have property *A*. They can only express that finitely many, in fact relatively few, things have property *A*.

16.14 The Role of Visual Logic in Knowledge

Both discursive and visual logic are essential to knowledge. But most of our sense-data are visual and our language is often inadequate to describe what we see. With respect to certain situations, one word is too much and a thousand words too little. In such situations, visual logic is more efficient than discursive logic.

Visual logic can play a role in knowledge in several ways. For example, it can synthesize data or fix concepts by means of icons when we must represent them, communicate them or show relations between them. It can extract data from icons. It can explain, illustrate or show the main steps required to solve a problem by means of icons.

That, in certain situations, visual logic is more efficient than discursive logic, explains the widespread use of diagrams in mathematics, for example, in the constructions of geometry or in the calculi of arithmetic and algebra. All mathematical diagrams have something in common. They consist in a spatial arrangement of objects and relations between their parts. They express relations by their very same structure, from which one may infer relations between the corresponding objects. They permit to express operations based on that structure, which enables one to transform, compose, decompose and combine visual representations.

16.15 Limitations of Visual Logic

Although, in certain situations, visual logic is more efficient than discursive logic, it has some limitations. Some of them have already been mentioned: visual logic does not permit disjunctive, negative or quantificational reasoning. Other limitations are the following.

1) Visual logic works only when the situation is not too complex.

2) Icons must be interpreted. An icon does not speak by itself, one has to intepret it by spotting the relevant data in it, which is difficult when the icon is complex.

3) An icon can often be read in several different ways. For example, as Wittgenstein points out, the icon

can be read "as a triangular hole, as a solid, as a geometrical drawing; as standing on its base, as hanging from its apex; as a mountain, as a wedge, as an arrow or pointer, as an overturned object which is meant to stand on the shorter side of the right angle, as a half parallelogram, and as various other things."[35] Reading an icon in one of these ways yields a reorganization of the data. As a result, certain features of the icon are perceived as front elements which would have been otherwise perceived as background ones.

4) Icons must be carefully handled. For example, diagrams in geometry must be accurately drawn since even small imperfections may lead to demonstrations of incorrect theorems. An example of this will be given in Chapter 21.

16.16 Complementarity of Discursive and Visual Logic

While different, discursive and visual logic are not opposed but rather complementary. This is apparent from the fact that visual logic is part not only of natural logic but also of artificial logic, which shows that the reduction of inference to propositional inference is unduly restrictive.

For example, many demonstrations of Euclid's *Elements* are a mix of diagrams and discursive reasoning, so they combine visual with discursive elements. They involve drawing diagrams whose parts are in relations that are homomorphic to the relations between the parts of the corresponding objects, making constructions on the diagrams, observing the resulting diagrams and reasoning about them to discover relations between their parts. The same can be said about several other mathematical demonstrations, from antiquity to present. For example, several demonstrations in the theory of categories use the fact that many mathematical properties can be unified and simplified representing them by arrow diagrams. They combine arrow diagrams and discursive reasoning.

Peirce even states that all "mathematical reasoning consists in constructing a diagram according to a general precept, in observing certain relations between parts of that diagram not explicitly required by the precept, showing that these relations will hold for all such diagrams, and in formulating this conclusion in general terms."[36] But even if not all mathematical reasoning consists in constructing a diagram, diagrams play a role in most of it.

---

[35]Wittgenstein (1958, II, § xi).
[36]Peirce (1931–1958, 1.54).

16.17 Logic and Reason

At the beginning of this chapter it has been said that logic has been traditionally viewed as a part of reason. This raises the question: Is logic a proper part of reason or the whole of it?

In the last century there has been an increasing tendency to consider logic as the whole of reason, or at least as its most distinctive feature. For example, Frege states that the laws of logic are "the most general laws, which prescribe universally the way in which one ought to think if one is to think at all."[37] If "beings were even found whose laws of thought flatly contradicted" the laws of logic, "I should say: we have here a hitherto unknown type of madness."[38] Thus, according to Frege, beings are rational only insofar as they obey the laws of logic, therefore logic is the whole of reason.

But, if logic is the whole of reason, then emotions, feelings or any biologically or culturally specific codes are excluded from the sphere of rationality. Any human act influenced by these factors will be termed as irrational. This is in conflict with the results of the neurosciences, which show that no human act is ever totally independent of all these factors, except perhaps in patients with a damaged ventromedial prefrontal cortex. The factors in question play an essential role in rationality, so excluding them would yield an impoverished concept of reason. Thus the concept of reason implicit in the view that logic is the whole of reason is inadequate for human beings, and does not account for the positive role that emotions, feelings or any biologically or culturally specific codes play in rationality. Therefore, logic cannot be the whole of reason but only a proper part of it.

That logic is not the whole of reason but only a proper part of it is the relation of logic to reason.

---

[37] Frege (1964, 12).
[38] *Ibid.*, 14.

Chapter 17
Logic, Method and Knowledge

17.1 Logic and Method

This chapter examines the relation of logic to method and knowledge. Let us first consider that of logic to method. Method is a means of solving problems, thus a means of discovery. There are various kinds of methods, but an important distinction is that between algorithmic and heuristic methods. While algorithmic methods guarantee to solve problems, heuristic methods do not guarantee that, but may serve as a guide towards that end. The formal literature on heuristics tends to suggest that the purpose of heuristics is to formulate mechanical rules that can be programmed on a computer. But this is misleading because the purpose of heuristics is rather to find non-mechanical rules that will guide one to solve problems, even if it takes some skill to apply them.

Clearly, there is a strict relation of logic to method because, as it has been stated in Chapter 16, both natural and artificial logic are problem solving capacities. Thus they are both means of solving problems. But the relation of logic to method is even stricter than that: logic arises from method. This is apparent, for example, from the fact that, as the methods of the sciences evolve, corresponding changes occur in logic. If logic arises from method, then method is the source of logic. Thus there is no basis for the divorce of logic from method originated by mathematical logic, which was considered in Chapter 13.

That method is the source of logic is the relation of logic to method.

17.2 Against Logic as a Normative Science

That method is the source of logic contrasts with the view of mathematical logic. As we have seen in Chapter 10, according to Frege, logic is a normative science, it tells men how they must think. Therefore, logic is a precondition of method.

In the last century, that logic is a normative science has been the prevailing view. This, however, is unjustified. As it has been argued in Chapter 4, deductive rules are not plausibility preserving, so the plausibility of a hypothesis obtained by means of a deductive rule can be guaranteed only by experience. A fortiori, the same can be said of non-deductive rules. Then it is experience that tells us what logical means may lead to fruitful discoveries. Their choice does not involve compliance with absolute norms but only with experience. Therefore, logic does not tell men how they must think and hence cannot be said to be a normative science.

As Dewey says, the claim "that experience only tells us how men have thought or do think, while logic is concerned" with "how men should think, is ludicrously inept."[1] In fact, "some sorts of thinking are shown by experience to have got nowhere," while "others have proved in manifest experience that they lead to fruitful and enduring discoveries."[2]

The relation of deductive and non-deductive rules to experience will be further discussed in Chapter 18.

17.3 Spinoza's Hammer-and-Iron Argument

If logic is a precondition of method, then method requires logic. Therefore, against the claim that logic arises from method, it might be objected that it leads to a circle or an infinite regress.

An answer to this objection is implicit in Spinoza's Hammer-and-Iron Argument. Spinoza observes that, against the claim that men can work iron, it might be objected that, "to work iron, a hammer is needed, and to have a hammer, it must be made. For this purpose there is need of another hammer and other tools, and again to get these there is need of other tools, and so on to infinity."[3] But this objection is invalid. For "at first, with the tools they were born with, men succeeded" in "making some very simple things; and when these were made they made other more complex things."[4] Thus, "advancing gradually from the simplest works to the making of tools, and from tools to other works and other tools, they have reached a point where they can make very many complex things."[5] Then there is no infinite regress.

Similarly, against the claim that logic arises from method, it might be objected that, to implement method, logical means are needed, and to have logical means, they must be made. For this purpose, there is need of another method and other logical means, and again to get these there is need of other logical means, and so on to infinity. But this objection is invalid. For at first, with the rudimentary methods of natural logic they were born with, men succeeded in making some very

---

[1] Dewey (2004, 78).
[2] Ibid.
[3] Spinoza (2002, 9).
[4] Ibid.
[5] Ibid.

simple logical means; and when these were made, they made other more complex logical means. Thus, advancing gradually from the simplest methods to the making of logical means, and from logical means to other methods and other logical means, they have reached a point where they can make very many complex logical means. Then there is no infinite regress.

That complex logical means evolve from less complex ones is no more paradoxical than that complex biological systems evolve from less complex ones.

17.4 Solving Problems and Knowledge

After considering the relation of logic to method, let us consider that of logic to knowledge. All knowledge arises from solving problems, where a problem is a goal that a person wants to attain but cannot immediately attain. At the origin of knowledge there is the fact that an organism has a problem. If the problem is important for the organism, it needs to find a solution. If the problem is crucial for the survival of the organism, finding a solution is vital for it.

'Problems' include both first-order problems, that is, problems arising directly from the world, and second-order problems, that is, problems arising from new theories or material tools developed to deal with the world. 'Problems' also include mathematical problems. Even Hilbert acknowledges that "mathematical research requires its problems. It is by the solution of problems that the strength of the investigator is hardened; he finds new methods and new outlooks, and gains a wider and freer horizon."[6]

Solving problems, when successful, produces knowledge, though knowledge that, as it will be argued later, is not certain and is always revisable. That solving problems, when successful, produces knowledge, means that there is a strict connection between knowledge and solving problems: knowledge arises from solving problems.

17.5 *Meno*'s Paradox

Against the claim that knowledge arises from solving problems, it might be objected that it is in conflict with *Meno*'s paradox. According to the latter, "it is impossible for a man to search either for what he knows or for what he does not know: for what he knows, because he already knows it and hence is in no need of searching for it; for what he does not know, because he does not even know what it is he is to search for."[7]

---

[6]Hilbert (2000, 241).
[7]Plato, *Meno*, 80 e 2–5.

Plato's solution to *Meno*'s paradox is that "our learning is nothing else but recollection."[8] Recollection "of the things which our soul once beheld when, journeying with the God, it looked down upon the things which we now say exist, and rose up into real being."[9] Since our soul once beheld such things, we have "knowledge of all those things before birth."[10] Then "those who, we say, are learning, are simply recollecting, and learning is but recollection."[11] Therefore, we are never taught anything new, but only reminded of things we already know.

This solution is unconvincing because it depends on the assumption that our soul once beheld the things in question. Such an assumption is unsupported by evidence, and moreover is unnecessary. For *Meno*'s paradox is not really a paradox, but only a sophistic argument arising from the ambiguity of the expression 'to know'.

Indeed, on the one hand, what a man knows are solutions to problems which have already been found. Then, since he already knows them, he is in no need of searching for them. Nevertheless, he is always in need of questioning them, since no solution to a problem is conclusive, the hypothesis used to solve a problem is in its turn a problem which needs to be solved. Therefore, it is unjustified to say that it is impossible for a man to search for what he knows because he already knows it and hence is in no need of searching for it. He never knows conclusively what he knows.

On the other hand, what a man does not know are the solutions to problems which have not been found yet. But the fact that he does not know them does not mean that he does not know what it is he is to search for. It only means that he has not found a solution yet, which does not exclude that he might find one at a later stage. Therefore, it is unjustified to say that it is impossible for a man to search for what he does not know because in that case he does not even know what it is he is to search for. He knows what he is searching for, but simply has not yet found it.

Therefore, *Meno*'s paradox cannot be used as an objection against the claim that knowledge arises from solving problems. Of course, one must have a prepared mind to be aware of a problem, to see that some hypothesis might yield a solution, to know the solutions which have already been found, and to be able to question them. But, as Gillies points out, in order to have a prepared mind, "the discoverer does not need a former existence to acquire the necessary partial, but not complete, knowledge. He can acquire this earlier in his own life."[12]

---

[8] Plato, *Phaedo*, 72 e 5–6.
[9] Plato, *Phaedrus*, 249 c 2–4.
[10] Plato, *Phaedo*, 75 d 4–5.
[11] *Ibid.*, 76 a 6–7.
[12] Gillies (2011, 43–44).

17.6 Analytic Method and Knowledge

That knowledge arises from solving problems brings up the question: How do human beings solve problems, in particular, scientific problems? In other words, what is the scientific method? Since antiquity, the latter has been identified with Aristotle's analytic-synthetic method. In particular, as we have seen in Chapter 8, this is the case of the originators of the Scientific Revolution of the seventeenth century. But identifying the scientific method with Aristotle's analytic-synthetic method is inadequate because, as it has been argued in Chapter 12, the analytic-synthetic method is incompatible with Gödel's first and second incompleteness theorems.

Luckily, however, since antiquity another method is known, the analytic method, described in Chapter 4, which is compatible with Gödel's results.

1) *The analytic method is compatible with Gödel's first incompleteness theorem.* For in such method the solution to a problem is obtained from the problem, and possibly other data already available, by means of hypotheses not necessarily belonging to the same field as the problem. Since Gödel's first incompleteness theorem implies that solving a problem of a given field may require hypotheses from some other field, Gödel's result even provides evidence for the analytic method.

2) *The analytic method is compatible with Gödel's second incompleteness theorem.* For in such method the hypotheses for the solution to a problem are not definitive, true and certain, but only provisional, plausible and uncertain, so no solution to a problem can be absolutely certain. Since Gödel's second incompleteness theorem implies that no solution to a problem can be absolutely certain, Gödel's result even provides evidence for the analytic method.

In view of this, the scientific method, and generally the method of solving problems, can be identified with the analytic method. Then knowledge is the result of solving problems by the analytic method. When solving problems is successful, it yields knowledge.

'Problems' include all sorts of problems, both first-order and second-order, in the sense explained above. In particular, 'problems' include the survival problem of our hunter-gatherer ancestors. As it has been stated in Chapter 14, scientific knowledge can be viewed as an extension of the activities by which our remotest ancestors solved their survival problem. Both the latter and the activities underlying scientific knowledge are based on essentially similar cognitive processes. Thus the analytic method is a continuity link between them.

17.7 Logic and Knowledge

A basic question about the analytic method is how hypotheses are obtained. Now, as it has been argued in Chapter 4, hypotheses are obtained from the problem, and possibly other data already available, by non-deductive rules. This means that the analytic method is a logical method. On the other hand, as it has been argued in the previous section, knowledge is the result of solving problems by the analytic method.

From the fact that the analytic method is a logical method and that knowledge is the result of solving problems by the analytic method, it follows that logic provides means to acquire knowledge. We do not reason in order to be logical, rather, we are logical in order to achieve our goals, first of all the goal of acquiring knowledge.

That logic provides means to acquire knowledge is the relation of logic to knowledge.

17.8 Non-ampliativity of Deductive Rules

That, in the analytic method, hypotheses are obtained from the problem, and possibly other data already available, by non-deductive rules, is motivated by the fact that, as it has been stated in Chapter 4, deductive rules are non-ampliative. As a fruit juicer cannot extract more from fruits than what is contained in them, deductive rules cannot extract more from premises than what is contained in them. Therefore, the conclusion of a deduction is contained in the premises.

Against this, however, some objections have been raised. Here are the main ones.

1) *Although the conclusion of a deduction is contained in the premises, extracting it from the premises requires labour, therefore deductive rules are ampliative.* For example, Frege states that, although conclusions "are in a way contained covertly in the whole set" of premises "taken together," this "does not absolve us from the labour of actually extracting them and setting them out in their own right."[13] For this reason "the conclusions we draw" from the premises may "extend our knowledge, and ought therefore, on Kant's view, to be regarded as synthetic."[14] For example, the *Begriffsschrift* proof of theorem 133 is "a proof of a proposition which might at first sight be taken for synthetic."[15] This objection, however, is unjustified because there is an algorithm for enumerating all deductions from given premises, thus deducing conclusions from the premises is in principle a purely mechanical business. Frege's claim that the conclusions we draw from the premises extend our knowledge is a form of psychologism, because it mistakes psychological novelty for logical novelty. The conclusions are psychologically surprising not because they are not contained in the premises, but rather because we are incapable of making even comparatively short deductions without the help of processes external to us. For such reason, extracting conclusions from the premises requires labour.

2) *If deductive rules were non-ampliative, someone who acknowledged that the axioms of a mathematical theory are true should thereby know all the theorems*

---

[13]Frege (1959, 23).

[14]*Ibid.*, 101.

[15]*Ibid.*, 103. This view of Frege is argued for in Macbeth (2012).

that can be deduced from them, which is absurd. For example, Dummett states that, if deductive rules were non-ampliative, "as soon as we had acknowledged the truth of the axioms of a mathematical theory, we should thereby know all the theorems. Obviously, this is nonsense."[16] Therefore, deduction must have the power "to yield knowledge that we did not previously possess."[17] This objection, however, is unjustified because, as it has been stated above, we are incapable of making even comparatively short deductions without the help of processes external to us. For this reason, we do not know all the theorems that can be deduced from the axioms of a mathematical theory as soon as we acknowledge that the axioms are true. This has nothing to do with ampliativity.

3) *The conclusion of a deductive inference, even when it only involves individuals mentioned in the premises, tells us something about them that the premises did not tell us.* For example, Russell states that, "if we already know that two and two always make four, and we know that Brown and Jones are two, and so are Robinson and Smith, we can deduce that Brown and Jones and Robinson and Smith are four."[18] Now, "this is new knowledge, not contained in our premisses, because the general proposition, 'two and two are four', never told us there were such people as Brown and Jones and Robinson and Smith, and the particular premises do not tell us that there were four of them."[19] This objection, however, is unjustified because the premise, 'Brown and Jones are two', told us that there were such people as Brown and Jones and that there were two of them. On the other hand, the premise, 'Robinson and Smith are two', told us that there were such people as Robinson and Smith and that there were two of them. Then they, together with the premise that two and two always make four, already told us that there were such people as Brown and Jones and Robinson and Smith, and that there were four of them.

17.9 The Paradox of Inference

Since, in the analytic method, hypotheses are obtained from the problem, and possibly other data already available, by non-deductive rules, they are obtained by inference rules which are not valid, that is, not truth preserving. This is necessary because non-deductive rules are ampliative, and ampliative rules cannot be valid.

That ampliative rules cannot be valid follows from the so-called "paradox of inference."[20] Like *Meno*'s paradox, the paradox of inference is not really a paradox. Unlike *Meno*'s paradox, however, it is not a sophistic argument but shows a basic property of inference rules. According to the paradox of inference, if in an inference

---

[16]Dummett (1991b, 195).

[17]*Ibid.*

[18]Russell (1997, 79).

[19]*Ibid.*

[20]Cohen and Nagel (1964, 173).

rule the conclusion is not contained in the premises, the rule cannot be valid; and if the conclusion does not possess novelty with respect to the premises, the inference rule cannot be ampliative; but the conclusion cannot be contained in the premises and also possess novelty with respect to them; therefore, an inference rule cannot be both valid and ampliative.

Since non-deductive rules are ampliative, from the paradox of inference it follows that they cannot be valid. Notice that the paradox of inference does not mean that an inference rule cannot be both non-valid and non-ampliative, but only that it cannot be both valid and ampliative. Indeed, as it will be argued in Chapter 18, there are inference rules which are both non-valid and non-ampliative.

17.10   Rules for Finding Hypotheses

The non-deductive rules by means of which hypotheses are obtained in the analytic method, are of many kinds. Several of them will be considered in the final part of this book. Which kind of non-deductive rule is to be used to find a hypothesis for solving a given problem, depends on the problem, and possibly other data already available. The problem and the other data already available are the basis for analysing the problem and deciding which non-deductive rule to use.

However, the problem and the other data already available do not uniquely determine which non-deductive rule is to be used. Different non-deductive rules may be used to solve one and the very same problem. This is a basic feature of the analytic method.

17.11   Knowledge and Certainty

Since knowledge is the result of solving problems by the analytic method, knowledge cannot be absolutely certain. For it is based on hypotheses which, as it has been argued in Chapter 4, are neither true nor certain. They can only be plausible, and plausibility does not guarantee truth or certainty. On the other hand, that knowledge cannot be absolutely certain does not mean, as the sceptics claim, that knowledge is impossible, but only that absolutely certain knowledge is impossible.

It might be objected that the assertion that knowledge cannot be absolutely certain is self-defeating, because it implies that such assertion cannot be absolutely certain itself. But it is not so. Rather, it is the objection that is self-defeating, because it implicitly acknowledges that absolutely certain knowledge is impossible.

In this connection it is interesting to cite Peirce: "A critic said of me that I did not seem to be absolutely sure of my own conclusions. Never, if I can help it, shall that critic's eye ever rest on what I am now writing; for I owe a great pleasure to him; and, such was his evident animus, that should he find that out, I fear the fires of hell would be fed with new fuel in his breast."[21] Indeed, by saying so, that critic had confirmed Peirce's claim that "we never can be absolutely sure of anything."[22]

17.12 Solving Problems and Intuition

Since knowledge is the result of solving problems by the analytic method, intuition is not necessary for knowledge. For, as it has been pointed out in Chapter 4, in the analytic method intuition plays no role in solving problems. This contrasts with the widespread view that, because of Gödel's incompleteness theorems, intuition is necessary. Turing and Gödel are significant representatives of this view.

1) Turing claims that "in pre-Gödel times it was thought by some" that "all the intuitive judgments of mathematics could be replaced by a finite number of" mechanical "rules. The necessity for intuition would then be entirely eliminated."[23] But Gödel's first incompleteness theorem showed "the impossibility of finding a formal logic which wholly eliminates the necessity of using intuition."[24] Now, Turing's claim is based on the assumption: either all problems can be solved by the mechanical rules of a given formal system, or intuition is necessary. Since, by Gödel's first incompleteness theorem, not all problems can be solved by the mechanical rules of a given formal system, from the assumption Turing concludes that intuition is necessary. The assumption, however, is unjustified because, since antiquity, it has been acknowledged that solving problems need not consist in using mechanical rules. Mathematics and medicine were the first areas where the need for procedures to solve problems arose, and the earliest such procedures of which we have notice, those of Hippocrates of Chios and Hippocrates of Cos, were non-mechanical. In particular, Plato points out that Hippocrates of Cos' procedure is opposed to the mechanical procedures of traditional medicine, following which "would be like walking with the blind."[25] Between the mechanicalness of the rules of formal systems and the inscrutability of intuition, there is an intermediate region inhabited by the heuristic procedures, which are neither mechanical nor intuitional. They play an essential role in knowledge, because the world is too complex to be comprehended in its entirety by organisms limited in space, time and cognitive resources such as human beings. They can make the world comprehensible to themselves only by resorting to heuristic procedures.

2) Gödel claims that his second incompleteness theorem implies that for the "axioms there exists no other rational (and not merely practical) foundation except

---

[21] Peirce (1931–1958, 1.10).
[22] *Ibid.*, 1.147.
[23] Turing (1939, 215).
[24] *Ibid.*, 216.
[25] Plato, *Phaedrus*, 270 d 9–e 1.

that" they "can directly be perceived to be true" by "an intuition of the objects falling under them."[26] In particular, we have "an intuition which is sufficiently clear to produce the axioms of set theory."[27] Such an intuition is obtained "focusing more sharply on the concepts concerned by directing our attention in a certain way, namely, onto our own acts in the use of these concepts, onto our powers in carrying out our acts, etc."[28] Thus we will get an "intuitive grasping of ever newer axioms."[29] Now, Gödel's claim that axioms can be directly perceived to be true by intuition is based on the assumption that knowledge must be absolutely certain. Since, by Gödel's second incompleteness theorem, the axioms cannot be proved to be true by absolutely reliable means, from the assumption Gödel concludes that they must be perceived to be true by intuition, thus intuition is necessary. The assumption, however, is unjustified because knowledge cannot be absolutely certain but only plausible. On the other hand, Gödel's claim that an intuition which is sufficiently clear to produce the axioms of set theory is obtained focusing more sharply on the concepts concerned, is based on the assumption that in this way the axioms can directly be perceived to be true. The assumption, however, is unjustified. For suppose that, by focusing more sharply on the concept of set σ, we directly perceive the axioms of a deductive theory S to be true of σ. Then σ is a model of S, so S is consistent, hence, by Gödel's first incompleteness theorem, there is a sentence G of S which is true of σ but undemonstrable in S. Let T be the deductive theory which is obtained from S by adding $\neg G$ as a new axiom. Since G is undemonstrable in S, the theory T is consistent, and hence has a model, say σ', which, being a model of S, is a concept of set. By focusing more sharply on the concept of set σ', we directly perceive the axioms of T, namely the axioms of S and $\neg G$, to be true of σ'. On the other hand, we directly perceive the axioms of S and G to be true of σ, and hence $\neg G$ to be false of σ. Then, is $\neg G$ true or false? Or, in other words, which of σ and σ' is the genuine concept of set? Intuition gives no answer.

17.13 Objections Against the Possibility of a Logic of Discovery

Since knowledge is the result of solving problems by the analytic method, the latter provides the basis for a logic of discovery. Thus the analytic method is the source of a logic of discovery. There are several objections against the possibility of such a logic, but they are unjustified. The main ones are the following.

1) *While there is a logic of justification based on mechanical rules, there can be no logic of discovery because discovery requires intuition, and hence cannot be*

---

[26]Gödel (1986–2002, III, 346–347).
[27]*Ibid.*, II, 268.
[28]*Ibid.*, III, 383.
[29]*Ibid.*, III, 385.

17.13 Objections Against the Possibility of a Logic of Discovery

based on mechanical rules. Carnap claims that there can be no logic of discovery because discovery requires "creative ingenuity," that is, intuition, so there cannot be "a computer into which we can put all the relevant observational sentences and get, as an output, a neat system of laws that will explain the observed phenomena."[30] Carnap's claim is based on the assumption: either discovery is obtained by mechanical rules or it requires intuition. The assumption, however, is unjustified because, as it has been argued in the previous section, between the mechanicalness of the rules of formal systems and the inscrutability of intuition, there is an intermediate region inhabited by the heuristic procedures. The purpose of a logic of discovery is not to dispense with the need for intelligence by use of mechanical rules, but rather to expand natural intelligence, providing it with tools capable of guiding it, though not infallibly.

2) *While there is a logic of justification based on rules that are completely objective, there can be no logic of discovery because the processes involved in discovery are purely subjective and psychological*. Reichenbach claims that there can be no logic of discovery because the process of discovery "evades distinct analysis."[31] The "context of discovery is left to psychological analysis, whereas logic is concerned with the context of justification."[32] Reichenbach's claim, however, is unjustified because the analytic method, on which the logic of discovery is based, has nothing subjective or psychological about it. The non-deductive rules by which the method is implemented, such as those discussed in the last part of this book, are as objective as the deductive rules of a logic of justification.

3) *While the rules for a logic of justification can be definitively stated, the same cannot be said about the rules for a logic of discovery*. Hilbert claims that the deductive rules for a logic of justification "form a closed system that can be discovered and definitively stated."[33] By 'deductive rules' Hilbert does not mean only those for first-order logic, but also those for second-order logic, because only by admitting the latter one may hope that "the axiom systems for number theory as well for analysis are complete."[34] Thus his consistency programme needs to establish consistency "relative to higher types of variables."[35] On the other hand, the rules for a logic of discovery cannot be definitively stated, because discovery is obtained "by separating and collecting ideas in fortunate ways."[36] Hilbert's claim, however, is unjustified because, as it has been pointed out in Chapter 12, by the strong incompleteness theorem for second-order logic, no consistent set of deductive rules would permit to deduce all second-order logical consequences from given hypotheses. Therefore, no set of rules for a logic of justification can

---

[30] Carnap (1966, 33).
[31] Reichenbach (1947, 1).
[32] *Ibid.*, 2.
[33] Hilbert (1967, 475).
[34] Hilbert (1998, 231).
[35] *Ibid.*
[36] Hilbert (2000, 243).

be definitively stated. Then one cannot blame a logic of discovery for not allowing rules that can be definitively stated. Even a logic of justification does not allow such rules.

4) *While justification is a logical process, discovery is not, being based on processes which are haphazard and illogical. Rather than discovery, logic can explain the organizational and verificational structure of science.* Feferman claims that "the creative and intuitive aspects of mathematical work evade logical encapsulation."[37] The "actual historical and individual processes of mathematical discovery appear haphazard and illogical."[38] Rather than discovery, logic can "explain what constitutes the underlying content of mathematics and what is its organizational and verificational structure."[39] Feferman's claim, however, is unjustified. Saying that discovery is based on processes which are haphazard and illogical contrasts with the fact that, since antiquity, mathematicians have used a method of discovery, the analytic method, in which hypotheses are found by non-deductive rules, so by logical means. Moreover, saying that logic can explain the organizational and verificational structure of a science is in conflict with Gödel's incompleteness theorems.

5) *While justification is an ordinary matter, discovery is a somewhat exceptional event, which comes about only by luck.* Quine claims that mathematicians make their discoveries "by unregimented insight and good fortune."[40] A demonstration is "discoverable in general only by luck."[41] Discovering it "is a hit and miss matter."[42] On the other hand, once a demonstration has been discovered, it "can be mechanically checked."[43] Quine's claim, however, is unjustified because, rather than a somewhat exceptional event, discovery is an ordinary one. Solving problems is a task that all organisms have to carry out to a certain extent, otherwise they could not survive. Moreover, discovery does not come about only by luck. As it has been argued in Chapter 13, it is the result of a long preparatory work which requires a prepared mind.

6) *While justification is based on reasoning which is definitive and establishes irrefutably the truth of the theorem, discovery is based on reasoning which is provisional and always open to possible refutation.* Pólya claims that the "logical type of reasoning" on which the justification of mathematical theorems is based, yields "rigorous demonstration," which "is definitive, it establishes irrefutably the truth of the theorem – once for all."[44] Conversely, the heuristic argument which guides discovery is "provisional; the one I find today increases my confidence

---

[37] Feferman (1998, 178).
[38] *Ibid.*, 77.
[39] *Ibid.*, 92.
[40] Quine (1981a, 87).
[41] *Ibid.*, 291.
[42] *Ibid.*, 6.
[43] *Ibid.*
[44] Pólya (1941, 450).

which may be shaken tomorrow by another heuristic" argument, "and definitively shattered the following day by the rigorous" logical "refutation of the theorem under consideration."[45] Pólya's claim, however, is unjustified because, by Gödel's second incompleteness theorem, logical reasoning is not definitive nor establishes irrefutably the truth of the theorem. Admittedly, the analytic method cannot yield absolutely certain knowledge, only plausible one. But this is the only kind of knowledge we can achieve.

17.14 Hypotheses and the *A Priori*

Knowledge which is the result of solving problems by the analytic method, is *a priori* – *a priori* not in the sense that it is totally independent of experience, but rather in the sense that it is based on hypotheses which go beyond experience.

Indeed, in the analytic method, hypotheses are obtained by non-deductive rules, so they are not contained in the premises. Thus, even when the premises depend on experience, the hypotheses go beyond it. Only testing them for plausibility depends on experience.

Knowledge which is *a priori* in this sense is not certain, and yet it is indispensable for the possibility of experience, because all sort of knowledge, including the perceptive one, is based on hypotheses.

17.15 The Evolution of the *A Priori*

It might be objected that the sense of *a priori* described in the previous section is in conflict with the traditional one. This, however, assumes that there is a traditional sense of *a priori*. Such an assumption is unjustified because, in the course of the centuries, the term *a priori* has had different senses.

As we have seen in Chapter 8, the term first occurs in the Scholastic tradition with reference to demonstration: *a priori* demonstration is that which descends from the cause to the effect. In the second half of the seventeenth century, in the Port-Royal Logic, one still reads that "demonstrating *a priori*" means "proving the effects from the causes."[46] Since then, this sense of *a priori* undergoes a number of changes, which involve a shift from demonstration to knowledge. We will consider three of them.

1) According to Kant, *a priori* knowledge is knowledge that occurs "absolutely independently of all experience."[47] It has the character of "strict universality," in the

---

[45] *Ibid.*
[46] Arnauld and Nicole (1992, 281).
[47] Kant (1997a, 137, B3).

sense that "no exception at all is allowed to be possible."[48] It has "the character of inner necessity."[49] And it is "certain."[50]

This sense of *a priori* knowledge, however, contrasts with the fact that no knowledge occurs absolutely independently of all experience, because all knowledge, including mathematical knowledge, arises from interaction with the external world. No knowledge has the character of strict universality, because exceptions are always possible, knowledge being at most plausible. No knowledge has the character of inner necessity, because all knowledge, being the product of our limited experience and our fallible biology, is always contingent. No knowledge is certain, because all knowledge, being at most plausible, is potentially fallible.

The sense of *a priori* knowledge described in the previous section is not subject to these limitations, because knowledge which is *a priori* in that sense, being based on hypotheses which derive their plausibility from experience, does not occur absolutely independently of all experience. It has no character of strict universality, because hypotheses, being only plausible, are not immunized from counterexamples. It has no character of inner necessity, because hypotheses, being only plausible, are contingent. It is not certain, because hypotheses, being only plausible, can be fallible.

2) According to Spencer, *a priori* knowledge consists of "cognitions that have been rendered organic by immense accumulations of experiences, received partly by the individual, but mainly by all ancestral individuals whose nervous systems he inherits."[51] Such experiences are "*a priori* for the individual, but *a posteriori* for that entire series of individuals of which he forms the last term."[52] In particular, Kant's "forms of intuition" are *a posteriori* for that entire series, because they consist in "certain pre-established relations answering to relations in the environment," which exist in the nervous system as a result of biological evolution and, "though independent of the experiences of the individual," have been "determined by the experiences of preceding organisms."[53]

This sense of *a priori* knowledge, however, contrasts with the fact that, if *a priori* knowledge is essential for the survival of organisms, then one cannot explain how our remotest ancestors could survive without it. To explain it one must admit that *a priori* knowledge was never *a posteriori*, it was *a priori* also for them. In particular, this holds of Kant's forms of intuition. If they had been *a posteriori* for our remotest ancestors, this would imply that, while we are unable to derive Euclid's fifth postulate from experience, our remotest ancestors were able to do so. This is absurd, because it would mean that our remotest ancestors had mental powers we no longer have.

---

[48] *Ibid.*, 137, B4.
[49] *Ibid.*, 127, A2.
[50] *Ibid.*
[51] Spencer (1893, 179, footnote).
[52] Spencer (1890, II, 195).
[53] *Ibid.*, I, 470.

The sense of *a priori* knowledge described in the previous section is not subject to these limitations because, in terms of it, even our remotest ancestors did not derive their knowledge from experience but through hypotheses obtained by non-deductive rules, so in that sense their knowledge was *a priori*.

3) According to Popper, *a priori* knowledge is the knowledge "which an organism has prior to sense experience; roughly speaking, it is inborn knowledge."[54] Such knowledge is not "valid *a priori*" but is only "genetically *a priori*," that is, "prior to all observational experience."[55] Moreover, it is very extensive, because "our knowledge is 99 per cent, or let us say 99.9 per cent, biologically innate. The rest is a modification, a revolutionary overturning of some previous knowledge."[56] The *a priori* knowledge is not obtained by induction but "by trial (hypothesis) and error (empirical refutation)."[57] The "trials correspond to the formation of competing hypotheses; and the elimination of error corresponds to the elimination or refutation of theories by way of tests."[58] This is "also the method used by living organisms in the process of adaptation."[59]

This sense of *a priori* knowledge, however, is in conflict with the fact that innate knowledge, being a result of biological evolution, which is slow, is necessarily limited. Then the claim that our knowledge is 99.9 per cent biologically innate is unrealistic. On the other hand, the claim that hypotheses are not obtained by induction but by trial and error, is in conflict with Popper's assertion that the success of trial and error "depends very largely on the number and variety of the trials: the more we try, the more likely it is that one of our attempts will be successful."[60] This means that its success depends on that very same induction which Popper rejects by saying that "there is no such thing."[61] Moreover, trial and error gropes along, and the number of trials that any organism can make is very limited. So, if hypotheses were found by trial and error, the chances of success of finding the right ones would be pretty low. Already Bacon warned that one must not only "seek and procure a greater abundance of experiments" but must also introduce a "method, order, and process for carrying on and advancing experience. For experience, when it wanders in its own track," is "mere groping in the dark."[62] Without method, human beings "wander and stray with no settled course, but only take counsel from things as they fall out," and so "make little progress."[63]

---

[54] Popper (1999, 69).
[55] Popper (1974, 47).
[56] Popper (1999, 54).
[57] *Ibid.*, 78.
[58] Popper (1972, 24).
[59] Popper (1974, 312).
[60] *Ibid.*
[61] Popper (2005, 168).
[62] Bacon (1961–1986, I, 203).
[63] *Ibid.*, I, 180.

The sense of *a priori* knowledge described in the previous section is not subject to these limitations, because knowledge which is *a priori* in that sense is the result not only of biological evolution, but also of cultural evolution. The latter is fast, so the *a priori* knowledge which it yields is very extensive. Moreover, hypotheses are not found by trial and error, which gives no indication as to how to obtain them, but by non-deductive rules, which serve as a guide towards obtaining them.

17.16 The Open World View of Science

As we have seen in Chapters 9 and 10, Kant proposes a closed world view of science according to which a science is a closed system, and Frege proposes a similar view of mathematics. Conversely if, as it has been suggested in this chapter, the scientific method is identified with the analytic method, this yields an open world view of science according to which a science is an open system.

An open system is a system which initially consists only of the problem to be solved, and possibly other data already available, and whose development consists in obtaining more and more hypotheses for solving the problem from the problem itself, and possibly other data already available, by non-deductive rules. The hypotheses are then checked by means of the plausibility test procedure. The other data already available from which hypotheses are possibly obtained come from other open systems, therefore the development of an open system involves interactions with other open systems. As Grosholz says, through such interactions "different traditions of representation are typically juxtaposed and superimposed."[64] The view that a science is an open system is an open world view just because the development of an open system involves interactions with other open systems. While closed systems are incapable of evolving, open systems can evolve through the introduction of new hypotheses or the modification or complete replacement of existing ones. They can evolve also through the introduction of new non-deductive rules for finding hypotheses.

The evolution of open systems can be compared to the biological evolution of species. Like species, open systems develop ceaselessly through interactions with other open systems. And, as the evolution of the species has not always the same speed but may have sudden breaks or accelerations, the evolution of open systems has not always the same speed but may have sudden breaks or accelerations. This occurs when, as a result of interactions with other systems, new hypotheses are introduced which involve a reorganization of the system.

---

[64]Grosholz (2007, 40).

Chapter 18
Classifying and Justifying Inference Rules

18.1 The Standard Classification of Inference Rules

In Chapters 4 and 17, deductive and non-deductive rules were distinguished in terms of the fact that non-deductive rules are ampliative while deductive rules are non-ampliative.

Is this the proper way of classifying inference rules? This is the question of the classification of inference rules.

In addition, two other questions naturally arise.

What justifies inference rules? This is the question of the justification of inference rules

What is the role of inference rules in knowledge? This is the question of the characterization of the role of inference rules in knowledge.

First we consider the question of the classification of inference rules. This is a basic logic task. Peirce even states that "the chief business of the logician is to classify arguments."[1] What can be termed the standard classification of inference rules, or inferences, is formulated by Hintikka and Sandu as follows: "Inferences can be either deductive, that is, necessarily truth preserving, or ampliative, that is, not necessarily truth preserving."[2]

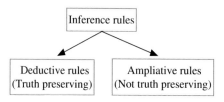

---

[1] Peirce (1931–1958, 2.619).
[2] Hintikka and Sandu (2007, 13).

This classification, however, is inadequate because, as we will see, there are inference rules which are neither deductive nor ampliative.

18.2 Abduction

It is widely held that one of the most important means of obtaining hypotheses is abduction, that is, the rule:

$$\text{(ABD)} \quad \frac{B \to A \quad A}{B}.$$

Clearly (ABD) is not truth preserving because, if A is true and B is false, then $B \to A$ is true, so both premises of (ABD) are true and the conclusion is B false. Indeed, compared with *modus ponens* (MP), abduction (ABD) is a fallacy which, as Aristotle points out, "is due to the idea that the relation of consequence is convertible."[3]

Since (ABD) is not truth preserving, in terms of the standard classification of inference rules, (ABD) would be considered to be ampliative. But this is in conflict with the fact that the conclusion, B, is literally a part of the major premise $B \to A$, thus it is contained in it. Therefore, (ABD) is non-ampliative.

Indeed, what generates new information is not (ABD), but rather the process that yields its major premise, $B \to A$, thus something prior to (ABD). As Frankfurt says, "clearly, if the new idea, or hypothesis, must appear in one of the premises of the abduction, it cannot be the case that it originates as the conclusion of such an inference; it must have been invented before the conclusion was drawn."[4]

Since (ABD), on the one hand, like deductive rules, is non-ampliative, and, on the other hand, like non-deductive rules, is not truth preserving, (ABD) is a counterexample to the standard classification of inference rules.

18.3 Peirce on the Status of Abduction

Even Peirce, who first formulated (ABD), acknowledges that (ABD) is non-ampliative. Admittedly, for some time Peirce entertains the idea that (ABD) is ampliative. For he states that (ABD) is "what Aristotle meant by *apagoge*."[5] Now, what Aristotle meant by *apagoge* is a process of discovery. For it is a way of finding premises for a given conclusion "when it is clear that the first term belongs to the

---

[3] Aristotle, *Sophistici Elenchi*, 34, 167 b 1–2.
[4] Frankfurt (1958, 594).
[5] Peirce (1992, 140).

middle and unclear that the middle belongs to the last term, though equally or more convincing than the conclusion; or when there are few middles between the last term and the middle."[6] Eventually, however, Peirce comes to recognize that the idea that (ABD) is ampliative is thin. He admits that his claim that (ABD) is what Aristotle meant by *apagoge* is based on "the doubtful theory, I confess, that the meaning" of *Prior Analytics*, B 25, "has been completely diverted from Aristotle's meaning by a single wrong word having been inserted by Apellicon," the first editor, "where the original word was illegible."[7]

Not only his assertion that (ABD) is what Aristotle meant by *apagoge* is based on a doubtful theory, but the idea that (ABD) is ampliative is positively wrong, because (ABD) is an inference of the form: "The surprising fact, A, is observed; But if B were true, A would be a matter of course; hence, there is reason to suspect that B is true."[8] Thus "B cannot be abductively inferred, or if you prefer the expression, cannot be abductively conjectured until its entire content is already present in the premiss, 'If B were true, A would be a matter of course'."[9]

Generally, "the entire logical matter of a conclusion must in any mode of inference be contained, piecemeal, in the premisses."[10] This includes abduction, because abduction "is logical inference, asserting its conclusion only problematically or conjecturally, it is true, but nevertheless having a perfectly definite logical form."[11] Since the entire logical matter of a conclusion must in any mode of inference be contained in the premisses, and abduction is logical inference, "quite new conceptions cannot be obtained from abduction."[12]

Thus Peirce recognizes that (ABD) is non-ampliative, since ampliative inference is an inference whose conclusion contains "something not implied in the premisses."[13]

18.4 Peirce on Abduction and Intuition

In addition to recognizing that (ABD) is non-ampliative, Peirce claims that the major premise of (ABD), $B \rightarrow A$, cannot be obtained by a process which can be subjected to logical analysis. For if we subjected it to logical analysis, "we should find that it terminated in what that analysis would represent as an abductive inference, resting

---

[6] Aristotle, *Analytica Priora*, B 25, 69 a 20–23.
[7] Peirce (1931–1958, 8.209).
[8] *Ibid.*, 5.189. For uniformity with the above formulation of (ABD), the letters C and A originally used by Peirce have been replaced with A and B, respectively.
[9] *Ibid.*
[10] *Ibid.*, 5.194.
[11] *Ibid.*, 5.188.
[12] *Ibid.*, 5.190.
[13] *Ibid.*, 6.40.

on the result of a similar process which a similar logical analysis would represent to be terminated by a similar abductive inference, and so on *ad infinitum*."[14] Ultimately, therefore, the major premise, $B \to A$, "must come from the uncontrolled part of the mind, because a series of controlled acts must have a first."[15] Specifically, it must be the result of an act of insight, then of intuition. The suggestion of the major premise, $B \to A$, "comes to us like a flash. It is an act of insight, although of extremely fallible insight."[16]

However, Peirce's claim that the major premise, $B \to A$, is the result of an act of insight, and hence cannot be subjected to logical analysis, is unjustified. The analytic method provides a counterexample to it, because it gives a logical analysis of the process of hypothesis formation.

18.5 Peirce's Classification of Inference Rules

(ABD) is a counterexample not only to the standard classification of inference rules, but also to Peirce's own classification of such rules. According to Peirce, inference rules may be divided into deductive or analytic, that is, non-ampliative, and synthetic, that is, ampliative. In their turn, synthetic rules "may be divided into induction and hypothesis."[17]

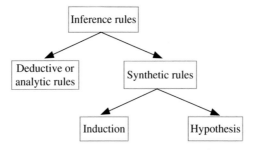

By 'hypothesis' Peirce means what he will later call 'abduction'. This is apparent from his example of hypothesis: "All the beans from this bag are white" and "These beans are white," therefore "These beans are from this bag."[18] This example is of the form: $\forall x(\text{bean-from-this-bag}(x) \to \text{white}(x))$, and $\text{white}(y)$, therefore bean-from-this-bag(y).

But, if 'hypothesis' means 'abduction', then, according to Peirce's classification of inference rules, (ABD) is synthetic, thus ampliative. This contradicts his

---

[14] *Ibid.*, 5.181.
[15] *Ibid.*, 5.194.
[16] *Ibid.*, 5.181.
[17] *Ibid.*, 2.641.
[18] *Ibid.*, 2.623.

statement, quoted above, that quite new conceptions cannot be obtained from abduction. The contradiction vanishes if one takes into account that Peirce's classification of inference rules belongs to an early phase of his thought, while his recognition that (ABD) is non-ampliative belongs to a later phase. The recognition that (ABD) is non-ampliative implies that Peirce's classification of inference rules is inadequate, because (ABD) is not a deductive rule, and yet is not synthetic.

Another problem with Peirce's classification of inference rules is that, while in an early phase of his thought Peirce does not sharply distinguish between the roles of induction and (ABD), in a later phase he considers (ABD) to be a means of introducing hypotheses, and induction only a means of verifying them. Indeed, he states that (ABD) "furnishes the reasoner with the problematic theory which induction verifies."[19] A theory "adopted by abduction could only be adopted on probation, and must be tested."[20] Induction is "the experimental testing of a theory," so it "never can originate any idea whatever."[21] Indeed, "induction adds nothing."[22] But the claim that induction is the experimental testing of a theory and verifies it, is unjustified. Scientific hypotheses are often universally quantified statements, so no finite number of experiments could verify them. Rather, induction is a means of introducing new hypotheses.

18.6 Objections to the Non-ampliativity of Abduction

Against the claim that (ABD) is non-ampliative some objections have been raised. Here are two of them.

1) (ABD) is ampliative because "the difficult part in discovery is the recognition that the hypothesis really is a viable way of solving this particular problem."[23] Namely, it is the recognition that the hypothesis "fits with those constraints and clues that are involved in the problem situation in question."[24] This objection is unjustified since it argues that (ABD) is ampliative because the difficult part in discovery is the recognition that the major premise, $B \to A$, holds. This amounts to saying that what generates new information is not really (ABD), but rather the process that yields the major premise, $B \to A$, thus something prior to (ABD).

2) (ABD) is ampliative because it "can 'interpret' the given data in a new vocabulary."[25] For example, suppose that, from the premises, 'If the patient has hepatitis, then the patient has jaundice' and 'The patient has jaundice', we infer

---

[19] *Ibid.*, 2.776.
[20] *Ibid.*, 7.202.
[21] *Ibid.*, 5.145.
[22] *Ibid.*, 7.217.
[23] Paavola (2004, 273).
[24] *Ibid.*, 274.
[25] Josephson and Josephson (1994, 13).

the conclusion, 'The patient has hepatitis'. Then "we have introduced into the conclusion a new term, 'hepatitis', which is from the vocabulary of diseases and not part of the vocabulary of symptoms. By introducing this term, we make conceptual connections with the typical progress of the disease, and ways to treat it, that were unavailable before."[26] This objection is unjustified since it argues that (ABD) is ampliative because it introduces into the conclusion, B, a new term which is not part of the vocabulary of the minor premise, A, thus establishing a conceptual connection between the two vocabularies. But the connection is made through the process that yields the major premise, $B \to A$, thus something prior to (ABD).

18.7 Inference to the Best Explanation

A generalization of abduction, called 'inference to the best explanation', has also been considered. It concerns the case when there are "several hypotheses which might explain the evidence."[27] In making this inference "one infers, from the premise that a given hypothesis would provide a 'better' explanation for the evidence than would any other hypothesis, to the conclusion that the given hypothesis is true."[28]

The concept of inference to the best explanation already occurs in Peirce. For he states that abduction "will include a preference for any one hypothesis over others which would equally explain the facts, so long as this preference is not based upon any previous knowledge bearing upon the truth of the hypothesis, nor on any testing of any of the hypotheses, after having admitted them on probation."[29]

Let $BE(B_i; A; B_1, \ldots, B_{i-1}, B_{i+1}, \ldots, B_n)$: B_i is a better explanation of the fact A than all of $B_1, \ldots, B_{i-1}, B_{i+1}, \ldots, B_n$. Then inference to the best explanation is the rule:

$$(\text{IBE}) \quad \frac{B_1 \to A \ \ldots \ B_n \to A \quad A \quad BE(B_i; A; B_1, \ldots, B_{i-1}, B_{i+1}, \ldots, B_n)}{B_i}.$$

Clearly, (ABD) is the special case of (IBE) with $n = 1$. Like (ABD), (IBE) is non-ampliative because B_i is literally a part of the premise $B_i \to A$. With respect to (ABD), however, (IBE) is problematic. For the premise $BE(B_1; A; B_1, \ldots, B_{i-1}, B_{i+1}, \ldots, B_n)$ raises the question of "how one is to judge that one hypothesis is sufficiently better than another hypothesis."[30] Answering this question requires a criterion for deciding which of two hypotheses is better. As Peirce points out, such

---

[26] *Ibid.*
[27] Harman (1965, 89).
[28] *Ibid.*
[29] Peirce (1931–1958, 6.525).
[30] Harman (1965, 89).

a criterion cannot be based on knowledge of the truth, or on testing, of any of the hypotheses. On the other hand, all other criteria that have been proposed are inadequate.

For example, one criterion is "based on considerations such as which hypothesis is simpler."[31] But why should the fact that a hypothesis is simpler be a reason to conclude that it is true? This would be justified only on the assumption that the universe is simple, which means, only on the assumption that the universe is organized for our convenience. But why should the universe be organized for our convenience? Galileo points out that natural matters do not "accommodate themselves to our comprehension," on the contrary, nature "first made things in her own way, and then made human reason skilful enough to be able to understand (but only by great labour) some of her secrets."[32] Kant points out that it is "not nature" that adjusts "to the conditions according to which we strive to obtain a concept of it," it is rather our "reflection on the laws of nature" that "adjusts itself to nature."[33] Then the simplicity criterion is inadequate. The same applies to all other criteria that have been proposed.

In view of the problematic character of (IBE), in what follows we will consider only (ABD).

18.8 An Alternative Classification of Inference Rules

Since (ABD) is a counterexample to the standard classification of inference rules, an alternative classification is necessary. To that purpose, all inference rules are divided into ampliative and non-ampliative. Ampliative rules consist of non-deductive rules and hence are not truth preserving. Non-ampliative rules are divided into deductive rules and (ABD), where the former are truth preserving while (ABD) is not truth preserving.

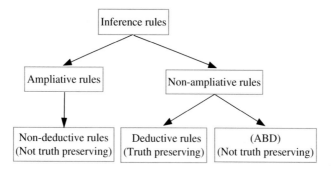

---

[31] *Ibid.*
[32] Galilei (1968, VII, 289).
[33] Kant (2007b, 15).

It is then clear why the standard classification of inference rules fails: (ABD) is both non-ampliative and not truth preserving. The only adequate classification of inference rules is in terms of ampliativity rather than truth preservation.

That non-deductive rules are not truth preserving is a consequence of their being ampliative. This follows from the paradox of inference, considered in Chapter 17. On the other hand, deductive rules can be truth preserving because they sacrifice ampliativity. Their conclusion contains no more, in fact usually less, than the premises. (ABD) belongs to a different category because, on the one hand, like deductive rules, it is non-ampliative, but, on the other hand, unlike them, it is not truth preserving. It is an open question whether, in addition to (ABD), there are other interesting inference rules that are both non-ampliative and not truth preserving.

18.9 Failures in Justifying Deductive Rules

After considering the question of the classification of inference rules, we now consider those of the justification of inference rules and the characterization of their role in knowledge. Let us first examine deductive rules. Several justifications of deductive rules have been proposed. Two especially significant ones are the truth-functional justification and the inferentialist justification.

1) According to the truth-functional justification, deductive rules are justified because they are truth preserving. For example, Frege states that the justification of *modus ponens*, ($\to$E), is: "From the propositions ' $\vdash \Delta \to \Gamma$' and ' $\vdash \Delta$' we may infer ' $\vdash \Gamma$'; for if Γ were not the True, then since Δ is the True, '$\Delta \to \Gamma$' would be the False."[34] This justification of ($\to$E), however, is circular because it is of the following kind. Suppose that $A \to B$ and A are true. Now, if $A \to B$ is true, then, if A is true, then B is true. Since $A \to B$ and A are true, from this, by two applications of ($\to$E), we conclude that B is true. Since this justification of ($\to$E) uses ($\to$E), it is circular.

Against the conclusion that the truth-functional justification of deductive rules is circular, two objections might be raised.

(i) The circularity involved in the truth-functional justification of deductive rules is not premise-circularity but rather rule-circularity. Premise-circularity occurs when the fact that a deductive rule is truth preserving is used as a premise in the justification of that rule. Rule-circularity occurs when a deductive rule is used in the course of the justification of the rule. Premise-circularity is harmful, because a premise-circular justification of a deductive rule has no force for anyone who does not already accept that such deductive rule is truth preserving. Rule-circularity is

---

[34]Frege (1964, 57). For convenience, Frege's two-dimensional notation has been replaced with the current one-dimensional one.

18.9 Failures in Justifying Deductive Rules

harmless, because a rule-circular justification of a deductive rule is not intended to persuade anyone of the truth of the conclusion of that deductive rule, but only to explain why the conclusion is true.

This objection, however, is untenable. For if rule-circularity is allowed, then one can give a truth-functional justification not only of ($\rightarrow$E), which is truth preserving, but also of (ABD), which is not truth preserving. The truth-functional justification of (ABD) is as follows. Suppose that $B \rightarrow A$ and A are true. Now, $B \rightarrow ((B \rightarrow A) \rightarrow A)$ is true. Moreover, if A is true, then $(B \rightarrow A) \rightarrow A$ is true. Since $B \rightarrow ((B \rightarrow A) \rightarrow A)$ and $(B \rightarrow A) \rightarrow A$ are true, by an application of (ABD) we conclude that B is true. It is no use to say that this is not a genuine justification of (ABD) because, while the truth-functional justification of ($\rightarrow$E) uses ($\rightarrow$E), which is truth preserving, the truth-functional justification of (ABD) uses (ABD), which is not truth preserving. For to justify that ($\rightarrow$E) is truth preserving is exactly the question at issue here.

(ii) The truth-functional justification of ($\rightarrow$E) involves use of ($\rightarrow$E) applied to the metalanguage, while the ($\rightarrow$E) being justified applies to the object language. Thus the rule being justified and the justifying rule belong to two distinct levels.

This objection, however, is untenable. For how will we justify the ($\rightarrow$E) of the metalanguage? By demonstrating that it is truth preserving, using ($\rightarrow$E) in the meta-metalanguage. The same question will then arise for the latter, and so on, *ad infinitum*. Thus we cannot argue that ($\rightarrow$E) is truth preserving without infinite regress. Moreover, the objection overlooks that if, by use of ($\rightarrow$E) in the metalanguage, we can justify use of ($\rightarrow$E) in the object language, then, as we have seen above, by use of (ABD) in the metalanguage, we can justify use of (ABD) in the object language. Thus, if ($\rightarrow$E) is justified, (ABD) too is justified.

Therefore, the truth-functional justification of deductive rules is inadequate.

2) According to the inferentialist justification, the introduction rules are self-justifying because they are the definitions of the symbols concerned, and the elimination rules are justified because they are the consequences of these definitions. As we have seen in Chapter 11, Gentzen proposes this view. Accordingly, he justifies ($\rightarrow$E) by saying that "we were able to introduce the formula $A \rightarrow B$ when there existed a derivation of B from the assumption formula A. If we then wished to use that formula by eliminating the $\rightarrow$-symbol," we "could do this precisely by inferring B directly, once A has been proved, for what $A \rightarrow B$ attests is just the existence of a derivation of B from A."[35]

This justification of ($\rightarrow$E), however, is circular because it is of the following kind. Suppose we have deductions of $A \rightarrow B$ and A. If we have a deduction of $A \rightarrow B$, then by Gentzen's definition of $A \rightarrow B$ we have a deduction of B from A. If we have a deduction of B from A, from the latter and the given deduction of A we obtain a deduction of B. Then by two applications of ($\rightarrow$E) we obtain a deduction of B. Since this justification of ($\rightarrow$E) uses ($\rightarrow$E), it is circular.[36]

---

[35] Gentzen (1969, 80–81).

[36] Howson claims that, using "a general deductive principle called 'Cut'," one can show that "there is a deductive justification for detaching the conclusion of a *modus ponens* inference," namely

Moreover, if ($\to$E) is justified since, if we have deductions of $A \to B$ and A, we can obtain a deduction of B, then (ABD) is justified in the same sense: If we have deductions of $B \to A$ and A, we can obtain a deduction of B.

To illustrate this point, let us consider Kepler's argument about Mars' orbit, which Peirce calls "the greatest piece" of abductive "reasoning ever performed."[37] According to Peirce, Kepler's argument is an example of (ABD). For let A: There are certain irregularities in the longitudes of Mars. Let B: The orbit of Mars is elliptical. Then Kepler's argument is: The surprising fact A is observed; but, if B, then A would be a matter of course, that is, $B \to A$; hence, there is reason to suspect that B is true. Now, for Kepler, a sufficient condition for asserting $B \to A$ is that, from the fact A, that there are certain irregularities in the longitudes of Mars, he deduces B, that the orbit of Mars is elliptical. Indeed, Kepler's argument is that the irregularities in question, on the one hand, are incompatible with a circular orbit, because the circle "sins by excess," and, on the other hand, are incompatible with a certain elliptical orbit, because the ellipse in question "sins by defect."[38] However, "between the circle and the ellipse there is nothing but another ellipse. Therefore the planet's orbit is an ellipse."[39] Thus, for Kepler, a sufficient condition for asserting $B \to A$ is the introduction rule:

$$(\text{ABD-I}) \, \dfrac{\begin{array}{c}[A]\\ \vdots\\ B\end{array}}{B \to A}.$$

Then a justification of (ABD) can be given as follows. Suppose we have deductions of $B \to A$ and A. If we have a deduction of $B \to A$, then, by Kepler's sufficient condition for asserting $B \to A$, (ABD-I), we have a deduction of B from A. From the latter and the given deduction of A we obtain a deduction of B. This is expressed by the following ABD-contraction rule, where for uniformity (ABD) has been renamed (ABD-E):

ABD-contraction

$$\begin{array}{l}(\text{ABD-I})\\ (\text{ABD-E})\end{array} \dfrac{\dfrac{\begin{array}{c}[A]\\ \vdots\\ B\end{array}}{B \to A} \quad \begin{array}{c}\vdots\\ A\end{array}}{B} \quad \Rightarrow \quad \begin{array}{c}[A]\\ \vdots\\ B\end{array}$$

Therefore, the inferentialist justification of deductive rules is inadequate.

($\to$E), which "need not employ *modus ponens* at all" (Howson 2000, 28). This claim, however, is unjustified; see Cellucci (2006).

[37] Peirce (1931–1958, 1.74).
[38] Kepler (1858–1871, III, 400).
[39] *Ibid.*

It can be shown that all other current justifications of deductive rules that have been proposed are also inadequate.[40] The inadequacy of all these justifications is due to the fact that none of them take into account the role of deductive rules in knowledge. Only by taking into account the role of deductive rules in knowledge it is possible to give a justification of such rules.

18.10 Validation and Vindication

In order to give a justification of an inference rule it is necessary first to explain what is meant by 'justification'. In this regard, it is convenient to use Feigl's distinction between validation and vindication. Validation is justification in the sense of an argument concerning "validating grounds."[41] Vindication is justification in the "sense of an argument concerning means with respect to ends."[42]

To validate an inference rule is to demonstrate that it can be derived from other inference rules. To vindicate an inference rule is to demonstrate that it is appropriate to a certain end.

18.11 Vindication and Truth Preservation

Since to validate a deductive rule is to demonstrate that it can be derived from other deductive rules, not all deductive rules can be validated, otherwise there would be an infinite regress or a vicious circle. Therefore, there must be some ultimate deductive rules that cannot be validated.

For such ultimate deductive rules we can only seek vindication, that is, we can only try to demonstrate that they are appropriate to a certain end. The question is: To what end? Feigl's answer is that they are appropriate to the end of deducing "true propositions from true premises."[43] This answer, however, is unsatisfactory because, as we have seen, we cannot demonstrate without circularity that ($\rightarrow$E) is appropriate to the end of deducing true propositions from true premises. The same applies to any other ultimate deductive rule. Therefore, we cannot demonstrate that the ultimate deductive rules are appropriate to that end. In addition, seeking to vindicate the ultimate deductive rules with respect to the end of deducing true propositions from true premises fails to take into account the role of deductive inferences in

---

[40]See Cellucci (2008a), Chapter 26; Haack (1996, 183–191).
[41]Feigl (1971, 128–129).
[42]*Ibid.*, 116.
[43]*Ibid.*

knowledge. For it overlooks that the premises on which our knowledge is based are not true but can only be plausible. Thus the end of deducing true propositions from true premises is a vacuous one. Therefore, the role of deductive rules in knowledge cannot be to deduce true propositions from true premises.

18.12 The Vindication of Deductive Rules

An alternative to Feigl's answer is that the ultimate deductive rules are appropriate to the following end:

(A) To make explicit all or part of what is contained in the premises.

That the ultimate deductive rules can be vindicated with respect to the end (A) follows from an analysis of the premises, which shows that the conclusion of a deductive rule is contained in them. For example, that ($\rightarrow$E) can be vindicated with respect to the end (A) follows from the observation that the conclusion B is literally a part of the major premise $A \rightarrow B$.

That the ultimate deductive rules can be vindicated with respect to the end (A) is consistent with the claim that only by taking into account the role of deductive rules in knowledge it is possible to give a justification of such rules. For that role is just (A). Deductive rules are non-ampliative, but that does not mean that they play no useful role in knowledge. Since the conclusion makes explicit all or part of what is contained in the premises, establishing that the conclusion is plausible facilitates the comparison of the premises with experience. Therefore, the end (A) agrees with the role of deductive rules in knowledge.

18.13 Vindication of Deductive Rules and Usefulness

That the ultimate deductive rules can be vindicated with respect to the end (A) does not ensure, however, that any specific deductive inference is useful.

For a deductive inference to be useful, one must know that its premises and conclusion are plausible. Knowing that its premises are plausible is not enough because, as we have seen in Chapter 4, deductive rules, while truth preserving, are not plausibility preserving.

Since, for a deductive inference to be useful, one must know that both its premises and conclusion are plausible, the usefulness of deductive rules essentially depends on experience, thus on something external to inference.

18.14 Failures in Justifying Non-deductive Rules

Let us now consider non-deductive rules. Several justifications have been proposed for them. An especially significant one is the intuitional justification. According to it, non-deductive rules are justified because they ultimately rest on intuition. For example, Kyburg states that "our justification of inductive rules must rest on an ineradicable element of inductive intuition."[44] When "we see that if all we know about in all the world is that all the A's we've seen have been B's, it is rational to expect that the next A will be a B."[45]

Such justification of non-deductive rules, however, is inadequate because intuition is fallible. In view of this, some proponents of the intuitional justification of non-deductive rules replace infallible intuition with fallible intuition. For example, Carnap states that the reasons for accepting non-deductive rules are based upon "inductive intuition."[46] Of course, inductive intuition is not "a source of knowledge that is infallible," it "may on occasion lead us astray."[47] But "the situation in deductive logic is exactly the same."[48] The reasons for accepting deductive rules are based upon deductive intuition because, in order to teach someone deduction, "you have to appeal to his deductive intuition."[49] Thus the "situation in inductive logic" is "not worse than that in deductive logic, but quite analogous to it."[50] That intuition is fallible simply means that the intuitive plausibility of a non-deductive inference "may be more or less strong; and in the course of the development of a system, there may be progress by an increase in plausibility."[51] Thus, a non-deductive inference can be "replaced by one or several more plausible" non-deductive inferences, or for a given non-deductive inference "more plausible reasons are found."[52] But then the reasons for accepting non-deductive rules ultimately depend on plausibility, and plausibility is based on argument, not on intuition. The same applies to deductive logic, if the reasons for accepting deductive rules are based on intuition.

Therefore, the intuitional justification of non-deductive rules is inadequate. It can be shown that all other justifications of non-deductive rules that have been proposed are also inadequate.[53] The inadequacy of all these justifications is due to the fact that

---

[44] Kyburg (1965, 276).
[45] *Ibid.*
[46] Carnap (1968, 265).
[47] *Ibid.*
[48] *Ibid.*
[49] *Ibid.*, 266.
[50] *Ibid.*
[51] *Ibid.*
[52] *Ibid.*
[53] See Cellucci (2008a), Chapter 25.

none of them take into account the role of non-deductive rules in knowledge. Only by taking into account the role of non-deductive rules in knowledge it is possible to give a justification of such rules.

18.15 The Vindication of Non-deductive Rules

To give a justification of non-deductive rules, Feigl's distinction between validation and vindication is once again useful. Since, to validate a non-deductive rule is to demonstrate that it can be derived from other non-deductive rules, not all non-deductive rules can be validated, otherwise there would be an infinite regress or a vicious circle. Therefore, there must be some ultimate non-deductive rules that cannot be validated. For such ultimate non-deductive rules we can only seek vindication, that is, we can only try to demonstrate that they are appropriate to a certain end. The question is: To what end? A natural answer is that the ultimate non-deductive rules are appropriate to the following end:

(B) To discover hypotheses.

That the ultimate non-deductive rules can be vindicated with respect to the end (B) follows from an analysis of the conclusion, which shows that the conclusion is not contained in the premises. This is essential for discovery.

That the ultimate non-deductive rules can be vindicated with respect to the end (B) is consistent with the claim that only by taking into account the role of non-deductive rules in knowledge one can give a justification of such rules. For that role is just (B). Non-deductive rules are ampliative because their conclusion essentially goes beyond the premises. For such reason they may provide a basis for discovery. Therefore, the end (B) agrees with the role of non-deductive rules in knowledge.

18.16 Vindication of Non-deductive Rules and Usefulness

That the ultimate non-deductive rules can be vindicated with respect to the end (B) does not ensure, however, that any specific non-deductive inference is useful. For a non-deductive inference to be useful, one must know that both its premises and conclusion are plausible. Knowing that its premises are plausible is not enough because, as we have seen in Chapter 4, non-deductive rules are not plausibility preserving.

Since, for a non-deductive inference to be useful, one must know that both its premises and conclusion are plausible, the usefulness of non-deductive rules essentially depends on experience, thus on something external to inference.

18.17 The Vindication of Abduction

Since (ABD) is non-ampliative, it cannot be vindicated with respect to the end (B), to discover hypotheses. Like deductive rules, it can be vindicated only with respect to the end (A), to make explicit all or part of what is contained in the premises.

To establish that (ABD) is appropriate to the end (A), we need only observe that the conclusion B is literally a part of the major premise $B \to A$, thus it is contained in it.

18.18 The Asymmetry View

It is commonly held that there is an asymmetry between deductive and non-deductive rules: While deductive rules can be justified, non-deductive rules cannot be justified. For example, Salmon states that deductive rules can be justified because, if we reflect upon a deductive rule such as ($\to$E), we "cannot conceive the possibility of any situation in which its use would lead from true premises to false conclusions."[54] So "we can find no grounds whatever for withholding the judgment" that ($\to$E) "is truth preserving."[55] Conversely, non-deductive rules cannot be justified because "we can, without difficulty, imagine all sorts of states of affairs in which practically all – if not absolutely all – of our future inductive inferences with true premises turn out to have false conclusions."[56]

Let us call this the 'asymmetry view'. Although common, this view is unwarranted, because the justifications of deductive and non-deductive rules raise similar problems and must be approached much in the same way. This is apparent from the following facts.

1) There must be both some ultimate deductive rules and some ultimate non-deductive rules that cannot be validated. For them one can only seek vindication.

2) Both deductive and non-deductive rules can be vindicated with respect to an end that agrees with their role in knowledge. Indeed, deductive rules can be vindicated with respect to the end (A), which is their role in knowledge. Non-deductive rules can be vindicated with respect to the end (B), which is their role in knowledge.

3) The usefulness of both deductive and non-deductive rules essentially depends on experience, thus on something external to inference.

These facts suggest symmetry, rather than asymmetry, between deductive and non-deductive rules.

---

[54] Salmon (1965a, 268).
[55] *Ibid.*
[56] *Ibid.*

18.19 Sextus Empiricus' Argument Concerning the Criterion of Truth

What is the origin of the asymmetry view? It cannot be attributed to Sextus Empiricus, because he produced an argument about the criterion of truth that immediately yields an argument for the impossibility of validating all inference rules – deductive or non-deductive.

Indeed, Sextus Empiricus states that "those who profess to judge the truth are bound to have a criterion of truth."[57] Now, this criterion of truth "either is not judged upon or has been judged upon. If it is not judged upon," it is untrustworthy, because "nothing that is disputed is trustworthy without judging. If it has been judged upon, again the thing which has judged upon it either is not judged upon or has been judged upon. And if it not judged upon, it is untrustworthy. If it has been judged upon, again the thing which has judged upon it either has been judged upon or is not judged upon, and so on *ad infinitum*."[58]

If we interpret 'criterion of truth' as 'inference rule', Sextus Empiricus' argument becomes: Those who profess to validate an inference rule are bound to have some inference rule to validate it. Now this inference rule either is not validated or has been validated. If it is not validated, then it cannot be trusted, for no matter of dispute is to be trusted without being validated. If it has been validated, the inference rule used to validate it, in its turn, either has been validated or has not been validated, and so on *ad infinitum*.

By this argument, it is impossible to validate all inference rules. So there must be some ultimate inference rules which cannot be validated. From this it is clear that the origin of the asymmetry view cannot be attributed to Sextus Empiricus.

18.20 Hume's Argument Concerning Induction

The origin of the asymmetry view can rather be attributed to Hume. This is apparent from his attitude towards induction and deduction. According to Hume, induction cannot be justified demonstratively, "since it implies no contradiction that the course of nature may change."[59] Induction could be justified only inductively or, as Hume says, 'by experience'. But to justify it by experience "is begging the question. For all inferences from experience suppose, as their foundation, that the future will resemble the past, and that similar powers will be conjoined with similar sensible qualities."[60] It "is impossible, therefore, that any arguments from experience can

---

[57] Sextus Empiricus, *Adversus Dogmaticos* (Mutschmann) I.340.
[58] *Ibid.*, I.340–341.
[59] Hume (2007, 25).
[60] *Ibid.*, 27.

prove this resemblance of the past to the future; since all these arguments are founded on the supposition of that resemblance."[61] If one claims that an argument from experience can prove it, then he "must be evidently going in a circle."[62]

Thus Hume's argument is that induction could be justified only inductively, but such justification is impossible because the purported justification, being itself inductive, would be circular. From this it is apparent that Hume's argument about induction is simply a special case of Sextus Empiricus' argument about the criterion of truth. As Weintraub points out, "Hume wasn't the first to cast doubt on the form of inference we call inductive," neither "was his argument original, initial appearances notwithstanding."[63] Even the terminology concerning induction is due to Sextus Empiricus rather than to Hume. Indeed, while Sextus Empiricus speaks of 'induction' [*epagoge*], Hume uses the terms 'by experience', or 'experimental', or 'causal', rather than 'induction', to refer to inductive arguments. Moreover, Sextus Empiricus' argument about the criterion of truth applies both to deductive and non-deductive rules, while Hume applies his argument only to induction.

18.21 Two Questions Concerning Hume

In view of this, the following two questions naturally arise:

1) Why did Hume apply his argument only to induction, refraining from extending it to deduction?

2) Since Hume's argument was not really original, what was his contribution?

As to 1), Hume distinguishes two kinds of justification: intuitional or inferential. Then he distinguishes two kinds of inferential justification: demonstrative or inductive. Now, for Hume, no inferential justification of deduction is possible. Indeed, on the one hand, no demonstrative justification of deduction is possible, because such justification would have to use those very same deductive rules that are being justified, and "the same principle cannot be both the cause and effect of another."[64] On the other hand, no inductive justification of deduction is possible, because induction itself cannot be justified. Since, for Hume, no inferential justification of deduction is possible, and, on the other hand, he does not claim that deduction cannot be justified, we may conclude that he tacitly assumes an intuitional justification of deduction, namely, that the validity of deductive rules is "discoverable at first sight."[65] Therefore, the recognition of the validity of deductive

---

[61] *Ibid.*
[62] *Ibid.*, 26.
[63] Weintraub (1997, 66).
[64] Hume (1978, 90).
[65] *Ibid.*, 70.

rules falls "under the province of intuition."[66] Then the reason why Hume applies his argument only to induction is that he tacitly assumes that deduction has an intuitional justification.

This assumption has been widely accepted since Hume. For example, Gödel states that, for ($\rightarrow$E), "there exists no other rational" justification except that it "can directly be perceived to be true (owing to the meaning of the terms or by an intuition of the objects falling under them)," because "the proposition stating" ($\rightarrow$E) is "an immediate datum."[67] Similarly, Kyburg states that "our justification of deductive rules must ultimately rest, in part, on an element of deductive intuition: we see" that ($\rightarrow$E) "is truth preserving – this is simply the same as to reflect on it and fail to see how it can lead astray."[68] The assumption in question, however, does not seem to be tenable. The intuitional justification of deduction is inadequate for the very same reason why the intuitional justification of induction is inadequate. Namely, intuition is fallible and, if one replaces infallible intuition with fallible intuition, then the justification of deductive rules ultimately depends on plausibility, and plausibility is based on argument, not on intuition.

As to 2), Hume's contribution was the asymmetry view. According to him, while deduction has an intuitional justification, the ground for an inductive inference "is not intuitive."[69]

Hume has strongly influenced later thought about induction, but his contribution does not consist in his argument about induction which, as we have seen, is a special case of Sextus Empiricus' argument about the criterion of truth. Hume's contribution consists rather in the asymmetry view: deductive rules can be justified, while non-deductive rules cannot be justified. The asymmetry view, however, is unjustified because, as we have seen, the justifications of deductive and non-deductive rules raise similar problems and must be approached much in the same way. But, if the asymmetry view is unjustified, there is no such thing as 'the problem of induction', because then there is nothing distinctively perplexing about induction as opposed to deduction. Therefore, there is no more a problem of induction than there is a problem of deduction.

---

[66] *Ibid.*
[67] Gödel (1986–2002, III, 346–347 and footnote 34).
[68] Kyburg (1965, 276).
[69] Hume (2007, 27).

Chapter 19
Philosophy and Knowledge

19.1 Philosophy in the Face of Modern Science

This chapter examines the relation of philosophy to knowledge. Such relation has been a fairly critical one since the Scientific Revolution of the seventeenth century, because science has invaded several areas which were traditionally part of philosophy, thus making the latter problematic and in need of legitimation. In fact, a great deal of philosophy since the Scientific Revolution has consisted in attempts to legitimize philosophy in the face of science.

One such attempt tries to legitimize philosophy by transforming it into a rigorous science with an object of its own. Thus Husserl states that philosophy must be founded "anew in the sense of rigorous science."[1] A science with an object of its own, consisting in "absolute subjectivity which constitutes everything that is, in its meaning and validity."[2] Its purpose will be, first, "the discovery of the necessary concrete manner of being of absolute subjectivity" in a "life of constant 'world-constitution'."[3] Secondly, "the new discovery, correlative to this, of the 'existing world'," which "results in a new meaning for what, in the earlier stages, was called world."[4] Husserl's attempt, however, fails because, starting from absolute subjectivity, he does not arrive at the discovery of the existing world, but only at the discovery of a world as a correlative of subjectivity.

Another attempt tries to legitimize philosophy by delegitimizing science, claiming that science deals merely with appearances, only philosophy penetrates to the underlying reality and reaches knowledge of the essence of things. Thus Heidegger

---
[1] Husserl (2002, 253).
[2] Husserl (1970, 199).
[3] *Ibid.*, 340.
[4] *Ibid.*

states that "science does not think."[5] It is "the disavowal of all knowledge of truth."[6] Therefore, "no one who knows will envy scientists – the most miserable slaves of modern times."[7] Their "insistence on what is demonstrable" blocks "the way to what is."[8] There is "no bridge" from science to thinking, "only the leap."[9] Only philosophy can make such a leap, since it is "knowledge of the essence of things."[10] Heidegger's attempt, however, fails because, with respect to science, philosophy has no unique means to give knowledge of the essence of things. There is no special source of knowledge which is accessible to philosophy but not to science.

19.2 Analytic Philosophy and Knowledge

A further attempt to legitimize philosophy is that of analytic philosophy.[11] According to it, philosophy does not advance knowledge, but only tries to clarify what we already know.

Thus Wittgenstein states that philosophy "neither explains nor deduces anything."[12] It "only states what everyone admits."[13] We "do not seek to learn anything new by it."[14] Philosophical work "consists essentially of elucidations."[15] Elucidations of what we already know. Therefore, "philosophy gives no pictures of reality."[16] And "philosophical problems are not solved by experience."[17] Rather, they are solved by logic, because "the object of philosophy is the logical clarification of thought."[18] That is, the object of philosophy is the logical analysis of propositions, since "in the proposition the thought is expressed perceptibly through the senses."[19] Now, "a proposition is completely logically analysed if its grammar

---

[5] Heidegger (1968, 8).
[6] Heidegger (1994, 5).
[7] Ibid., 6.
[8] Heidegger (1972, 72).
[9] Heidegger (1968, 8).
[10] Heidegger (1994, 5).
[11] As stated in the Introduction, here by 'analytic philosophy' is meant 'classical analytic philosophy'.
[12] Wittgenstein (1958, I, § 126).
[13] Ibid., I, § 599.
[14] Ibid., I, 89.
[15] Wittgenstein (1922, 4.112).
[16] Wittgenstein (1979, 106).
[17] Wittgenstein (2001, I.1).
[18] Wittgenstein (1922, 4.112).
[19] Ibid., 3.1.

is made completely clear."[20] Therefore, ultimately a philosophical "investigation is a grammatical one."[21]

This extends Frege's view of the relation of logic to knowledge to the whole of philosophy. Just as, according to Frege, logic does not advance knowledge, according to analytic philosophy, philosophy does not advance knowledge. This extension of Frege's view is quite natural because analytic philosophy is strictly related to mathematical logic. Indeed, on the one hand, as Dummett states, analytic philosophy is "written by people to whom the basic principles of the representation of propositions in the quantificational form that is the language of mathematical logic are as familiar as the alphabet."[22] On the other hand, mathematical logic is not philosophically neutral, because it depends on assumptions that are at the basis of analytic philosophy, such as Frege's assumptions that logic must be restricted to the context of justification, to deduction and to propositional inferences.

The view that philosophy does not advance knowledge but only tries to clarify what we already know, characterizes analytic philosophy and has been repeatedly reaffirmed since Wittgenstein. For example, Wisdom states that "the analytic philosopher, unlike the scientist, is not one who learns new truths, but one who gains new insight into old truths."[23] Dummett states that philosophy "is concerned with reality, but not to discover new facts about it: it seeks to improve our understanding of what we already know."[24] Maddy states that "the best confirmation of success" of a philosophy of mathematics "would be for the mathematician to shrug and say, 'Of course, everybody knows that'. I think there is a non-trivial link between this fact and Wittgenstein's remark that 'Philosophy only states what everyone admits'."[25]

But the view that philosophy does not advance knowledge has negative implications for the status of philosophy. Russell himself, while being one of the originators of analytic philosophy, laments that the latter seems "to have abandoned, without necessity, that grave and important task which philosophy throughout the ages has hitherto pursued," that is, "to understand the world."[26] It "seems to concern itself, not with the world and our relation to it, but only with the different ways in which silly people can say silly things."[27] In particular, Wittgenstein makes philosophy, "at best, a slight help to lexicographers, and at worst, an idle tea-table amusement."[28] But, "if this is all that philosophy has to offer, I cannot think that it is a worthy subject of study."[29]

---

[20] Wittgenstein (1975, 51).
[21] Wittgenstein (1958, I, § 90).
[22] Dummett (1991a, 2–3).
[23] Wisdom (1934, 2).
[24] Dummett (2010, 10).
[25] Maddy (1998, 137).
[26] Russell (1995b, 170).
[27] Ibid.
[28] Ibid., 161.
[29] Ibid., 170.

19.3 The Armchair View of Philosophy

The reason why analytic philosophy has abandoned the task of understanding the world is that it conceives philosophy as an armchair subject – a subject which needs no input from experience and is the product of thought alone. According to analytic philosophy, in this respect philosophy is similar to mathematics. For example, Dummett states that philosophy "is a discipline that makes no observations, conducts no experiments, and needs no input from experience: an armchair subject, requiring only thought."[30] It is like "another armchair discipline: mathematics. Mathematics likewise needs no input from experience: it is the product of thought alone."[31] Williamson states that "the traditional methods of philosophy are armchair ones: they consist of thinking, without any special interaction with the world beyond the chair."[32] Now, "mathematics is a science if anything is; it is done in an armchair if anything is," and, "if mathematics is an armchair science, why not philosophy too?"[33]

This is unjustified. Mathematics is not an armchair subject, because several mathematical problems have an extra-mathematical origin; several mathematical concepts are formulated to deal with extra-mathematical questions; several mathematical theories are developed to meet extra-mathematical needs and are evaluated in terms of their capacity to meet those needs. Therefore, mathematics essentially involves interactions with the world beyond the armchair. A fortiori, philosophy is not an armchair subject. Indeed if, as Russell states, it is an important task of philosophy to understand the world, then philosophy necessarily involves interactions with the world beyond the armchair, therefore it needs inputs from experience.

19.4 Implications of the Armchair View

That analytic philosophy conceives philosophy as an armchair subject has several implications.

1) Claiming that philosophy neither explains nor deduces anything but only states what everyone admits, analytic philosophy confines itself to minute inessential questions, rather than pursuing great essential ones. Wittgenstein states that in philosophy "there are no great essential problems in the sense of science."[34] But, by confining itself to minute inessential questions, analytic philosophy promotes

---

[30]Dummett (2010, 4).
[31]*Ibid.*
[32]Williamson (2007, 1).
[33]*Ibid.*, 4.
[34]Wittgenstein (2005, 301).

a technical style that is absorbed with minutiae, and destroys all interest in the subject by severing its connection to basic human concerns. This leads analytic philosophers to inhabit a small corner of the field, and to confine themselves to modifying existing arguments a little here and there. Students are "trained to repeat the tricks" after their instructors, "so that sometimes in the future they may perhaps be able to become trainers themselves, modifying the tricks a little here and there (this is called 'original research'), and being equally stern in the propagation of their knowledge (this is called 'professional conscience')."[35] Rather than confining itself to minute, inessential questions, philosophy must deal with great essential problems in the sense of science. And it must not restrict itself to local questions, but must have a global view because, as Plato says, "anyone who can have a global view is a philosopher, and anyone who cannot is not."[36]

2) Claiming that philosophical work consists essentially of elucidations of what we already know, analytic philosophy makes philosophy a rather fruitless activity. Wittgenstein states that "philosophy is a tool which is useful only against philosophers."[37] But then what is the point of philosophy? The search for elucidation is rewarding only if it is used to deal with problems arising from the world, not to restate what we already know in other terms.

3) Claiming that philosophy gives no pictures of reality, analytic philosophy becomes a self-referential subject. Moore states: "I do not think that the world or the sciences would ever have suggested to me any philosophical problem. What has suggested philosophical problems to me is things which other philosophers have said."[38] But, by becoming a self-referential subject, analytic philosophy looses contact with the world. Even Dummett admits: "The layman or non-professional expects philosophers to answer deep questions of great import for an understanding of the world."[39] And "the layman is quite right: if philosophy does not aim at answering such questions, it is worth nothing. Yet he finds most writing by philosophers of the analytical school disconcertingly remote from these concerns," and this complaint "is understandable."[40] Somewhat inconsequently, however, Dummett concludes that the complaint in question is "unjustified," because "philosophy can take us no further than enabling us to command a clear view of the concepts by means of which we think about the world, and, by so doing, to attain a firmer grasp of the way we represent the world in our thought."[41] But, in order to enable us to command a clear view of the concepts by means of which we think about the world, philosophy must refer such concepts to the world, and hence must give a picture of

---

[35] Feyerabend (1999, 386).
[36] Plato, *Respublica*, VII 537 c 7.
[37] Wittgenstein (1932, 11).
[38] Moore (1952, 14).
[39] Dummett (1991a, 1).
[40] *Ibid.*
[41] *Ibid.*

the world. Then how can philosophy enable us to attain a firmer grasp of the way we represent the world in our thought if it gives no pictures of reality?

4) Claiming that philosophical problems are not solved by experience, analytic philosophy is bound to appeal to intuition rather than to experience as the source for their solution. This makes intuition the ultimate arbiter of philosophical questions. Russell claims that "all our knowledge of truths depends upon our intuitive knowledge."[42] Kripke even states: "I think" that "something's having intuitive content" is "very heavy evidence in favor of anything, myself. I really don't know, in a way, what more conclusive evidence one can have about anything, ultimately speaking."[43] But, being subjective and arbitrary, intuition cannot be very heavy evidence in favor of anything. Asserting that a statement is true on the basis of intuition amounts to saying: I feel it is so; therefore it must be so. But two persons may say 'I feel it is so' about opposite views, and this leaves no criterion to choose between them.

5) Claiming that philosophical problems are solved by logic because the object of philosophy is the logical clarification of thought, analytic philosophy bases philosophy on logic. Wittgenstein states that "philosophy consists of logic and metaphysics: logic is its basis."[44] But this hinges on the illusion that basing philosophy on logic will provide philosophy not only with rigour but also with substance. That this is an illusion has been pointed out by several people. For example, Halmos states: "If you think that your paper is vacuous, | Use the first-order functional calculus. | It then becomes logic, | And, as if by magic, | The obvious is hailed as miraculous."[45] Rota states that "the fake philosophical terminology of mathematical logic has misled philosophers into believing that mathematical logic deals with the truth in the philosophical sense."[46] But it is not so. The "snobbish symbol-dropping found nowadays in philosophical papers raises eyebrows among mathematicians, like someone paying his grocery bill with Monopoly money."[47] Even Kripke admits that, although "logical investigations can obviously be a useful tool for philosophy," it "should not be supposed that the formalism can grind out philosophical results in a manner beyond the capacity of ordinary philosophical reasoning. There is no mathematical substitute for philosophy."[48]

6) Claiming that a philosophical investigation is a grammatical one, analytic philosophy establishes the primacy of grammar, on the assumption that grammar expresses essence. Wittgenstein states that "philosophy as custodian of grammar can in fact grasp the essence of the world."[49] For "grammar tells what kind of

---

[42] Russell (1997, 109).
[43] Kripke (1980, 42).
[44] Wittgenstein (1979, 106).
[45] Halmos (1985, 216).
[46] Rota (1997, 93).
[47] *Ibid*.
[48] Kripke (1976, 416).
[49] Wittgenstein (1975, § 54).

object anything is."⁵⁰ Therefore "essence is expressed by grammar."⁵¹ But this is unjustified, because philosophical problems are not questions of words, they are questions of things. In particular, claiming that a philosophical investigation is a grammatical one, analytic philosophy establishes the primacy of the dictionary. Indeed, Austin states that, to carry out a philosophical investigation, "first we may use the dictionary – quite a concise one will do."⁵² We may "read the book through, listing all the words that seem relevant," or we may "start with a widish selection of obviously relevant terms, and to consult the dictionary under each."⁵³ Definitions, "I should add, explanatory definition, should stand high among our aims."⁵⁴

19.5 The Demise of Philosophy

The claim that philosophy is an armchair discipline raises serious doubts about the relevance of the subject. If philosophy needs no input from experience, how can it possibly contribute to the knowledge of reality? And, if it doesn't, why should one continue to practice it? Perhaps "philosophy is" really "that thing, with which and without which everything remains the same anyway."⁵⁵

This seems to confirm the opinion of several scientists, that philosophy is a by now rather futile activity. Thus Hawking states that "philosophy is dead."⁵⁶ While, "in the eighteenth century, philosophers considered the whole of human knowledge, including science, to be their field," in the nineteenth and twentieth centuries they "reduced the scope of their inquiries."⁵⁷ So much so that Wittgenstein "said, 'The sole remaining task for philosophy is the analysis of language'. What a comedown from the great tradition of philosophy from Aristotle to Kant!"⁵⁸ Mullis states that "chemists always believe they're smarter than biochemists. Of course, physicists think they're smarter than chemists, mathematicians think they're smarter than physicists."⁵⁹ And, "for a while, philosophers thought they were smarter than mathematicians, until they found out" in the twentieth "century that they really didn't have anything much to talk about."⁶⁰ Gowers states that "the questions

---

⁵⁰Wittgenstein (1958, I, § 373).

⁵¹*Ibid.*, I, § 371,

⁵²Austin (1970, 186).

⁵³*Ibid.*

⁵⁴*Ibid.*, 189.

⁵⁵Old Italian proverb.

⁵⁶Hawking and Mlodinow (2010, 9).

⁵⁷Hawking (1988, 185).

⁵⁸*Ibid.*

⁵⁹Mullis (1998, 38).

⁶⁰*Ibid.*

considered fundamental by philosophers are the strange, external ones that seem to make no difference to the real, internal business of doing mathematics."[61] Following Wittgenstein, one may say that philosophy is like "a wheel that can be turned though nothing else moves with it."[62]

19.6 An Alternative Philosophy Paradigm

If philosophy is to be legitimized in the face of science, an alternative philosophy paradigm is necessary. Contrary to the view of analytic philosophy, philosophy is not an armchair subject nor something radically different from science. It arises from the need to respond to problems with which human beings are confronted in the world, and a solution to such problems essentially requires knowledge about the world. Therefore philosophy is first of all an inquiry into the world, and hence aims primarily at knowledge.

In Chapter 17 it has been argued that logic provides means to acquire knowledge, and this is the relation of logic to knowledge. The view that philosophy is first of all an inquiry into the world, and hence aims primarily at knowledge, extends this to the whole of philosophy. On this view, philosophy provides means to acquire knowledge, and this is the relation of philosophy to knowledge. This is consistent with the original meaning of the term *philosophia*: the striving towards knowledge. Plato even states that "philosophy is the acquiring of knowledge [*ktesis epistemes*]."[63]

The kind of knowledge to which philosophy aims differs from scientific knowledge in no essential respect, and is not restricted to any area. Like Descartes states, philosophy aims at acquiring knowledge "of all things that mankind is capable of knowing."[64] Then, the object of philosophy is not essentially different from that of science. The only difference is that philosophy deals with questions which are beyond the present sciences. The latter are about what we know, philosophy is about what we still do not know. Here 'questions which are beyond the present sciences' does not mean 'open questions of some of the existing sciences', but rather 'open questions of none of the existing sciences'. To deal with them requires new ideas, and it is the task of philosophy to try to find them. By means of them, philosophy aims at discovering new lands, and, when successful, it may give rise to new sciences. In this sense, philosophy is a midwife of sciences.

This is what philosophy has been since the seventeenth century, giving rise to new sciences, from physics to cognitive science. The title of Newton's main work, *Philosophiae Naturalis Principia Mathematica*, underlines the origin of physics

---

[61] Gowers (2006, 198).

[62] *Ibid*. Wittgenstein's quote is from Wittgenstein (1958, I, § 271).

[63] Plato, *Euthydemus*, 288 d 8.

[64] Descartes (1996, IX–2, 2).

from philosophy. The expression 'natural philosopher' was of current use until 1833, when Whewell first used the expression 'scientist'. There is no evidence that philosophy might not discover new lands also in the future. Indeed, philosophy must continue to do so if it is to remain fruitful. What we still do not know is so extensive that it leaves ample scope for philosophy. To make just an example, the study of the extended mind, mentioned in Chapter 14, involves questions which go far beyond psychology or any of the existing sciences.

This contrasts with the view of analytic philosophy, that "no practicing philosopher would explain the value of the subject merely as a matrix out of which new disciplines could develop."[65] This leads analytic philosophy to identify philosophy with "what is left when the disciplines to which it gave birth have left the parental home."[66] And it leads analytic philosophy to claim that "it was not until the nineteenth century that it made sense to ask for an example of a philosophical problem, as opposed to a problem of some other kind."[67] But if, as Descartes says, philosophy aims at acquiring knowledge of all things that mankind is capable of knowing, philosophical problems are not opposed to problems of some other kind. That philosophy is about what we still do not know does not make philosophical problems qualitatively different from the scientific ones. The latter were once genuinely philosophical problems, since they were about what, at the time, human beings still did not know. Therefore, it is unjustified to say that it was not until the nineteenth century that it made sense to ask for an example of a philosophical problem, as opposed to a problem of some other kind.

In order to discover new lands, philosophy must sail away from the known shores, always risking a shipwreck. But this is necessary, because only so philosophy may possibly give rise to new sciences.

19.7 Distinguishing Features of Philosophy

In what has been said above it is implicit that a philosophy which wants to be legitimized in the face of science ought to have the following distinguishing features.

1) *Philosophy aims primarily at knowledge.* Being an inquiry into the world, its object is not essentially different from that of science.

2) *Philosophy has a global view.* Since its object is not essentially different from that of science, it cannot be based on a local view.

3) *Philosophy is continuous with science.* Once again, this follows from the fact that its object is not essentially different from that of science. The only difference between philosophy and science is that philosophy deals with questions which are beyond the present sciences.

---

[65]Dummett (2010, 4).
[66]*Ibid.*
[67]*Ibid.*, 8.

4) *Philosophy makes use of results of science.* Aiming primarily at knowledge, it makes use of all the knowledge available. This is not accessory but essential to its progress since, in order to acquire new knowledge, one must start from the existing one.

5) *Philosophy is based on the same method as science.* Being continuous with science, its method cannot be essentially different from that of science. This is already underlined by Plato who, as we have seen in Chapter 4, identifies the method of philosophy with the analytic method, which was the method used by Hippocrates of Chios and Hippocrates of Cos for solving problems in mathematics and medicine, respectively.

6) *Philosophy aims at finding new rules of discovery.* Aiming primarily at knowledge, philosophy is naturally interested in finding such rules. All the more so as it deals with questions which are beyond the present sciences, and there is no guarantee that the hypotheses needed to deal with them could be obtained by the present non-deductive rules.

7) *Philosophy makes use of the experience of philosophers of the past.* Only so it can avoid trying routes which have already proved fruitless. Moreover, some ideas of philosophers of the past, suitably reinterpreted, may have a powerful suggestive value. For example, as we have seen in Chapter 4, such are Plato's views about the analytic method.

8) *Philosophy introduces new idioms.* Old idioms are the stratification of beliefs based on obsolete world views, or simply on prejudices. Philosophy needs new idioms, adequate to the new questions being considered.

9) *Philosophy never arrives at definitive solutions.* This follows from the fact that it is continuous with science. Scientific problems are never definitively solved, since each solution is based on hypotheses which are always provisional and bound to be replaced sooner or later by deeper ones. The same applies to philosophical problems.

19.8 An Alternative View of Epistemology

A philosophy with the features described above involves a view of epistemology essentially different from that of analytic philosophy. According to the latter, epistemology no longer has a central place in philosophy.

Thus Searle states that "it seems reasonable that in the seventeenth century" Descartes "saw his task as providing a secure foundation for knowledge," because at that time "the very existence of knowledge was in question," so "the possibility of certain, objective, universal knowledge seemed problematic."[68] Therefore Descartes "took epistemology as the central element of the entire philosophical enterprise."[69]

---

[68] Searle (2008, 4).
[69] *Ibid.*

19.8 An Alternative View of Epistemology

As a result, "we had three and a half centuries in which epistemology was at the centre of philosophy."[70] But today, "because of the sheer growth of certain, objective, and universal knowledge, the possibility of knowledge is no longer a central question in philosophy," therefore epistemology no longer lies "at the heart of the philosophical enterprise."[71] Dummett states that Descartes made epistemology "the foundation of philosophy because he had conceived the task of philosophy as being that of introducing rigour into science," intended as "the whole body of things we conceive ourselves to know."[72] But he was wrong, because "the fundamental part of philosophy which underlies all others" is "the theory of meaning."[73] Epistemology deals with questions of justification, but "until we have first achieved a satisfactory analysis of the meanings of the relevant expressions, we cannot so much as raise questions of justification," because "we remain unclear about what we are attempting to justify."[74] By making "the theory of meaning" the "foundation of all philosophy, and not epistemology, as Descartes misled us into believing," Frege "effected a revolution in philosophy," therefore we can "date a whole epoch in philosophy as beginning with the work of Frege."[75]

This is unjustified. Being an inquiry into the world, philosophy aims primarily at knowledge, thus epistemology necessarily has a central place in philosophy. The purpose of epistemology is not to inquire into the possibility of certain, objective, universal knowledge, because there is no such knowledge. As it has been argued in the Introduction, even mathematical knowledge is not absolutely certain. The purpose of epistemology is rather to inquire into the means for acquiring knowledge, fallible knowledge and yet knowledge. This transfers epistemology from the context of justification to that of discovery, which includes the context of justification because, in the process of discovery, hypotheses are accepted only when they are shown to be plausible. Moreover, the theory of meaning cannot be the foundation of philosophy, because meaning is a question of words, while basic philosophical problems are always questions of things. As Kant states, "in matters over which one has quarreled over a long period of time, especially in philosophy, there has never been at the basis a quarrel of words but always a true quarrel over things."[76] As regards Frege, until the end his intended purpose was to give a secure foundation for mathematics, which is a question of justification within Descartes' epistemological tradition.[77] As Descartes conceived the task of philosophy as being that of introducing rigour into science, Frege conceived the task of philosophy as being that of introducing rigour in mathematics. For in order

---

[70] *Ibid.*, 5.
[71] *Ibid.*
[72] Dummett (1981, 676).
[73] *Ibid.*, 669.
[74] *Ibid.*, 667.
[75] *Ibid.*, 669.
[76] Kant (2007a, 179).
[77] For a criticism of Dummett's interpretation of Frege, see Cellucci (1995).

to achieve a secure foundation for mathematics he asked that "the fundamental propositions of arithmetic should be proved, if in any way possible, with the utmost rigour."[78]

19.9 Comparison with Other Views of Philosophy

The view of philosophy described above differs from the others mentioned earlier in this chapter.

1) It differs from Husserl's view, because it does not assume that philosophy can become a rigorous science with an object of its own. Philosophy has no object of its own, because it aims at knowing all things that mankind is capable of knowing. It cannot become a rigorous science, because it ventures into as yet largely unexplored areas, with respect to which there are no established standards. What can be rigorous are only the new sciences to which philosophy possibly gives rise.

2) It differs from Heidegger's view, because it does not assume that philosophy can give knowledge of the essence of things. Philosophy has no special means to give such knowledge.

3) It differs from the view of analytic philosophy, because it does not assume that it is of the essence of philosophical investigation that we do not seek to learn anything new by it. Philosophy must seek to learn something new about what we still do not know, otherwise it is a somewhat futile exercise.

4) It differs even from Russell's view. Admittedly, Russell states that philosophy "aims primarily at knowledge."[79] A knowledge that "does not differ essentially from scientific knowledge."[80] For "what concerns philosophy is the universe as a whole."[81] By this, however, Russell only means to say that philosophy "examines critically the principles employed in science."[82] It does so in order "to see whether they are mutually consistent and whether the inferences employed are such as seem valid to a careful scrutiny."[83] This seems to be unrealistic. Scientists don't have to wait for philosophers to examine critically the principles employed in their sciences, in order to see whether they are mutually consistent and whether the inferences employed are valid. This is an integral part of their work, and they are much more competent to the task than philosophers, who do not have the necessary qualification. Moreover, a philosophy of this kind is unlikely to give rise to new sciences.

---

[78]Frege (1959, 4).
[79]Russell (1997, 154).
[80]*Ibid.*, 149.
[81]Russell (1995a, 189).
[82]Russell (1997, 149).
[83]Russell (1995a, 239).

19.10 Good and Bad Philosophy?

The view of philosophy described above is meant to indicate what kind of philosophy is likely to be legitimized in the face of science. This does not mean that this kind of philosophy is good philosophy and other kinds of philosophy are bad philosophy – for example, philosophies oriented towards ethical, political or aesthetical issues. It only means that other kinds of philosophy cannot be expected to be legitimized in the face of science, which does not rule out that they could be legitimized in the face of something else.

The problem with analytic philosophy is that, on the one hand, as it is apparent from Hawking, Mullis and Gowers, it cannot be considered to be legitimized in the face of science, and, on the other hand, it is unclear in the face of what it could be considered to be legitimized. Even some analytic philosophers implicitly recognize that there is a problem here. For example, Dummett states: "If universities had been an invention of the second half of the twentieth century, would anyone have thought to include philosophy among the subjects that they taught and studied? It seems very doubtful."[84] It "would be easy to conclude that" such inclusion "is an anachronism."[85] Indeed, philosophy is an anachronism if it does not contribute to the advancement of knowledge.

19.11 The Way of Naturalism

The view of philosophy described above, according to which philosophy aims primarily at knowledge, is to be seen on the background of the view of knowledge that has been presented in Chapter 14. According to the latter, in addition to a cultural role, knowledge has a biological role and is a natural phenomenon which occurs in all organisms. When saying that philosophy aims primarily at knowledge, 'knowledge' is to be meant in this sense. Of course, this is a form of naturalism. There are several forms of naturalism. The one assumed here is that the world does not include supernatural entities or events, and no aspect of the world, including ourselves, is to be explained in terms of supernatural entities or events – entities or events that stand outside the world and whose doing cannot be understood as part of it.

From the viewpoint of this form of naturalism, there are several misconceptions about naturalism.

1) *Naturalism is the view that the solution to philosophical problems is to be based on the present science.* Quine states that "the only point of view" the naturalist

---

[84]Dummett (2010, 2).
[85]*Ibid.*

philosopher "can offer" is "the point of view of our own science."[86] He "begins his reasoning within the inherited world theory" and "tries to improve, clarify, and understand the system from within."[87] But this seems to be unrealistic because, as it has been stated above with respect to Russell, improving, clarifying, understanding the inherited world theory is an integral part of the scientists' work, and scientists are much more competent to the task than philosophers. Rather, philosophy deals with problems in areas that the present science cannot handle, therefore, the solutions to philosophical problems cannot be based on the present science. A philosophy dealing with problems that can be approached on the basis of the present science would be reduced to recording the pronouncements of scientists. Moreover, such a philosophy could not be expected to give rise to new sciences if, as Quine states, philosophy "is contained in natural science, as a chapter of psychology."[88]

2) *Naturalism is the view that natural science is not answerable to any external tribunal, and the same goes for mathematics.* Maddy states that naturalism is the view "that the practice of natural science is not answerable to the epistemic standards of any external" standpoint, "that legitimate criticisms of scientific method can only come from within scientific practice itself," and that "the same goes for mathematics."[89] The problem with this view is that there is nothing specifically naturalistic about it, rather, it is concerned with the question of the justification of the present science. Moreover, Maddy contravenes her own characterization of naturalism when she states: "Suppose mathematicians decided to reject the old maxim against inconsistency – so that both '$2+2=4$' and '$2+2=5$' could be accepted – on the grounds that this would have a sociological benefit for the self-esteem of school children."[90] If mathematicians themselves insisted that "this goal overrides the various traditional goals, I find nothing in the mathematical naturalism presented here that provides grounds for protest."[91] Patently, such a decision would be made from a standpoint external to mathematics.

3) *Naturalism is the view that there is no a priori knowledge.* Ruse states that naturalism means "that you cannot just think things through *a priori*."[92] This is based on the assumption that '*a priori* knowledge' is to be identified with knowledge which occurs absolutely independently of all experience. But, as it has been argued in Chapter 17, *a priori* knowledge must rather be identified with knowledge based on hypotheses which go beyond experience. This not only is not incompatible with, but is also required by naturalism. Indeed to assume, like Spencer, that all *a priori* knowledge is *a priori* for the individual but *a posteriori* with respect to the species,

---

[86] Quine (1981b, 181).
[87] *Ibid.*, 72.
[88] Quine (1969, 83).
[89] Maddy (1998, 136).
[90] Maddy (1997, 198, footnote 9).
[91] *Ibid.*
[92] Ruse (1995, 2).

19.11 The Way of Naturalism

would imply, for example, that, while we cannot derive Euclid's fifth postulate directly from experience, our ancestors could do so, which is absurd.

4) *Naturalism is opposed to anthropocentrism, thus it makes it impossible to explain the effectiveness of mathematics in the natural science.* Steiner states that naturalism is "opposition to anthropocentrism," whereas the effectiveness of mathematics can be explained only by adopting "an anthropocentric point of view."[93] Such effectiveness depends on a correspondence "between the human brain and the physical world as a whole."[94] Since mathematics is the product of a mind and is applicable to the physical world, the latter too must be the product of a mind. It is this that makes our universe "a universe which allows our species to discover things about it."[95] The effectiveness of mathematics depends on this "relation between Mind and the Cosmos."[96] This explanation is "consistent with natural theology."[97] Now, this argument is reminiscent of the claims by Greek philosophers, considered in Chapter 2, that the universe is governed by a divine mind, and that the human mind mirrors the divine mind, which makes it potentially capable of acquiring knowledge of the universe. Nevertheless, it is invalid because, from the fact that mathematics is the product of a mind and is effective in the natural science, it does not follow that the physical world is the product of a mind. As it has been argued in Chapter 8, human beings are capable of gaining knowledge of the physical world by means of mathematics, not because the physical world is the product of a mind, but rather because of the nature of Galileo's philosophical revolution, and ultimately because of biological and cultural evolution.

5) *Naturalism is a strong form of atheism.* Plantinga states that naturalism is the view that "there is no such person as God or anything much like God."[98] We "might call it 'Atheism Plus' or perhaps 'High Octane Atheism'."[99] But naturalism is not concerned with the existence of God, it simply complies with the mediaevals' warning, mentioned in Chapter 14, that a philosopher should not make explanatory recourse to God. In the fourteenth century Oresme stated that, in trying "to show the causes of some effects which seem to be marvels," there is "no reason to take recourse" to "our glorious God as if He would produce these effects directly."[100] This agrees with naturalism. Now, Oresme was no atheist, he was a believer and even a bishop. Simply, like other mediaevals, he rejected any explanatory recourse to God in world matters.

---

[93] Steiner (1998, 55).
[94] *Ibid.*, 176.
[95] *Ibid.*, 8.
[96] *Ibid.*, 45.
[97] *Ibid.*, 10.
[98] Plantinga (2006, 29).
[99] *Ibid.*
[100] Hansen (1985, 137).

19.12 The Ultimate Reason of Supernaturalism

Naturalism has been variously criticized. All objections, however, can be ultimately traced back to supernaturalism, the view that some aspects of the world can be explained only in terms of some supernatural entities or events. Supernaturalism is popular because it gives human beings the comfort of believing that the world is an orderly, stable and safe place, owing to the intervention of some supernatural entities or events. This is an illusion, the world is a rather messy, unstable and unsafe place, in which human beings and non-human animals try to make a living. People are aware of this, and therefore have fear – fear of the unknown.

Fear of the unknown played a role in the origin of religion. The first Gods were a response to it, but it was not the fear of Gods that gave rise to them, rather, the fear of the unknown led human beings to take refuge in them. Expiatory, propitiatory, sacrificing offerings to the first Gods were aimed at getting their favour, help and protection in the face of the unknown. Fear of the unknown played a key role also in the origin of philosophy and science. People sought a defence from this fear in world-views which assumed the intrinsic rationality of the universe, the uniformity of nature, the existence of universal and necessary laws – all reassuring views.

Of course, philosophy and science are responses to the fear of the unknown quite different from religion. While religion professes to embody eternal and absolutely certain truth and is based on faith, philosophy and science aim at provisional and fallible knowledge of the world and are based on evidence. Despite this difference, however, neither religion nor philosophy nor science can eliminate the rather messy, unstable and unsafe character of the world. An asteroid coming dangerously close to the Earth, a tornado, virus or bacterium threatening death and destruction, suffice to generate uncontrolled fear. Religion, philosophy, science are different ways of exorcising this fear, but cannot completely remove it, because they cannot completely abolish its causes which are often beyond present human capacities of control.

Part IV
Rules of Discovery

Chapter 20
Induction and Analogy

20.1 The Rules of Discovery

In this final part of the book several rules of discovery are considered, that is, non-deductive rules for finding hypotheses to solve problems. Of course, finding hypotheses is not a sufficient condition for discovery. The latter requires hypotheses to be plausible, and the plausibility test procedure of Chapter 4 involves operations beyond simple hypothesis formation. Nevertheless, finding hypotheses is a necessary condition for discovery and, in that sense, one may speak of rules of discovery. The latter are not a closed set, given once for all, but rather an open set which can always be extended as research develops. Each such extension is a development of the analytic method, which grows as new non-deductive rules are added. As Bacon says, "the art of discovery may grow with discoveries."[1]

Although the rules of discovery are not a closed set, the rules considered in this final part of the book are quite basic. To illustrate them, some historical examples are considered. They are meant in the spirit of Pólya: "I cannot tell the true story how the discovery did happen, because nobody really knows that. Yet I shall try to make up a likely story how the discovery could have happened. I shall try to emphasize" the "inferences that led to it."[2]

That nobody really knows the true story how the discovery did happen is due to the fact that discoverers generally do not reveal their way to discovery. They do so not because, as Descartes suggests, they conceal it with a kind of pernicious cunning, but rather because either they are not fully aware of how they arrived at their discoveries, or feel uneasy to reveal that their way to discovery was not rigorously deductive. In the spirit of Pólya, the examples considered in this final part of the book are conjectures as to the rule of discovery that could have led to the

---

[1] Bacon (1961–1986, I, 223).
[2] Pólya (1954, I, vi–vii).

hypothesis on which the discovery is based. In some cases it will be clear that other rules of discovery could have led to the hypothesis, and which rules.

In this chapter, two of the oldest and better known rules of discovery are considered: induction and analogy.

20.2 Induction from a Single Case

Induction is a kind of reasoning which infers, from the fact that some things of a given kind have a certain property, that all things of that kind have that property. Several kinds of induction can be distinguished, but the main ones are induction from a single case and induction from multiple cases.

Induction from a single case is an inference of the form: a thing a of kind A is B, therefore all things of kind A are B. So it is an inference by the rule:

$$(\text{ISC}) \frac{A(a) \quad B(a)}{\forall x (A(x) \to B(x))}.$$

This kind of induction is already considered by Aristotle, according to whom, as we have seen in Chapter 7, the number of particulars from which induction starts need not be large, sometimes even a single particular will do.

An example of use of (ISC) is the discovery, by an unknown Chinese author thought to be anterior to Pythagoras, that the square of the diagonal of a rectangle is equal to the sum of the squares of two adjacent sides. The *Chou pei*, the earliest extant Chinese text on astronomy and mathematics, states: "Let us cut a rectangle (diagonally), and make the width 3 (units) wide, and the length 4 (units) long. The diagonal between the (two) corners will then be 5 (units) long."[3] Now, let us draw "a square on this diagonal," and let us "circumscribe it by half-rectangles like that which has been left outside, so as to form a (square) plate."[4] That is, so as to form a larger square of side 7, and hence of area 49. Thus "the (four) outer half-rectangles of width 3, length 4, and diagonal 5, together make two rectangles (of area 24); then (when this is subtracted from the square plate of area 49) the remainder is of area 25. This (process)" is quite general and "is called 'piling up the rectangles'."[5]

---

[3] Swetz and Kao (1977, 14).
[4] *Ibid.*
[5] *Ibid.*

20.3 Induction from Multiple Cases

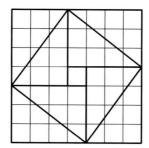

In the specific case of the rectangle considered in the figure, 'rectangle' refers to any of the four 3 by 4 corner rectangles, 'half-rectangles' refers to the 3 by 4 by 5 right triangles which result from cutting them diagonally, and 'square on this diagonal' refers to the 5 by 5 square. To 'circumscribe it by half-rectangles' means to surround the 5 by 5 square with four 3 by 4 by 5 right triangles identical to the one we started with. This forms the 'larger square of side 7, and hence area of 49'. Subtracting from this larger square the area of the four triangles, we get $49 - 24 = 25$, the area of the 5 by 5 square on the diagonal. Therefore, the square on the diagonal of the 3 by 4 rectangle, 25, is equal to the sum of the squares, 9 and 16, of two adjacent sides, 3 and 4, respectively. From this, by (ISC), the unknown Chinese author infers that the square of the diagonal of any rectangle is equal to the sum of the squares of two adjacent sides.

Thus the argument pattern is as follows. Let a be the rectangle with two adjacent sides 3 and 4. Let $A(x)$: x is a rectangle. Let $B(x)$: the square of the diagonal of the rectangle x is equal to the sum of the squares of two adjacent sides of x. Then $A(a)$ and $B(a)$. From this, by (ISC), it follows $\forall x(A(x) \to B(x))$.

20.3 Induction from Multiple Cases

Induction from multiple cases is a straightforward generalization of induction from a single case. It is also known as 'induction by enumeration'.

Induction from multiple cases is an inference of the form: things $a_1, \ldots, a_n$ of kind A are B, therefore all things of kind A are B. So it is an inference by the rule:

$$(\text{IMC}) \frac{A(a_1) \wedge \ldots \wedge A(a_n) \quad B(a_1) \wedge \ldots \wedge B(a_n)}{\forall x (A(x) \to B(x))}.$$

An example of use of (IMC) is Goldbach's discovery that, considering 1 to be a prime number, "every number greater than 2 is an aggregate," or the sum, "of three prime numbers."[6] Goldbach verifies that this holds for numbers up to a certain k, for example, $3 = 1+1+1$, $4 = 1+1+2$, $5 = 1+1+3$, $6 = 1+2+3$, etc. From

---

[6]Fuss (1843, I, 127 footnote).

this, by (IMC), he infers that every number greater than 2 is the sum of three prime numbers.

Thus the argument pattern is as follows. Let $A(x)$: x is a number greater than 2. Let $B(x)$: x is the sum of three prime numbers. Then $A(3) \wedge \ldots \wedge A(k)$ and $B(3) \wedge \ldots \wedge B(k)$. From this, by (IMC), it follows $\forall x(A(x) \rightarrow B(x))$.

20.4 Some Misconceptions Concerning Induction

There are some misconceptions concerning induction that are an obstacle to understanding its nature.

1) *There is no such thing as induction and there is no need for it.* Science is concerned with falsification rather than verification, and falsification requires only deductive logic. Thus Popper states that "there is no such thing as induction."[7] Induction is unnecessary in science. It is unnecessary for discovery, because discovery is obtained by a creative intuition, in Bergson's sense. It is unnecessary for justification, because "we test for truth, by eliminating falsehood."[8] That is, by falsification. Now, "falsification presupposes no inductive inference, but only the tautological transformations of deductive logic whose validity is not in dispute."[9] This, however, is unjustified, because falsification is no adequate replacement for induction. Indeed, Popper states that a theory is "falsified only if we discover a reproducible effect which refutes the theory," that is, "if a low-level empirical hypothesis which describes such an effect is proposed."[10] This hypothesis "must be empirical, and so falsifiable."[11] But the hypothesis is falsified only if we discover a reproducible effect which refutes the theory, namely, if a low-level empirical hypothesis which describes such an effect is proposed. And so on. This leads to an infinite regress. Popper denies that there is an infinite regress. He claims that every test of a theory must "stop at some basic statement or other which we decide to accept."[12] Specifically, it must stop at some "statement asserting that an observable event is occurring."[13] The "basic statements at which we stop" have "admittedly the character of dogmas" since we "desist from justifying them by further arguments (or by further tests)."[14] They "are accepted as the result of a decision or agreement; and to that extent they are conventions."[15] But if the basic statements at which

---

[7] Popper (2002, 18).
[8] Popper (1972, 30).
[9] Popper (2002, 20).
[10] *Ibid.*, 66.
[11] *Ibid.*, 67.
[12] *Ibid.*, 86.
[13] *Ibid.*, 85.
[14] *Ibid.*, 87.
[15] *Ibid.*, 88.

20.4 Some Misconceptions Concerning Induction

we stop are conventions, then falsification lapses into a matter of convention, and science becomes a matter of convention. This conflicts with Popper's claim, considered in Chapter 8, that the aim of science is truth. Moreover, falsification presupposes that the future will be conformable to the past, being based on the assumption that a theory which is falsified at a certain time will remain falsified at any later time. This amounts to assuming induction, which contrasts with the fact that Popper claims that science is concerned with falsification just because he wants to dispense with induction.

2) *Induction is closely linked to probability*. An inductive argument is one in which there is a certain probability that the conclusion is true if the premises are true. Thus Carnap states that "all inductive reasoning" is "reasoning in terms of probability," therefore "inductive logic, the theory of the principles of inductive reasoning, is the same as probability logic."[16] This, however, is unjustified, because induction is essentially different from probability. On the one hand, there are hypotheses which are obtained by induction from a single case, (ISC), and are plausible. Such is the case of the hypothesis about the square of the diagonal of a rectangle by an unknown Chinese author considered earlier in this chapter. This contrasts with the fact that, on the classical concept of probability as ratio between winning and possible cases, a conclusion obtained by (ISC) has zero probability when the number of possible cases is infinite. Such is the case of the hypothesis by the unknown Chinese author. The same holds on other concepts of probability, such as the subjective concept, according to which the probability of a hypothesis is the rate at which an individual is willing to bet on the truth of that hypothesis. An individual who bets on the truth of a hypothesis obtained by (ISC) can never win the bet, because it can never be established with certainty that the conclusion is true. He can only lose the bet if some b is observed such that $A(b) \wedge \neg B(b)$. Therefore, the only reasonable betting rate for the individual to adopt is zero. On the other hand, there are hypotheses which are obtained by induction from multiple cases, (IMC), and are not plausible. Such is the case of the hypothesis that all swans are white. Until the end of the seventeenth century, all swans observed were white. From this, by (IMC), it was inferred that all swans are white. But in 1697 black swans were discovered in Western Australia. Since then, the hypothesis that all swans are white has zero probability. This contrasts with the fact that, on the classical concept of probability, a conclusion obtained by (IMC) has non-zero probability when the number of possible cases is not infinite. Such is the case of the hypothesis that all swans are white.

3) *Induction is a means of justification*. It determines the probability of a hypothesis. Thus Carnap states that "an inductive inference does not, like a deductive inference, result in the acquisition" of a hypothesis (or conclusion) "but in the determination of its degree of confirmation."[17] That is, of its probability, because "the concept of probability on which inductive logic is to be based" is "the degree

---

[16] Carnap (1962, v).
[17] *Ibid.*, 206.

of confirmation of a hypothesis (or conclusion) on the basis of some given evidence (or premises)."[18] In many cases, it is even "possible to determine, by mechanical procedure, the logical probability, or degree of confirmation."[19] This, however, is unjustified, because we are generally unable to determine the probability of our hypotheses about the world, let alone to determine it by a mechanical procedure. Moreover, applying the calculus of probability to our hypotheses about the world would involve making substantial assumptions about the working of the world. Then, if our hypotheses were justified by showing that they are probable, they would not be really justified by induction, but rather by our assumptions about the working of the world. Such assumptions could not be justified in terms of the calculus of probability, because it would be impossible to account for them in purely mathematical terms.

4) *Induction ultimately depends on intuition.* There is nothing else on which it could ultimately depend, therefore intuition is indispensable. Thus Salmon states: "Reluctant as I am to admit inductive intuition, I must concede that it may be necessary in the last analysis to depend upon it. If inductive intuition does prove indispensable, then accept it we must."[20] This, however, is unjustified, because hypotheses which someone considers to be true on the basis of his inductive intuition, someone else will consider to be false on the basis of his own inductive intuition. Then if induction is ultimately justified by appeals to intuition, one will find himself in a situation of 'It is your intuition against mine'.

20.5 Analogy

Analogy is a kind of reasoning which infers, from the fact that two things are similar in certain respects and one of them has a certain property, that the other has that property.

Let $a \approx b$: a is similar to b in certain respects. Analogy is an inference of the form: $a \approx b$ and a is A, therefore b is A. So it is an inference by the rule:

$$(\text{AN}) \frac{a \approx b \quad A(a)}{A(b)}.$$

Aristotle states (AN) as follows: "Among similars, what is true of one is true of the rest."[21] Clearly, (AN) is a generalization of substitutivity of equality:

---

[18] *Ibid.*, v.
[19] Carnap (1966, 34).
[20] Salmon (1965b, 280).
[21] Aristotle, *Topica*, A 18, 108 b 13–14.

$$\text{(SE)} \frac{a = b \quad A(a)}{A(b)}.$$

However, while (SE) is a deductive rule, (AN) is a non-deductive rule. Nevertheless, (AN) is only a general schema of analogical reasoning, and is vacuous if one does not specify what meaning is to be attached to 'a is similar to b'. Indeed, any two things can be viewed as having some property in common – for example, the property of being a thing – and hence as being similar with respect to that property.

Depending on the meaning attached to 'a is similar to b', several kinds of analogy can be distinguished. The main ones are analogy by quasi-equality, analogy by separate indistinguishability, inductive analogy, proportional analogy, analogy by agreement, and analogy by agreement and disagreement.

20.6 Analogy by Quasi-Equality

Two things are said to be quasi-equal if, while not identical, they are a very close approximation to each other. This is the kind of similarity that holds, for example, between twins.

Let $a \cong b$: a is quasi-equal to b. Analogy by quasi-equality is an inference of the form: $a \cong b$ and a is A, therefore b is A. So it is an inference by the rule:

$$\text{(AQE)} \frac{a \cong b \quad A(a)}{A(b)}.$$

An example of use of (AQE) is Antiphon's discovery that the area of a circle with circumference c and radius r is equal to the area of the triangle with base c and height r, that is, $(1/2)cr$. The hypothesis that the area of a circle with circumference c and radius r is $(1/2)cr$ occurs in Archimedes.[22] But it must have been much older, because it follows almost immediately from Antiphon's remark that the area of a circle can be approximated arbitrarily closely by the areas of inscribed regular polygons with an ever increasing number of sides. Indeed "Antiphon, having drawn a circle, inscribed in it one of the polygons that can be inscribed therein"[23] Then, by bisecting the sides of the inscribed polygon, he formed a polygon of twice as many sides; and doing the same again and again, he concluded that in this manner "a polygon would be inscribed in the circle whose sides would by and large coincide with the circumference of the circle."[24] In this sense we may speak of 'Antiphon's discovery'.

---

[22] See Archimedes (1880–81, I, 258.2–4).
[23] Simplicius, *In Aristotelis Physicorum Libros Quattuor Priores Commentaria* (Diels), 54.20–22.
[24] *Ibid.*, 55.7–8.

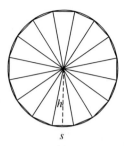

Given a circle with circumference c and radius r, let us inscribe a regular n-sided polygon with side length s in it. Such a polygon can be viewed as consisting of n isosceles triangles with the same base s and the same height h, thus with the same area $(1/2)sh$. Let p be the perimeter of the polygon, so that $p = ns$. Then the area of the polygon is $n(1/2)sh = (1/2)nsh = (1/2)ph$. As n increases, the perimeter p of the polygon will approximate more and more closely the circumference c of the circle, and the height h of the triangles will approximate more and more closely the radius r of the circle. Therefore, for a sufficiently large n, the polygon and the circle will be quasi-equal. Then, from the fact that the area of the polygon is $(1/2)ph$, by (AQE), Antiphon infers that the area of the circle is $(1/2)cr$.

Thus the argument pattern is as follows. Let a be an n-sided polygon inscribed in a circle b. Let $A(x)$: area of $x = (1/2) \cdot (\text{perimeter of } x) \cdot (\text{height of } x)$ where, if x is a circle, 'perimeter of x' is to mean 'circumference of x', and 'height of x' is to mean 'radius of x'. Then, for a suitably large n, we have $a \cong b$, and $A(a)$. From this, by (AQE), it follows $A(b)$.

20.7 Analogy by Separate Indistinguishability

Two things are said to be indistinguishable when observed separately if, as Leibniz states, they "cannot be distinguished when observed in isolation from each other," in the sense that "nothing can be observed in one, viewed by itself, which cannot be equally observed in the other."[25] This is the kind of similarity that holds, for example, between two circles of different diameters.

Let $a \sim b$: a and b are indistinguishable when observed separately. Analogy by separate indistinguishability is an inference of the form: $a \sim b$ and a is A, therefore b is A. So it is an inference by the rule:

$$(\text{ASI}) \frac{a \sim b \quad A(a)}{A(b)}.$$

---

[25]Leibniz (1971, V, 181).

An example of use of (ASI) is Thales' discovery that a diameter bisects the circle. Let *PQR* be a circle and *PQ* a diameter. Apply one part of the circle to the other by folding it over along the diameter *PQ*.

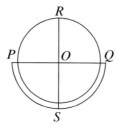

Suppose that this part is not equal to the other. Then "it falls either inside or outside it."[26] If it falls inside it, then a shorter line *OR* will be equal to a longer line *OS* since "all the lines from the centre to the circumference are equal. Thus the line that extends beyond will be equal to the line that falls short. This is impossible. The one part, then, fits the other, so that they are equal."[27] The same applies if the part which is not equal to the other falls outside it. Thus "the diameter bisects the circle."[28] Now, any two circles are indistinguishable when observed separately. Then, from the fact that a diameter *PQ* bisects the particular circle *PQR* represented by the diagram, by (ASI), Thales infers that a diameter bisects any circle.

Thus the argument pattern is as follows. Let *PQR* be the particular circle represented by the diagram, and *UVW* another circle. Let $A(x)$: a diameter bisects the circle *x*. Then $PQR \sim UVW$ and $A(PQR)$. From this, by (ASI), it follows $A(UVW)$.

20.8 Inductive Analogy

A number of things are said to be inductively analogous if they have two properties in common.

Inductive analogy is an inference of the form: Things $a_1, \ldots, a_n$ are *A* and *B*, and *b* is *A*, therefore *b* is *B*. So it is an inference by the rule:

$$(\text{IA}) \frac{A(a_1) \wedge \ldots \wedge A(a_n) \quad B(a_1) \wedge \ldots \wedge B(a_n) \quad A(b)}{B(b)}$$

An example of use of (IA) is Herschel's discovery that the new celestial object called Uranus is "a primary planet of our solar system."[29] The orbits of Mercury,

---

[26] Proclus, *In Primum Euclidis Elementorum Librum Commentarii* (Friedlein), 157.20.
[27] Ibid., 157.22–158.1.
[28] Ibid., 158.1–2.
[29] Herschel (2008, 73).

Venus, Earth, Mars, Jupiter, Saturn are like the orbit of a planet, Mercury, Venus, Earth, Mars, Jupiter, Saturn are planets, and the orbit of Uranus is like the orbit of a planet. From this, by (IA), Herschel infers that Uranus is a planet.

Thus the argument pattern is as follows. Let $a_1, \ldots, a_6$ be Mercury, Venus, Earth, Mars, Jupiter, Saturn, respectively, and let b be Uranus. Let $A(x)$: the orbit of x is like the orbit of a planet. Let $B(x)$: x is a planet. Then $A(a_1) \wedge \ldots \wedge A(a_6)$ and $B(a_1) \wedge \ldots \wedge B(a_6)$ and $A(b)$. From this, by (IA), it follows $B(b)$.

Calling (IA) 'inductive analogy' is justified, because (IA) can be derived from induction from multiple cases (IMC) as follows:

$$(\to E) \frac{\displaystyle (\text{IMC}) \frac{A(a_1) \wedge \ldots A(a_n) \quad B(a_1) \wedge \ldots B(a_n)}{(\forall E) \frac{\forall x (A(x) \to B(x))}{A(b) \to B(b)}} \quad A(b)}{B(b)}$$

20.9 Proportional Analogy

Four things a, b, c, d are said to be proportionally analogous if a is to b as c is to d. For example, old age, life, evening, day are proportionally analogous since, as Aristotle says, "old age is to life as evening is to day."[30]

Proportional analogy is a generalization of mathematical proportion, $a{:}b = c{:}d$. It is a strict generalization because, if three terms of one mathematical proportion are respectively equal to the three corresponding terms of another mathematical proportion, the remaining term of one must be equal to the remaining term of the other. On the contrary, in proportional analogy this does not hold. For example, in addition to saying that old age is to life as evening is to day, one may also say that old age is to life as sunset is to day. For one may say "old age to be the evening of life, or the sunset of life."[31] Being a strict generalization of mathematical proportion, proportional analogy cannot have all properties of mathematical proportion. Nevertheless, it has three properties in common with it: inversion, permutation of the middles, and permutation of the extremes. Accordingly, one may distinguish three kinds of proportional analogy: by inversion, by permutation of the middles, by permutation of the extremes. Let $a|b :: c|d$: a is to b as c is to d.

Proportional analogy by inversion is an inference of the form: $a|b :: c|d$, therefore $b|a :: d|c$. So it is an inference by the rule:

$$(\text{PAI}) \frac{a|b :: c|d}{b|a :: d|c}$$

---

[30] Aristotle, *Poetica*, 1457 b 22–23.
[31] *Ibid.*, 1457 b 23–24.

20.9 Proportional Analogy

Proportional analogy by permutation of the middles is an inference of the form: $a|b :: c|d$, therefore $a|c :: b|d$. So it is an inference by the rule:

$$(\text{PAPM}) \frac{a|b :: c|d}{a|c :: b|d}$$

Proportional analogy by permutation of the extremes is an inference of the form: $a|b :: c|d$, therefore $d|b :: c|a$. So it is an inference by the rule:

$$(\text{PAPE}) \frac{a|b :: c|d}{d|b :: c|a}$$

For instance, let us consider (PAPM). An example of use of (PAPM) is Hippocrates of Chios discovery of the hypothesis, considered in Chapter 4, that circles are as the squares on their diameters. For a given circle PQ let RS be the square on its diameter circumscribed to the circle. For a given circle UV let WX be the square on its diameter circumscribed to the circle.

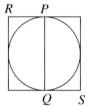

Then the circle PQ is to the square RS as the circle UV is to the square WX. From this, by (PAPM), Hippocrates of Chios infers that the circle PQ is to the circle UV as the square RS is to the square WX.[32]

Thus the argument pattern is as follows. $PQ|RS :: UV|WX$. From this, by (PAPM), it follows $PQ|UV :: RS|WX$.

In addition to (PAI), (PAPM), (PAPE), one may also consider another kind of proportional analogy, proportional analogy by transfer.

Proportional analogy by transfer is an inference of the form: $a|b :: c|d$ and c and d are in the relation A, therefore a and b are in the relation A. So it is an inference by the rule:

$$(\text{PAT}) \frac{a|b :: c|d \quad A(c,d)}{A(a,b)}.$$

An example of use of (PAT) is Rutherford's discovery of a model of the atom. An electron is to the nucleus as a planet is to the Sun. Now, a planet is bound to the Sun by a force, gravitation, which is proportional to $1/r^2$, where r is the

---

[32] See Leibniz (1971, V, 182).

distance of the orbiting object from the centre. From this, by (PAT), Rutherford infers that an electron is bound to the nucleus by a force, the electric Coulomb force, which is proportional to $1/r^2$. Specifically, if an atom has a positive charge Ne at its centre, and is surrounded by a distribution of negative electricity Ne uniformly within a sphere of radius R, "the electric force X" in question is "given by $X = Ne(\frac{1}{r^2} - \frac{r}{R^3})$."[33]

Thus the argument pattern is as follows. Let a, b, c, d be an electron, the nucleus, a planet, and the Sun, respectively. Let $A(x,y)$: x is bound to y by a force that is proportional to $1/r^2$. Then $a|b :: c|d$ and $A(c,d)$. From this, by (PAT), it follows $A(a,b)$.

20.10 Analogy by Agreement

Two things are said to be analogous by agreement if they have certain properties in common.

Analogy by agreement is an inference of the form: a and b are $A_1, \ldots, A_n$ and a is C, therefore b is C. So it is an inference by the rule:

$$(\text{AA}) \frac{A_1(a) \wedge \ldots A_n(a) \quad A_1(b) \wedge \ldots \wedge A_n(b) \quad C(a)}{C(b)}.$$

An example of use of (AA) is Franklin's conjecture that lightning is attracted by pointed conductors. Franklin observes that electricity and lightning agree in the following properties: 1) Giving light; 2) Colour of the light; 3) Crooked direction; 4) Swift motion; 5) Being conducted by metals; 6) Crack or noise in exploding; 7) Subsisting in water or ice; 8) Rending bodies it passes through; 9) Destroying animals; 10) Melting metals; 11) Firing inflammable substances; 12) Sulphurous smell. He also observes that electricity is attracted by pointed conductors. From this, by (AA), Franklin infers that lightning too is attracted by pointed conductors, so electricity and lightning "agree likewise in this."[34]

Thus the argument pattern is as follows. Let a be electricity and b lightning. Let $A_i(x)$: x has property i), $1 \leq i \leq 12$. Let $C(x)$: x is attracted by pointed conductors. Then $A_1(a) \wedge \ldots \wedge A_{12}(a)$ and $A_1(b) \wedge \ldots \wedge A_{12}(b)$ and $C(a)$. From this, by (AA), it follows $C(b)$.

While, as we have seen, (IA) can be derived from induction from multiple cases (IMC), (AA) can be derived from induction from a single case (ISC) as follows:

---

[33]Rutherford (1911, 671).
[34]Franklin (1859, II, 295).

$$(\to E) \frac{A_1(b)\wedge\ldots\wedge A_n(b) \quad (\forall E) \frac{(ISC) \frac{A_1(a)\wedge\ldots\wedge A_n(a) \quad C(a)}{\forall x(A_1(x)\wedge\ldots\wedge A_n(x)\to C(x))}}{A_1(b)\wedge\ldots\wedge A_n(b)\to C(b)}}{C(b)}$$

20.11 Analogy by Agreement and Disagreement

Two things are said to be analogous by agreement and disagreement if they have certain properties in common, but other properties are known which they do not have in common.

Analogy by agreement and disagreement is an inference of the form: a and b are $A_1, \ldots, A_n$ but a is $B_1, \ldots, B_k$ while b is not all of $B_1, \ldots, B_k$, and moreover a is C, therefore b is C. So it is an inference by the following rule, where $A^*(x)$ and $B^*(x)$ are short for $A_1(x) \wedge \ldots \wedge A_n(x)$ and $B_1(x) \wedge \ldots \wedge B_k(x)$, respectively:

$$(AAD) \frac{A^*(a) \quad A^*(b) \quad B^*(a) \quad \neg B^*(b) \quad C(a)}{C(b)}.$$

Rule (AAD) is subject to the condition that $\neg B^*(b)$ must not be incompatible with the conclusion $C(b)$.

An example of use of (AAD) is Maxwell's discovery of the dynamic theory of gases. Maxwell observes that a gas can be viewed as consisting of a "number of small, hard, and perfectly elastic spheres acting on one another only during impact."[35] Both gas particles and billiard balls are capable of motion and of impact, so these are properties which they have in common. On the other hand, billiard balls are red or white, hard and shiny, whereas gas particles do not have such properties, so these are properties which we know they do not have in common. Moreover, billiard balls obey the laws of mechanics. Furthermore, that gas particles do not have the properties of being red or white, hard and shiny, is not incompatible with the fact that gas particles obey the laws of mechanics, since the properties in question are irrelevant to the behaviour of gas particles. From this, by (AAD), Maxwell infers that gas particles obey the laws of mechanics.

Thus the argument pattern is as follows. Let a be a billiard ball and b a gas particle. Let $A_1(x)$: x is capable of motion. Let $A_2(x)$: x is capable of impact. Let $B(x)$: x is red or white, and hard and shiny. Let $C(x)$: x obeys the laws of mechanics. Then $A_1(a) \wedge A_2(a)$ and $A_1(b) \wedge A_2(b)$ and $B(a)$ and $\neg B(b)$ and $C(a)$. From this, by (AAD), it follows $C(b)$. This is justified because $\neg B(b)$ is not incompatible with $C(b)$.

---

[35]Maxwell (1965, I, 377–378).

20.12 A Refinement of Analogy by Agreement

Analogy by agreement and disagreement, (AAD), is a refinement of analogy by agreement, (AA). This appears from the following example suggested by Mill.

The Moon agrees with the Earth in: 1) Being a solid; 2) Being opaque; 3) Being nearly spherical substance; 4) Appearing to contain, or to have contained, active volcanoes; 5) Receiving heat and light from the Sun; 6) Revolving on its axis; 7) Being composed of materials which gravitate; 8) Obeying all the various laws resulting from that property. In addition, the Earth has the property that there are inhabitants on it. Now, if the properties 1)–8) "were all that was known of the Moon," we might infer, by (AA), that the Moon too has the property that there are inhabitants on it, thus there are "inhabitants in that luminary."[36]

Indeed, let a be the Earth and b the Moon. Let $A_1(x)$: x has the i-th property among 1)–8). Let $C(x)$: x has inhabitants on it. Then $A_1(a) \wedge \ldots \wedge A_8(a)$ and $A_1(b) \wedge \ldots \wedge A_8(b)$ and $C(a)$. From this, by (AA), we might infer $C(b)$.

But, while the Earth and the Moon have in common the properties 1)–8), the Earth has water while the Moon has "no water."[37] Thus the Earth and the Moon do not have in common the property of having water. Now, the fact that the Moon has no water is incompatible with the conclusion that the Moon has inhabitants on it, because the property of having water is "among those which, on the Earth, are found to be indispensable conditions of animal life."[38] Therefore, we are not entitled to infer, by (AAD), that the Moon has inhabitants on it. Since "life cannot exist" on the Moon "in the manner in which it exists" on the Earth, we have no reason "to believe that" the Moon "can contain life."[39]

Indeed, let a be the Earth and b the Moon. Let $A_1(x)$: x has the i-th property among 1)–8). Let $B(x)$: x has water. Let $C(x)$: x has inhabitants on it. Then $A_1(a) \wedge \ldots \wedge A_8(a)$ and $A_1(b) \wedge \ldots \wedge A_8(b)$ and $B(a)$ and $\neg B(b)$ and $C(a)$. From this, however, we are not entitled to infer $C(b)$ by (AAD), because the premise $\neg B(b)$ is incompatible with the conclusion $C(b)$.

Since (AAD) does not permit to draw this conclusion which is not plausible, this justifies the claim that (AAD) is a refinement of (AA).

20.13 Some Misconceptions Concerning Analogy

There are some misconceptions concerning analogy that are an obstacle to understanding its nature.

---

[36] Mill (1963–1986, VII, 557).
[37] Ibid.
[38] Ibid., VII, 557–558.
[39] Ibid.,VII, 558.

20.13 Some Misconceptions Concerning Analogy

1) *Analogy is a special case of induction.* It is an induction with respect to properties. Thus Kant states that an "inference according to an analogy" is "nothing other than an induction, only an induction in respect of the predicate."[40] For according to it, if two things "have come together in respect of all attributes that I have been able to cognize in them, then they will also come together in the remaining attributes."[41] This, however, is unjustified. Of course, as we have seen above, (AA) can be derived from (ISC), but derivability does not extend to other kinds of analogy. In fact, there is a substantial difference between analogy and induction. While (AAD) takes account of properties that two things do not have in common, (ISC) and (IMC) take no account of them. This makes a difference because, as we have seen, inferences that would be legitimate by (AA), which takes no account of properties that two things do not have in common, are not legitimate by (AAD), which takes account of them.

2) *Induction is a special case of analogy.* It is based on the similarity between the things considered. Thus Hume states that all inductive arguments "are founded on the similarity, which we discover among natural objects, and by which we are induced to expect effects similar to those, which we have found to follow from such objects."[42] What is relevant in inductive arguments is the similarity among the instances, not the number of instances considered. For there is no "process of reasoning which, from one instance, draws a conclusion, so different from that which it infers from a hundred instances, that are nowise different from that single one."[43] This, however, is unjustified. For in inductive inference one generally considers instances which are different in some respects. The point of increasing the number and kind of instances is just to make differences apparent, bringing out non-uniform instances. Hume himself observes that there is "nothing so like as eggs; yet no one, on account of this appearing similarity, expects the same taste and relish in all of them."[44] Even things which are as similar in many respects as eggs, may differ in other respects, depending, for example, on the breed of chickens, on the feed chickens are given, or on whether they have been treated using chemicals to make them last longer. Increasing the number and kind of instances can make such differences apparent, bringing out non-uniform instances of eggs. Of course, as Hume states, there is no process of reasoning which, from one instance, draws a conclusion different from that which it infers from a hundred instances, if the latter are nowise different from that single one. But the point is that they must be nowise different from that single one, and only rarely one knows that this is the case. Inductive inference is especially useful when we know many instances, but do not know in what ways they differ from one another, that is, we do not know what properties they do not have in common. Then an increase in the number

---

[40] Kant (1992, 232).
[41] *Ibid.*
[42] Hume (2007, 26).
[43] *Ibid.*
[44] *Ibid.*

and kind of instances may help to make the differences clear, bringing out non-uniform instances. Conversely, analogical inference is especially useful when we know a limited number of instances, but know accurately enough in what ways those instances are similar and differ from one another – what properties they have in common and what properties they do not have in common. For this reason, (AAD) is important.

3) *Analogy is strictly related to probability.* The probability of the conclusion of (AAD) is directly proportional to the known points of agreement between a and b, and inversely proportional to the known points of disagreement between them. Thus Mill states that, in analogy, every "resemblance which can be pointed out between b and a, affords some degree of probability, beyond what would otherwise exist, in favour of the conclusion drawn from it."[45] On the other hand, "every dissimilarity which can be proved between them furnishes a counter-probability of the same nature on the other side."[46] There will, therefore, be "a competition between the known points of agreement and the known points of difference in a and b; and according as the one or the other may be deemed to preponderate, the probability derived from analogy will be for or against b's having the property C."[47] This, however, contrasts with Mill's own example concerning the existence of inhabitants on the Moon, considered in the previous section. In that example, the Earth and the Moon have eight known points of agreement and one known point of disagreement, so the known points of agreement preponderate. And yet the probability of the conclusion that there are inhabitants on the Moon is zero, because such conclusion is incompatible with the property of the Moon of having no water.

---

[45] Mill (1963–1986, VII, 556).
[46] *Ibid.*, VII, 557.
[47] *Ibid.*

Chapter 21
Other Rules of Discovery

21.1 Expanding the Rules of Discovery

In Chapter 20 two of the oldest and better known rules of discovery have been considered: induction and analogy.

In this chapter other rules of discovery are considered: generalization, specialization, metaphor, metonymy, definition as abbreviation, definition as analysis, diagrams.

21.2 Generalization

Generalization is passing from the consideration of a given set to that of a larger set, containing the given set as a subset.

Inference by generalization is an inference of the form: $b \subseteq a$ and b is A, therefore a is A. So it is an inference by the rule:

$$(\text{GEN}) \frac{b \subseteq a \quad A(b)}{A(a)}.$$

An example of use of (GEN) is Newton's discovery that there is a power of gravity pertaining to all bodies. Planets are bodies and there is a power of gravity pertaining to all planets. From this, by (GEN), Newton infers that "there is a power of gravity pertaining to all bodies."[1]

---

[1] Newton (1972, II, 576).

Thus the argument pattern is as follows. Let b be the set of planets and a the set of bodies, so that $b \subseteq a$. Let $A(x)$: There is a power of gravity pertaining to all members of the set x. Then $A(b)$. From $b \subseteq a$ and $A(b)$, by (GEN), it follows $A(a)$.

(GEN) is useful because, to find a hypothesis, it is often convenient to consider first a special case.

21.3 Specialization

Specialization is passing from the consideration of a given set to that of a smaller set, contained as a subset in the given set.

Inference by specialization is an inference of the form: $a \subseteq b$ and b is A, therefore a is A. So it is an inference by the rule:

$$\text{(SPE)} \frac{a \subseteq b \quad A(b)}{A(a)}.$$

An example of use of (SPE) is Gauss's discovery, at the age of nine, of a solution to the problem: find the sum of all numbers in the set $\{1,2,3,\ldots,100\}$. Sartorius, the original source for Gauss' discovery, narrates that the schoolmaster had "barely stated" the problem "before Gauss threw his slate" with his solution "on the table," saying: "There it lies."[2] Sartorius does not say that the problem the schoolmaster gave to his class concerned the sum of all numbers in $\{1,2,3,\ldots,100\}$, but only that it concerned "the summing of an arithmetical series."[3] Moreover, he gives no hint of the procedure used by Gauss. Nevertheless, the problem and the procedure are now part of the Gauss folklore, according to which, to solve the problem, 'find the sum of all numbers in the set $\{1,2,3,\ldots,100\}$', Gauss considers the general problem, 'find the sum of all numbers in the set $\{1,2,3,\ldots,n\}$, for arbitrary n'.[4] He imagines the numbers in such set to be displayed in two rows in reverse order:

1	2	3	...	$n-1$	n
n	$n-1$	$n-2$	...	2	1

The sum of each column is $n+1$ and there are n columns, so the total sum is $n(n+1)$, therefore the sum of all numbers in the set $\{1,2,3,\ldots,n\}$ is $n(n+1)/2$. From this, by (SPE), Gauss infers that the sum of all numbers in the set $\{1,2,3,\ldots,100\}$ is $100 \cdot 101/2 = 5,050$.

Thus the argument pattern is as follows. Let $a = \{1,2,3,\ldots,100\}$ and $b = \{1,2,3,\ldots,n\}$ for $n \geq 100$, so that $a \subseteq b$. Let $A(x)$: The sum of all numbers

---

[2] Sartorius von Wantershausen (1856, 12).
[3] Ibid.
[4] See, for example, Graham et al. (1994, 6–7).

in the set x is $n(n+1)/2$, where n is the largest number in x. Then $A(b)$. From $a \subseteq b$ and $A(b)$, by (SPE), it follows $A(a)$.

(SPE) is useful because, to find a hypothesis, it is often convenient to consider first a more general case.

21.4 Metaphor

Metaphor is asserting that things of one domain, called the 'target domain', are to be considered as if they were things of another domain, called the 'source domain'. The implication is that, if the things of the source domain have a certain property, the things of the target domain will also have that property. Thus metaphor transfers properties of objects of the source domain to objects of the target domain. In fact 'metaphor' derives from the Greek *metaphora* which means 'transfer'.

For example, if the target domain consists of words and the source domain of stones, then 'Words are stones' is a metaphor, because it asserts that words are to be considered as if they were stones.[5] The implication is that, since stones may cause injuries, also words may cause injuries.

Let S be the source domain and T the target domain. Let $T \mapsto S$: The elements of T are to be considered as if they were elements of S. Metaphor is an inference of the form: $T \mapsto S$, $a \in T$, and from $x \in S$ it follows that x is A, therefore a is A. So, it is an inference by the rule:

$$(\text{MTA}) \frac{T \mapsto S \quad a \in T \quad \overset{[x \in S]}{A(x)}}{A(a)}.$$

As in the case of Gentzen's rules considered in Chapter 11, the assumption class $[x \in S]$ written above the premise $A(x)$ indicates that assumptions belonging to that class may occur above that premise and may be discharged by the rule.

An example of use of (MTA) is Newton's discovery of a solution to the problem: "Given any relationship whatever of fluent quantities, to find the relationship of their fluxions."[6] Fluent quantities are growing quantities $x, y, z, \ldots$ and fluxions are the speeds, $\dot{x}, \dot{y}, \dot{z}, \ldots$ with which they grow. In order to solve this problem, Newton states: "I consider" mathematical "quantities as though they were generated by continuous increase in the manner of a space which a moving object describes in its course."[7] Thus Newton introduces the metaphor, 'Mathematical quantities are to be considered as if they were physical quantities generated by a continuous motion', where the target domain consists of mathematical quantities, and the source domain

---

[5] *Words are stones* is the title of Levi (2005).
[6] Newton (1967–1981, VIII, 93).
[7] *Ibid.*, III, 73.

consists of physical quantities generated by a continuous motion. Let us examine, for instance, the case of two fluents x, y in the relationship $y = x^2$. The problem is to find the relationship, or ratio, of their fluxions, $\dot{y}/\dot{x}$. Let o be a time interval. Since space = time × speed, in the time interval o the fluents x and y will grow by $o\dot{x}$ and $o\dot{y}$, respectively. Since the relationship between fluents holds instant by instant, it will be $y + o\dot{y} = (x + o\dot{x})^2$. Now, fluents can "be expressed by any lines whatever which are proportional to them."[8] Then the following diagram shows that $(x + o\dot{x})^2 = x^2 + 2xo\dot{x} + o\dot{x}o\dot{x}$.

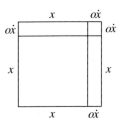

Therefore, $y + o\dot{y} = x^2 + 2xo\dot{x} + o\dot{x}o\dot{x}$. Since $y = x^2$, from the latter by subtraction it follows $o\dot{y} = 2xo\dot{x} + o\dot{x}o\dot{x}$, and hence, dividing both members of the equation by o, $\dot{y} = 2x\dot{x} + o\dot{x}\dot{x}$. Now, let o "come to vanish."[9] Then $\dot{y} = 2x\dot{x} + o\dot{x}\dot{x}$ becomes $\dot{y} = 2x\dot{x}$. Therefore $2x\dot{x}$ is "the speed with which the space y" proceeds "to be described" when the space x "increases with uniform speed."[10] Since $\dot{y} = 2x\dot{x}$, it follows $\dot{y}/\dot{x} = 2x$. From this, by (MTA), Newton concludes that, if two fluents x, y are in the relationship $y = x^2$, the relationship, or ratio, of their fluxions, $\dot{y}/\dot{x}$, is $2x$.

Thus the argument pattern is as follows. Let S be the domain of physical quantities generated by a continuous motion, and T the domain of mathematical quantities. Let us consider the elements of T as if they were elements of S, so that $T \mapsto S$. Let $w \in T$. Let $A(x)$: the ratio of the fluxions of x^2 and x is $2x$. Let $x \in S$. Then $A(x)$. From $T \mapsto S$ and $w \in T$ and the fact that from $x \in S$ it follows $A(x)$, by (MTA), it follows $A(w)$.

Newton's approach to the calculus of infinitesimals is an example of what in the Introduction has been called the bottom-up approach to mathematics. For it develops the calculus of infinitesimals from below, from problems concerning physical quantities, and develops it by the analytic method.

---

[8] Ibid., VIII, 125.
[9] Ibid., VIII, 129.
[10] Ibid., III, 73.

21.5 Some Misconceptions Concerning Metaphor

There are some misconceptions concerning metaphor that are an obstacle to understanding its nature.

1) *Metaphor is giving a thing a name that belongs to something else.* Thus Aristotle states that "metaphor is giving a thing a name that belongs to another thing."[11] This, however, is unjustified. For it makes metaphor only a way of naming something that could have been named otherwise. On this view, metaphor has merely an ornamental function, it replaces literal expressions with fancier and more appealing ones. But metaphor has not merely an ornamental function, it has a cognitive function since it permits to find new hypotheses.

2) *Metaphor is a kind of analogy.* It is based on some pre-existing similarity between two things, which is made explicit by comparing their properties. Thus Aristotle states that "metaphor makes what is signified somehow familiar on account of the similarity; for those who make metaphors do so on account of some similarity."[12] This, however, is unjustified because it makes metaphor vacuous. For example, on this view, Newton's metaphor, that mathematical quantities are to be considered as if they were physical quantities generated by a continuous motion, would mean that mathematical quantities are to be considered as similar to physical quantities generated by a continuous motion. But, since this statement does not indicate with respect to which properties they are similar, the metaphor would be vacuous. This is akin to the problem concerning the general schema for analogical reasoning, (AN), considered in Chapter 20. Any two things can be viewed as having some property in common, and hence as being similar with respect to that property. Moreover, even when one specifies with respect to which properties the two things are similar, such properties may not mean the same thing in the target domain and in the source domain. For example, in the metaphor, 'Words are stones', words and stones have both the property that they may cause injuries, but this does not mean the same thing in the domains of words and stones. While stones may cause injuries in the sense that they can hurt the flesh, words can cause injuries in the sense that they can hurt feelings. Saying that words are stones creates a similarity, because it suggests that words and stones are similar insofar as they can both cause injuries. So it is the metaphor that creates a similarity, rather than being based on a pre-existing similarity. In addition, while similarity is symmetrical, metaphor is not symmetrical. For example, 'Words are stones' is a metaphor, but 'Stones are words' does not make sense. And yet, if metaphor were a type of analogy, it would have to be symmetrical.

---

[11] Aristotle, *Poetica*, 1457 b, 6–7.
[12] Aristotle, *Topica*, Z 2, 140 a 9–12.

21.6 Metonymy

Metonymy is letting one thing stand for another thing which is associated with it. Thus the statement 'I like to read Auden', is a metonymy because it lets 'Auden' stand for Auden's poems.

Metonymy is the basis of all mathematical symbolism. For example, 'Let ABC be a triangle' is a metonymy, because it lets ABC stand for a triangle. Being the basis of all mathematical symbolism, metonymy is omnipresent in mathematics and is involved in virtually every mathematical discovery.

Let $a \Rightarrow b$: Let a stand for b. Metonymy is an inference of the form: $a \Rightarrow b$ and a is A, therefore b is A. So, it is an inference by the rule:

$$(\text{MTO}) \frac{a \Rightarrow b \quad A(a)}{A(b)}$$

An example of use of (MTO) is the Pythagoreans' discovery that the three angles of a triangle are equal to two right angles. Eudemus "says that" the Pythagoreans "demonstrated it as follows."[13] Let PQR be a triangle, and through P draw a line ST parallel to QR.

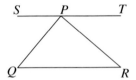

Since QR, ST are parallel, the alternate angles SPQ, PQR are equal, and so are the alternate angles TPR, PRQ. Therefore the sum of the angles SPQ, TPR is equal to the sum of the angles PQR, PRQ. Add to each the angle QPR. Then the sum of the angles SPQ, TPR, QPR, which is two right angles, is equal to the sum of the angles PQR, PRQ, QPR, the three angles of the triangle. From this, by (MTO), the Pythagoreans conclude that "the three angles of a triangle are equal to two right angles."[14]

Thus the argument pattern is as follows. Let PQR stand for a triangle b, so that $PQR \Rightarrow b$. Let $A(x)$: the three angles of x are equal to two right angles. Then $A(PQR)$. From $PQR \Rightarrow b$ and $A(PQR)$, by (MTO), it follows $A(b)$.

It might seem improper to consider metonymy to be a procedure for finding hypotheses, but it is not so. For metonymy permits to reason on concrete objects and then transfer properties established on them to abstract objects. This may have great heuristic value. Thus, in the case of the Pythagoreans' discovery, metonymy

---

[13] Proclus, *In Primum Euclidis Elementorum Librum Commentarii* (Friedlein), 379.5–6.
[14] *Ibid.*, 379.15–16.

permits to reason on the concrete object *PQR*, a drawn figure, and then to transfer the property of having the three angles equal to two right angles, established on this concrete object, to an abstract object – everything satisfying the definition of a triangle. This has great heuristic value, because it would be extremely difficult, if not impossible, to discover such a property on the basis of the definition of a triangle alone.

Thus Kant states: "Give a philosopher the concept of a triangle, and let him try to find out," merely on the basis of the definition of a triangle, "how the sum of its angles might be related to a right angle."[15] He "may reflect on this concept as long as he wants, yet he will never produce anything new."[16] Conversely, "let the geometer take up this question. He begins at once to construct a triangle" and constructs a line on it, then through a chain of inferences "he arrives at a fully illuminating and at the same time general solution of the question."[17] In fact, drawing the figure *PQR* and constructing a line *ST* parallel to *QR* on it, make the discovery straightforward. The property has been discovered by reasoning on the concrete object *PQR*, then transferring it to an abstract object.

21.7 Definition

As we have seen in Chapter 3, Aristotle considers two concepts of definition, definition of thing and definition of name, although in his view the definition of thing is the only genuine kind of definition.

There are several kinds of definition of name, but the one especially relevant here is definition as abbreviation. A definition as abbreviation is a declaration that a certain word or combination of words is to mean the same as a certain other combination of words of which the meaning is already known. This kind of definition is not subject to contradiction and can always be eliminated.

There are also several kinds of definition of thing, but the one especially relevant here is definition as analysis. A definition as analysis is a characterization of a concept through an analysis of data already available. This kind of definition is subject to contradiction if the analysis is inadequate, and cannot be eliminated.

21.8 Definition as Abbreviation

While definition as abbreviation is an instance of definition of name, that for Aristotle is not a genuine definition, for Pascal definition as abbreviation is the only genuine definition. Indeed, Pascal states that, "in geometry, only those definitions

---

[15] Kant (1997a, 631, B 744).
[16] *Ibid.*, 631–632, B 744.
[17] *Ibid.*, 632, B 744–745.

are recognized which logicians call definitions of name, that is, only the impositions of names to things which have been clearly designated," and "it is of these alone that I speak."[18] They "impose names on things to abbreviate discourse."[19] Being only impositions of names, they "are completely free, and are never subject to contradiction."[20] Moreover, being only abbreviations, they are inessential, and can always be eliminated if "one always mentally substitutes in the demonstration the definitions for the things defined."[21] Nevertheless, they are useful in practice, because they permit to "abbreviate discourse, in expressing by the single name that has been imposed what could otherwise be only expressed by several terms."[22]

This view of definition has become quite widespread in the modern and contemporary age. Thus Frege states that "a definition is an arbitrary stipulation by which a new sign" is "introduced to take the place of a complex expression whose sense we know."[23] Its only purpose "is to bring about an extrinsic simplification by stipulating an abbreviation."[24] It is completely free and is never subject to contradiction. Thus one may define "the concept of a right-angled equilateral pentagon," and the fact that it "contains a contradiction does not make it inadmissible."[25] Moreover, a definition is "wholly inessential and dispensable" because, "if the definiens occurs in a sentence and we replace it by the definiendum, this does not affect the thought at all."[26] Thus no definition "extends our knowledge."[27] However, a definition is useful in practice, because it "makes for ease and simplicity of expression."[28] Hilbert and Bernays state that a definition is "the introduction of an abbreviating symbol for a complex expression."[29] Popper states that "in science, only nominalist definitions occur, that is to say, shorthand symbols or labels are introduced in order to cut a long story short."[30]

In a sense, definition as abbreviation is a form of metonymy. For, by declaring that a certain word or combination of words is to mean the same as a certain other combination of words of which the meaning is already known, it lets one thing stand for another thing.

Let $b \triangleright a$: b is an abbreviation of a. Definition as abbreviation is an inference of the form: $b \triangleright a$ and a is A, therefore b is A. So, it is an inference by the rule:

---

[18]Pascal (1904–1914, IX, 242–243).
[19]*Ibid.*, IX, 244.
[20]*Ibid.*, IX, 243–244.
[21]*Ibid.*, IX, 278.
[22]*Ibid.*, IX, 243.
[23]Frege (1979, 211).
[24]Frege (1967, 55).
[25]Frege (1979, 179).
[26]*Ibid.*, 208.
[27]Frege (1984, 274).
[28]Frege (1979, 208).
[29]Hilbert and Bernays (1968–1970, I, 292).
[30]Popper (1945, II, 13).

$$\text{(DAB)} \quad \frac{b \triangleright a \quad A(a)}{A(b)}.$$

An example of use of (DAB) is Pascal's discovery that the space left by the descent of the mercury in a glass tube is void. Let 'void space' be an abbreviation for "a space having length, width, and depth, immovable and capable of receiving and containing a body of the same length and shape."[31] Now, what is left by the descent of the mercury in a glass tube is a space having length, width, and depth, immovable and capable of receiving and containing a body of the same length and shape. From this, by (DAB), Pascal infers that what is left by the descent of the mercury in a glass tube is a void space.

Thus the argument pattern is as follows. Let b be 'void space', and a 'a space having length, width, and depth, immovable and capable of receiving and containing a body of the same length and shape', so that $b \triangleright a$. Let $A(x)$: x is what is left by the descent of the mercury in a glass tube. Then $A(a)$. From this, by (DAB), it follows $A(b)$.

Being strictly related to metonymy, definition as abbreviation may serve as a means of discovery, but is somewhat problematic.

1) A definition as abbreviation is supposed not to be subject to contradiction. But it is not so. For example, let us stipulate that division '$x/y = z$' is to mean the same as '$y \neq 0$ and $x = y \cdot z$'. This leads to a contradiction because $1/0 = 1/0$, so there is a z such that $1/0 = z$. Then, by our definition, $0 \neq 0$ and $1 = 0 \cdot z$, which is absurd.

2) A definition as abbreviation is supposed to be always eliminable. But it is not so. For example, let us declare that '$x/y = z$' is to mean the same as 'if $y \neq 0$ then $x = y \cdot z$'. Then division is not eliminable from contexts such as $1/0 \neq 2$ because, on the basis of this definition, we cannot decide whether $1/0 = 2/0$.

21.9 Definition as Analysis

Greek mathematics provides plenty of examples of definition as analysis. Such is Definition 15 of a circle in Euclid's *Elements*. A circle is a plane figure contained by one line, which is called its circumference, such that all the straight lines falling upon the circumference from one point of those lying inside the figure, which is called the centre of the circle, are equal to one another. Such definition is based on an analysis of the concept of a circle derived from the experience of round shapes that human beings had from the very beginning, for example, the Moon or the Sun. But definition as analysis is also used to characterize abstract concepts. For example, Eilenberg and MacLane characterize the concept of 'category' through an analysis of "the common formal properties of" certain "aggregates."[32]

---

[31] Pascal (1904–1914, II, 103).
[32] Eilenberg and MacLane (1945, 237).

Even some supporters of the view that definition as abbreviation is the only genuine kind of definition, acknowledge the importance of definition as analysis. Thus Whitehead and Russell, on the one hand, state that definitions "are, strictly speaking, mere typographical conveniences" and "are theoretically superfluous."[33] But, on the other hand, they acknowledge that definitions "often convey more important information than is contained in the propositions in which they are used."[34] In such cases, "the definition contains an analysis of a common idea, and may therefore express a notable advance" since it "gives definiteness to an idea which had previously been more or less vague. For these reasons" the "definitions are what is most important."[35]

Let $a \triangleleft b$: a is an analysis of b. Definition as analysis is an inference of the form: $a \triangleleft b$ and a is A, therefore b is A. So, it is an inference by the rule:

$$\text{(DAN)} \quad \frac{a \triangleleft b \quad A(a)}{A(b)}.$$

An example of use of (DAN) is Thales' discovery that a point on the circumference of a circle sees the endpoints of a diameter of the circle as a right angle. Pamphile says that Thales "was the first to describe a right-angled triangle in a circle."[36] This seems to suggest that Thales was the first to make the above discovery, but it does not tell us how. The way described below seems to be the most likely explanation, because it does not use the theorem that the sum of the angles of a triangle is two right angles, whose discovery, at least in Greece, had to wait for the Pythagoreans.

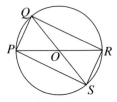

Let a circle be given. Let PR be a diameter of the circle and Q a point on the circumference. Draw QP and QR, and draw a line from Q through the centre of the circle O to S. Then QS is a diameter of the circle. By Euclid's definition of circle, all diameters of the circle are equal, so PR and QS are equal, hence the diagonals of the quadrilateral $PQRS$ are equal. Therefore $PQRS$ is a rectangle, and so its angles are right angles. Then in particular PQR is a right angle. From this, by (DAN), Thales infers that a point on the circumference of a circle sees the endpoints of a diameter of the circle as a right angle.

---

[33] Whitehead and Russell (1925–1927, I, 11).
[34] Ibid.
[35] Ibid., I, 12.
[36] Diogenes Laertius, *Vitae Philosophorum*, I.24.

Thus the argument pattern is as follows. Let b be 'circle' and a 'a figure satisfying Euclid's definition of a circle', so that $a \triangleleft b$. Let $A(x)$: a point on the circumference of x sees the endpoints of a diameter of x as a right angle. Then $A(a)$. From $a \triangleleft b$ and $A(a)$, by (DAN), it follows $A(b)$.

21.10 Diagrams

In Chapter 20 and the present one, several diagrams have been utilized to illustrate use of non-deductive rules. But diagrams are not only auxiliary means, they are also an important source of non-deductive inferences on their own.

In a sense, also the use of diagrams is a form of metonymy, because it is letting a figure stand for another thing which is associated with it. In this respect, the use of diagrams is like that of any symbolism. In addition, however, a diagram is supposed to have a certain likeness to the things which is associated with it. This is the advantage of diagrams over symbols.

One may distinguish between various kinds of likeness of a diagram to the thing which is associated with it. The most common is iconicity, or likeness of physical appearance, which occurs when a diagram contains elements that physically resemble elements of the thing which is associated with the diagram. The kind of likeness more useful to discovery is relational similarity, which occurs when the relation between elements of the diagram corresponds to the relation between elements of the thing which is associated with the diagram.

Let $a \gg b$: Let the figure a stand for b. Diagrammatic inference is an inference of the form: $a \gg b$ and $A(a)$, therefore $A(b)$. So, it is an inference by the rule:

$$(\text{DR}) \quad \frac{a \gg b \quad A(a)}{A(b)}.$$

In relational similarity, the relation between elements of the thing which is associated with the diagram may be either static or dynamic.

1) An example of use of (DR) where the relation is static is the discovery by an unknown Egyptian author that the area of a triangle is half the base times the height. Problem 51 of the Rhind papyrus states: "Example of calculating a triangle of land. If it is said to you: What is the area of a triangle of 10 khet on the height of it and 4 khet on the base of it?" you will proceed as follows: "Take 1/2 of 4, namely, 2, in order to get its rectangle. Multiply 10 times 2; this is its area."[37] The key to the discovery is the remark that one should take 1/2 half of 4 in order to get its rectangle. Such remark refers to the hypothesis that is the key to the discovery that the area of a triangle is half the base times the height, that is, the hypothesis that a triangle is

---

[37]Clagett (1999, 163). 'Khet' is an ancient Egyptian unit of measure for length, equal to 100 cubits.

half the size of a rectangle with the same base and the same height. Let the figure *PQR* stand for a triangle.

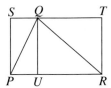

Let *PSTR* stand for a rectangle with the same base and the same height as *PQR*. Then the height *QU* divides the triangle *PQR* into two right-angled triangles, *PQU* and *RQU*, each of which can be moved so as to form the rectangle *PSQU* or *RTQU*, respectively, and hence is half the size of the latter. Thus the triangle *PQR* is half the size of the rectangle *PSTR*. Therefore the area of the triangle *PQR* is half the base times the height. From this, by (DR), the unknown Egyptian author concludes that the area of a triangle is half the base times the height.

Thus the argument pattern is as follows. Let the figure *PQR* stand for a triangle *b*, so that *PQR* » *b*. Let *A(x)*: the area of the triangle *x* is half the base times the height of *x*. Then *A(PQRS)*. From *PQRS* » *b* and *A(PQRS)*, by (DR), it follows *A(b)*.

2) An example of use of (DR) where the relation is dynamic is Galileo's discovery that a body which is carried by "a motion compounded of a horizontal uniform motion and a downward" uniformly "accelerated motion" describes "a semi-parabolic line."[38] This uses Galileo's previous discovery of the law of the falling bodies: "The spaces described by a body falling with a uniformly accelerated motion are to each other as the squares of the time-intervals employed in traversing these distances."[39] Let *ab* stand for an elevated horizontal line or plane along which a body moves with uniform speed. Suppose this plane to end abruptly at *b*. Then the body, lacking the support of the plane, in addition to the uniform horizontal motion, will acquire a downward uniformly accelerated motion. Draw the line *be* along the line *ab*. The line *be* is to stand for the flow of time. On *be* lay off any segment *bc* as unit, and then segments *cd*, *de*, each equal to *bc*. All these segments are to stand for equal intervals of time. From the points *b*, *c*, *d*, *e* draw lines perpendicular to *be*. On the perpendicular from *b* lay off any segment *bo* as unit, and then segments *bg*, *bl* such that *bg* is four times *bo*, *bl* nine times *bo*. All these segments stand for displacements which, by the law of falling bodies, stand to *bo* as the squares 1, 4, 9 of the time-intervals 1, 2, 3.

---

[38] Galilei (1968, VIII, 269).
[39] *Ibid.*, VIII, 209.

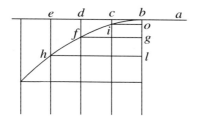

Then the points i, f, h will be such that df is four times ci, eh nine times ci, therefore such points "will lie on one and the same parabola."[40] More precisely, they will lie on a semi-parabolic line. From this, by (DR), Galileo infers that a body which is carried by a motion compounded of a horizontal uniform motion and a downward uniformly accelerated motion describes a semi-parabolic line.

Thus the argument pattern is as follows. Let $bifh$ stand for the path p followed by a body which is carried by a motion compounded of a horizontal uniform motion and a downward uniformly accelerated motion, so that $bifh \gg p$. Let $A(x)$: x is a semi-parabolic line. Then $A(bifh)$. From $bifh \gg p$ and $A(bifh)$, by (DR), it follows $A(p)$.

As Grosholz points out, the novelty of Galileo's "diagram is the perpendicular juxtaposition of line $bogl$ with $abcde$."[41] Through such juxtaposition the diagram can express that the resulting motion of the body is "compounded of a uniform horizontal and a vertical naturally accelerated motion."[42]

21.11 Some Misconceptions Concerning Diagrams

There are some misconceptions concerning diagrams that are an obstacle to understanding their nature.

1) *Diagrams involve intuition.* Thus Hilbert states that "geometrical figures are signs or mnemonic symbols of space intuition and are used as such by all mathematicians."[43] This, however, is unjustified. Geometrical figures involve visual perception which, as it has been argued in Chapter 16, is the result of inference and hence has nothing to do with intuition. For example, let us reconsider the discovery by an unknown Egyptian author that the area of a triangle is half the base times the height. Because of the limitations of our visual system, in order to visualize the diagram shown in the previous section, we must move the eye to scan different

---

[40] *Ibid.*, VIII, 273.
[41] Grosholz (2007, 15).
[42] Galilei (1968, VIII, 268).
[43] Hilbert (1996b, 1100).

parts of the diagram, then we must integrate the data thus obtained. For example, the successive partial glimpses we get in the course of scanning the diagram might be:

Then there is the problem of keeping track of the successive partial glimpses and integrating them into a single figure. This involves going beyond the data, therefore, it involves inference.

2) *Diagrams do not yield genuine demonstrations, because the latter must be deductions from axioms.* Thus Hilbert states that "a theorem is only proved when the proof is completely independent of the figure. The proof must call step by step on the preceding axioms"[44] Therefore, although using figures can be helpful, "we will never rely on them."[45] This, however, is unjustified. First, if a theorem were only demonstrated when the demonstration is completely independent of the figure, then one should conclude that Euclid's propositions are not demonstrated, because Euclid's demonstrations essentially rely on figures. But this conclusion would be improper, because Euclid's demonstrations are not faulty instances of the concept of demonstration as deduction from axioms. Rather, they are based on a different concept of demonstration, according to which: 1) Postulates are not merely starting points of deductions, but principles of construction of diagrams that fix what one is allowed to draw, for example, to draw a straight line from any point to any point, or to draw a circle with any centre and distance; 2) From the diagram one may gather properties of the objects involved. Secondly, it is unjustified to say, as Hilbert does, that he never relies on geometrical figures. As Hadamard points out, in working out his *Foundations of Geometry*, Hilbert "has been constantly guided by his geometrical sense."[46] To see this, one "ought simply to cast one glance at Hilbert's book. Diagrams appear at practically every page."[47] Thirdly, and more importantly, in Hilbert's *Foundations of Geometry* diagrams are often essential to demonstrations, including the very first demonstration in the book.[48] This contradicts Hilbert's intended purpose, "to establish for geometry a complete, and as simple as possible, system of axioms and to deduce from them the most important geometrical theorems."[49] Using diagrams in an essential way, his demonstrations are not really deductions from his axioms.

---

[44]Hilbert (2004a, 75).
[45]*Ibid.*, 541.
[46]Hadamard (1954, 88).
[47]*Ibid.*
[48]For details, see Cellucci (2008a), Chapter 9.
[49]Hilbert (1962, 1).

3) *Diagrams do not permit to establish general propositions.* Thus Tennant states that they can cause "the mistake of assuming as given information that is true only of the triangle that one has happened to draw, but which could well be false of other triangles that one equally well might have drawn in its stead."[50] But this does not mean that diagrams do not permit to establish general propositions. A diagrammatic demonstration is schematic, that is, it is an argument-schema that, given any object in the domain, will yield a demonstration specific to that object, without structural changes in the demonstration. That a diagrammatic demonstration is schematic does not mean, as Tennant states, that an expression such as "'Triangle *ABC*' is no more than a placeholder in schematic reasoning," and the diagram "stands for no particular triangle."[51] The expression in question is not a mere placeholder, and the diagram stands for a particular triangle, and therefore, for "an individual object."[52] That a diagrammatic demonstration is schematic means that the demonstration is repeatable, replacing an individual object by another individual object throughout the demonstration, without structural changes in the latter. The repeatability of the demonstration provides the basis for the generality of the proposition. This suggests replacing Gentzen's restriction on the rule ($\forall$I), stated in Chapter 11, with the following alternative restriction: the individual variable y must be such that if, in the deduction of the premise A_y^x, we replace y throughout with another individual variable z not occurring in the deduction, we obtain a deduction of A_z^x from the same assumptions. It can be easily seen that Gentzen's restriction on the rule ($\forall$I) and the above alternative restriction are, if not intensionally, at least "extensionally equivalent."[53]

4) *Diagrams are unreliable because, when incorrectly drawn, they can lead to errors.* Thus Klein states that "there is real danger that a pupil of Euclid may, because of a falsely drawn figure, come to a false conclusion."[54] For example, consider the following demonstration of the incorrect proposition: From a point not on a line two distinct perpendiculars can be drawn to the line. Draw any two circles, intersecting at points P and Q, and draw the diameters PR and PS. Then draw RS. Let T and U be the points where RS intersects the circles. Draw PT and PU. Since PUR and PTS are both triangles in a semicircle, they are right-angled. Therefore PT and PU must both be perpendiculars to the line RS from a point P not on the line RS. This is impossible.

---

[50]Tennant (1986, 304).

[51]*Ibid.*

[52]Cellucci (2009, 13). Tennant speaks of the 'Triangle *ABC*' as the "general triangle" (Tennant 1986, 304). Thus he links his view with Locke's. For Locke claims that 'Triangle *ABC*' does not stand for a particular object but rather for the 'general triangle', that is, "the general idea of a triangle," which "must be neither oblique, nor rectangle, neither equilateral, equicrural, nor scalenon; but all and none of these at once" (Locke 1975, 596). But the idea of general triangle is an impossible one, because it can be shown that "general objects cannot exist" (Cellucci 2009, 5).

[53]*Ibid.*, 14.

[54]Klein (2004, 201).

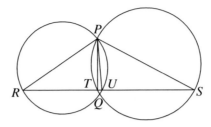

The error arises from the fact that the figure is incorrectly drawn: *PR* is not really a diameter of the corresponding circle. This leads to the improper intersections *T* and *U* of *RS* and the two circles. But it is unjustified to say that examples of this kind support the view that diagrams are unreliable. Errors such as this one arise from misapplications of diagrams, and can be avoided by taking care that the figures are carefully drawn and properly analysed. The situation is similar to that of errors like Russell's paradox, which arise from misapplications of discursive reasoning, and can be avoided by taking care that concepts are carefully expressed and properly analysed. Errors arising from misapplications of discursive reasoning are ubiquitous in mathematics. Then, if one says that diagrams, being unreliable, do not yield genuine demonstrations, one must be prepared to say that discursive reasoning, being unreliable, does not yield genuine demonstrations – a bizarre conclusion.

5) *Diagrams are never reliable when used to deal with limits of infinite processes.* Thus Giaquinto states that "visualizing is never reliable when used to discover the nature of the limit of an infinite process."[55] For example, consider the following diagram which shows a sequence of curves: the first curve is a semicircle on a diameter; the second curve results from dividing the diameter into 2 equal parts and forming semicircles on each of these parts, alternatively over and under; the third curve results from dividing the diameter into 2^2 equal parts and forming semicircles on each of these parts, alternatively over and under; and so on.

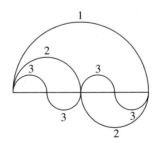

The curves get closer and closer to the diameter, and, for large *n*, the *n*-th curve will be a wiggly line "becoming barely distinguishable from the diameter. The curve lengths too seem to approach that of the diameter, so that the limit of the curve lengths will be the length of the diameter. But this is wrong. The length of all

---

[55] Giaquinto (2007, 174).

21.11 Some Misconceptions Concerning Diagrams

curves in the sequence is the same."[56] Indeed, if the diameter has length d, then the first curve – the semicircle – has length $\pi \cdot d/2$; the second curve has length $2(\pi \cdot d/4) = \pi \cdot d/2$; the third curve has length $4(\pi \cdot d/8) = \pi \cdot d/2$; and so on. On this basis Giaquinto concludes that visualizing is never reliable when used to discover the nature of the limit of an infinite process. This, however, is unjustified because, as Bråting and Pejlare point out, "visualization can be interpreted in more than one way, giving different results."[57] In this case, we can look at the lengths of the curves and take the limit, or we can consider the length of the limit function. Now, "if we look at the lengths of the curves and take the limit we get the result $\pi \cdot d/2$. But if we instead consider the length of the limit function, then the result is the length of the diameter, that is, the result is d."[58] With experience we can learn to interpret a diagram in different ways and choose the appropriate one, just as with experience we can learn to interpret a concept in different ways and choose the appropriate one.

6) *Diagrams can be legitimate components in valid deductive reasoning.* Thus Avigad, Dean and Mumma state that "any fact obtained by a direct diagram inference is contained in the set of first-order consequences of the set of our universal axioms" – of a formal system for Euclid's *Elements* – "and the set of literals constituting the diagram."[59] Moreover, "our formal system is sound and complete for an appropriate semantics."[60] With such formal system, "the role of the singular – that is, the particular diagram – drops out of the story entirely; we focus only on the diagrammatic features that are generally valid in a given context, and say nothing about a particular instantiation."[61] Now, the formulation of this formal system, or of any other formal system of a similar kind, is part of the attempt to fit diagrams into the axiomatic method.[62] The attempt has the effect that the particular diagram 'drops out of the story entirely'. But the attempt conflicts with the fact that, as Dieudonné emphasizes, "a strict adherence to axiomatic methods" requires "abstaining from introducing any diagram."[63] What is more important, it conflicts with the fact that, as we have seen in the Introduction, Gödel's first incompleteness theorem refutes the assumption that the method of mathematics is the axiomatic method. Rather than in the axiomatic method, diagrams naturally fit in the analytic method, where diagrammatic inference, (DR), is one of basic the rules of discovery.

---

[56] *Ibid.*
[57] Bråting and Pejlare (2008, 354).
[58] *Ibid.*
[59] Avigad et al. (2009, 758).
[60] *Ibid.*, 760.
[61] *Ibid.*, 764.
[62] This is also clear from Mancosu (2008), a sort of manifesto for the attempt to fit not only diagrams, but all mathematical practice into the axiomatic method. For a criticism of this manifesto, see Cellucci (2013b), section 2.
[63] Dieudonné (1969, ix).

Chapter 22
Conclusion

Logic is generally considered to be the study of the principles of valid inference, thus a subject, like papyrology or botany. But logic is not only that, it is also that problem solving capacity that virtually all organisms have as a result of biological evolution, and without which they could not survive. Thus logic is not only a subject, but also a basic ability of all organisms. This contrasts with Frege's view that logic is a primordial body of laws that are fixed and absolute, and with which human beings must comply. Such laws, the laws of logic, descended from some rational heaven and hence have some sort of sovereign, transcendental validity.

Contrary to Frege's view, the laws of logic are neither fixed nor absolute, nor descended from any rational heaven. At least some of them are implicit in the evolutionary processes from which life originated. They are in no sense prior to those processes, and it is out of the latter that the tendency to comply with them emerges. This means that logic is not peculiar to human beings. Biological evolution has endowed not only human beings, but virtually all organisms, with a natural logic through which they manage to survive. Thus natural logic is not an arbitrary creation, but a response to certain basic facts and features of the world, and a response which is essential for life. Thus *logos* arises in the service of *bios*.

On the other hand, logic does not reduce to natural logic, and hence to evolutionary theory, because by means of natural logic alone human beings would be unable to cope with situations that did not occur in their evolutionary past. In addition to natural logic, an artificial logic is necessary, namely, that problem solving capacity that human beings have as a result of cultural evolution. Natural and artificial logic are distinct, and the latter does not reduce to the former. Thus, while arising in the service of *bios*, *logos* does not reduce to it.

That natural and artificial logic are distinct does not mean, however, that they are opposed. Since cultural evolution depends on capacities that human beings have as a result of biological evolution, cultural evolution ultimately depends on biological evolution.

Both natural and artificial logic serve to solve problems, starting with that of survival, so they are means of discovery. Thus logic is essentially a logic of discovery, and hence has a strict relation to method. Indeed, logic arises from method, so method is the source of logic. In particular, the analytic method is the source of the logic of discovery, because it permits to find hypotheses by means of non-deductive rules, which are the engines of discovery.

Hilbert's programme of mechanizing discovery must be replaced with a programme of naturalizing discovery, which considers discovery as a natural phenomenon occurring in virtually all organisms. Such a programme builds on the fact that, as a result of biological evolution, virtually all organisms have a natural logic, and, as a result of cultural evolution, human beings also have an artificial logic.

Since logic is essentially a logic of discovery, the basic assumptions of mathematical logic 1)–5) considered in the Introduction, must be replaced with the following alternative assumptions:

1) *The purpose of logic is to give means for acquiring new knowledge.* Only so it can be considered to be fruitful.

2) *Logic pursues this purpose through the study of the method of mathematics, and science generally.* This will show how new knowledge can be acquired.

3) *The method of mathematics, and science generally, is the analytic method.* One starts from problems and finds hypotheses to solve them by means of non-deductive rules.

4) *Logic must express all that is necessary for the analytic method.* For it must consider expressing anything that is significant for acquiring new knowledge.

5) *Logic can actually give means for acquiring new knowledge.* For it can provide the non-deductive rules by means of which one may find hypotheses for solving problems.

These assumptions show the difference between the view of logic proposed in this book and mathematical logic.

References

Albert of Saxony. 1986. *Questiones Subtilissime in Libros Aristotelis de Caelo et Mundo – Questiones Subtilissime super Libros Posteriorum.* Hildesheim: Georg Olms.
Archimedes. 1880–1881. *Opera Omnia*, ed. Johnan Ludvig Heiberg. Leipzig: Teubner.
Arnauld, Antoine, and Pierre Nicole. 1992. *La logique ou l'art de penser*, ed. Charles Jourdain. Paris: Gallimard.
Austin, John Langshaw. 1970. *Philosophical papers*, ed. James Opie Urmson and Geoffrey James Warnock. Oxford: Oxford University Press.
Avigad, Jeremy, Edward Dean, and John Mumma. 2009. A formal system for Euclid's *Elements. The Review of Symbolic Logic* 2: 700–768.
Bacon, Francis. 1961–1986. *Works*, ed. James Spedding, Robert Leslie Ellis, and Douglas Denon Heath. Stuttgart Bad Cannstatt: Frommann Holzboog.
Bailey, Dominic. 2006. Plato and Aristotle on the unhypothetical. *Oxford Studies in Ancient Philosophy* 30: 101–126.
Barendregt, Henk. 2009. Proofs of correctness in mathematics and industry. In *Encyclopedia of computer science and engineering*, ed. Benjamin Wan-Sang Wah, 2284–2290. New York: Wiley.
Barnes, Jonathan. 1993. Commentary. In Aristotle, *Posterior Analytics*, ed. Jonathan Barnes, 81–271. Oxford: Oxford University Press.
Barnes, Jonathan. 2003. Argument in ancient philosophy. In *The Cambridge companion to Greek and Roman philosophy*, ed. David Sedley, 20–41. Cambridge: Cambridge University Press.
Bechara, Antoine, Hanna Damasio, and Antonio Damasio. 2000. Emotion, decision making and the orbitofrontal cortex. *Cerebral Cortex* 10: 295–307.
Belnap, Nuel D. 1962. Tonk, plonk and plink. *Analysis* 22: 130–134.
Bennett, Maxwell R., and Peter Michael Stephan Hacker. 2003. *Philosophical foundations of neuroscience.* Oxford: Blackwell.
Berkeley, George. 1948–1957. *Works*, ed. Arthur Aston Luce and Thomas Edmund Jessop. London: Nelson.
Blanché, Robert. 1970. *La logique et son histoire, d'Aristote à Russell.* Paris: Armand Colin.
Boger, George. 2004. Aristotle's underlying logic. In *Handbook of the history of logic*, vol. 1: *Greek, Indian and Arabic logic*, ed. Dov M. Gabbay and John Woods, 101–246. Amsterdam: Elsevier.
Boghossian, Paul A. 2003. Blind reasoning. *Proceedings of the Aristotelian Society Supplementary Volume* 77: 225–248.
Bourbaki, Nicolas. 1949. Foundations of mathematics for the working mathematician. *The Journal of Symbolic Logic* 14: 1–8.

Bourbaki, Nicolas. 1996. The architecture of mathematics. In *From Kant to Hilbert: A source book in the foundations of mathematics*, vol. 2, ed. William Bragg Ewald, 1265–1276. Oxford: Oxford University Press.
Bråting, Kajsa, and Johanna Pejlare. 2008. Visualization in mathematics. *Erkenntnis* 68: 345–358.
Byers, William. 2007. *How mathematicians think. Using ambiguity, contradiction, and paradox to create mathematics*. Princeton: Princeton University Press.
Calvino, Italo. 1974. *The invisible cities*. San Diego: Harcourt Brace.
Calvino, Italo. 1985. *Mr. Palomar*. San Diego: Harcourt Brace.
Capozzi, Mirella. 2002. *Kant e la logica*, vol. 1. Naples: Bibliopolis.
Capozzi, Mirella. 2006. Kant on heuristics as a desirable addition to logic. In *Demonstrative and non-demonstrative reasoning in mathematics and natural science*, ed. Carlo Cellucci and Paolo Pecere, 123–181. Cassino: Edizioni dell'Università degli Studi di Cassino.
Capozzi, Mirella. 2011. Le inferenze del giudizio riflettente nella logica di Kant: l'induzione e l'analogia. *Studi Kantiani* 24: 11–48.
Carnap, Rudolf. 1962. *Logical foundations of probability*. Chicago: The University of Chicago Press.
Carnap, Rudolf. 1966. *Philosophical foundations of physics. An introduction to the philosophy of science*. New York: Basic Books.
Carnap, Rudolf. 1968. Inductive logic and inductive intuition. In *The problem of inductive logic. Proceedings of the international colloquium in the philosophy of science, London 1965*, vol. 2, ed. Imre Lakatos, 258–267, 307–314. Amsterdam: North-Holland.
Cellucci, Carlo. 1992. Existential instantiation and normalization in sequent natural deduction. *Annals of Pure and Applied Logic* 58: 111–148.
Cellucci, Carlo. 1995. Frege e le origini della logica matematica. In Gottlob Frege, *Leggi fondamentali dell'aritmetica*, ed. Carlo Cellucci, ix–lxvi. Rome: Teknos.
Cellucci, Carlo. 1998. *Le ragioni della logica*. Rome: Laterza.
Cellucci, Carlo. 2003. *Filosofia e matematica*. Rome: Laterza. English translation of the introduction in *18 unconventional essays on the nature of mathematics*, ed. Reuben Hersh (2006), 17–36. Berlin: Springer.
Cellucci, Carlo. 2006. The question Hume didn't ask: Why should we accept deductive inference? In *Demonstrative and non-demonstrative reasoning in mathematics and natural science*, ed. Carlo Cellucci and Paolo Pecere, 207–235. Cassino: Edizioni dell'Università degli Studi di Cassino.
Cellucci, Carlo. 2007. *La filosofia della matematica del Novecento*. Rome: Laterza.
Cellucci, Carlo. 2008a. *Perché ancora la filosofia*. Rome: Laterza.
Cellucci, Carlo. 2008b. Why proof? What is a proof? In *Deduction, computation, experiment. Exploring the effectiveness of proof*, ed. Rossella Lupacchini and Giovanna Corsi, 1–27. Berlin: Springer.
Cellucci, Carlo. 2009. The universal generalization problem. *Logique & Analyse* 52: 3–20.
Cellucci, Carlo. 2011. Classifying and justifying inference rules. In *Logic and knowledge*, ed. Carlo Cellucci, Emily Rolfe Grosholz, and Emiliano Ippoliti, 93–106. Newcastle upon Tyne: Cambridge Scholars Publishing.
Cellucci, Carlo. 2012. Reason and logic. In *Reason and rationality*, ed. Maria Cristina Amoretti and Nicla Vassallo, 199–216. Frankfurt: Ontos Verlag.
Cellucci, Carlo. 2013a. Philosophy of mathematics: Making a fresh start. *Studies in History and Philosophy of Science* 44: 32–42.
Cellucci, Carlo. 2013b. Top-down and bottom-up philosophy of mathematics. *Foundations of Science* 18: 93–106.
Cellucci, Carlo. (forthcoming). Explanatory and non-explanatory demonstrations. In *Logic, methodology and philosophy of science. Proceedings of the fourteenth international congress*, ed. Pierre Edouard Bour and Peter Schroeder-Heister (to appear). London: College Publications.
Chen, Ludwig C.H. 1992. *Acquiring knowledge of the ideas. A study of Plato's methods in the Phaedo, the Symposium and the central books of the Republic*. Stuttgart: Steiner.

References

Chisholm, Roderick M. 1989. *Theory of knowledge*. Englewood Cliffs: Prentice-Hall.
Church, Alonzo. 1936. An unsolvable problem in elementary number theory. *American Journal of Mathematics* 58: 345–363.
Clagett, Marshall. 1999. *Ancient Egyptian science. A source book*, vol. 3: *Ancient Egyptian mathematics*. Philadelphia: American Mathematical Society.
Coffa, Alberto. 1991. *The semantic tradition from Kant to Carnap. To the Vienna station*. Cambridge: Cambridge University Press.
Cohen, I. Bernard. 1971. *Introduction to Newton's 'Principia'*. Cambridge: Cambridge University Press.
Cohen, I. Bernard. 1985. *Revolution in science*. Cambridge: Harvard University Press.
Cohen, Morris Raphael, and Ernest Nagel. 1964. *An introduction to logic and scientific method*. London: Routledge.
Cooper, William S. 2001. *The evolution of reason. Logic as a branch of biology*. Cambridge: Cambridge University Press.
Cornford, Francis Macdonald. 1932. Mathematics and dialectic in the *Republic* VI-VII. *Mind* 41: 37–52.
Couturat, Louis (ed.). 1961. *Opuscules et fragments inedits de Leibniz*. Hildesheim: Georg Olms.
Curry, Haskell Brooks. 1977. *Foundations of mathematical logic*. Mineola: Dover.
Damasio, Antonio. 2003. *Looking for Spinoza. Joy, sorrow, and the feeling brain*. London: Heinemann.
Davidson, Donald. 2001. *Subjective, intersubjective, objective*. Oxford: Oxford University Press.
Davies, Edward Brian. 2008. Interview. In *Philosophy of mathematics: 5 questions*, ed. Vincenta Fella Hendricks and Hannes Leitgeb, 87–99. New York: Automatic Press/VIP.
Davis, Philip J. 2006. *Mathematics and common sense. A case of creative tension*. Natick: A K Peters.
de l'Hospital, Guillaume François Antoine. 1696. *Analyse des infiniment petits*. Paris: Imprimerie Royale.
Dehaene, Stanislas, and Laurent Cohen. 2007. Cultural recycling of cortical maps. *Neuron* 56: 384–398.
Descartes, René. 1996. *Œuvres*, ed. Charles Adam and Paul Tannery. Paris: Vrin.
Devlin, Keith. 2005. *The math instinct. Why you're a mathematical genius (along with lobsters, birds, cats, and dogs)*. New York: Thunder's Mouth Press.
Dewey, John. 1916. *Essays in experimental logic*. Chicago: The University of Chicago Press.
Dewey, John. 1938. *Logic. The theory of inquiry*. New York: Holt.
Dewey, John. 2004. *Reconstruction in philosophy*. Mineola: Dover.
Diels, Hermann Alexander, and Walther Kranz (eds.). 1964. *Die Fragmente der Vorsokratiker*. Berlin: Weidmann.
Dieudonné, Jean. 1964. Recent developments in mathematics. *The American Mathematical Monthly* 71: 239–248.
Dieudonné, Jean. 1969. *Foundations of modern analysis*. New York: Academic Press.
Dieudonné, Jean. 1979. The Bourbaki choice. *Mathematical Medley* 7(2–3): 28–36.
Dilthey, Wilhelm. 1989. *Introduction to the human sciences*. Princeton: Princeton University Press.
Dirac, Paul Adrien Maurice. 1951. A new classical theory of electrons. *Proceedings of the Royal Society of London*, Series A, 209: 291–296.
Dirac, Paul Adrien Maurice. 1958. *The principles of quantum mechanics*. Oxford: Oxford University Press.
Dirac, Paul Adrien Maurice. 1963. The evolution of the physicist's picture of nature. *Scientific American* 208(5): 43–53.
Dummett, Michael Anthony Eardley. 1981. *Frege: Philosophy of language*. London: Duckworth.
Dummett, Michael Anthony Eardley. 1991a. *The logical basis of metaphysics*. Cambridge: Harvard University Press.
Dummett, Michael Anthony Eardley. 1991b. *Frege: Philosophy of mathematics*. London: Duckworth.
Dummett, Michael Anthony Eardley. 1993. *The seas of language*. Oxford: Oxford University Press.

Dummett, Michael Anthony Eardley. 2010. *The nature and future of philosophy.* New York: Columbia University Press.
Eilenberg, Samuel, and Saunders MacLane. 1945. General theory of natural equivalences. *Transactions of the American Mathematical Society* 58: 231–294.
Einstein, Albert. A testimonial. In Jacques Hadamard, *The psychology of invention in the mathematical field*, 142–143. Mineola: Dover.
Euclid. 1883–1916. *Opera Omnia*, ed. Johnan Ludvig Heiberg and Heinrich Menge. Leipzig: Teubner.
Eutocius of Ascalon. 1881. *Commentarii in Libros de Sphaera et Cylindro. Ut Menechmus.* In Archimedes, *Opera Omnia*, vol. 3, ed. Johnan Ludvig Heiberg, 92–99. Stuttgart: Teubner.
Favaro, Antonio. 1968. Avvertimento. In Galileo Galilei, *Opere*, vol. IV, ed. Antonio Favaro, 5–16. Florence: Barbera.
Feferman, Solomon. 1998. *In the light of logic.* Oxford: Oxford University Press.
Feigl, Herbert. 1971. De principiis non disputandum...? On the meaning and the limits of justification. In *Philosophical analysis. A collection of essays*, ed. Max Black, 113–147. New York: Books for Libraries Press.
Feyerabend, Paul. 1999. Letters to the Director of the Department of Philosophy. In Imre Lakatos and Paul Feyerabend, *For and against method*, 382–393. Chicago: The University of Chicago Press.
Floyd, Juliet, and Hilary Putnam. 2000. A note on Wittgenstein's 'notorious paragraph' about the Gödel theorem. *The Journal of Philosophy* 97: 624–632.
Fodor, Jerry Alan. 1981. *Representations. Philosophical essays on the foundations of cognitive science.* Brighton: Harvester Press.
Fodor, Jerry Alan, and Zenon W. Pylyshyn. 1981. How direct is visual perception? Some reflections on Gibson's 'ecological approach'. *Cognition* 9: 139–196.
Frankfurt, Harry Gordon. 1958. Peirce's notion of abduction. *The Journal of Philosophy* 55: 593–597.
Franklin, Benjamin. 1859. *Memoirs.* New York: Derby and Jackson.
Franzén, Torkel. 2005. *Gödel's theorem. An incomplete guide to its use and abuse.* Wellesley: A K Peters.
Frege, Gottlob. 1959. *The foundations of arithmetic. A logico-mathematical enquiry into the concept of number.* Oxford: Blackwell.
Frege, Gottlob. 1964. *The basic laws of arithmetic. Exposition of the system*, ed. Montgomery Furth. Berkeley/Los Angeles: University of California Press.
Frege, Gottlob. 1967. *Begriffsschrift*, a formula language, modeled upon that of arithmetic, for pure thought. In *From Frege to Gödel. A source book in mathematical logic, 1879–1931*, ed. Jean van Heijenoort, 5–82. Cambridge: Harvard University Press.
Frege, Gottlob. 1969. *Nachgelassene Schriften*, ed. Hans Hermes, Friedrich Kambartel, and Friedrich Kaulbach. Hamburg: Meiner.
Frege, Gottlob. 1979. *Posthumous writings*, ed. Hans Hermes, Friedrich Kambartel, and Friedrich Kaulbach. Oxford: Blackwell.
Frege, Gottlob. 1980. *Philosophical and mathematical correspondence*, ed. Gottfried Gabriel, Hans Hermes, Friedrich Kambartel, Christian Thiel, and Albert Veraart. Oxford: Blackwell.
Frege, Gottlob. 1984. *Collected papers on mathematics, logic, and philosophy*, ed. Brian McGuinness. Oxford: Blackwell.
Fuss, Paul Heinrich (ed.). 1843. *Correspondance mathématique et physique de quelques célebres géomètres du XVIIIème siècle.* Saint Pétersbourg: Académie Impériale des Sciences.
Galilei, Galileo. 1968. *Opere*, ed. Antonio Favaro. Florence: Barbera.
Gentzen, Gerhard. 1969. *Collected papers*, ed. Manfred E. Szabo. Amsterdam: North-Holland.
Gershon, Michael. 1998. *The second brain.* New York: Harper Collins.
Giaquinto, Marcus. 2007. *Visual thinking in mathematics. An epistemological study.* Oxford: Oxford University Press.
Gibson, James Jerome. 1986. *The ecological approach to visual perception.* New York: Psychology Press.

Gillies, Donald. 2011. *Meno*-like discoveries in mathematics and science. *Paradigmi* 29(3): 29–44.
Gödel, Kurt. 1986–2002. *Collected works*, ed. Solomon Feferman et al. Oxford: Oxford University Press.
Gowers, William Timothy. 2002. *Mathematics: A very short introduction*. Oxford: Oxford University Press.
Gowers, William Timothy. 2006. Does mathematics need a philosophy? In *18 unconventional essays on the nature of mathematics*, ed. Reuben Hersh, 182–200. Berlin: Springer.
Graham, Ronald L., Donald E. Knuth, and Oren Patashnik. 1994. *Concrete mathematics*. Reading: Addison-Wesley.
Grosholz, Emily Rolfe. 2000. The partial unification of domains, hybrids, and the growth of mathematical knowledge. In *The growth of mathematical knowledge*, ed. Emily Rolfe Grosholz and Herbert Breger, 81–91. Dordrecht: Kluwer.
Grosholz, Emily Rolfe. 2007. *Representation and productive ambiguity in mathematics and the sciences*. Oxford: Oxford University Press.
Haack, Susan. 1996. *Deviant logic, fuzzy logic. Beyond the formalism*. Chicago: The University of Chicago Press.
Hadamard, Jacques. 1954. *The psychology of invention in the mathematical field*. Mineola: Dover.
Hallett, Michael, and Ulrich Majer (eds.). 2004. *David Hilbert's lectures on the foundations of geometry (1891–1902)*. Berlin: Springer.
Halmos, Paul Richard. 1985. *I want to be a mathematician. An automathography*. Berlin: Springer.
Hamming, Richard Wesley. 1980. The unreasonable effectiveness of mathematics. *The American Mathematical Monthly* 87: 81–90.
Hamming, Richard Wesley. 1998. Mathematics on a distant planet. *The American Mathematical Monthly* 105: 640–650.
Hansen, Bert. 1985. *Nicole Oresme and the marvels of nature. A study of his De causis mirabilium with critical edition, translation, and commentary*. Toronto: Pontifical Institute of Mediaeval Studies.
Harman, Gilbert. 1965. The inference to the best explanation. *Philosophical Review* 74: 88–95.
Hawking, Stephen William. 1988. *A brief history of time. From the big bang to black holes*. New York: Bantam Books.
Hawking, Stephen William, and Leonard Mlodinow. 2010. *The grand design*. New York: Bantam Books.
Heidegger, Martin. 1968. *What is called thinking?* New York: Harper and Row.
Heidegger, Martin. 1972. *On time and being*. New York: Harper and Row.
Heidegger, Martin. 1994. *Basic questions of philosophy. Selected 'problems' of 'logic'*. Bloomington: Indiana University Press.
Heidegger, Martin. 1998. *Pathmarks*. Cambridge: Cambridge University Press.
Heidegger, Martin. 2009. *Logic as the question concerning the essence of language*. Albany: State University of New York Press.
Hempel, Carl Gustav. 2000. *Selected philosophical essays*, ed. Richard Carl Jeffrey. Cambridge: Cambridge University Press.
Herschel, William. 2008. Letter to Sir Joseph Bank. In James Sime, *William Herschel and his work*, 73–74. Charleston: BiblioBazaar.
Hilbert, David. 1962. *Grundlagen der Geometrie*. Stuttgart: Teubner.
Hilbert, David. 1967. The foundations of mathematics. In *From Frege to Gödel. A source book in mathematical logic, 1879–1931*, ed. Jean van Heijenoort, 464–479. Cambridge: Harvard University Press.
Hilbert, David. 1980. Letter to Frege 29.12.1899. In Gottlob Frege, *Philosophical and mathematical correspondence*, ed. Gottfried Gabriel, Hans Hermes, Friedrich Kambartel, Christian Thiel, and Albert Veraart, 38–41. Oxford: Blackwell.
Hilbert, David. 1983. On the infinite. In *Philosophy of mathematics. Selected readings*, ed. Paul Benacerraf and Hilary Putnam, 183–201. Cambridge: Cambridge University Press.

Hilbert, David. 1996a. On the concept of number. In *From Kant to Hilbert: A source book in the foundations of mathematics*, vol. 2, ed. William Bragg Ewald, 1092–1095. Oxford: Oxford University Press.

Hilbert, David. 1996b. Axiomatic thought. In *From Kant to Hilbert: A source book in the foundations of mathematics*, vol. 2, ed. William Bragg Ewald, 1107–1115. Oxford: Oxford University Press.

Hilbert, David. 1998. Problems of the grounding of mathematics. In *From Brouwer to Hilbert. The debate on the foundations of mathematics in the 1920s*, ed. Paolo Mancosu, 227–233. Oxford: Oxford University Press.

Hilbert, David. 2000. Lecture at the international congress of mathematicians, Paris 1900. In Jeremy John Gray, *The Hilbert challenge*, 240–282. Oxford: Oxford University Press.

Hilbert, David. 2004a. Die Grundlagen der Geometrie. In *From Kant to Hilbert: A source book in the foundations of mathematics*, vol. 2, ed. William Bragg Ewald, 72–81. Oxford: Oxford University Press.

Hilbert, David. 2004b. Grundlagen der Geometrie. In *David Hilbert's lectures on the foundations of geometry (1891–1902)*, ed. Michael Hallett and Ulrich Majer, 540–606. Oxford: Oxford University Press.

Hilbert, David, and Wilhelm Ackermann. 1950. *Principles of mathematical logic*. New York: Chelsea.

Hilbert, David, and Paul Bernays. 1968–1970. *Grundlagen der Mathematik*. Berlin: Springer.

Hintikka, Jaakko. 1996. *The principles of mathematics revisited*. Cambridge: Cambridge University Press.

Hintikka, Jaakko. 2000. *On Gödel*. Belmont: Wadsworth.

Hintikka, Jaakko, and Unto Remes. 1974. *The method of analysis. Its geometrical origin and its general significance*. Dordrecht: Reidel.

Hintikka, Jaakko, and Gabriel Sandu. 2007. What is logic? In *Philosophy of logic*, ed. Dale Jacquette, 13–39. Amsterdam: North-Holland.

Hippocrates. 2005. *On ancient medicine*. Leiden: Brill.

Hönigswald, Richard. 1980. Letter to Frege 24.04.1925. In Gottlob Frege, *Philosophical and mathematical correspondence*, ed. Gottfried Gabriel, Hans Hermes, Friedrich Kambartel, Christian Thiel, and Albert Veraart, 53–54. Oxford: Blackwell.

Howson, Colin. 2000. *Hume's problem. Induction and the justification of belief*. Oxford: Oxford University Press.

Hrbacek, Karel, and Thomas Jech. 1999. *Introduction to set theory*. New York: Marcel Dekker.

Hume, David. 1978. *A treatise of human nature*, ed. Lewis Amherst Selby-Bigge and Peter Harold Nidditch. Oxford: Oxford University Press.

Hume, David. 2007. *An enquiry concerning human understanding*, ed. Lewis Amherst Selby-Bigge and Peter Harold Nidditch. Oxford: Oxford University Press.

Husserl, Edmund. 1970. *The crisis of European sciences and transcendental phenomenology*. Evanston: Northwestern University Press.

Husserl, Edmund. 2001. *Logical investigations*. London: Routledge.

Husserl, Edmund. 2002. Philosophy as rigorous science. *The New Yearbook for Phenomenology and Phenomenological Philosophy* 2: 249–295.

Ivancevic, Vladimir G., and Tijana T. Ivancevic. 2008. *Quantum leap. From Dirac and Feynman, across the universe, to human body and mind*. Singapore: World Scientific.

Jaffe, Arthur. 1997. Proof and the evolution of mathematics. *Synthese* 111: 133–146.

Josephson, John R., and Susan G. Josephson (eds.). 1994. *Abductive inference. Computation, philosophy, technology*. Cambridge: Cambridge University Press.

Kac, Mark, Gian-Carlo Rota, and Jacob T. Schwartz. 1992. *Discrete thoughts. Essays on mathematics, science, and philosophy*. Boston: Birkhäuser.

Kant, Immanuel. 1900–. *Gesammelte Schriften (Akademie Aausgabe)*. Berlin: Königlich Preußischen Akademie der Wissenschaften.

Kant, Immanuel. 1992. *Lectures on logic*, ed. J. Michael Young. Cambridge: Cambridge University Press.

Kant, Immanuel. 1997a. *Critique of pure reason*, ed. Paul Guyer and Allen W. Wood. Cambridge: Cambridge University Press.

Kant, Immanuel. 1997b. *Lectures on metaphysics*, ed. Karl Ameriks and Steve Naragon. Cambridge: Cambridge University Press.

Kant, Immanuel. 1998. *Logik-Vorlesung. Unveröffentlichte Nachschriften*, ed. Tillmann Pinder. Hamburg: Meiner.

Kant, Immanuel. 1999a. *Practical philosophy*, ed. Mary J. Gregor. Cambridge: Cambridge University Press.

Kant, Immanuel. 1999b. *Correspondence*, ed. Arnulf Zweig. Cambridge: Cambridge University Press.

Kant, Immanuel. 2002. *Theoretical philosophy after 1781*, ed. Henry Allison and Peter Heath. Cambridge: Cambridge University Press.

Kant, Immanuel. 2003. *Theoretical philosophy 1755–1770*, ed. David Walford and Ralf Meerbote. Cambridge: Cambridge University Press.

Kant, Immanuel. 2005. *Notes and fragments*, ed. Paul Guyer. Cambridge: Cambridge University Press.

Kant, Immanuel. 2007a. *Anthropology, history, and education*, ed. Günter Zöller and Robert B. Louden. Cambridge: Cambridge University Press.

Kant, Immanuel. 2007b. *Critique of judgment*, ed. Nicholas Walker. Oxford: Oxford University Press.

Kepler, Johannes. 1858–1871. *Opera Omnia*, ed. Christian Frisch. Frankfurt/Erlangen: Heyder & Zimmer.

Klein, Christian Felix. 2004. *Elementary mathematics from an advanced standpoint: Geometry*. Mineola: Dover.

Kneale, William, and Martha Kneale. 1962. *The development of logic*. Oxford: Oxford University Press.

Knorr, Wilbur Richard. 1993. *The ancient tradition of geometric problems*. Mineola: Dover.

Kripke, Saul Aaron. 1976. Is there a problem about substitutional quantification? In *Truth and meaning: Essays in semantics*, ed. Gareth Evans and John Henry McDowell, 325–419. Oxford: Oxford University Press.

Kripke, Saul Aaron. 1980. *Naming and necessity*. Cambridge: Harvard University Press.

Kyburg, Henry Ely. 1965. Comments on Salmon's inductive evidence. *American Philosophical Quarterly* 2: 274–276.

Leibniz, Gottfried Wilhelm. 1948. *Textes inédits d'après les manuscripts de la Bibliothèque provinciale de Hanovre*, ed. Gaston Grua. Paris: Presses Universitaires de France.

Leibniz, Gottfried Wilhelm. 1965. *Die Philosophischen Schriften*, ed. Carl Immanuel Gerhardt. Hildesheim: Georg Olms.

Leibniz, Gottfried Wilhelm. 1966. *Handschriften*, ed. Eduard Bodemann. Hildesheim: Georg Olms.

Leibniz, Gottfried Wilhelm. 1971. *Mathematische Schriften*, ed. Carl Immanuel Gerhardt. Hildesheim: Georg Olms.

Leibniz, Gottfried Wilhelm. 1988. *Opuscules et fragments inédits*, ed. Louis Couturat. Hildesheim: Georg Olms.

Levi, Carlo. 2005. *Words are stones. Impressions of Sicily*. London: Hesperus Press.

Lewis, David Kellogg. 1996. Elusive knowledge. *Australasian Journal of Philosophy* 74: 549–567.

Löb, Martin Hugo. 1955. Solution of a problem of Leon Henkin. *The Journal of Symbolic Logic* 20: 115–118.

Locke, John. 1975. *An essay concerning human understanding*, ed. Peter Harold Nidditch. Oxford: Oxford University Press.

Macbeth, Danielle. 2012. Diagrammatic reasoning in Frege's *Begriffsschrift*. *Synthese* 186: 289–314.

Mach, Ernst. 1976. *Knowledge and error. Sketches on the psychology of enquiry*. Dordrecht: Reidel.

Maddy, Penelope. 1997. *Naturalism in mathematics*. Oxford: Oxford University Press.

Maddy, Penelope. 1998. V=L and maximize. In *Logic colloquium 1995*, ed. Johann A. Makowsky and Elena V. Ravve, 134–152. Berlin: Springer.
Maier, Heinrich. 1896–1900. *Die Syllogistik des Aristoteles*. Tübingen: Lauppsche.
Mancosu, Paolo (ed.). 2008. *The philosophy of mathematical practice*. Oxford: Oxford University Press.
Maor, Eli. 2007. *The Pythagorean theorem. A 4,000-year history*. Princeton: Princeton University Press.
Maxwell, James Clerk. 1965. *Scientific papers*, ed. William Davidson Niven. Mineola: Dover.
McCarthy, John. 1963. A basis for a mathematical theory of computation. In *Computer programming and formal systems*, ed. Paul Braffort and Dan Hirschberg, 33–70. Amsterdam: North-Holland.
Menn, Stephen. 2002. Plato and the method of analysis. *Phronesis* 47: 193–223.
Mill, John Stuart. 1963–1986. *Collected works*, ed. John M. Robson. Toronto: University of Toronto Press.
Moore, George Edward. 1952. An autobiography. In *The philosophy of G. E. Moore*, ed. Paul Arthur Schilpp, 3–39. New York: Tudor.
Mullis, Kary. 1998. *Dancing naked in the mind field*. New York: Vintage.
Murawski, Roman. 1999. *Recursive functions and metamathematics. Problems of completeness and decidability, Gödel's theorems*. Dordrecht: Kluwer.
Nagel, Thomas. 1986. *The view from nowhere*. Oxford: Oxford University Press.
Nagel, Thomas. 1997. *The last word*. Oxford: Oxford University Press.
Naylor, Arch W., and George R. Sell. 2000. *Linear operator theory in engineering and science*. Berlin: Springer.
Newton, Isaac. 1952. *Opticks, or a treatise of the reflections, refractions, inflections & colours of light*. Mineola: Dover.
Newton, Isaac. 1959–1977. *Correspondence*, ed. Alfred Rupert Hall and Laura Tilling. Cambridge: Cambridge University Press.
Newton, Isaac. 1967–1981. *The mathematical papers*, ed. Derek Thomas Whiteside. Cambridge: Cambridge University Press.
Newton, Isaac. 1972. *Philosophiae Naturalis Principia Mathematica. Facsimile of third edition (1726) with variant readings*, ed. Alexandre Koyré, I. Bernard Cohen, and Anne Whitman. Cambridge: Cambridge University Press.
Novalis (von Hardenberg, Friedrich). 2007. *Notes for a romantic encyclopedia. Das Allgemeine Brouillon*. Albany: State University of New York Press.
Nowak, Leszek. 2000. Galileo-Newton's model of free fall. In Izabella Nowakowa and Leszek Nowak, *Idealization X: The richness of idealization*, 17–62. Amsterdam: Rodopi.
Oaksford, Mike, and Nick Chater. 2007. *Bayesian rationality. The probabilistic approach to human reasoning*. Oxford: Oxford University Press.
Paavola, Sami. 2004. Abduction as a logic and methodology of discovery: The importance of strategies. *Foundations of Science* 9: 267–283.
Pappus of Alexandria. 1876–1878. *Collectio*, ed. Friedrich Otto Hultsch. Berlin: Weidmann.
Pascal, Blaise. 1904–1914. *Oeuvres*, ed. Léon Brunschvicg and Pierre Boutroux. Paris: Hachette.
Peirce, Charles Sanders. 1931–1958. *Collected papers*, ed. Charles Hartshorne, Paul Weiss, and Arthur W. Burks. Cambridge: Harvard University Press.
Peirce, Charles Sanders. 1992. *Reasoning and the logic of things. The Cambridge conference lectures of 1898*, ed. Kenneth Laine Ketner. Cambridge: Harvard University Press.
Penrose, Roger. 1991. *The Emperor's new mind. Concerning computers, minds, and the laws of physics*. London: Penguin.
Piccolomini, Alessandro. 1547. *In mechanicas quaestiones Aristotelis – Commentarium de certitudine mathematicarum disciplinarum*. Rome: Antonio Blado.
Pinker, Steven. 1995. *The language instinct*. New York: Harper-Collins.
Plantinga, Alvin. 2006. How naturalism implies skepticism. In *Analytic philosophy without naturalism*, ed. Antonella Corradini, Sergio Galvan, and E. Jonathan Lowe, 29–44. London: Routledge.

Plotkin, Henry. 1997. *Darwin machines and the nature of knowledge*. Cambridge: Harvard University Press.
Poincaré, Henri. 1914. *Science and method*. London: Nelson.
Poincaré, Henri. 1958. *The value of science*. Mineola: Dover.
Pólya, George. 1941. Heuristic reasoning and the theory of probability. *The American Mathematical Monthly* 48: 450–465.
Pólya, George. 1954. *Mathematics and plausible reasoning*. Princeton: Princeton University Press.
Pólya, George. 1981. *Mathematical discovery. On understanding, learning and teaching problem solving*. New York: Wiley.
Pólya, George. 1990. *How to solve it. A new aspect of mathematical method*. London: Penguin.
Popper, Karl Raimund. 1945. *The open society and its enemies*. London: Routledge.
Popper, Karl Raimund. 1972. *Objective knowledge. An evolutionary approach*. Oxford: Oxford University Press.
Popper, Karl Raimund. 1974. *Conjectures and refutations. The growth of scientific knowledge*. London: Routledge.
Popper, Karl Raimund. 1996. *In search of a better world. Lectures and essays from thirty years*. London: Routledge.
Popper, Karl Raimund. 1998. *The world of Parmenides. Essays on the presocratic enlightenment*, ed. Arne F. Petersen and Jørgen Mejer. London: Routledge.
Popper, Karl Raimund. 1999. *All life is problem solving*. London: Routledge.
Popper, Karl Raimund. 2000. *Realism and the aim of science*, ed. William Warren Bartley III. London: Routledge.
Popper, Karl Raimund. 2002. *The logic of scientific discovery*. London: Routledge.
Popper, Karl Raimund. 2005. *Unended quest. An intellectual autobiography*. London: Routledge.
Post, Emil Leon. 1965. Absolutely unsolvable problems and relatively undecidable propositions. Account of an anticipation. In *The undecidable*, ed. Martin Davis, 340–433. New York: Raven Press.
Posy, Carl J. 2000. Epistemology, ontology and the continuum. In *The growth of mathematical knowledge*, ed. Emily Rolfe Grosholz and Herbert Breger, 199–219. Dordrecht: Kluwer.
Prawitz, Dag. 1971. Ideas and results in proof theory. In *Proceedings of the second Scandinavian logic symposium*, ed. Jens Erik Fenstad, 235–307. Amsterdam: North-Holland.
Prawitz, Dag. 2006. *Natural deduction. A proof-theoretical study*. Mineola: Dover.
Prawitz, Dag. 2011. Proofs and perfect syllogisms. In *Logic and knowledge*, ed. Carlo Cellucci, Emily Rolfe Grosholz, and Emiliano Ippoliti, 385–402. Newcastle upon Tyne: Cambridge Scholars Publishing.
Pylyshyn, Zenon W. 2003. *Seeing and visualizing. It's not what you think*. Cambridge: The MIT Press.
Quine, Willard Van Orman. 1946. Concatenation as a basis for arithmetic. *The Journal of Symbolic Logic* 11: 105–114.
Quine, Willard Van Orman. 1969. *Ontological relativity and other essays*. New York: Columbia University Press.
Quine, Willard Van Orman. 1981a. *Mathematical logic*. Cambridge: Harvard University Press.
Quine, Willard Van Orman. 1981b. *Theories and things*. Cambridge: Harvard University Press.
Raussen, Martin, and Christian Skau. 2004. Interview with Michael Atiyah, and Isadore Singer. *European Mathematical Society Newsletter* 53: 24–30.
Read, Stephen. 2010. General-elimination harmony and the meaning of the logical constants. *Journal of Philosophical Logic* 39: 557–576.
Reichenbach, Hans. 1947. *Elements of symbolic logic*. New York: Macmillan.
Reid, Thomas. 1863. *Works*, ed. William Hamilton and Dugald Stewart. Edinburgh: MacLachlan and Stewart.
Renfrew, Andrew Colin. 2008. Neuroscience, evolution and the sapient paradox: The factuality of value and of the sacred. *Philosophical Transactions of the Royal Society B* 363: 2041–2047.
Rescher, Nicholas. 1988. *Rationality. A philosophical inquiry into the nature and the rationale of reason*. Oxford: Oxford University Press.

Rescher, Nicholas. 2009. *Unknowability*. Lanham: Lexington Books.
Ribet, Kenneth Alan. 1990. From the Taniyama-Shimura conjecture to Fermat's last theorem. *Annales de la Faculté des Sciences de Toulouse – Mathématiques* 11: 116–139.
Robbin, Joel W. 2006. *Mathematical logic. A first course*. Mineola: Dover.
Robinson, Richard. 1936. Analysis in Greek geometry. *Mind* 45: 464–473.
Rota, Gian-Carlo. 1991. *The end of objectivity. The legacy of phenomenology. Lectures at MIT*. Cambridge: MIT Mathematics Department.
Rota, Gian-Carlo. 1997. *Indiscrete thoughts*, ed. Fabrizio Palombi. Boston: Birkhäuser
Rota, Gian-Carlo. 1999. *Lezioni napoletane*. Naples: La Città del Sole.
Rubbia, Carlo. 1997. Asking nature. In *Passionate minds. The inner world of scientists*, ed. Lewis Wolpert and Alison Richards, 195–202. Oxford: Oxford University Press.
Ruse, Michael. 1995. *Evolutionary naturalism*. London: Routledge.
Russell, Bertrand 1949. Answer to questionnaire. In Eliot Dole Hutchinson, *How to think creatively*, 110–112. New York: Abingdon-Cokesbury Press.
Russell, Bertrand. 1954. *Human society in ethics and politics*. London: Allen & Unwin.
Russell, Bertrand. 1971. *Autobiography*. London: Allen & Unwin.
Russell, Bertrand. 1994. *Mysticism and logic*. London: Routledge.
Russell, Bertrand. 1995a. *An outline of philosophy*. London: Routledge.
Russell, Bertrand. 1995b. *My philosophical development*. London: Routledge.
Russell, Bertrand. 1996. *Why I am not a Christian*. London: Routledge.
Russell, Bertrand. 1997. *The problems of philosophy*. Oxford: Oxford University Press.
Russell, Bertrand. 1999. *Our knowledge of the external world*. London: Routledge.
Russell, Bertrand. 2004. *History of Western philosophy*. London: Routledge.
Rutherford, Ernest. 1911. The scattering of α and β particles by matter and the structure of the atom. *Philosophical Magazine* 21: 669–688.
Salmon, Wesley Charles. 1965a. The concept of inductive evidence. *American Philosophical Quarterly* 2: 265–270.
Salmon, Wesley Charles. 1965b. Rejoinder to Barker and Kyburg. *American Philosophical Quarterly* 2: 277–280.
Sartorius von Wantershausen, Willem. 1856. *Gauss: zum Gedächtnis*. Leipzig: Hirzel.
Sayre, Kenneth M. 1969. *Plato's analytic method*. Chicago: University of Chicago Press.
Schiefsky, Mark J. 2005. Introduction. In Hippocrates, *On ancient medicine*, 1–71. Leiden: Brill.
Scholz, Heinrich. 1961. *Concise history of logic*. New York: Philosophical Library.
Schwartz, Stephen P. 2012. *A brief history of analytic philosophy. From Russell to Rawls*. Chichester: Wiley-Blackwell.
Searle, John Rogers. 2008. *Philosophy in a new century*. Cambridge: Cambridge University Press.
Shoesmith, David John, and Timothy John Smiley. 1978. *Multiple-conclusion logic*. Cambridge: Cambridge University Press.
Simpson, Stephen G. 1988. Partial realizations of Hilbert's program. *The Journal of Symbolic Logic* 53: 349–363.
Smith, Robin. 1989. Notes. In Aristotle, *Prior Analytics*, ed. Robin Smith, 105–228. Indianapolis: Hackett.
Smith, Robin. 1995. Logic. In *The Cambridge companion to Aristotle*, ed. Jonathan Barnes, 27–65. Cambridge: Cambridge University Press.
Song, Jinwoong, Sook-Kyoung Cho, and Byung-Hoon Chung. 1997. Exploring the parallelism between change in students' conceptions and historical change in the concept of inertia. *Research in Science Education* 27: 87–100.
Spelke, Elizabeth Shilin. 2011. Natural number and natural geometry. In *Space, time and number in the brain*, ed. Stanislas Dehaene and Elizabeth Merrit Brannon, 287–317. London: Elsevier.
Spencer, Herbert. 1890. *The principles of psychology*. London: Williams & Norgate.
Spencer, Herbert. 1893. *First principles*. London: Williams & Norgate.
Spinoza, Benedictus. 2002. *Complete works*, ed. Michael L. Morgan. Indianapolis: Hackett.
Steiner, Mark. 1998. *The applicability of mathematics as a philosophical problem*. Cambridge: Harvard University Press.

Sterne, Laurence. 1997. *The life and opinions of Tristram Shandy, gentleman.* London: Penguin.
Striker, Gisela. 2009. Introduction. In Aristotle, *Prior Analytics. Book I*, ed. Gisela Striker. Oxford: Oxford University Press.
Sullivan, Philip Richard. 2009. Objects limit human comprehension. *Biology and Philosophy* 24: 65–79.
Suppes, Patrick. 1984. *Probabilistic metaphysics.* Oxford: Blackwell.
Swetz, Frank J., and T.I. Kao. 1977. *Was Pythagoras Chinese? An examination of right triangle theory in ancient China.* University Park: The Pennsylvania State University Press.
Tarski, Alfred. 1944. The semantic conception of truth and the foundations of semantics. *Philosophy and Phenomenological Research* 4: 341–376.
Tarski, Alfred. 1969. Truth and proof. *Scientific American* 220(6): 63–77.
Tarski, Alfred. 1983. *Logic, semantics, metamathematics*, ed. John Corcoran. Indianapolis: Hackett.
Tarski, Alfred. 1994. *Introduction to logic and to the methodology of deductive sciences*, ed. Jan Tarski. Oxford: Oxford University Press.
Tennant, Neil. 1986. The withering away of formal semantics? *Mind and Language* 1: 302–318.
Turing, Alan Mathison. 1936–1937. On computable numbers, with an application to the *Entscheidungsproblem. Proceedings of the London Mathematical Society*, Series 2, 42: 230–265; 43: 544–546.
Turing, Alan Mathison. 1939. Systems of logic based on ordinals. *Proceedings of the London Mathematical Society*, Series 2, 45: 161–228.
Ungar, Anthony M. 1992. *Normalization, cut-elimination and the theory of proofs.* Stanford: CSLI.
van Benthem, Johan. 2008. Interview. In *Philosophy of mathematics: 5 questions*, ed. Vincenta Fella Hendricks and Hannes Leitgeb, 29–43. New York: Automatic Press/VIP.
von Helmholtz, Hermann Ludwig Ferdinand. 1867. *Handbuch der Physiologischen Optik.* Leipzig: Voss.
von Helmholtz, Hermann Ludwig Ferdinand. 1995. *Science and culture. Popular and philosophical essays.* Chicago: The University of Chicago Press.
Wagner, Gerd. 1991. Ex contradictione nihil sequitur. In *IJCAI'91 proceedings of the 12th international joint conference on artificial intelligence*, vol. 1, ed. John Mylopoulos and Raymond Reiter, 538–543. San Francisco: Morgan Kaufmann.
Wallas, Graham. 1926. *The art of thought.* London: Cape.
Wang, Hao. 1974. *From mathematics to philosophy.* London: Routledge.
Wansing, Heinrich. 2006. Connectives stranger than tonk. *Journal of Philosophical Logic* 35: 653–660.
Weiner, Joan. 1990. *Frege in perspective.* Ithaca: Cornell University Press.
Weintraub, Ruth. 1997. *The sceptical challenge.* London: Routledge.
Weisberg, Robert W. 2006. *Creativity. Understanding innovation in problem solving, science, invention, and the arts.* New York: Wiley.
Whitehead, Alfred North, and Bertrand Russell. 1925–1927. *Principia Mathematica.* Cambridge: Cambridge University Press.
Wigner, Eugene Paul. 1960. The unreasonable effectiveness of mathematics in the natural sciences. *Communications on Pure and Applied Mathematics* 13: 1–14.
Williamson, Timothy. 2007. *The philosophy of philosophy.* Oxford: Blackwell.
Wisdom, John. 1934. *Problems of mind and matter.* Cambridge: Cambridge University Press.
Witt, Charlotte. 1989. *Substance and essence in Aristotle. An interpretation of Metaphysics VII-IX.* Ithaca: Cornell University Press.
Wittgenstein, Ludwig. 1922. *Tractatus logico-philosophicus.* London: Kegan Paul.
Wittgenstein, Ludwig. 1932. Muss sich denn nicht . . . . In *Wittgenstein's Nachlass*, TS 219.
Wittgenstein, Ludwig. 1958. *Philosophical investigations.* Oxford: Blackwell.
Wittgenstein, Ludwig. 1975. *Philosophical remarks*, ed. Rush Rhees. Oxford: Blackwell.
Wittgenstein, Ludwig. 1976. *Lectures on the foundations of mathematics, Cambridge, 1939*, ed. Cora Diamond. Brighton: Harvester Press.

Wittgenstein, Ludwig. 1978. *Remarks on the foundations of mathematics*, ed. Georg Henrik von Wright, Rush Rhees, and Gertrude Elizabeth Margaret Anscombe. Oxford: Blackwell.
Wittgenstein, Ludwig. 1979. *Notebooks 1914–1916*, ed. Gertrude Elizabeth Margaret Anscombe and Georg Henrik von Wright. Oxford: Blackwell.
Wittgenstein, Ludwig. 2001. *Lectures, Cambridge, 1932–1935*, ed. Alice Ambrose. Amherst: Prometheus Books.
Wittgenstein, Ludwig. 2005. *The big typescript TS 213*, ed. C. Grant Luckhardt and Maximilian A. E. Aue. Oxford: Blackwell.
Zabarella, Iacopo. 1608. *Opera Logica*. Frankfurt: Zetner.
Zimmermann, Ernst. 2002. Peirce's rule in natural deduction. *Theoretical Computer Science* 275: 561–574.

Name Index

A
Ackermann, Wilhelm, 2
Adelson, Edward H., 273
Albert of Saxony, 137, 138
Alexander of Aphrodisias, 34, 80, 91, 133
Alhazen, 272
Amphinomous, 69
Anaxagoras, 32
Antiphon, 337, 338
Aphrodite, 38
Apollo, 33
Archimedes, 337
Argos, 38
Aristotle, 18, 21, 25–30, 33–37, 45–53, 65, 68, 72, 75–83, 88–93, 95–133, 137–139, 141, 143, 146, 147, 149–152, 154, 157, 158, 188, 189, 202, 203, 208, 215–216, 218–219, 225, 227, 239, 241, 244, 253, 263, 265–267, 283, 296, 297, 319, 332, 336, 340, 351, 353
Arnauld, Antoine, 291
Atiyah, Michael, 62
Auden, Wystan Hugh, 352
Austin, John Langshaw, 19, 319
Avigad, Jeremy, 363

B
Bacon, Francis, 14–17, 21, 157–160, 293, 331
Bailey, Dominic, 44
Barendregt, Henk, 68
Barnes, Jonathan, 20, 34, 52, 216, 217
Bechara, Antoine, 261
Belnap, Nuel D., 213
Bennett, Maxwell R., 274
Bergson, Henri-Louis, 228, 334
Berkeley, George, 149
Bernays, Paul, 2, 220, 354
Blanché, Robert, 16, 227
Blanshard, Brand, 20
Boger, George, 95, 96
Boghossian, Paul A., 224
Bourbaki, Nicolas, 11–13, 73
Bråting, Kajsa, 363
Buridan, Jean, 260
Byers, William, 153, 234, 236

C
Calvino, Italo, 9, 247
Capozzi, Mirella, 57, 152, 173, 180
Carnap, Rudolf, 19, 289, 307, 335, 336
Cassandra, 33
Castelli, Benedetto, 138, 139
Cellucci, Carlo, 3, 4, 10, 11, 59, 68, 151, 210, 217, 218, 220, 221, 223, 246, 247, 304, 305, 307, 323, 360, 361, 363
Chater, Nick, 11
Chen, Ludwig C.H., 43
Chisholm, Roderick M., 41
Church, Alonzo, 10, 11
Cicero, Marcus Tullius, 34, 132, 257
Clagett, Marshall, 357
Clement of Alexandria, 29
Coffa, Alberto, 193
Cohen, I. Bernard, 137, 143
Cohen, Laurent, 248
Cohen, Morris Raphael, 285
Commandino, Federico, 88
Cooper, William S., 268
Copernicus, Nicolaus, 232
Cornford, Francis Macdonald, 65

Coulomb, Charles Augustin de, 342
Couturat, Louis, 171
Curry, Haskell Brooks, 4

D

Damasio, Antonio, 257
Davidson, Donald, 270
Davies, Edward Brian, 10
Davis, Philip J., 17, 64
Dean, Edward, 363
Dehaene, Stanislas, 248
de l'Hospital, Guillaume François Antoine, 10
Democritus, 33
Descartes, René, 14–18, 20, 21, 157, 161–168, 170–172, 194, 250, 320–323, 331
Devlin, Keith, 256
Dewey, John, 19, 20, 129, 241, 247, 280
Diels, Hermann Alexander, 26–30, 32, 37, 61, 70, 92, 337
Dieudonné, Jean, 12–14, 363
Dilthey, Wilhelm, 272
Diogenes Laertius, 34, 133, 356
Diophantus of Alexandria, 161
Dirac, Paul Adrien Maurice, 11, 150, 232, 261
Dummett, Michael Anthony Eardley, 19, 153, 194, 285, 315–317, 321, 325

E

Eilenberg, Samuel, 355
Einstein, Albert, 270
Empedocles, 29, 70
Epicurus, 230
Euclid, 68, 69, 78, 79, 85, 86, 88, 128, 129, 186, 277, 292, 327, 355–357, 360, 361, 363
Eudemus, 352
Eudoxus, 61
Euripides, 32
Eutocius of Ascalon, 59

F

Favaro, Antonio, 139
Feferman, Solomon, 290
Feigl, Herbert, 305, 306, 308
Fermat, Pierre de, 72, 73
Feyerabend, Paul, 317
Floyd, Juliet, 6–7
Fodor, Jerry Alan, 248, 274
Fraenkel, Abraham Adolf, 8
Frankfurt, Harry Gordon, 296
Franklin, Benjamin, 342

Franzén, Torkel, 8
Frege, Gottlob, 1, 2, 14, 16, 17, 20, 21, 154, 155, 181, 183–197, 199, 201, 213, 215–220, 222–225, 227, 229, 250, 267, 268, 278, 279, 284, 294, 302, 315, 323, 324, 354, 365
Freud, Sigmund, 251
Fuchs, Lazarus Immanuel, 233
Fuss, Paul Heinrich, 333

G

Galilei, Galileo, 14, 137–140, 144, 147, 151, 232, 258, 301, 358, 359
Gellius, Aulus, 133
Geminus, 75
Gentzen, Gerhard, 21, 186, 199–213, 215, 217, 225, 303, 340, 361
Gershon, Michael, 262
Giaquinto, Marcus, 362, 363
Gibson, James Jerome, 274
Gillies, Donald, 282
Gödel, Kurt, 1–12, 17, 18, 20, 21, 73, 153, 196, 217–223, 225, 232, 283, 287–288, 290, 291, 312, 363
Goldbach, Christian, 333
Gowers, William Timothy, 5, 320, 325
Graham, Ronald L., 223, 348
Grosholz, Emily Rolfe, 12, 294, 359

H

Haack, Susan, 305
Hacker, Peter Michael Stephan, 274
Hadamard, Jacques, 270, 360
Halmos, Paul Richard, 318
Hamming, Richard Wesley, 69
Hansen, Bert, 327
Harman, Gilbert, 300
Hawking, Stephen William, 319, 325
Heidegger, Martin, 242, 269, 313, 314, 324
Helen, 38, 188
Hempel, Carl Gustav, 19, 227
Heraclitus, 30
Hering, Ewald, 272, 273
Herschel, William, 339–340
Hersh, Reuben, 7
Hilbert, David, 2, 68, 216, 217, 219–223, 225, 234, 281, 289, 354, 359, 360, 366
Hintikka, Jaakko, 83, 223, 224, 295
Hippocrates of Chios, 30, 35, 36, 59, 61, 62, 65, 73, 90, 115, 116, 287, 322, 341
Hippocrates of Cos, 30, 35, 36, 44–45, 70, 115, 116, 287, 322

Name Index

Homer, 38, 253
Hönigswald, Richard, 197
Howson, Colin, 303, 304
Hrbacek, Karel, 262
Hume, David, 154, 229, 310–312, 345
Husserl, Edmund, 65, 147, 273, 313, 324

I
Ivancevic Tijana T., 240
Ivancevic, Vladimir G., 240

J
Jaffe, Arthur, 64
Jech, Thomas, 262
Josephson, John R., 299
Josephson, Susan G., 299

K
Kac, Mark, 17
Kant, Immanuel, 2, 18, 21, 56, 57, 152, 157, 172–181, 183, 187, 192, 193, 195, 197, 216, 218, 220, 252, 266–268, 284, 291, 292, 294, 301, 319, 323, 345, 353
Kao, T.I., 332
Kepler, Johannes, 232, 261, 304
Klein, Christian Felix, 361
Kneale, Martha, 15, 227
Kneale, William, 15, 227
Knorr, Wilbur Richard, 80, 90
Kranz, Walther, 26–30, 32, 70
Kripke, Saul Aaron, 318
Kublai Kahn, 9
Kyburg, Henry Ely, 307, 312

L
Lakatos, Imre, 20
Leibniz, Gottfried Wilhelm, 10, 21, 88, 157, 168–173, 194–195, 217–219, 223, 231, 338, 341
Levi, Carlo, 349
Lewis, David Kellogg, 64
Löb, Martin Hugo, 4
Locke, John, 14–15, 17, 361

M
Macbeth, Danielle, 284
Mach, Ernst, 255
MacLane, Saunders, 355
Maddy, Penelope, 315, 326

Maier, Heinrich, 96
Mancosu, Paolo, 363
Maor, Eli, 93
Maxwell, James Clerk, 343
McCarthy, John, 13, 14
Menaechmus, 59, 60, 69, 73
Menn, Stephen, 83
Mill, John Stuart, 181, 344, 346
Mlodinow, Leonard, 319
Moore, George Edward, 19, 317
Mullis, Kary, 319, 325
Mumma, John, 363
Murawski, Roman, 5

N
Nagel, Ernest, 252, 267, 285
Nagel, Thomas, 252, 267, 285
Naylor, Arch W., 10
Neurath, Otto, 19
Newton, Isaac, 11, 21, 142–144, 150, 162, 234, 235, 320, 347, 349–351
Nicole, Pierre, 291
Novalis, 234
Nowak, Leszek, 144

O
Oaksford, Mike, 11
Odysseus, 38
Oresme, Nicole, 327

P
Paavola, Sami, 299
Padoa, Alessandro, 68
Palomar, 247–248
Pamphile of Epidaurus, 356
Pappus of Alexandria, 21, 72, 75, 83–85, 87–89, 91, 93, 138–139, 144, 161, 219
Parmenides, 25–30, 35, 37–39, 65, 92, 117, 154, 208, 225, 239, 265
Pascal, Blaise, 68, 353–355
Peano, Giuseppe, 4, 218, 223
Peirce, Charles Sanders, 210, 211, 232, 240, 277, 286, 287, 295–300, 304
Pejlare, Johanna, 363
Penrose, Roger, 262
Perelman, Chaim, 20
Pericles, 32
Piccolomini, Alessandro, 78
Pinker, Steven, 243
Plantinga, Alvin, 327

Plato, 18, 21, 25–31, 35–37, 39–45, 48, 51, 55, 63, 65–72, 82–83, 115–119, 150, 154, 215, 225, 239, 265, 281, 282, 287, 317, 320, 322
Plotkin, Henry, 252
Poincaré, Jules Henri, 229–231, 233, 234, 262
Polo, Marco, 9
Pólya, George, 56, 57, 89, 90, 229, 290, 291, 331
Popper, Karl Raimund, 67, 151, 228, 229, 263, 293, 334, 335, 354
Post, Emil Leon, 6
Posy, Carl J., 178
Prawitz, Dag, 202, 203, 205, 207–209, 211, 212
Proclus, 69, 339, 352
Ptah, 30
Ptolemy, Claudius, 272
Putnam, Hilary, 6, 7
Pylyshyn, Zenon W., 274, 275
Pythagoras, 332

Q
Quine, Willard Van Orman, 7, 290, 325–326

R
Raphael, 232
Raussen, Martin, 62
Read, Stephen, 212
Reichenbach, Hans, 19, 289
Reid, Thomas, 235
Remes, Unto, 83
Renfrew, Andrew Colin, 246
Rescher, Nicholas, 241, 252
Ribet, Kenneth Alan, 72, 73
Robbin, Joel W., 224
Robinson, Richard, 85, 285
Rosser, John, Barkley, 7
Rota, Gian-Carlo, 17, 262, 318
Rubbia, Carlo, 261
Ruse, Michael, 326
Russell, Bertrand, 4, 5, 9, 10, 19, 194–196, 212, 215, 219, 224, 241, 257, 260, 285, 315, 316, 318, 324, 326, 356, 362
Rutherford, Ernest, 341, 342
Ryle, Gilbert, 19

S
Salmon, Wesley Charles, 309, 336
Sandu, Gabriel, 295

Sartorius von Wantershausen, Willem, 348
Sayre, Kenneth M., 83
Schiefsky, Mark J., 70
Schlick, Moritz, 19
Scholz, Heinrich, 1, 172, 218
Schultz, Johann Friedrich, 192
Schwartz, Stephen P., 19
Searle, John Rogers, 322
Sell, George R., 10
Sextus Empiricus, 33, 310–312
Shabaka, 30, 31
Shimura, Goro, 72, 262
Shoesmith, David John, 210
Simplicius, 61, 92, 337
Simpson, Stephen G., 9
Skau, Christian, 62
Smiley, Timothy John, 210
Smith, Robin, 96, 101, 120, 285
Socrates, 36, 98, 117–119
Solon, 32
Song, Jinwoong, 140
Spelke, Elizabeth Shilin, 256
Spencer, Herbert, 292, 326
Speusippus, 69
Spinoza, Benedictus, 222, 280–281
Steiner, Mark, 327
Sterne, Laurence, 22
Strawson, Peter Frederik, 19
Stricker, Gisela, 95
Sullivan, Philip Richard, 252
Suppes, Patrick, 253
Swetz, Frank J., 332

T
Taniyama, Yutaka, 72, 262
Tarski, Alfred, 2, 3, 20, 51, 63, 64, 132, 152–154, 217, 225, 227, 231
Thales, 339, 356
Toulmin, Stephen Edelston, 20
Turing, Alan Mathison, 11, 287

U
Ungar, Anthony M., 210

V
van Benthem, Johan, 20
Viéte, François, 88
von Helmholtz, Hermann Ludwig Ferdinand, 272

Name Index

W
Wagner, Gerd, 9
Wallas, Graham, 230
Wang, Hao, 13, 17
Wansing, Heinrich, 212
Weiner, Joan, 193
Weintraub, Ruth, 311
Weisberg, Robert W., 233
Whewell, William, 321
Whitehead, Alfred North, 356
Wigner, Eugene Paul, 150
Wiles, Andrew John, 72, 73, 262
Williamson, Timothy, 316
Wisdom, John, 315
Witt, Charlotte, 81
Wittgenstein, Ludwig, 8, 9, 19, 239, 240, 276, 277, 314–320

Z
Zabarella, Iacopo, 266
Zermelo, Ernst Friedrich Ferdinand, 8
Zeus, 33, 133, 253
Zimmerman, Ernst, 211

Subject Index

A

Abduction
    inference to the best explanation and, 300–301
    inferentialist justification of, 302–304
    non-ampliativity of, 296–297
    Peirce view of, 296–298
    vindication of, 309
Alternative logic paradigm
    characters of, 18–19
    need for, 17–18
    towards an, 18
Analogy
    by agreement, 342–343
    by agreement and disagreement, 343
    and induction, 345
    inductive, 339–340
    inference by, 336
    Kant's views on, 179–180
    misconceptions concerning, 344–346
    and probability, 346
    proportional, 340–342
    proportional by inversion, 340
    proportional by permutation of the extremes, 341
    proportional by permutation of the middles, 341
    proportional by transfer, 341
    by quasi-equality, 337–338
    by separate indistinguishability, 338–339
Analytic method
    vs. analytic-synthetic method, 93–94
    vs. axiomatic method, 69
    Aristotle's changes to, 75
    Aristotle's criticism of, 75
    basic features of, 62–63
    and bottom-up approach, 10–12
    definition of, 55
    double movement of, 58
    fortune of, 72
    infinite regress in, 63–64
    and intuition, 63, 67
    and method of medicine, 70–71
    origin of, 59–62
    original formulation of, 65–67, 71
    and plausibility test procedure, 56
    and reduction to the impossible, 90–91
Analytic philosophy
    classical, 19, 314–319, 322–324
    neo-analytic, 19
A priori
    definition of, 291
    demonstration, 137–138
    evolution of, 291–294
    hypotheses and, 291
    Kant's view of, 291–292
    Popper's view of, 293–294
    Spencer's view of, 292–293
Aristotle's analytic-synthetic method
    abandonment of, 216–217
    definition of, 76
    direction of analysis in, 80
    example of, 78–79
    Galileo and, 137–138
    heuristic procedure for, 126
    inadequacy of, 218–219
    original formulation of, 76–78
    and reduction to the impossible, 90–91
    role of intuition in, 81
Aristotle's logic
    deductivist view of, 95–96, 112–114
    heuristic procedure for, 120–126
    heuristic view of, 119–120
    limitations of, 129–132

Aristotle's logic (*cont.*)
  as a logic of discovery, 129
  plausibility and, 126–129
  proximate sources of, 117–119
  Stoic logic and, 132–133
  ultimate sources of, 115–116
Assertions
  A, E, I, O, 99
  Aristotle's analysis of, 97–99
  compound, 97
  contradictories, 100
  contraries, 99
  Frege's analysis of, 188–189
  indeterminate, 98
  particular, 97
  simple, 97
  subcontraries, 100
  universal, 97
Axiomatic method
  definition of, 68
  Hippocrates of Cos' criticism of, 44–45
  as a part of the analytic-synthetic method, 89–90
  Plato's criticism of, 43–44
  and top-down approach, 10–12

B

Bottom-up approach
  and analytic method, 11–12
  to mathematics, 10–11
  to science, 11–12

C

Closed world view
  Frege's, 187–188
  inadequacy of, 218
  Kant's, 177–178
Consistency
  and truth, 221–222
  and Wittgenstein's rule, 8–9
Contractions
  abduction, 304
  detour, 203–204
  permutation, 204–206
  simplification, 206

D

Deduction
  direct, 106–108
  Frege's analysis of, 190
  Gentzen's analysis of, 200–201, 207–208
  ideal of atomizing, 185, 213
  indirect, 106–108
  normal, 207–208
Deductive rules
  Frege's, 190
  Gentzen's, 200–201, 207–208
  Hume's justification of, 311–312
  inferentialist justification of, 303–305
  intuitional justification of, 311–312
  for negation, 207–208
  non-ampliativity of, 55–56, 284–285
  plausibility preservation of, 57–58
  truth-functional justification of, 302–303
  validation of, 305
  vindication of, 306
Definition
  as abbreviation, 353–355
  as analysis, 355–357
  and metonymy, 354
Demonstration
  analytic notion of, 58–59
  axiomatic notion of, 68–69
  direct, 108
  indirect, 108
Diagrams
  as representing a dynamic relation, 357–358
  as representing a static relation, 357–358
  and metonymy, 357
  misconceptions concerning, 359–363
Discovery
  logic of (*see* Logic, of discovery)
  programme of mechanizing, 171, 222–223
  mathematical logic and, 16
  prejudices against a logic of, 288–291
  psychology of, 229–232

E

Emotion
  choice of problems or hypotheses and, 260–261
  as a compensation for the limitations of reason, 258
  doubt and, 264
  error and, 262–263
  knowledge and, 258–259
  reason and, 257–258
  mathematical knowledge and, 262
  scientific knowledge and, 261
  solving problems and, 259–260
Endoxa
  definition of, 81–82
  and plausibility, 81–82

Subject Index

Evolution
  biological, 243–244
  cultural, 243–244
Extended mind
  brain plasticity and, 248–249
  origin of, 247
  world and, 247–248

F
Function
  current notion of, 188
  eighteenth century notion of, 188

G
Generalization
  inference by, 347–348
  use of, 348

H
Human nature
  anti-biologism and, 242–243
  biological evolution and, 243–244
  cultural evolution and, 243–244

I
Ideal
  of atomizing deduction, 185, 213
  of a calculus of reasoning, 217–218
  of a universal language, 217
Incompleteness theorem
  Gödel's first, 4–6, 218–219, 222
  Gödel's second, 4–9, 219, 221
  Gödel's third, 220
  strong, 217–218, 223
Induction
  and analogy, 345–346
  and Aristotle's analytic-synthetic method, 123–126
  Hume's argument concerning, 310–311
  Kant's views on, 179–180
  misconceptions concerning, 334–336
  from multiple cases, 333–334
  and probability, 335
  from a single case, 332–333
Inference rules
  alternative classification of, 301–302
  asymmetry view of, 309
  Hume's view of, 310–311
  Peirce's classification of, 298–299
  standard classification of, 295–296
  validation of, 305
  vindication of, 305
Inferentialism
  definition of, 202–203
  and justification of deductive rules, 303–305
  limitations of, 208–213, 224
Intuition
  analytic method vs., 235–236
  analytic philosophy and, 318
  Aristotle and role of, 47–48
  Parmenides on role of, 38–39
  Plato on role of, 42
  solving problems and, 287–288

K
Knowledge
  analytic method and, 283
  analytic philosophy and, 314–315
  a priori, 291–294
  biological role of, 249–250
  certainty and, 286–287
  consciousness and, 250–251
  cultural role of, 254
  logic and, 283–284
  mathematical, 255–256
  purpose of, 253–254
  role of visual logic in, 276
  scientific, 255
  solving problems and, 281
  things in themselves and, 251–253
  unconscious, 251

L
Logic
  anti-evolutionism in, 267–268
  Aristotle and role of, 47–48
  Aristotle's names for, 34–35
  artificial, 265–266, 269
  Bacon's view of, 160
  Descartes' view of, 161–167
  discursive, 275–277
  of discovery, 28, 129, 161–163, 168–169, 179–181, 183–184, 229–230, 288–291
  Frege's foundation of, 193–194, 196–197
  Frege's primitive laws of, 195
  Frege's view of, 183–185
  Gentzen's view of, 201–202
  Kant's view of, 172–175
  Leibniz's view of, 168–172
  language and, 269–270
  and method, 227–229

Logic (*cont.*)
   natural, 265–267
   normativity of, 174–175, 184–185, 279–280
   origin of, 29–30
   origin of the name, 33–34
   Parmenides and role of, 38–39
   Plato and role of, 42
   reason and, 278
   reconstruction of, 19–20
   restricted to the study of deduction, 132–133, 183–184
   visual, 275–277
Logicism
   Frege's, 194–196, 219
   Leibniz's, 194–195

M

Mathematical logic
   basic assumptions of, 1–5
   high expectations on, 224–225
   intended purpose of, 1
   limitations of, 3–5, 217–224
   modest returns of, 224–225
   and Scholastic logic, 15–16
   seeking another role for, 13–14
Mathematics
   artificial, 255–256
   bottom-up approach to, 10–11
   effectiveness of, 150–151
   Frege's view of, 187–188, 191–193
   Galileo's book of the world and, 147
   Galileo's revolution and, 146–147
   Hilbert's view of, 220–223
   influence of emotion on, 262
   loss of certainty of, 7–10
   natural, 256
   need for a new kind of, 149–150
   top-down approach to, 10–11
   and truth, 153
Metaphor
   and analogy, 351
   inference by, 349
   misconceptions concerning, 351
   source domain of, 349
   target domain of, 349
Metonymy
   inference by, 352
   and mathematical symbolism, 352
Method
   analytic (*see* Analytic method)
   of ancient medicine, 70–71
   Aristotle's analytic-synthetic (*see* Aristotle's analytic-synthetic method)
   Bacon's, 157–159
   divorce of logic from, 227
   example of Galileo's, 139–142
   Galileo's, 137–142
   logic and, 279
   negation of, 228–229
   Newton's, 142–143
   origin of the name, 35–36
   Pappus' analytic-synthetic (*see* Pappus' analytic-synthetic method)

N

Naturalism
   definition of, 325
   Maddy's view of, 326
   Plantinga's view of, 327
   Quine's view of, 325–326
   Ruse's view of, 326–327
   Steiner's view of, 327
   and supernaturalism, 328
Non-deductive rules
   ampliativity of, 55–56
   intuitional justification of, 307–308
   plausibility preservation of, 57
   vindication of, 308

P

Pappus' analytic-synthetic method
   definition of, 83
   direction of analysis in, 87–88
   example of, 85–87
   fortune of, 88–89
   Galileo and, 138–139
   Newton and, 144
   original formulation of, 84–85
   and reduction to the impossible, 90–91
Paradox
   of inference, 285–286
   Meno's, 281–282
   Russell's, 195–196
   sapient, 246
Perception as inference
   irresistibility of, 272–273
   non-propositional character of, 271
   objection to, 273–275
   origin of, 272
Philosophy
   alternative view of, 320–324
   analytic (*see* Analytic philosophy)

Subject Index   389

armchair view of, 316–319
demise of, 319–320
features of, 321–322
Heidegger's view of, 313, 324
Husserl's view of, 313, 324
Russell's view of, 324
Wittgenstein's view of, 314–315
Plausibility
    and analytic method, 55–56
    and analytic-synthetic method, 126–127
    definition of, 56
    and *endoxa*, 81–82
    essence and, 128
    guaranteed only by experience, 57–58
    in place of truth, 154–155
    and probability, 56–57
    test procedure, 56
Primary and secondary qualities
    Galileo's distinction, 148
    limitations of Galileo's distinction, 149, 273
Programme
    Frege's logicist, 194–195
    Hilbert's conservation, 220–221
    Hilbert's consistency, 221
    of mechanizing discovery, 171, 222–223

R

Reason
    artificial, 245
    definition of, 240–241
    logic and, 278
    natural, 245
    origin of logic and, 239–240
    rationality and, 240–241
    relativity of the concept of, 244–245
Reduction to the impossible
    analytic method and, 90–91
    analytic-synthetic method and, 90–91
    definition of, 28
    reason for use of, 91–92
    strong, 105, 111–112

S

Science
    Aristotle's conception of, 45–46
    bottom-up approach to, 12
    and emotion, 261
    finished, 128–129
    Galileo's revolution in, 146

    idealization in, 144–145
    Kant's conception of, 177–178
    in the making, 128–129
    open world view of, 294
    Parmenides' conception of, 37–38
    philosophy in the face of, 313–314
    Plato's conception of, 39–41
    top-down approach to, 11–12
    and truth, 151–152
Scholastic logic
    criticism of, 14–15
    and mathematical logic, 15–16
Specialization
    inference by, 348
    use of, 349
Syllogism
    Aristotle's definition of, 100–101
    completion of, 107–108
    conversion of, 105–107
    demonstrative, 131
    dialectical, 101, 128
    figures of, 102
    formal theory of, 110–112
    from a hypothesis, 130–131
    heuristic procedure for, 120–122
    inductive, 123–126
    moods of, 102–103
    name of, 101–102
    reduction of, 108–110
    scientific, 128

T

Top-down approach
    and axiomatic method, 10–11
    to mathematics, 10–11
    to science, 11
Truth
    Aristotle on, 51–52
    concept of, 152–153
    and consistency, 221–222
    as correspondence, 51–52, 151–152
    criterion of, 152–153, 310
    as intuition of the essence, 52
    Kant on, 151–152
    mathematics and, 153
    modern science and, 151–152
    Plato on, 51–52
    plausibility in place of, 154–155
    Tarski on, 152–153
    unknowability of, 219

Made in United States
North Haven, CT
14 October 2022